"An authoritative guide and must-buy for
the area and owns a mountain bike."

— *Mountain Bike* magazine on c
companion guide, *Mountain 1
Southern California's Best 100 Trails*

"Mandatory reading for locals and visitors alike, *Mountain
Biking Northern California's Best 100 Trails* is the cyclist's most
thorough guide yet to the beauty of Northern California."

— *Mountain Biking* magazine

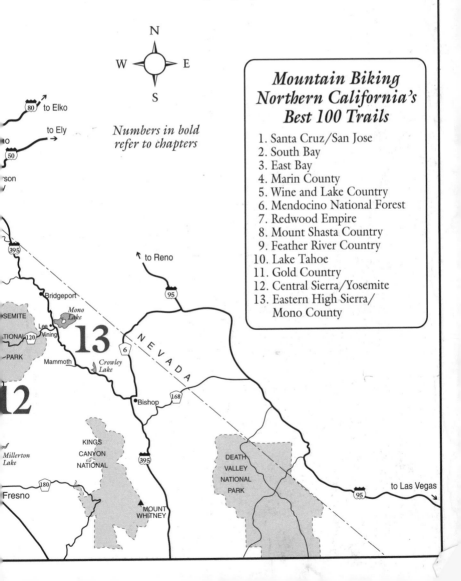

*Numbers in bold
refer to chapters*

Mountain Biking
Northern California's
Best 100 Trails

1. Santa Cruz/San Jose
2. South Bay
3. East Bay
4. Marin County
5. Wine and Lake Country
6. Mendocino National Forest
7. Redwood Empire
8. Mount Shasta Country
9. Feather River Country
10. Lake Tahoe
11. Gold Country
12. Central Sierra/Yosemite
13. Eastern High Sierra/
    Mono County

MOUNTAIN BIKING
Northern California's
BEST **100** TRAILS

Second Edition

Delaine Fragnoli & Robin Stuart

With Chapters By

R.W. Miskimins, Carol Bonser, Réanne Hemingway-Douglass,

Mark Davis, & Don Douglass

MOUNTAIN
BIKING
PRESS.COM

FINE EDGE
Productions LLC

IMPORTANT LEGAL NOTICE AND DISCLAIMER

Credits:

book design: Melanie Haage
copy editing: Cindy Kamler
diagrams: Sue Irwin, Sue Athmann
cover photo: © Jason Houston
all other photos by the authors, except as noted

Library of Congress Cataloging-in-Publication Data

Fragnoli, Delaine, 1962–
    Mountain biking northern California's best 100 trails / by Delaine Fragnoli & Robin Stuart with contributions by R.W. Miskimins ... [et al.].--2nd ed.
      p.   cm.
    Includes bibliographical references and index.
    ISBN 0-938665-73-1
      1. All terrain cycling--California, Northern--Guidebooks.
2. California, Northern--Guidebooks. I. Title: Northern California's best 100 trails. II. Stuart, Robin. III. Title.
GV1045.5.C22 C2545 2000
917.9404'54--dc21   00-025433

ISBN 0-938665-73-1

Mountain Biking Press™, FineEdge.com,
13589 Clayton Lane, Anacortes, WA 98221
www.FineEdge.com

TABLE OF CONTENTS

Chapter 1: Santa Cruz/San Jose
By Robin Stuart

Chapter 2: South Bay
By Robin Stuart

Chapter 3: East Bay
By Robin Stuart

Chapter 4: Marin County
By Robin Stuart

Chapter 5: Wine and Lake Country
By Robin Stuart

Chapter 6: Mendocino National Forest
By Robin Stuart

Chapter 7: Redwood Empire
By Delaine Fragnoli

Chapter 8: Mount Shasta Country
By Delaine Fragnoli

Chapter 9: Feather River Country
By Delaine Fragnoli

Chapter 10: Lake Tahoe
By R.W. Miskimins and Carol Bonser

Chapter 11: Gold Country
By Delaine Fragnoli

Chapter 12: Central Sierra/Yosemite
By Delaine Fragnoli

Chapter 13: Eastern High Sierra/Mono County
By Réanne Hemingway-Douglass, Mark Davis, and Don Douglass

Appendix

Miskimins

Lake Tahoe: The Great Flume Ride

Acknowledgments

The authors wish to thank Ray Miskimins and Carol Bonser for their help in documenting the great riding around Lake Tahoe. Thanks also go out to Réanne Douglass for her oversight of the project, to book designer Melanie Haage for her skill and dedication, and to map maker Sue Irwin for her hard work in producing this book.

We are indebted to the many United States Forest Service, Bureau of Land Management, National Park, State Park and other land management personnel at all levels for their cooperation and encouragement during a time of increased demand for recreation and decreased funding to meet those demands. Thanks, too, to the many bike shop employees and bike club members who volunteered a favorite trail.

On a personal note, Delaine Fragnoli would like to thank her husband, Jim MacIntyre, for his companionship on and off the trail and her daughter, Whitney, who has already had more adventures than she will ever know.

Robin Stuart sends her thanks to Cathy Jensen for literally riding through fires with her, and to Sierra, who missed her daily walks on the beach while we were out riding.

Delaine Fragnoli and Robin Stuart
Quincy, California
February 2000

Stuart/Jensen

Stuart/Jensen

Safety and Precautions

One of the joys of mountain biking on dirt is the freedom to experience nature. However, mountain biking in the backcountry involves unavoidable hazards and risks that each cyclist accepts when leaving the pavement behind. You can increase your safety by being aware of potential dangers, preparing ahead and respecting and remaining alert to the environment in all its variety and changes. Just because a trail is described in this book does not mean it will be safe or suitable for you.

Trails in this book cover an unusually wide range of terrain, elevation, and weather patterns that require different levels of skill and conditioning. A route that is safe for one rider may not be safe for another. It is important that you know and heed your own limitations, that you condition properly both physically and mentally, and that you give thought to your equipment as well as to trail and weather conditions.

En route, take appropriate action, including turning back at any time your judgment and common sense dictates. This book is not a substitute for detailed mountain survival or for cycling texts or courses. We recommend that you consult appropriate resources or take courses before you attempt the more strenuous or remote routes. When you have a question about route suitability or safety, consult local bike shops and land management offices.

This warning and the legal disclaimer herein are not given to discourage your enjoyment, but to remind you to take responsibility for yourself so your feeling of satisfaction comes truly from being independent and self-sufficient.

RULES OF THE TRAIL
International Mountain Bicycling Association

Thousands of miles of dirt trails have been closed to mountain bicycling because of the irresponsible riding habits of a few riders. Do your part to maintain trail access by observing the following rules of the trail:

1. **Ride on open trails only.** Respect trail and road closures (ask if not sure), avoid possible trespass on private land, obtain permits and authorization as may be required. Federal and State wilderness areas are closed to cycling. Additional trails may be closed because of sensitive environmental concerns or conflicts with other users. Your riding example will determine what is closed to all cyclists!

2. **Leave no trace.** Be sensitive to the dirt beneath you. Even on open trails, you should not ride under conditions where you will leave evidence of your passing, such as on certain soils shortly after a rain. Observe the different types of soils and trail construction; practice low-impact cycling. This also means staying on the trail and not creating any new ones. Be sure to pack out at least as much as you pack in.

3. **Control your bicycle!** Inattention for even a second can cause disaster. Excessive speed maims and threatens people; there is no excuse for it!

4. **Always yield trail.** Make known your approach well in advance. A friendly greeting (or bell) is considerate and works well; startling someone may cause loss of trail access. Show your respect when passing others by slowing or even stopping. Anticipate that other trail users may be around corners or in blind spots.

5. **Never spook animals.** All animals are startled by an unannounced approach, a sudden movement, or a loud noise. This can be dangerous for you, others, and the animals. Give animals extra room and time to adjust to you. In passing, use special care and follow the directions of horseback riders (ask if uncertain). Running cattle and disturbing wild animals is a serious offense. Leave gates as you found them or as marked.

6. **Plan ahead.** Know your equipment, your ability, and the area in which you are riding, and prepare accordingly. Be self-sufficient at all times, keep your machine in good repair, and carry necessary supplies for changes in weather or other conditions. A well-executed trip is a satisfaction to you and not a burden or offense to others. Keep trails open by setting an example of responsible cycling for all mountain bicyclists.

Dedicated to the appreciation of and access to recreational lands, non-profit IMBA welcomes your support. Please contact IMBA, P.O. Box 7578, Boulder, CO 80306-7578
Phone: (303) 545-9011
Fax: (303) 545-9026
E-mail: info@imba.com or membership@imba.com
Website: www.imba.com

WELCOME TO MOUNTAIN BIKING NORTHERN CALIFORNIA

Celebrated as the birthplace of mountain biking, Northern California holds a special appeal to mountain bikers. It was here that the sport's pioneers transformed the balloon-tired bike into the mountain bike. In doing so, they revolutionized both the bicycle industry and backcountry recreation.

No one who has experienced Northern California's trails should be surprised by this. There is plenty of inspiration to be found in the area's natural lands. From the rolling oak woodlands of San Jose to the fabled headlands of Marin, from the volcanic splendor of Mt. Lassen and Mt. Shasta to the holy quiet of a redwood forest, from the alpine serenity of Lake Tahoe to the granite glory of Yosemite, there is scenery and terrain for all abilities and tastes.

Working with land management personnel, bike shop employees and local trail experts, we have compiled Northern California's top rides, many of which have never before been documented in print. We can say with confidence that this is the most thorough, wide-ranging mountain bike guidebook yet published for the area.

HOW TO USE THIS BOOK

With so many great trails to choose from, selecting the best was difficult. (This book could easily have become Mountain Biking Northern California's Best 200 Trails.) Obviously *best* means different things to different people. Some rides were included for their outstanding scenic value, others for their historical significance, others simply for their high fun factor. A few were selected because they represented the quintessential California in some way.

We have also attempted to include a variety of terrain and levels of difficulty, as well as a certain geographic diversity, although we have erred on the side of accessibility. Thus we have included numerous rides in the heavily-populated and highly-visited areas of Northern California, namely the San Francisco Bay Area and the greater Lake Tahoe region.

We have organized all this information in an easy-to-use way. Each chapter is dedicated to a particular area, usually a distinct geographic region. The chapters are organized in a loop starting, appropriately enough, in the birthplace of mountain biking, the San Francisco Bay area, before moving north up the coast to the redwood parks, east to Mount Shasta and the Klamath National Forest and back down along Interstate 5 to Lake Tahoe. We complete the loop by circling back to Sacramento and the Gold Country before visiting Yosemite National Park and the Eastern Sierra. Within each chapter we have grouped together rides that are in the same vicinity.

At the beginning of each ride you will find capsule information to let you decide quickly if a ride is for you or not. Ride **distance** is included, as is a rating of **difficulty**. Mileages shown are approximate and may vary among riders and odometers. We rated the rides for strenuousness (from easy to very strenuous) and for technical difficulty (from not technical to extremely technical). The ratings are a subjective assessment of what the average fit rider (acclimatized to elevation) might consider the route.

If you are a racer, you might find some of our difficult rides to be moderate. If you are new to the sport, you may find our mildly technical rides challenging. Know your limits and be honest in evaluating your skill level. We also recommend that you check with local bike shops and land managers for their evaluation of your fitness for a particular ride. We do not know your skill level and consequently cannot be responsible for any losses you may incur using this information. Please see the important legal notice and disclaimer in the front portion of this book.

For **elevation** we include whatever elevation information seems pertinent to that particular ride, usually net elevation gain and loss. Rides at high elevation will include such information. **Ride type** lets you know if the ride is a loop, an out-and-back trip, a multiple-day tour or if it requires a car shuttle. It also tells you the trail surface; for example, "fire road loop with singletrack return." Next, we suggest the best **season** for riding each route. Then, we recommend the best **maps** of the area. Unless otherwise indicated, the map names refer to USGS 7.5-minute topographical maps. Last, in **comments** we tell you where you can find water, restrooms and other amenities on the ride or nearby.

If, after reading the capsule information, you are not sure if a ride is for you, the text of each ride description should give you additional information with which to make a decision. The **highlights** section contains general information on the area and describes the ride's best features. **Getting there** directs you to the trailhead, and the **route** portion gives you a turn-by-turn guide to the ride.

Please note that the routes described in this book are not patrolled and contain natural hazards. Trail conditions and surfaces are constantly changing. Also be aware that the trail access situation is very volatile in certain regions, particularly in the San Francisco area. Some areas are just now turning on to mountain biking and may have new trails and information by the time you read this. Check with local land managers for the latest trail and access conditions. A complete list of pertinent agencies, visitor centers and clubs is included in the Appendix.

Throughout we have tried to be consistent in presentation. We have made an effort, however, to retain some of the character and tone of each individual author. Mountain biking is a very individualistic sport, and we think that should be reflected in any writing about the sport. Remember also that each odometer gives different results and yours may vary from each author's.

We hope you think of this book as a group of friends getting together to tell you about the best riding they've discovered. But enough talk. Get on your bike and start discovering Northern California for yourself. You've got 100 trails to explore and the best trail guide available.

KNOW BEFORE YOU GO:
SPECIAL CONSIDERATIONS

To enhance your pleasure and safety we ask that you observe the following Special Considerations:

1. **Courtesy.** Extend courtesy to all other trail users and follow the golden rule. Observe the IMBA Rules of the Trail. The trails and roads in Northern California are popular with many user groups: hikers, equestrians, fishermen, ranchers, 4WD enthusiasts, hunters, loggers and miners. Mountain bikers are the newest user group, so set a good example.

2. **Preparations.** Plan your trip carefully; develop and use a check list. Know your equipment, your ability, and the area in which you are riding and prepare accordingly. Be self-sufficient at all times, wear a helmet, keep your machine in good repair, and carry necessary supplies for changes in weather or other conditions. A well-executed trip is a pleasure to you and not a burden or offense to others.

3. **Mountain Conditions.** Be sensitive at all times to the natural environment: the land, beautiful and enjoyable, can also be frightening and unforgiving. The areas covered by this book often encompass extremes in elevation, climate and terrain. If you break down, it may take you longer to walk out than it took you to ride in. Check with your local Red Cross, Sierra Club, or mountaineering textbooks for detailed mountain survival information. Know how to deal with dehydration, hypothermia, altitude sickness, sunburn and heatstroke. Always be prepared for:

Intense Sun: Protect your skin against the sun's harmful rays by wearing light-colored, long-sleeved shirts or jerseys. Some of the rides in this book are at relatively high altitude, and the higher you go, the more damaging the sun becomes. Use sunscreen with a sufficient rating. Wear sunglasses that offer adequate protection. Guard against heatstroke by riding in early morning or late afternoon when the sun's rays are less intense.

Low Humidity: East-facing slopes and high elevation usually have low humidity. To avoid headaches or cramps, start each trip with a minimum of two or more full quart water bottles or a full Camelbak-type water bladder . (Gallons of water may not be sufficient for really hot weather or hard rides.) Force yourself to drink before you feel thirsty. Carry water from a known source or treat water gathered from springs, streams and lakes. Untreated drinking water may cause Giardiasis or other diseases.

Variations in Temperature and Weather Conditions: Carry extra clothing —a windbreaker, gloves, dry socks—and use the multi-layer system so you can quickly adapt to different weather conditions. You may find it cool and foggy on the coastal side of a ridge, and hot and dry on the other. Afternoon thundershowers occur frequently in the high country, so keep an eye on changing cloud and wind conditions and prepare accordingly.

Fatigue: Sluggish or cramping muscles and fatigue indicate the need for

A mechanical problem can ruin your whole day. Here the culprit is a broken chain.

calories and liquids. Carry high-energy snack foods such as granola bars, dried fruits and nuts, Powerbars or Clif Bars, packets of Power Gel or Gu, and try an energy drink such as Gatorade to maintain strength and warmth. To conserve energy, add clothing layers as the temperature drops or the wind increases.

Closures: Many mountain and foothill areas are closed to the public during times of high fire danger. Other areas may be temporarily closed during hunting season or because of logging activity. Please check ahead of time with local authorities, and observe such closures. Always be very careful with fire.

4. Maps and Navigation. The maps in this book are not intended for navigation but as guides to the appropriate forest or USGS topographic maps which we recommend you carry and use. Have a plan ready in advance with your cycling group in case you lose your way (it's easy to do!). En route, record your position on the map(s), noting the times you arrive at known places. Be sure to look back frequently in the direction from which you came, in case you need to retrace your path. Do not be afraid to turn back when conditions change or if the going is tougher than you expected.

In certain cases, it may be difficult to determine which roads and trails are open to public travel. When in doubt, make local inquiries. Follow signs and leave all gates either opened or closed, as you found them, or as signed. Park off the road, even in remote areas, so you do not block possible emergency vehicles.

Before you leave on a ride, tell someone where you're going, when you expect to return, and what to do in case you don't return on time. Ask that person to call the proper officials if you are more than six hours overdue, giving full details about your vehicle and your trip plans.

5. Horses and Pack Animals. Some of the trails in Northern California are used by recreational horse riders as well as cyclists and hikers. Some horses are spooked easily, so make them aware of your presence with a friendly greeting or bell *well in advance of the encounter.* A startled horse can cause serious injuries both to a rider and to itself.

If you come upon horses moving *toward* you, yield the right-of-way, even when it seems inconvenient. Carry your bike to the downhill side and stand quietly, well off the trail in a spot where the animals can see you clearly. If you come upon horses *moving ahead of you in the same direction,* stop well behind them. Do not attempt to pass until you have alerted the riders and asked for permission. Then, pass on the downhill side of the trail, talking to the

Author atop Mt. Ingalls; Smith Peak (Ride #62) behind her on the right; Lake Davis (Ride #61) behind her on the left.

horse and rider as you do. It is your responsibility to ensure that such encounters are safe for everyone. Do not disturb grazing sheep or cattle.

6. Respect the Environment. Minimize your impact on the natural environment. Remember, *mountain bikes are not allowed in Wilderness Areas and in certain other restricted areas.* You are a visitor, so ask when in doubt. Leave plants and animals alone; historic and cultural sites untouched. Stay on established roads and trails, do not create any new ones, and do not enter private property. Follow posted instructions and use good common sense. If you plan to camp, you may need a permit. Contact the nearest land management agency for information.

Be sensitive to the dirt beneath you. Even on open trails, you should not ride under conditions where you will leave evidence of your passing, such as on certain soils shortly after a rain. Observe the different types of soils and trail construction; practice low-impact cycling. Be sure to pack out at least as much as you pack in.

7. Control and Safety. Crashes usually don't cause serious injury, but they occasionally can and do. Stay under control and slow down for the unexpected. Wear protective gear—helmet, gloves and glasses—to protect yourself from scrapes and impacts with rocks, dirt and brush. Guard against excessive speed. Avoid overheated rims and brakes on long or steep downhill rides. Lower your center of gravity by lowering your seat on downhills. Lower your tire pressure on rough or sandy stretches. In late summer and fall, avoid opening weekend of hunting season, and inquire at the appropriate land management agency as to which areas are open to hunting. Carry first aid supplies and bike tools for emergencies. *Avoid solo travel in remote areas.*

8. **Trailside Bike Repair.** Minimum equipment: pump, spare tube, glueless patches, and a good multi-tool with a full set of Allen wrenches, a chain tool and a spoke wrench. Don't forget some duct tape as well. Tools may be shared with others in your group. Correct tire inflation, wide tires, and avoiding rocks will prevent most flats. Grease, lube, and proper adjustment prevent most mechanical failures. Frequent stream crossings wash out chain lube, so carry extra.

9. **First Aid.** Carry first aid for your body as well as your bike. If you have allergies, be sure to bring your medicine, whether it's for pollen or bee stings. Sunscreen saves your skin, and insect repellent increases your comfort in many seasons. Bring bandages and ointment for cuts and scrapes, and aspirin for aches that won't go away. Additional first-aid items you might carry in your kit are antiseptic swabs, moleskin, a single-edged razor blade, a needle, elastic bandage, Tums or other stomach remedy, and waterproof matches. For expedition trips, consult mountaineering texts on survival for more suggestions.

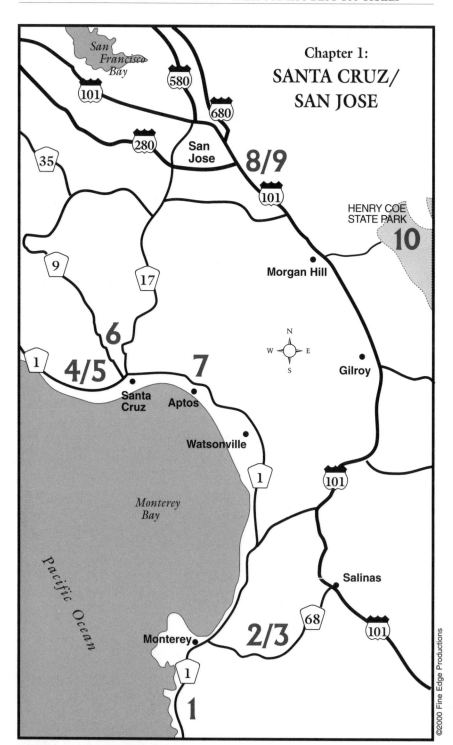

Chapter 1:
SANTA CRUZ/
SAN JOSE

CHAPTER 1

Santa Cruz/San Jose

By Robin Stuart

Thanks to the Santa Cruz Mountains, the lands bordering the Bay Area to the south are the most beautiful in the region. On the western side of the range, you find breathtaking ocean views and the university town of Santa Cruz, with its famous beach and boardwalk. The eastern slopes surround San Jose, the heart of the Silicon Valley and face inland toward the rolling hills of the East Bay. Although the Santa Cruz and San Jose areas are sides of the same mountain range, they are as different as night and day, with only one thing in common: killer singletrack. On the ocean side, you find dense, often moist forests of redwood and eucalyptus. The inland side tends to be drier, favoring oak, laurel, and pine. One thing's for sure: it smells good down here.

Although geographically considered to be part of the South Bay (see Chapter 2), this area deserves special attention. The trails in the parks around Santa Cruz and San Jose are among the best in northern and southern California. (I've also included one ride from farther south for those of you who want a taste of riding in Big Sur.) But don't just take my word for it—go out and ride! On any given day you may see test riders for Rock Shox, Specialized and Fox, along with scores of locals out enjoying these rides.

So what makes this area so great? If you're a beginner, unfortunately not much. Most of the trails are at least a little technical in nature, generally due to rocks. Once you've mastered those basic handling skills, however, you'll find trails as technical as you can stand, including long and winding fire roads rolling over ridges and topping mountain peaks, and some of the sweetest singletrack rolling down, over, and through aromatic forests.

You can thank the local mountain biking community for continued access to the singletrack here, and the best way to show your gratitude is by behaving yourself. Clubs and organizations such as ROMP (Responsible Organized Mountain Pedallers) work long and hard to keep the trails open and available to us. Please don't give land managers and landowners any reasons to consider banning mountain bikes from these trails.

1 Monterey/The Old Coast Road

Distance: 10.5 miles one way; 18.5 miles as a loop; 21 miles out and back
Difficulty: One way or as a loop, it is strenuous and mildly technical; as an out-and-back venture, very strenuous and mildly technical
Elevation: Over 1,800' one way or as a loop; more than 3,700' out and back
Ride Type: One-way shuttle on dirt road; loop on dirt road and pavement; out-and-back on dirt road
Season: Year-round. Spring, with wildflowers and without lots of tourists, is best
Map: AAA Monterey Bay Region
Water: At Andrew Molera State Park
Comments: Nearest facilities are at the road's southern end in Andrew Molera State Park. The road is open to vehicle traffic. After the first mile, be sure to stay on the road as all land beyond that point is private (and emphatically signed as such).

Highlights: Before the Bixby Bridge was completed in 1932, the Old Coast Road was the main route from Big Sur into Carmel. Today the graceful bridge is not only a lovely concrete structure, but it lets cars zoom through on Highway 1, leaving the Old Coast Road to you and me and our two-wheeled friends.

The Old Road can be ridden from Andrew Molera State Park in the south to Bixby Bridge in the north or vice versa. I prefer to start at AMSP. The parking situation at AMSP is better, there are facilities available in nearby Big Sur, the view as you descend to Bixby Bridge is spectacular, and on your return route down Highway 1, the ocean is on your right and the wind is, usually, at your back.

Either way, you do plenty of steep climbing as you make your way up and through the ranch land of the Big Sur Valley, into and out of the old-growth redwoods of the Little Sur drainage, and into and out of the Bixby drainage on your way to the ocean at Bixby Landing.

I prefer the loop option, but you can arrange to have a friend pick you up at Bixby Landing if the vehicle traffic on Highway 1 makes you nervous. As an out-and-back, the Old Coast Road is a burly undertaking— although I know people who have done it.

Getting There: AMSP is 22 miles south of Carmel on Highway 1. It's a short 10-minute drive north from Pfeiffer Big Sur State Park, an excellent choice for camping. The parking lot is on the west side of the highway, or you can park at one of the walk-in gates along PCH north of the main park entrance.

Route: From the parking lot, climb 0.1 mile back out to and across Highway 1. The Old Coast Road takes off from the dirt pull-out directly across the highway. You can't miss it. There's a street sign which reads *Coast Highway/Cabrillo Highway* and several yellow signs declaring *Entering State Park Property* and *Impassable When Wet.*

The road climbs immediately. About 0.1 mile up, a trail takes off to the right. It's signed as being open to bikes, but a quick hike up it convinced me it's not particularly rideable—at least uphill. At 0.3 mile you begin to get views of the coast. A turnout at

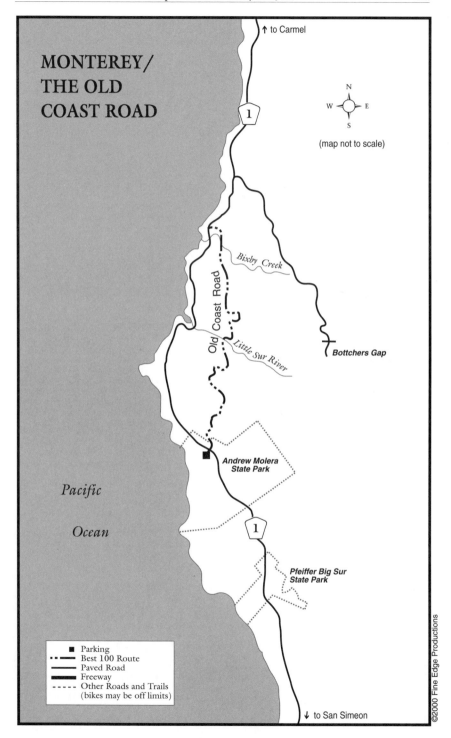

MONTEREY/
THE OLD
COAST ROAD

↑ to Carmel

1

N
W ⊕ E
S

(map not to scale)

Bixby Creek

Old Coast Road

Little Sur River

Bottchers Gap

■ Andrew Molera
State Park

Pacific

Ocean

1

Pfeiffer Big Sur
State Park

■ Parking
▪▪▪ Best 100 Route
── Paved Road
━━ Freeway
---- Other Roads and Trails
(bikes may be off limits)

↓ to San Simeon

©2000 Fine Edge Productions

View of Bixby Bridge and the Pacific Ocean from the Old Coast Road.

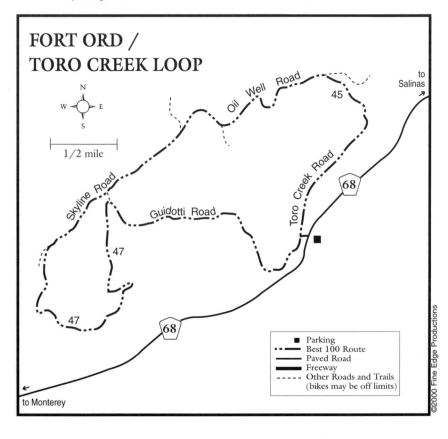

0.6 mile offers a nice vista of the beach and ocean. The hard-packed gravel road turns inland just beyond here.

At 0.8 mile, you cross a cattle-guard and gate with signs indicating private property on both sides of the road for the next 6 miles. In other words: Stay on the road. Route-finding for the rest of the ride is easy as there are no other roads or trails you can take.

At 1.5 miles the grade lessens a bit before pitching upward again. One more mile and you top out and begin a 2-mile downhill. It's over at 4.5 miles as you begin the ride's toughest climb. You grunt through several steep, tight switchbacks with loose gravel and rocks. You will loathe these. To add to the misery factor, this portion of the climb lacks any shade.

Fortunately, the agony lasts "only" 2 miles. When you top out at 6.5 miles, you are greeted by an awesome 3-mile descent through a cool, old-growth redwood forest. These are the best trees on the ride. Although the coastal views are long gone, this is my favorite part of the route. In my mind, this is the main reason for doing the ride.

At 9.5 miles you have one final climb. Thankfully, it is shorter than the earlier ones. Just under 10 miles, you can see Bixby Bridge and the ocean—a great photo op.

At 10.1 miles, start your descent to Highway 1. A left turn onto the highway and an 8-mile spin back to your car completes the loop. Or, if you've arranged a shuttle pickup, your ride ends here.

2 Fort Ord/Toro Creek Loop

Distance: 9.5 miles
Difficulty: Moderately strenuous, seasonally technical
Elevation: 1,000' gain/loss
Ride Type: Loop on fire roads and singletrack
Season: Year-round
Map: Free at trail gates
Comments: There are no amenities available, no water and no bathrooms. This area gets very hot in the summer and most of this ride is exposed. Bring as much water as you can carry and hydrate like crazy. The heat can turn this into a very strenuous ride.

Highlights: Fort Ord is the latest jewel in the mountain biking crown of the South Bay/Central Coast region. Once home to 25,000 army and civilian personnel, Fort Ord was founded as a cavalry post in 1917 and served as a major training ground during World War II. Two-thirds of the 28,000-acre former military holdings were conveyed to the Bureau of Land Management by the U.S. Army after the base closed in 1994.

Primarily devoted to preserving wildlife habitat, the area currently boasts 50 miles of multi-use roads, fire roads, tank tracks and singletrack. The trails offer a diverse playground of opportunities, from family-oriented paved roads to steep and twisting singletrack roller coasters. Local riders

Stuart/Jensen

Some of Fort Ord's many miles of singletrack.

Getting There: Fort Ord is 2 hours south of San Francisco, butted by Highway 1 on the west and Highway 68 on the east. From San Francisco, take Highway 1 south to the Reservation Road exit in Seaside. Follow Reservation Road through Seaside to Highway 68/Monterey. Highway 68 very quickly turns into a fast two-lane road. The park entrance is approximately one mile from the beginning of the two-lane. A small gate in a large clearing on the right serves as a parking lot. If you blink as you pass, you'll miss it. If you reach the Toro Cafe (on the left side of the road), you've gone about 100 yards too far.

Route: From the gate at Highway 68, follow the spur to catch Toro Creek Road, a smooth and sandy fire road. Get used to the sand, you're on it most of the ride. Take a left onto Toro Creek and enjoy the manzanita and live oak shade while it lasts. After a fun and easy downhill section, at 1.4 miles the road veers to the left and becomes Guidotti Road.

A short grunt of a climb is quickly rewarded with a downhill. Near the bottom, at 2.3 miles, turn left onto the singletrack marked "47." Trail 47 alternates between steep and winding, sometimes it's both. Bear left at the trail junction with Trail 48 at 3.4 miles to stay on 47. In another mile, near the park's southern boundary, the two trails briefly join forces. At the split, make a sharp left

regard the entire land mass as "the best." Their advice is just to show up and go play—trails are generally well signed. The following two rides are mere introductions to what Fort Ord has to offer.

One warning, though; pay heed to the signs surrounding the explosives area. Unexploded mines and an assortment of artillery lurk beneath the ground's surface. The good news: the land that the open trails traverse is completely safe. Nothing more exciting than the random bullet has been found for some time by any of the thousands of recreational users who descend on this area every weekend.

to continue on 47. As 47 climbs up and out of the valley, bid farewell to the cover of the trees. At least you have spectacular views to look forward to. After a last big push, 47 ends at Skyline Road at 5.8 miles.

Catch your breath and look around in awe at the Monterey Bay, then turn right onto Skyline to enjoy a ridgeline roller coaster. Sheep regularly graze around this area, guarded by several dogs. Keep your water bottle handy in case a blast at an overly-protective muzzle is required.

At 6.1 miles, stay left at the intersection with Guidotti and continue on Skyline Road. The trail starts down, sometimes steeply, back into the valley toward Toro Creek. You pass a couple of inviting trails on the left. These are fine as long as you bear in mind that what goes down must go back up, sometimes uncomfortably. On this ride, though, keep following Skyline to about 7.9 miles.

At the junction with Trail 45, turn right onto 45 for a steep descent to a seasonal water crossing. If the creek is running, SLOW DOWN. Wheels have been known to get stuck in the bog. Just past the creek, Trail 45 ends at Toro Creek Road. Turn right to head back to the gate and parking area.

3 Fort Ord/Oil Well Road

Distance: 11 miles
Difficulty: Strenuous, slightly technical
Elevation: 1,100' gain/loss
Ride Type: Loop on singletrack, some fire road
Season: Year-round
Map: Free at trail gates
Comments: There are no amenities available, no water and no bathrooms. This area gets very hot in the summer and most of this ride is exposed. Bring as much water as you can carry and hydrate like crazy. The heat can turn this into a very strenuous ride.

Highlights: This ride will introduce you to the singletrack wonders awaiting at Fort Ord. The loop takes you through one of the more wooded areas in the northeast corner of the park.

Getting There: Follow the directions for the previous ride.

Route: From the Toro Creek gate, follow the spur to catch Toro Creek Road, a smooth and sandy fire road. Turn right from the spur onto Toro Creek Road. Wave a little hello to Trail 45 (see Ride 2) as you bear right to stay on the fire road.

At 1.6 miles, the road ends at Oil Well Road. Turn left onto Oil Well Road. You're greeted almost immediately by a short steep climb. Our old friend Trail 45 greets you on the left just as the trail levels off. Stay on the fire road for another short, not so steep climb.

At 2.6 miles, turn right onto Trail 10. This singletrack starts innocuously enough with a not-altogether unpleasant little climb, after which it becomes a wild roller-coast-

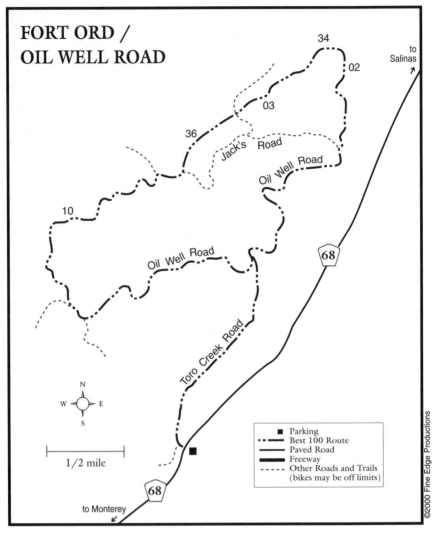

er ride—steep descents followed by steeper climbs, rewarded with more steep downhills. It can get a little slippery due to summer sand and winter mud.

At the trail junction at 3.2 miles, bear left, then make a sharp right to stay on 10, although you may not be happy about it. Still with me? A granny-gear gut-buster is the thanks you get, followed by another steepish descent.

At the next fork, at 3.9 miles, bear right and climb up to the paved Jack's Road. Ah, pavement, you think, this part should be easy. Not so fast, bucko. It's another climb. Fortunately, a short one.

At the top, at about 4.3 miles, turn left back onto the dirt of Trail 36. Trail 36 takes you parallel to the pavement back into the wilds of single-track country, ending at a crossroads just a hair under the 5-mile mark.

Cross the fire road to catch another climb—on Trail 03—which I'm sure you'll greet cheerfully. At the top, you enter a maze of crisscrossing-crossing trails. The good news is that the trails are marked. Keep following 03 until the turn-off for Trail 34 at 5.7 miles.

Turn right onto 34 for a rollicking downhill to the trail's end at Trail 02 at 5.9 miles. Turn right onto 02 and continue your downhill mania for about another mile.

The trail ends at the fire road portion of Jack's Road. Turn left and follow the fire road as it meanders around a lake and climbs gradually (whew) back to Oil Well Road.

At 8.6 miles, the road turns into Oil Well Road. You'll know it by the downhill leading back to the crossroads with Toro Creek Road. Turn left onto Toro Creek to get back to the gate.

Stream crossing at Wilder Ranch.

4 Wilder Ranch Loop

Distance: 9.5 miles
Difficulty: Moderately strenuous, technical sections
Elevation: 800' gain/loss
Ride Type: Loop on fire roads and singletrack
Season: Year-round
Map: Free at the ranger kiosk
Comments: Restrooms and drinking water are available in the parking lot.

Highlights: Wilder Ranch is a favorite with regional mountain bikers, well worth the hour or so drive from the Bay Area. Located on Santa Cruz's northwest border, the Wilder Ranch State Park and Cultural Preserve is considered to be the local version of a mountain bike park. Nestled within Wilder's 3,900 acres are 28 miles of roller-coaster fire roads,

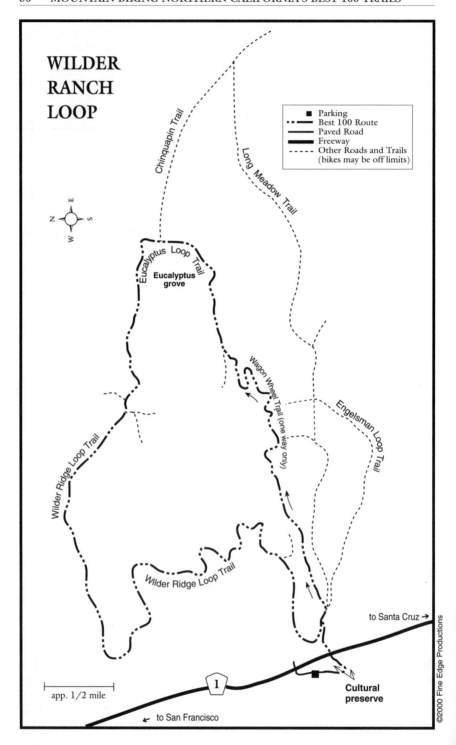

WILDER
RANCH
LOOP

Chinquapin Trail

Long Meadow Trail

Parking
Best 100 Route
Paved Road
Freeway
Other Roads and Trails
(bikes may be off limits)

Eucalyptus Loop Trail

Eucalyptus grove

Wagon Wheel Trail (one way only)

Engelsman Loop Trail

Wilder Ridge Loop Trail

Wilder Ridge Loop Trail

to Santa Cruz →

1

Cultural preserve

app. 1/2 mile

← to San Francisco

©2000 Fine Edge Productions

View of ocean, Wilder Ranch

twisting and technical singletrack, water crossings, rockbeds, loose and steep climbs and descents; just about everything the fat-tire heart desires. And thanks to the tireless efforts of the local mountain biking community, it's all legal.

Wilder Ranch also offers a bit of historical enrichment as well. The cultural preserve is a sort of living history center; a collection of restored buildings and artifacts found within the park's boundaries depict its early days as a Native American habitat to its later life as a Spanish ranch during the mission period. In the late nineteenth century, the park was the site of a thriving dairy ranch, which continued through the early twentieth century. To illustrate its past, a small number of livestock are raised on the grounds as part of the exhibit.

Past the cultural preserve and into the parklands, the trails wind through stands of eucalyptus, windswept chaparral overlooking the ocean, and dense forests of oak and redwoods. There are a number of awesome trails and combinations to be ridden here; the following is a favorite short loop which introduces some of Wilder's best features. Few of the trails are signed and nobody seems to know the names anyway, so pay attention to the route directions.

Wilder Ranch

Wilder Ranch boasts a variety of terrain—including plenty of rocy stream crossings.

Stuart/Jensen

Getting There: From San Francisco, take Highway 1 south toward Santa Cruz, about 60 miles. Wilder Ranch is on Highway 1, just past Davenport and about a mile north of Santa Cruz. The park entrance and parking lot are on the right, well signed with their own turning lane. Parking is $6, a little high, but the increased parking fee has kept the park open. Smile as you pay it.

Route: From the south end of the parking lot, follow the path leading through the gate past the restrooms. The path runs into a paved service road; turn right and head down, turning left into the cultural preserve. The preserve is a popular picnic spot so ride slowly or walk through. Veer left at the fork. The path leads through a tunnel (beneath Highway 1) which deposits you onto a fire road at the trailhead.

Head straight on the fire road, ignoring the hairpin turn to the left. Make the next left onto the single-track and head into the woods. The first half-mile or so takes you through a meadow flanked by stands of oak. The trees get thicker and the terrain gets rockier as you approach the red-wood-studded creek.

Your first test, should you accept it, is the amazing all-rock creek crossing. In the winter, the water level rises significantly, making this crossing even more exciting. The trail smoothes out (a little) on the other side, although you're not out of the rocks just yet. At about 1.5 miles, the large, chain-ring-bashing rocks get smaller as you start the long climb up to the ridge. The farther from the water you climb, the drier and looser the trail becomes as it snakes its way up through and around the red-woods.

As you close in on the 2-mile mark, the incline gets a little less steep and the rocky trail gets clear. A last tight S-turn around two trees and you pop out onto the fire road. Turn left for an easy climb to the next singletrack turnoff, about a quarter-mile straight ahead. There's no sign marking the trail, just a small clearing in front of a dense oak patch. The fire road veers off to the right, but you go straight onto the sometimes barely noticeable singletrack, taking to the trees once again.

If you regarded the first single-track as work, then this one's your payoff—a rollicking, rocky and steep descent deep into the redwoods. The trail hugs the wall above another creek that, yes, you will be crossing. In the summer, there's barely a trickle of water through here, maybe ankle-deep in the winter. Slow way down as you approach the final drop-

Fragnoli

Wilder Ranch

off into the creek. On the other side is a tricky, steep hairpin switchback. Once you've negotiated that bit of frivolity, the rest of the singletrack is a smooth cruise up and out of the woods. You end up once again on the main fire road at 3.2 miles.

Catch your breath, boast to your friends about how easy that was, then turn right onto the fire road for an easy climb up to the eucalyptus grove. Once past the mighty, if lonely, stand of trees, the trail pitches into

a short, steepish descent before it veers left and rolls for about a half-mile. You're then treated to a double-header, a long straight-away downhill broken up by a short level spot in the middle of the descent. Use caution as you reach the bottom—a sand trap awaits your arrival. In the winter, it doesn't get muddy, exactly . . . more like wet sand.

Follow the fire road as it winds easily up around to the left. You hit a short patch of pavement at about 6

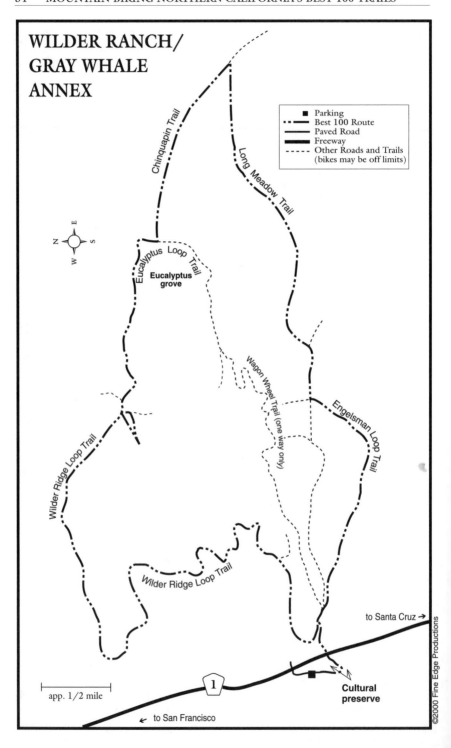

WILDER RANCH/
GRAY WHALE
ANNEX

Chinquapin Trail

Long Meadow Trail

Parking
Best 100 Route
Paved Road
Freeway
Other Roads and Trails
(bikes may be off limits)

Eucalyptus Loop Trail
Eucalyptus grove

Wagon Wheel Trail (one way only)

Engelsman Loop Trail

Wilder Ridge Loop Trail

Wilder Ridge Loop Trail

to Santa Cruz →

1

app. 1/2 mile

Cultural preserve

← to San Francisco

©2000 Fine Edge Productions

miles. Keep your eyes open for an unsigned singletrack turnoff at the apex of the paved bend. Take a left onto the singletrack, a short but fun little rocky roller that ends at the Wilder Ridge fire road. Turn left onto Wilder Ridge, which rolls gently along a chapparal ridge. After a short straight-away that parallels the ocean, the trail makes a left turn and descends deceptively quickly. Around the bend, the pitch gets downright steep as it rounds a granite-encrusted S-turn. This marks the beginning of a no-doubt-about-it, all-downhill-all-the-time (okay, so there's a little blip of a climb that you can sail up using momentum alone) return to the main fire road that leads back to the parking lot.

5 Wilder Ranch/Gray Whale Annex

Distance: 10.5 miles
Difficulty: Moderate, not technical
Elevation: 800' gain/loss
Ride Type: Loop on fire roads
Season: Year-round
Map: Free at the ranger kiosk
Comments: Restrooms and drinking water available in the parking lot

Highlights: One of the pleasures of this loop is that it seems to contain more downhilling than climbing, without requiring a shuttle. It also highlights the reasons why the 1997 annexation of Gray Whale Ranch, previously a privately-owned cattle ranch, caused a celebration among area mountain bikers. Although the trails here are not terribly technical, the additional 2,100 acres teem with towering conifers rising from a rugged and rocky surface not usually experienced this far west of the Sierras.

Getting There: Follow the directions for the previous ride.

Route: From the south end of the parking lot, take the service road to the visitor's center, turning left and walking your bike through the cultural preserve. On the other side of the tunnel, follow the fire road to the first hairpin where you turn left and start climbing the Wilder Ridge Loop Trail. Follow Wilder Ridge as it rolls steeply toward the ocean overlook, after which it becomes a pleasant, if rocky, cruise to the crossroads at the bottom of the rock-cluttered descent at 3.5 miles.

Turn right onto the Eucalyptus Loop Trail. It starts off as asphalt which quickly gives way to dirt just around the bend. Make your choice between the fire road and the singletrack, which reconnect at the bottom of the hill. I choose singletrack. Watch your speed at the bottom; in the summer, it's a sand trap and in the winter, it's a mud pit.

Turn right at the bottom of the descent, back onto the fire road and get ready to grunt. Winter conditions often make this part of the fire road seem a lot more like singletrack. Let's all remember to yield the good line to the climbers, kids. After the first initial steepy, there are enough level spots and short descents to make the majority of the climb toward the Eucalyptus Grove seem like less work than it is.

As you close in on the Eucalyptus Grove at 4.6 miles, turn left through the gate into the Gray Whale Annex and onto the Chinquapin Trail. (I dare you to pronounce it out loud). This fire road is really more of a doubletrack that rolls so gently downhill that it takes a while to realize you're not pedaling very much. Pine trees suddenly surround you at the trail crossing at 5.5 miles.

Make a very sharp right, nearly doubling backward, onto the well-marked Long Meadow Trail. Leave all thoughts of the coast behind you for a while as you continue descending through a pine-studded forest along dry and rocky doubletrack. About 0.5 mile into it, the trail smoothes out and becomes a rollicking downhill. The pines give way to redwoods just before you roll through a clearing that offers you a knock-out view of the ocean and the southern Santa Cruz Mountains. The trail picks up more of a downward tilt and, at 7.6 miles, gets downright steep for a short, seasonally technical (i.e. muddy) descent.

You find yourself deposited in a clearing at 7.7 miles, just you and the decaying brick foundations of abandoned lime kilns. Hang a right for an easy climb up to Engelsman Loop Trail at 7.8 miles. Turn left and get used to going downhill. The fire road rolls and sweeps you back down to the Wilder Ridge Loop trailhead at 9.6 miles. Stay left to head back to the cultural preserve and the parking lot.

6 Henry Cowell Redwoods State Park

Distance: 6.5 miles
Difficulty: Moderate, mildly technical
Elevation: 600' gain/loss
Ride Type: Loop on fire roads and pavement
Season: Year-round
Map: Available at the park for $1
Comments: Water is available at the trailhead.

Highlights: Located off Highway 1 in Santa Cruz, this 1,600-acre park epitomizes the Northern California coast with its towering redwoods, cool river canyons and wide open ridges. Its namesake, Henry Cowell, owned pretty much all of Santa Cruz in the late 1800s. Drawn from Massachusetts by the gold rush, Cowell and his brother operated a drayage service that hauled equipment from the Bay Area to the minefields in the Sierra Nevada foothills. As his success grew, so did his business interests until he became the richest man in Santa Cruz County. Cowell's son made a gift of land to the State of California in 1953. It became a state park in 1954.

The trails are fairly easy, with some sand and rocks, and wind through amazing forests of redwoods, along the San Lorenzo River, and up to an

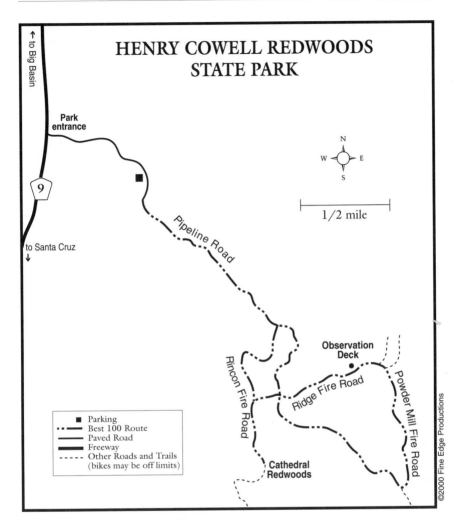

HENRY COWELL REDWOODS STATE PARK

to Big Basin

Park entrance

9

to Santa Cruz

Pipeline Road

N
W — E
S

1/2 mile

Observation Deck

Rincon Fire Road

Ridge Fire Road

Powder Mill Fire Road

Cathedral Redwoods

■ Parking
•—■—• Best 100 Route
——— Paved Road
▅▅▅ Freeway
- - - - Other Roads and Trails
(bikes may be off limits)

©2000 Fine Edge Productions

overlook with an expansive view of the coastal mountains and valleys.

Getting There: From San Francisco, take 280 south to Highway 1 and follow it to Santa Cruz. Turn left onto Highway 9 and follow it for 5 miles. The park entrance is on the right. Parking is $5.

Route: The trailhead is just past the Nature Center. Follow the paved Pipeline Road past an impressive stand of redwoods and through the trees. After passing under a railroad bridge, the trail begins to climb, getting markedly steeper after crossing Eagle Creek. At the top of the rise, the trail rolls the rest of the way through forests of pine and fir.

At about 2.5 miles, you come to an intersection with the Powder Mill Fire Road. Turn left onto Powder Mill and begin the steady climb up to the Observation Deck. Parts of the fire road get pretty sandy, especially in

Forest of Nisene Marks, epicenter of the 1989 Loma Prieta earthquake.

the later summer months. The worst of the climb is over as you reach the crossroads with the Ridge Fire Road. Stay left and follow Ridge the last quarter-mile to the Observation Deck.

After looking around and oohing and ahhing, it's all downhill from here. And kind of steep. The Ridge Trail is a loose and bumpy fire road back down to Pipeline. Keep going past Pipeline to the trail's end at the Rincon Fire Road. Turn left onto Rincon—there's something you gotta see.

Rincon gently descends to the Cathedral Redwoods. This is a stand of redwoods like you've only heard about and well worth the side trip. After feeling appropriately humbled by nature, turn around and go back up Rincon. Keep going past the intersection with Ridge, following Rincon as it winds and descends to Pipeline. Turn left on Pipeline and keep your speed in check as you head back down the pavement to the parking lot.

7 Forest of Nisene Marks/ Sand Point Overlook

Distance: 17 miles
Difficulty: Moderately strenuous, mildly technical
Elevation: 1,400' gain/loss
Ride Type: Out-and-back on fire road
Season: Year-round
Map: Available at the park for $1
Comments: No services are available at the trailhead.

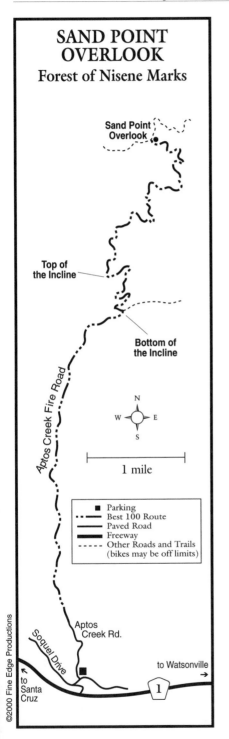

SAND POINT OVERLOOK

Forest of Nisene Marks

Sand Point Overlook

Top of the Incline

Bottom of the Incline

Aptos Creek Fire Road

N
W — E
S

1 mile

■ Parking
·—·— Best 100 Route
—— Paved Road
▬▬ Freeway
- - - - Other Roads and Trails
(bikes may be off limits)

Aptos Creek Rd.

Soquel Drive

to Watsonville →

to Santa Cruz

1

Highlights: The Forest of Nisene Marks State Park is a popular attraction for mountain bikers and hikers. Its rugged terrain is much like its original state. Shaped by fault lines that bisect the park, the area's narrow canyons and winding ridges make it undesirable to developers. Even the Ohlone tribes that inhabited neighboring regions kept their distance. In 1883, though, it got touched. Rather severely.

The property was sold to a lumber company that had joined forces with the Southern Pacific Railroad. Using a variety of means, everything from trestles to pack animals, they succeeded in clear-cutting the entire forest by 1923. Cut and stacked logs still remain in some of the remote areas of the park—just because they could cut it down didn't mean they could get it out. When the last of the valuable timber was gone, the loggers moved on.

In the 1950s, the Marks family, Salinas Valley farmers, purchased the land. In 1963, the Marks children donated the acreage to the state in their mother's name.

An interesting little side note: the Marks placed a deed restriction on equestrian access. So, while mountain bikes are not allowed on singletrack, oddly enough, horses aren't even allowed past the first couple of miles of fire road.

Today, a new generation of trees, including redwoods, eucalyptus, madrone and fir, have taken hold. But it will be a long time before the forest is completely restored.

Home seismologists and current events fans take note: the epicenter of the 1989 Loma Prieta quake, which rocked the Bay Area as the players took the field in the third game of the World Series, is located off the main fire road near the park's southeast boundary. I mention the game because it's responsible for saving the lives of countless numbers of Bay Area residents who had left work early to catch the 5:00 p.m. play time; the quake hit at 5:04, causing major damage (some still not repaired) to freeways and the collapse of a section of the Bay Bridge.

Getting There: From San Francisco, take 280 south to Highway 1 and follow it past Santa Cruz. Turn left at the Aptos turnoff and make the first right onto Soquel Drive. Follow Soquel for about half a mile and turn left onto Aptos Creek Road. Park in the large dirt turnout on the right.

Route: From the parking area, follow Aptos Creek Road for a little under a mile. At that point, it turns to dirt (welcome to the park) and becomes the Aptos Creek Fire Road. You follow this trail all the way up to the Sand Point Overlook. The trail starts out fairly level as it carries you inland,

over the steel bridge, where you can look down into a deep and narrow gorge, and past the remains of the loggers' turn-of-the-century housing.

At about 4.5 miles, you reach a point known as the Bottom of the Incline. This marks the end of the gentle ride. To the right is the hiking trail that leads to the Loma Prieta quake epicenter, about 0.5 mile up. Ahead, the going gets a little on the steep side as you enter into a series of switchbacks that climb about 600 feet in a little under a mile.

At about 6 miles, just past the Top of the Incline, the trail straightens out a bit and continues uphill at an easier grade. As you make your way up, the views start to get nice, especially as you close in on Sand Point. You reach the Sand Point Overlook at 8.5 miles or so. Feel free to ogle at will the coast and Monterey Bay, the Santa Cruz Mountains and Big Basin.

Turn around here for the fun and frolicking downhill ride back to your car.

8 Grant Ranch Loop

Distance: 9.6 miles
Difficulty: Strenuous, moderately technical (sand, loose rock, seasonal water crossing)
Elevation: 1,000' gain/loss
Ride Type: Loop on sometimes narrow fire roads
Season: Year-round; heavy rains may temporarily close some trails
Map: Lick Observatory. (Not all trails appear on the USGS map, so pick up a County Parks and Recreation map of Grant Ranch at the Visitor Center.)
Comments: Helmets required; water available at the Visitor Center area. Please close all gates behind you.

Highlights: Located at the base of Mount Hamilton in San Jose is the Joseph D. Grant County Park, better known as Grant Ranch. The largest recreational area in Santa Clara

County, the 9,522-acre park boasts over 20 miles of trails open to mountain bikers.

The park is named for the family which held the land from 1880 until

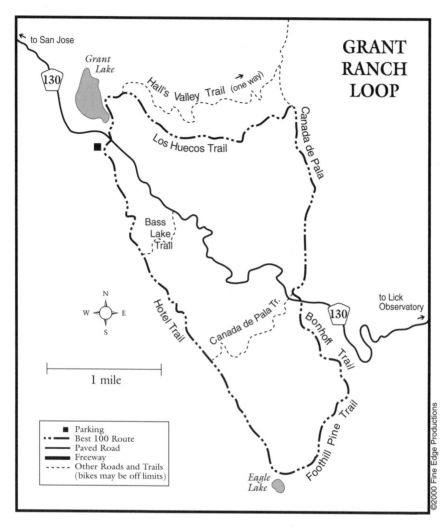

GRANT RANCH LOOP

to San Jose

Grant Lake

130

Hall's Valley Trail (one way)

Los Huecos Trail

Canada de Pala

Bass Lake Trail

N
W E
S

Hotel Trail

Canada de Pala Tr.

Bonhoff Trail

130

to Lick Observatory

1 mile

Foothill Pine Trail

■ Parking
Best 100 Route
Paved Road
Freeway
Other Roads and Trails
(bikes may be off limits)

Eagle Lake

©2000 Fine Edge Productions

1972, at which time the property was willed to the Save-the-Redwoods League and the Menninger Foundation. Santa Clara County purchased the land in 1975.

Most of the trails follow the peninsula mold of long and sometimes gnarly climbs, but here you are rewarded with equally long and downright thrilling descents. A local favorite, this playground is a popular site on the Northern California race circuit.

The loop ride, which follows several trails, illustrates the best that Grant Ranch has to offer: rolling, gentle and not-so-gentle climbs and descents by mountain lakes, through meadows and along panoramic ridges, all populated with oak and pine woodlands.

Getting There: From San Francisco, San Jose is about an hour's drive down either southbound 101 or 280. Both have an Alum Rock turnoff. Head east on Alum Rock for about 2

Stuart/Jensen

Grant Ranch

tures can soar above 100 degrees), walking is not only permissible, it may be required.

Stop to admire the view (i.e., catch your breath) before bearing left at the lake and following the Foothill Pine Trail as it drops blissfully down a short hill before climbing up again for another 1.1 miles, bringing your total to 4.3 miles. Hang a left at the next trail intersection onto the Bonhoff Trail, and enjoy or endure (depending on how you look at it) the next steep ascent. Fortunately, it's over fairly quickly and the trail levels off for a bit along the ridge before dropping down to the cattleguard at Mt. Hamilton Road (Highway 130).

Go across the road, through the gate on the other side, and continue north for a nasty little ascent up Canada de Pala Trail. Upon reaching the ridge line, after you stop swearing, you can see the Santa Clara Valley laid out below and all around you.

Now you're at the good part. The trail rolls along the ridge until you reach the 7.1-mile point in your journey and come to the intersection with the Los Huecos Trail. Turn left here for the payoff you so well deserve. All that lovely elevation you have gained is lost in 1.8 miles of rollicking downhill.

The trail ends at Grant Lake; turn left to head to the parking lot.

miles, turning right onto Mt. Hamilton Road/Highway 130. The park entrance is on the right, 8 miles up Mt. Hamilton Road. The park charges a $3 day-use fee.

Route: Starting from the visitor's center, turn right and head down the Hotel Trail. Follow the trail as it makes its way gently up to the Circle Corral, 1.4 miles. Past the corral, the going gets a bit steeper as you climb up to Eagle Lake, which you reach at 3.2 miles. There are several steep climbs along this route; since heat is often a factor in these parts (tempera-

9 Grant Ranch/Antler Point

Distance: 11.2 miles
Difficulty: Strenuous, moderately technical
Elevation: 1,400' gain/loss
Ride Type: Loop on sometimes narrow fire roads
Season: Year-round
Maps: Lick Observatory, Mt. Day. (Not all Grant Ranch trails appear on the USGS map, so pick up a County Parks and Recreation map of the park at the Visitor Center.)
Comments: Helmets required; water available at the visitor center area.

Highlights: This is the ride of choice for thrill seekers at both ends of the fat-tire spectrum—mountain goats who like the views from the highest attainable point and the downhill types who enjoy viewing the world through saucer-shaped pupils. On this ride, you traverse the trails leading to Antler Point, at 2,995 feet, Grant Ranch's highest peak. As you might guess, the views are spectacular. The ride also incorporates many

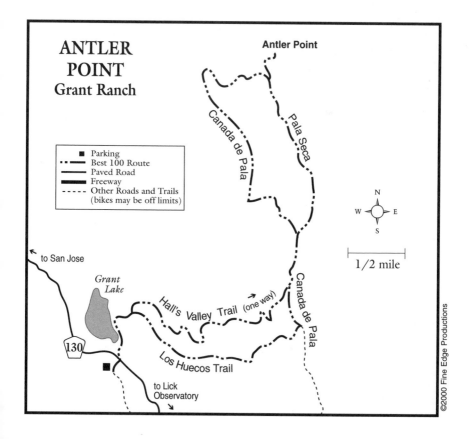

ANTLER POINT
Grant Ranch

Antler Point

Canada de Pala

Pala Seca

■ Parking
Best 100 Route
Paved Road
Freeway
Other Roads and Trails
(bikes may be off limits)

to San Jose

Grant Lake

Hall's Valley Trail (one way)

Canada de Pala

130

Los Huecos Trail

to Lick Observatory

N
W   E
S

1/2 mile

©2000 Fine Edge Productions

people's favorite downhill, the ever-lovin' Los Huecos Trail.

Getting There: Follow the directions for the previous ride.

Route: Starting from the visitor's center, head left and cross Mt. Hamilton Road to Grant Lake. Follow the trail to Hall's Valley Trail. The Hall's Valley Trail is open to bikes going uphill only; it's a popular route to the Canada de Pala Trail that is not as long as the Hotel to Bonhoff Trail and not as steep as the Los Huecos Trail. Bear left on Hall's Valley Trail and begin the climb toward the ridge. At about 1.3 miles, the grade steepens a bit for the next 0.25 mile, suddenly gaining 200 feet. Take heart, however; the next 200-foot gain comes with twice the distance.

The trail meanders around and up to the 2.7-mile point, when it ascends sharply to the junction with Canada de Pala. Turn left here and follow the trail as it ascends slightly to the next intersection of Canada de Pala and the Pala Seca Trail.

Bear right and head up the Pala Seca Trail. After a steep but brief climb, it rolls along the high ridge. When you've gone 4.9 miles, you come to a very steep trail going up on your right. Feel free to walk it, but you just have to go the 0.2 mile to see the world from almost 3,000 feet. This is Antler Point.

After spending a few moments, or a long time, feeling that top-of-the-world feeling, go back down to the Pala Seca Trail and turn right. The trail drops steeply to a line shack, used for herding the cattle that sometimes graze here. Bear left at the shack and continue descending to the stream.

You are now back on the Canada de Pala Trail which follows the stream until the junction with the Washburn Trail—off limits to bikes. Bear left and stay on the Canada de Pala Trail. This all starts looking familiar as you approach first the intersection with Pala Seca, then Hall's Valley. Stay on Canada de Pala; you've got a date with a downhill.

When you reach the trail marker for Los Huecos at 8.7 miles, turn right and get ready for the fun. At the bottom, turn left and follow along the lake to get back to the parking lot.

10 Henry Coe State Park/ Middle Ridge Loop

Distance: 9.5 miles
Difficulty: Strenuous, moderately technical
Elevation: 1,900' gain/loss
Ride Type: Loop on fire roads and singletrack
Season: Spring through fall
Maps: Mount Sizer, Mississippi Creek. (The Pine Ridge Association produces a map, available at the park, with suggested mountain bike routes and trail mileages.)
Comments: Water is available at park headquarters. All park singletrack is closed for 48 hours after a half-inch or more of rain. There's a 15-mph speed limit on roads.

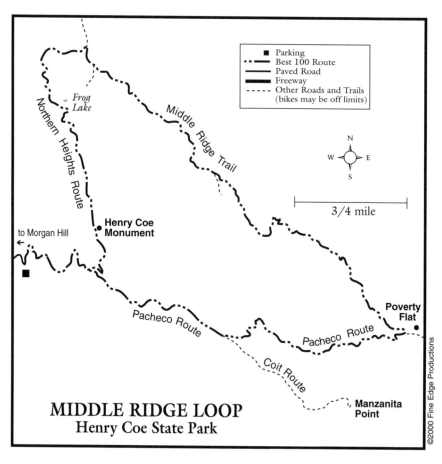

MIDDLE RIDGE LOOP
Henry Coe State Park

Map labels: Parking; Best 100 Route; Paved Road; Freeway; Other Roads and Trails (bikes may be off limits); Frog Lake; Northern Heights Route; Middle Ridge Trail; Henry Coe Monument; to Morgan Hill; Pacheco Route; Coit Route; Poverty Flat; Manzanita Point; 3/4 mile; N W E S; ©2000 Fine Edge Productions

Highlights: At over 79,000 acres, Henry Coe is California's largest state park. Some 22,000 of those acres are designated wilderness and, thus, closed to bikes. Look on the bright side—that still leaves 57,000 acres to explore. The land is an amalgamation of ranch lands acquired by the state, beginning with Henry Coe's Pine Ridge Ranch. In 1953, Pine Ridge Ranch was donated to the county by Henry Coe's daughter in her father's name. The county park was bought by the state in 1958, which then added to it as the state acquired the neighboring ranch properties.

What exists now is a wonderland of challenging, well-marked trails and pristine wilderness with over 70 lakes and ponds. The trails take you through forests of oak and pine, mountain meadows lush with seasonal wildflowers, creek crossings, and cool canyons. The park's rolling hills dotted with oaks are as classic a California landscape as the Sierras or the redwoods. This is quintessential Northern California.

Most of the riding in this park is strenuous with very steep climbs and descents. (Beginning mountain bikers may want to try the relatively easy 5.4-mile trip out to Manzanita Point instead of this ride.) The Middle

Fragnoli

Good friends will always snap a photo of your crash before helping you up.

Ridge Loop is a short loop and, by far, the most popular loop trail in the park. It's got everything—classic singletrack, tight switchbacks, challenging climbs and descents, rocks, sand, water crossings, you name it.

Whenever you ride at Henry Coe, keep your eyes peeled for riders on high-tech bikes. The park is a favorite testing ground for employees of nearby Specialized Bicycle Components.

Getting There: From San Francisco, take 101 south to Morgan Hill and take the East Dunne Avenue exit. Head east on East Dunne, following the signs to the park entrance, about 13 miles. The park charges a $5 per vehicle day-use fee.

Route: Starting from the park headquarters, make a left turn onto the Northern Heights Route, 0.7 mile from the gate. At the top of Pine Ridge, you pass a monument to Henry Coe. Give him your regards and descend to and cross Little Fork Coyote Creek on your way to Frog Lake. Just past the lake and up a small climb, at 3.0 miles, turn right onto the Middle Ridge Trail. This singletrack delight rolls along the ridge with a few short, steep climbs.

Just over 4.0 miles, you pass a junction with Fish Trail. Stay on the Middle Ridge Trail. At 4.7 miles, after passing through a meadow, the trail pitches steeply downhill along a forested ridge. Keep your speed under control and be prepared for the steep, tight switchbacks that begin about halfway down.

The wild ride ends at Poverty Flat, the ride's low point of 1,200 feet. At about the 6.2-mile mark, cross Coyote Creek and take a few deep breaths; you're about to pay for all that fun. Bear right onto the Pacheco Route and granny it up a steep, 1,400-foot, dang-blasted hill.

When you pass the trail junction with Coit Route, at 8.0 miles, the worst is over. Mercifully the last 1.5 miles are an easy spin back to Pacheco Route gate and the parking lot.

Fragnoli

Peak bagging, especially when there's a lookout tower, is one of Northern California's great pastimes.

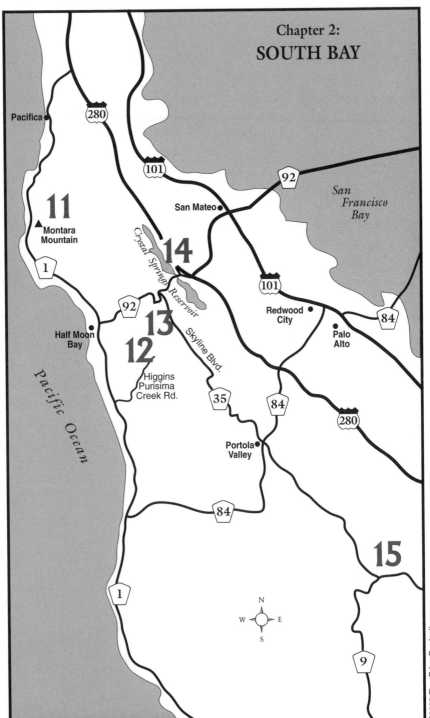

CHAPTER 2

South Bay

by Robin Stuart

Mountain bikers who enjoy San Francisco's South Bay have a lost Spaniard with poor navigation skills to thank. In 1769, Gaspar de Portola "discovered" the San Francisco Bay from a spot near what is now San Pedro State Beach on the Bay Area peninsula. De Portola had actually been hunting for Monterey, about 100 or so miles south, but he must have been distracted on his trek north from San Diego. His mistake was to our advantage. With only a little imagination, it's still possible to see what Gaspar saw in his unplanned discovery. Much of the area down the peninsula remains undeveloped as protected land, open space, national parks and game preserves.

Within 30 minutes drive south of San Francisco, literally hundreds of miles of trails await your tire treads. Driving down Highway 1, past and through the laid-back coastal communities between Pacifica and Half Moon Bay, you have the Pacific Ocean on your right and the western-most end of the Santa Cruz Mountains on your left. The terrain varies from windswept and weather-carved sandstone and granite to redwood rain forests.

Thanks to the marine layer, the weather is fairly pleasant year-round, with temperatures ranging from the forties to the sixties in the winter, and the sixties through eighties in the summer months. In the winter and early spring, wearing removable layers of clothing is strongly recommended as the temperature can vary as much as 10 degrees on a 1,000-foot climb. Particularly in redwood forests, the farther you get away from the valley floor, the warmer it gets.

Those preferring warmer climes and drier conditions need only turn left at Half Moon Bay and head a few minutes east. On the inland side of the coastal range lies the South Bay region. Home of Silicon Valley, political conservatives and great weather, the South Bay also boasts a smorgasbord of trails ranging from long, easy spins to lung-busting climbs. The parks, open spaces and game preserves are all heavily forested with redwood, eucalyptus and several species of pine.

On weekends, the trails in this region are sometimes crowded, but so far everyone is well-behaved, if not downright polite. There's plenty of great riding and hiking for all.

11 Old San Pedro Mountain Road/ North Peak

Distance: 12.4 miles
Difficulty: Strenuous, mildly technical
Elevation: 1,800' gain/loss
Ride Type: Out-and-back on access roads
Season: Year-round
Map: Montara Mountain
Comments: There's no water on this ride, but there are outhouses.

Highlights: Awesome views and a wild downhill make this one of the most popular rides in the area. The top of North Peak (1,898') offers a 360-degree panorama of the entire Bay Area. On clear days, you can see as far north as Point Reyes and Napa County, as far south as Santa Cruz, and as far east as the Sierras hiding behind Mount Diablo. To the west, the Farallon Islands are the only land mass interrupting the Pacific Ocean.

Old San Pedro Mountain Road runs north along the western side of Montara Mountain from the town of Montara to Pacifica. As the name suggests, it was once an automobile route between San Francisco and Half Moon Bay. Known as Coastside Boulevard, it opened in 1915 and was abandoned in 1937 in favor of the "new" state highway, Highway 1, although some folks used it until after World War II. The trail that exists now is made up of sandstone and deteriorating asphalt. Every winter, a little more of the asphalt gives way to dirt.

The top of Old San Pedro Mountain Road becomes North Peak Access Road, a jeep trail used by park

The climb to North Peak.

Stuart/Jensen

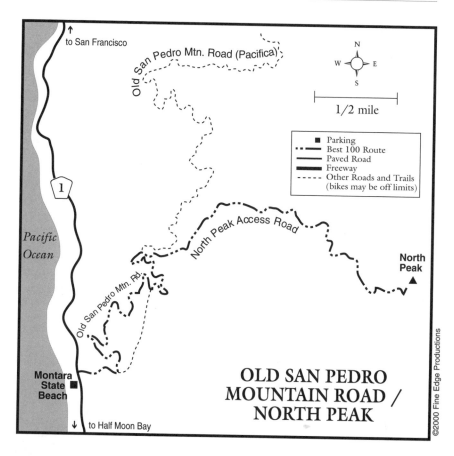

to San Francisco

Old San Pedro Mtn. Road (Pacifica)

N
W E
S

1/2 mile

■ Parking
Best 100 Route
Paved Road
Freeway
Other Roads and Trails
(bikes may be off limits)

1

Pacific
Ocean

North Peak Access Road

North
Peak

Old San Pedro Mtn. Rd.

Montara
State
Beach

to Half Moon Bay

OLD SAN PEDRO
MOUNTAIN ROAD /
NORTH PEAK

©2000 Fine Edge Productions

rangers and various agencies to reach the communications towers at the top. The trail turns into an all-sandstone adventure in traction at this point, rolling steeply to the Peak. The descent is what makes this trail famous—a high-speed roller coaster on a surface that sometimes feels like marbles.

The Old San Pedro Mountain Road portion of the trail is the busiest, used year-round by mountain bikers, hikers and equestrians. The closer you get to North Peak, the more traffic thins out.

Getting There: From San Francisco, drive 22 miles south on Highway 1.

The trailhead is on the left side of the highway just past Devil's Slide, easily identified by a metal gate and trail marker. Although the area in front of the gate will accommodate only four cars, the Montara State Beach parking lot is almost directly across the highway (with much easier access both in and out).

Route: Follow the trail of broken asphalt, rocks and sand to the first fork at the ranger's house. Hang a left here and keep following the gradually disintegrating trail of broken pavement. Don't worry, about halfway up, it gives way completely to dirt.

Along the way, you come across

several singletrack offshoots, none of which are signed and all but one of which are legal for bikes (the exception has a circle-slash-bike marker). Almost all of these dead-end within a mile but they make a nice diversion. On this particular ride, however, you need to save your strength.

About 1.0 mile up, you come to a fun little S-shaped whoop-de-do. In the winter, it becomes a whoop-de-wet, filling with rainwater runoff. Continue snaking your way up the mountain.

As you gain elevation, you can see behind you the towns of Montara and Moss Beach. A little higher up, you can see Half Moon Bay and Pillar Point Harbor, marked by the radar tower which is used to track satellites.

You also notice a couple of over-turned rusting automobiles dotting the mountain side, remnants of what once was.

At 2.5 miles, you come to another fork. To the left, Old San Pedro Mountain Road continues on, descending into Pacifica. On this ride, keep going straight and shift into your granny gear. You're about to climb a loose, steep section known lovingly as "The Wall." The Wall ascends 500 feet in 0.5 mile. The thought that keeps your legs moving is knowing that you get to ride down this sucker.

Past The Wall, the trail gets a lot more interesting. The foliage flanking the trail becomes more dense with coastal scrub and manzanita, and there are just enough short descents

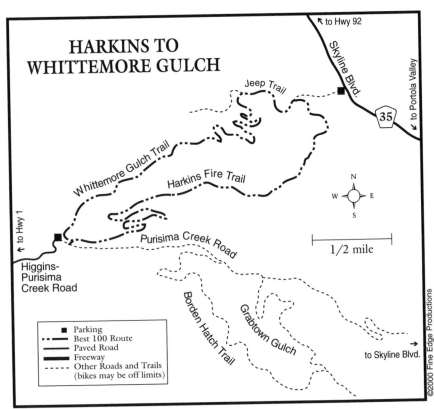

to keep your spirits up as you continue to gain altitude. And then, of course, there are the views. As you wind your way up to the ridge line, you see alternately the north coast (San Francisco, Mount Tam and Point Reyes) on the left and the south coast (Half Moon Bay, Pescadero and Santa Cruz) to the right.

You know you're just about there when you reach the first communication tower, which is basically a bunch of antennas and generators. Keep heading straight past the first tower and head up to the next one. When you see the sharp left turn, take it. It will be obvious. This is followed by a deeply-rutted right turn. Within a few feet, you find yourself in a small clearing, sharing level ground with the fenced-in communication setup. There's a short, narrow trail of loose granite rocks rising up to the left. Follow it to the dead end, about 10 feet. Look around. Amazing, huh?

After ample gawking time comes the best part; you get to go back down. There is no speed limit, but in the warm spring and summer months, keep your speed in check because you will likely encounter other bicyclists and hikers. In the wet winter months, when traction is at its best, use caution but don't expect to see too many other fools like you traipsing around up here.

12 Harkins Fire Trail to Whittemore Gulch

Distance: 6.8 miles
Difficulty: Strenuous, somewhat technical
Elevation: 1,400' gain/loss; begin/end 400'; high point 1,800'
Ride Type: Loop on fire road and singletrack
Season: Harkins, year-round; Whittemore Gulch, spring through fall
Map: Woodside. The Midpeninsula Open Space District produces a brochure with trail map available by calling 650-691-1200. Trail map also available on site.
Comments: Helmets required. Speed limit of 15 mph suggested but currently not enforced. Whittemore Gulch Trail is closed to bikes and equestrians during the rainy season. No water at trailheads, but outhouses at upper and lower trailheads. This route saw a lot of trail work and bridge repair during 1999, but the bridge should be in place by summer 2000.

Highlights: Nestled on the western slopes of the Santa Cruz Mountains just east of Half Moon Bay is the Purisima Creek Redwoods Open Space Preserve. The 2,519-acre park offers a variety of bike trails, including one of the region's most awesome singletracks, the Whittemore Gulch Trail. This is what mountain biking is all about: tight switchbacks, precarious dropoffs, negotiating through rocks and winding around trees, all in a spectacular redwood forest.

The Harkins Fire Trail is no slouch, either. Its name is deceiving; this "fire trail" has two stretches of singletrack, a wide fire road section and the rest which is roughly the width of doubletrack. Harkins presents you with fast sweeping turns, steep technical sections through loose rocks and tree roots, seasonal bouts with mud, and a climb that tests your levels of fitness and determination.

Jensen

Ride #12

preserve's main entrance and parking lot is on Highway 35/Skyline Boulevard, 4.5 miles south of 92.

To get to the preserve's lower entrance, take 92 down to Highway 1. Turn left onto Highway 1 and left again onto Higgins-Purisima Creek Road, about 1 mile south of Half Moon Bay. Keep going straight at the fork. The parking lot is about 2 miles past the fork, on the right.

Route: The traffic on the trail system at Purisima seems to move counterclockwise or by shuttle. This is due to the elevation changes; if you want to do a loop, you have to climb one trail to get to the other. Because I prefer going out with a bang instead of a whimper, I suggest starting from the lower parking lot and climbing up Harkins Fire Trail. This also makes a convenient segue to the next ride.

So, from the lower gate, pedal 50 yards or so along Purisima Creek Road, the main trail along Purisima Creek, and turn left onto the wooden bridge. On the other side of the bridge, turn right onto Harkins (all of the trails at Purisima are well marked). The climb begins in the cool shade of towering redwoods, accompanied by Purisima Creek.

As you climb out of the redwoods, the trail turns from mud to dry powder while the temperature goes up a few degrees. The landscape changes from lush rain forest to the wide-open feeling of the Sierras. If you can take your eyes off of the pine, scrub and wildflowers flanking the trail, you have views of the neighbor-

Whittemore Gulch is a popular hiking trail and, as always, bicyclists are at the bottom of the right-of-way pecking order. Although there are signs of the presence of horses, the most likely place that you will encounter equestrians is on the Harkins Fire Trail.

Both trails afford ample views of the Pacific and the lower coastal hills. Most of your riding time, however, is spent among the redwoods and Douglas fir. It's a great place to enjoy being alive.

Getting There: From San Francisco, take Highway 280 south to Highway 92, about 27 miles. From 92, take the Highway 35/Skyline Boulevard turnoff, which comes up quickly. The

The climb up Harkins Fire Trail.

Stuart/Jensen

Jensen

Ride #13

ing Santa Cruz Mountains while the ocean is behind you.

The trail narrows and widens, alternating between gentle rolling slopes and steep, out-of-the-saddle grunters. The last 0.5 mile is an easy wall-hugging singletrack that offers a beautiful view of the coast.

The trail ends at a jeep trail. To the right is the upper parking lot. Turn left and keep your eyes peeled for the Whittemore Gulch trailhead, about 0.5 mile down. The trailhead is on the left; if you go by too fast, you'll miss it. It's set back off the jeep trail a couple of feet, in a thickly wooded area, and is identified by a wooden fence with a trail marker.

Now for some serious fun. The trail starts with a

gentle downslope through the trees and leads to a test of your switchback skills. The first 1.5 miles are tricky due to half-a-dozen very tight switchbacks that wind down the face of the mountain. After the last switchback, the trail goes from an open meadow to an E-ticket roller coaster through the redwoods. The scenery, if you take time to notice, is impossibly beautiful with huge redwoods and ferns everywhere.

Too quickly, you find yourself back at the bridge by the lower parking lot. Turn right and cross it to get back to the parking lot.

13 Borden Hatch to Grabtown Gulch

Distance: 6 miles
Difficulty: Strenuous, somewhat technical
Elevation: 1,200' gain/loss; begin/end 400'; high point 1,600'
Ride Type: Loop on jeep trails
Season: Year-round
Map: Woodside. The Midpeninsula Open Space District produces a brochure with trail map available by calling 650-691-1200. Trail map also available on site.
Comments: Helmets required. Speed limit of 15 mph suggested but not enforced.

Stuart/Jensen

Fern-lined singletrack along Borden Hatch.

Highlights: Although it's short, this is the second most popular ride in Purisima Creek Redwoods Open Space Preserve. The Borden Hatch Trail is a 3.5-mile climb along a canyon wall through a forest of redwoods and eucalyptus. If you go to the end of the trail, you will find yourself at a country road that takes you to another park, Skeggs Point. Borden Hatch also leads to Grabtown Gulch, a hair-raising 1.25-mile descent back down the canyon to Purisima Creek. As if the grade didn't make it lively enough, there are water bars every 50-100 feet for those who prefer to fly.

This loop is most populated by bicyclists; Borden Hatch, albeit one of the

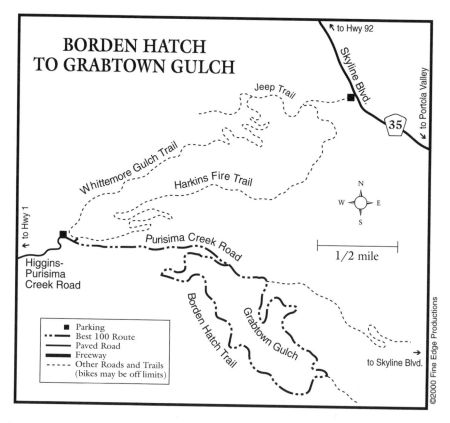

BORDEN HATCH TO GRABTOWN GULCH

to Hwy 92

Skyline Blvd.

Jeep Trail

to Portola Valley

35

Whittemore Gulch Trail

Harkins Fire Trail

N W E S

to Hwy 1

Purisima Creek Road

1/2 mile

Higgins-Purisima Creek Road

Borden Hatch Trail

Grabtown Gulch

to Skyline Blvd.

■ Parking
— ·— ·— Best 100 Route
——— Paved Road
▬▬▬ Freeway
------ Other Roads and Trails
       (bikes may be off limits)

©2000 Fine Edge Productions

prettiest trails in the park, is considered an out-and-back by loop-happy hikers for whom the steep Grabtown Gulch holds little appeal. Once in a while you may encounter hearty souls making their way up Grabtown Gulch, but not often.

Because this loop is short, most riders incorporate it into other rides. Therefore, it gets less populated later in the day. Depending on the time of year, the terrain is almost-but-not-quite dry to very muddy.

Getting There: This loop can be directly accessed only from the lower parking lot. Of course, you can ride across the park from the upper lot to get to the trailhead. Follow the driving directions for the previous ride.

Route: From the gate at the lower parking lot, follow Purisima Creek Road for 1.0 mile to the Borden Hatch trailhead, on the right. You begin to climb immediately, but the severity of the grade eases past the first turn. After that point, it alternates from "this isn't so bad," to kind of hard, to downright steep. There are also several coasting sections and a couple of downhills just to keep things interesting. You get to use pretty much all of your gears on this trail.

The only time you do not have towering trees as a ceiling is when you come to a trail junction in a small meadow, 3.5 miles up. Turn left onto Grabtown Gulch and quickly descend back into the trees. The turns on this

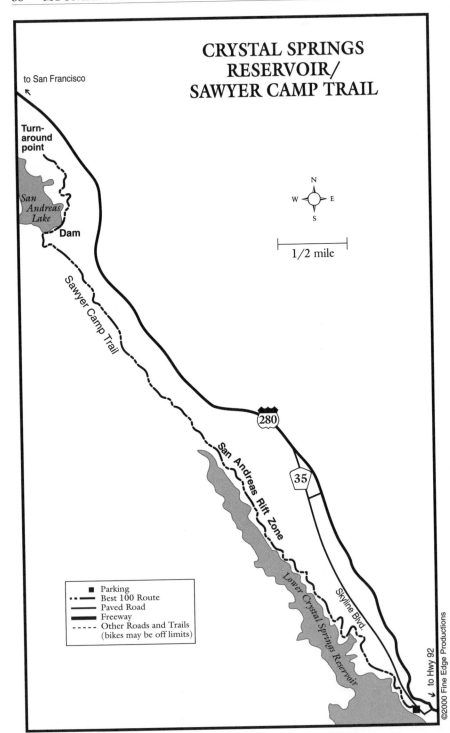

CRYSTAL SPRINGS RESERVOIR/ SAWYER CAMP TRAIL

to San Francisco

Turn-around point

San Andreas Lake

Dam

Sawyer Camp Trail

N
W   E
S

1/2 mile

280

35

San Andreas Rift Zone

Lower Crystal Springs Reservoir

Skyline Blvd.

to Hwy 92

■ Parking
┅ Best 100 Route
— Paved Road
▬ Freeway
┅┅ Other Roads and Trails
     (bikes may be off limits)

©2000 Fine Edge Productions

trail are mostly blind, and the water-bars seem to get taller the farther down you go. It also gets slippery in spots. Again, it is a beautiful trail, guarded by redwoods, eucalyptus and ferns.

The last two waterbars are the steepest and may require a bit of lifting to get your front wheel onto them. The trail ends back on Purisima Creek Road, about 0.25 mile from the Borden Hatch trailhead. Turn left onto Purisima Creek Road to get back to the parking lot.

14 Crystal Springs Reservoir/ Sawyer Camp Trail

Distance: 12 miles
Difficulty: Easy, not technical
Elevation: 300' gain/loss
Ride Type: Out-and-back on pavement
Season: Year-round
Maps: Montara Mountain, San Mateo
Comments: Mosquito repellent is a must. Enforced speed limits. Water and bathrooms available throughout ride.

Highlights: Although not a "real" mountain bike trail, under the strictest definition, the Sawyer Camp Trail warrants attention because it's such a great family trail; an easy, rolling out-and-back with plenty of benches and bathrooms. In fact, families are the dominant user-group, so keep an eye out for wandering toddlers and small children wobbling on their first bikes.

This trail is also a popular winter destination for local mountain bikers, when rains close the nearby trails, or as an easy spin on warm summer evenings. At any given time, you're as likely to see the latest in full-suspension high-zoot technology as you are a kid on a Big Wheel. The path winds along the lower branch of the Crystal Springs Reservoir and the southern end of San Andreas Lake. Beneath the lake is the site where our old friend, Gaspar de Portola, camped after making his exhausting discovery. The surrounding land is now a fish and game reserve; woodland creatures may shadow you on the hillside above the trail as you make your way through stands of live oak, Monterey pine, eucalyptus and laurel.

Speaking of laurel, you'll be passing by the oldest and largest one. Over 600 years old, the Jepson Laurel is named for California botanist Willis Linn Jepson. Signs in both directions point out the tree.

The Sawyer Camp Trail parallels the infamous San Andreas Fault, which was responsible for the "Great Earthquake" of 1906 that devastated San Francisco. Most of the trail runs approximately a mile parallel to the fault, although once you cross the dam, you're just a few feet away.

Getting There: From San Francisco, drive 27 miles south on Highway 280 to the Bunker Hill exit and veer right. Turn right onto Skyline Boulevard. The reservoir entrance is about

0.5 mile away, on the left. There's a small parking lot just south of the gate, or you can park on the road.

Route: The minute you pass through the reservoir's main gate, you're on the trail. There are no turns or tricky parts, making this one of the all-time easiest trails to follow. Scattered alongside the paved path are several taste-tempting morsels of singletrack. Unfortunately, as a multitude of signs and your fellow trail users will gleefully point out, these are strictly off-limits to bikes. Violators are not only subject to fines, but to serious doses of poison oak and insect bites as well.

You share the trail with walkers and in-line skaters until about the 3.0-mile mark, at which point the crowds thin out. The famed Jepson Laurel towers off to your left at 3.5 miles. Its moss-shrouded cousins keep you

company for the next 1.0 mile or so, until you start a mild climb.

At the top of the rise, just past the 5.0-mile mark, you ride along the San Andreas Dam at the southeast end of San Andreas Lake. The dam was built in 1869 and its claim to fame is its strength; it survived the 1906 earthquake unscathed, although pipes leading in and out of it sheared right off. The dam also serves as a scenic overlook. As you cross it, Crystal Springs Valley is laid out to the right. From this point of view, there's no sign of civilization, or even the bike path you just came up, only rolling green hills and lots of trees.

On the other side of the dam, an easy 0.5-mile climb takes you to the end of the path at the park's north gate. Turn around here and head back, keeping in mind that foot traffic starts getting heavy again at about the halfway mark.

Stuart/Jensen

Saratoga Gap

15 Saratoga Gap

Distance: 13.6 miles
Difficulty: Strenuous, somewhat technical, unrideable in one short section (no matter how good you are)
Elevation: 1,200' gain/loss
Ride Type: Loop on fire roads and singletrack
Season: Year-round; heavy rain closes portions of the trail
Maps: Mindego Hill, Cupertino (Existing topos do not show the Saratoga Gap Trail or the Canyon Trail/Charcoal Road junction that leads over Table Mountain.)
Comments: There are no amenities, no water or restrooms. This trail gets very hot and dry in the summer months, so bring plenty of water.

Highlights: This is one of the most popular loops in the Bay Area. A series of trails lead through grasslands and forest, replete with pine, oak and the ever-present ferns. The terrain rolls, steeply at times, along the ridges

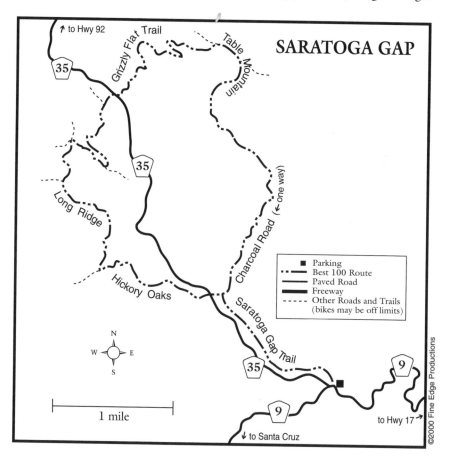

and down the canyon to Stevens Creek and back up, making for a truly scenic adventure.

The trails join together three open-space areas: Saratoga Gap, Montebello and Long Ridge. While each open-space preserve offers its own share of mountain biking opportunities, this particular loop provides a sort of sampler plate.

Getting There: The trailhead is located at the junction of Highways 9 and 35. From San Francisco, take 280 south to the Highway 92 turnoff. Head west on 92 to Highway 35 (Skyline Boulevard), which pops up right away. Turn left onto Skyline and follow it to the parking lot at the junction with Highway 9, about 25 miles.

Route: From the gate, follow the first stretch of singletrack, the Saratoga Gap Trail. If you're observant, you may notice a Y at 0.6 mile; stay right and follow the main singletrack to a sandy clearing. At this point, you're faced with four choices: the extreme right dead-ends immediately and the extreme left leads out to Highway 35. Bearing right takes you onto the Charcoal Road Trail. Tantalizing as it is, especially for those who know what's in store, Charcoal Road is only legal to uphill bike traffic (you'll climb it at the end of the ride). That leaves just one choice: cross the sand pit bearing left (but not sharp left) to continue on the Saratoga Gap singletrack.

At 2.1 miles, the singletrack ends at Highway 35. Cross the road to pick up the Hickory Oaks Trail. You can take either the main fire road or the singletrack option on the right; they converge around the bend at the Hickory Oaks fire road. After they

converge, turn right at the fire road for an easy climb, bearing right at the first Y at 2.3 miles. At the top of the climb, enjoy the panoramic view of the South Bay before dropping onto a mile or so of chapparal roller coaster.

At 3.1 miles, bear right followed by a left turn at 3.3 miles, following the markers for the Long Ridge Trail. Just past the street sign (no, I'm not kidding), go straight into the forest and onto Long Ridge. You reach another fork at 3.9 miles; bear right to stay on Long Ridge. The singletrack winds its way back down into the valley. Ignore the spurs that you see on the right and continue straight through until you reach a trail crossing at 5.4 miles. Make a sharp left here for a gradual climb, following the signs for the Grizzly Flat trail.

You find yourself back at Highway 35 at 5.9 miles; cross the road and pick up the Grizzly Flat fire road on the other side. Grizzly Flat is a long, fast and sweeping descent from a chapparal and manzanita ridge into cool redwoods. Turn left at the unmarked crossing at 7.0 miles to continue down. At the bottom, around 7.9 miles, turn left along a short singletrack that leads to Peters Creek, seasonally more like a river. If you can ride across it, you are officially a stud. Humans will have to portage through it, using the rocks strategically placed by the rangers.

On the other side of the creek, say good-bye to downhill for a while. The climb begins with a series of tight singletrack switchbacks. At 8.2 miles, turn right toward Stevens Canyon Road. You get a brief respite from climbing which ends at another water crossing, much smaller and easier to negotiate depending on the weather.

Bear right on the other side, at 8.6 miles, onto Table Mountain

Trail. This is a steep, technical single-track with really nice scenery. Right around the 9-mile mark, a short length of the trail has eroded into a narrow ditch filled with gnarled tree roots and rocks—a trail restoration project waiting to happen. Mortals will have to walk this section. At least it's very short.

Back on the bike, continue the singletrack climb until it ends at 9.9 miles at a fire road. This is a popular catch-your-breath spot. Turn right to continue on the last leg of the Table Mountain Trail. This part of the trail is a roller with a short but very welcome downhill.

At 10.3 miles, gear down and get comfy. Remember that uphill-only trail you saw near the beginning of the ride? You're about to get friendly with it. You turn right onto Charcoal Road, a fire road climb with a couple of extra steeps thrown in. At 11.0 miles, turn right to stay on Charcoal.

The brutality ends at 11.9 miles when you drop back into the sand pit clearing at the trail junction with the Saratoga Gap Trail. Turn left onto the blessedly shaded and frolicking singletrack to return to the parking lot.

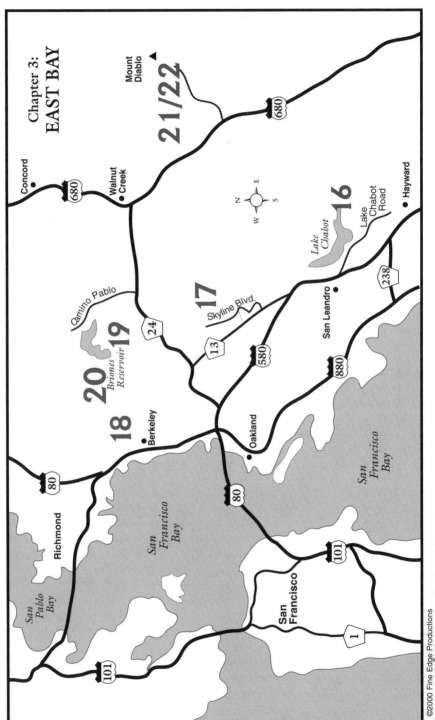

Chapter 3:
EAST BAY

©2000 Fine Edge Productions

CHAPTER 3

East Bay

by Robin Stuart

If you live in the Bay Area, the chances are that you or someone you love lives in the East Bay. Just across the Bay Bridge from San Francisco proper, this sprawling suburbopolis is comprised of dozens of mini-suburbs with names like Hayward, San Leandro and Castro Valley; upscale bedroom communities like Danville, Pleasant Hill and Blackhawk; and the cities-within-the-suburbs of Oakland, Richmond and Berkeley. Doesn't exactly sound like a mountain biker's paradise, does it?

Don't be fooled. Lurking within and beyond each of the aforementioned locales are several of the most popular trails in Northern California. The allure of the East Bay parks is their knack for containing some of the most spectacular ridge rides this side of the Sierras. On any given trail, the views may range from the Bay to Yosemite. The trails themselves are visions in eucalyptus and live oak, with smatterings of pine and redwood.

Another likely reason for the East Bay's popularity is the accessibility of its trails; while some of the climbs and descents may be, shall we say, invigorating, few of them are technically difficult. Tree roots and loose rocks pop up here and there, but the most common technical challenge is sand-like pulverized soil. The later it gets in the season, the looser the trails become, owing to the region's arid summer and fall months.

One of the drawbacks of the East Bay is its lack of legal singletrack. However, as the number of mountain bikers continues to grow, hopefully, so too will our clout. In the meantime, there are plenty of fire roads, jeep trails and doubletrack with spectacular views to keep us busy and breathless.

16 Lake Chabot Loop

Distance: 11.2 miles
Difficulty: Moderately strenuous, mildly technical
Elevation: 600' gain/loss
Ride Type: Loop on fire roads
Season: Year-round
Map: Olmsted & Bros. Rambler's Guide to the Trails of the East Bay Hills (Central). The East Bay Regional Park District makes a free brochure and trail map available at the park or by calling 510-562-PARK.
Comments: Water is available at each entrance and along the paved portions of the path. Bells are required.

Highlights: This loop is an area favorite with riders of all abilities. Beginners will find a couple of the climbs challenging, but they are paid for in spades by the overall roller-coaster ride around the lake and through forests of madrone, pine and live oak in the park's southern end, and eucalyptus, bay and pine in the north.

The ride follows a circuit around the 4,900-acre Anthony Chabot Regional Park, better known as Lake Chabot. The park sits on the boundaries of Castro Valley, San Leandro and Oakland and has entrances in each city. The lake itself is actually a reservoir built in 1875 by a placer mining engineer, Anthony Chabot. It's now used as an emergency water supply for the East Bay.

Lake Chabot, one of the East Bay's most popular rides.

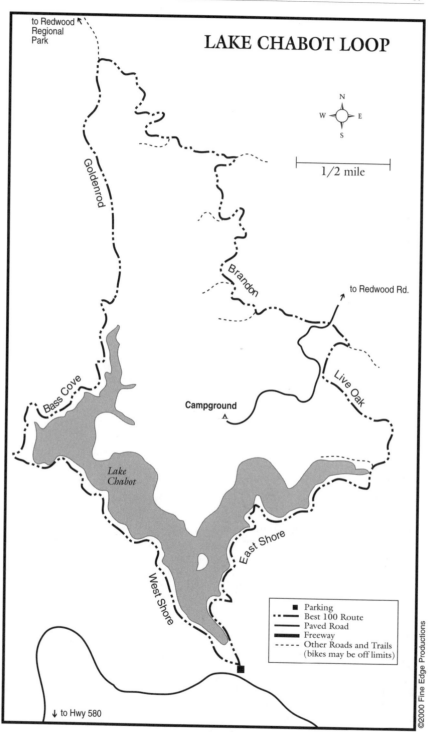

LAKE CHABOT LOOP

to Redwood Regional Park

Goldenrod

to Redwood Rd.

Brandon

Bass Cove

Live Oak

Campground

Lake Chabot

East Shore

West Shore

1/2 mile

N
W E
S

■ Parking
∙–∙∙ Best 100 Route
—— Paved Road
▬▬ Freeway
----- Other Roads and Trails
(bikes may be off limits)

↓ to Hwy 580

©2000 Fine Edge Productions

Getting There: From the Bay Bridge, head east on 580 toward Hayward. Take the Fairmont Drive exit, turning left at the second light onto Fairmont. Follow Fairmont over the hill into Castro Valley where the road becomes Lake Chabot Road. Just past the first left is the left turn into the park. Expect to pay a $3.50 day-use fee during the summer and on weekends, and a $1 fee for dogs— not allowed on trails.

Route: Starting from the main parking lot, follow the paved footpath into the barbecue area at the marina. Make the first right turn over a small bridge and turn left onto the East Shore path. This is a popular walking path with a bike speed limit of 15 mph. Keep right and be alert around blind turns for fishermen holding their poles straight out in front of them.

At about 1.5 miles, you reach a gate that signifies the end of the pavement as well as the foot traffic. Just past the gate, turn left and walk down the narrow steps to the bridge. On the other side of the bridge, gear down and get ready for the worst climb of the day.

Bear right and bear with the Live Oak Trail. It's graded regularly which ensures loose conditions. To the right is the southwestern boundary of the Willow Park Golf Course. As you creep your way up, you can feel superior to the golfers until you round a bend which hides the plaid bunch from view. To the left, you have a great view of Honker Bay and the southern half of Lake Chabot.

The worst of the climbing is over as you reach the 2.5-mile point. The trail levels for a short while, ending at a road that leads to a campground. Turn right on the trail that parallels

the road, and follow it as it winds up to the ridge.

At the top, at about 3.0 miles, make a hairpin turn to the left onto the Brandon Trail. The trail quickly leads to a gate and another parking lot. Go out the gate, cross the parking lot and the road, and pick up Brandon through the gate on the other side. The next 1.0 mile or so is a washboard, the result of being a popular thoroughfare for equestrians. Keep an eye out for them.

At approximately 3.5 miles, you come to an intersection; bear right to stay on the Brandon Trail. A second intersection quickly follows; again, stay right. About this time, you'll probably notice the sound of gunfire. On the other side of the ridge is a shooting range. Although it is disconcerting, you're not in any danger.

The trail dives down, then swoops back up again, which is a recurring pattern for the rest of the ride. At the top of the first brief climb, you reach the next intersection; bear right and keep on Brandon. Within 0.5 mile, at the next intersection, turn left. Believe it or not, you're still on Brandon.

Not all trails are signed, so in late spring through fall, the trail intersections are marked with white arrows painted on the ground; the arrows point in the direction of the Brandon Trail to minimize the confusion.

After a few more swoops, the trail leads down a rocky hill. At the bottom of the hill, at about 6.0 miles, you come to a stone bridge. If you turn right, you can follow the East Bay Skyline Trail to the Redwood Regional Park. On this ride, though, turn left and out of the oak and begin the climb through the eucalyptus up the Goldenrod Trail. The climb levels at 6.6 miles and rolls along the northwestern ridge before diving back down toward the lake. This ridge skirts the back side of a eucalyptus forest; it smells good but you won't see much.

At approximately 8.0 miles, the trail dead ends at a paved path used by golf carts (this time, it's the Lake Chabot Golf Course). Turn left for a quick paved descent, then left again at the bottom and back to the dirt to catch the Bass Cove Trail. This trail is a fun stretch of twisting downhill leading back to the water's edge.

You come to a fork at 9.1 miles; bear left followed by a quick right to the trail's end at the paved West Shore Trail and the dam. Turn left and follow the rolling path back to the marina and the parking lot.

17 Redwood Regional Park/ West Ridge to East Ridge Loop

Distance: 9.0 miles
Difficulty: Moderately strenuous, some technical sections
Elevation: 900' gain/loss
Ride Type: Loop on fire roads
Season: Year-round
Map: Olmsted & Bros. Rambler's Guide to the Trails of the East Bay Hills (Central Section). The East Bay Regional Park District makes a free brochure and trail map available at the park or by calling 510-562-PARK.
Comments: Water is available at park entrances; bells are required. Watch for dogs on trails near parking areas as this park has become quite popular with dog owners.

Highlights: Slightly north of Lake Chabot (and connected by the East Bay Skyline Trail) is the regal Redwood Regional Park. As the name implies, one of the park's highlights is its inviting forest of redwoods; the West/East Loop begins and ends under their cool canopy. Believe me, in the heat of summer, it's very much appreciated.

Although shorter, this trail is a little more exciting than the Lake Chabot Loop, which is why riders with the time and energy like to combine the two (such a loop would be 22.5 miles). Here in Redwood Regional, the loop begins on a redwood-forested ridge, drops into the canyon and climbs back up. Sounds simple enough, right?

What makes this ride so popular is that it starts with a few tree roots and drops along great slabs of rock which lead to a loose and dusty screaming downhill. You have a chance to catch your breath on the level traipse across the canyon floor to a grunting uphill followed by a roller-coaster ride back to the car.

Although some people have different names for it, nearly every Bay Area rider you talk to mentions this ride as one of their favorites.

Getting There: From the Bay Bridge, take 580 to 24 (Walnut Creek). From 24, take Highway 13 (Warren Freeway) south to the Joaquin Miller Road exit. Head east on Joaquin Miller to Skyline Boulevard. Turn left on Skyline and follow it for approximately 3 miles to the

REDWOOD REGIONAL PARK
West Ridge to East Ridge Loop

to Berkeley ↑

Skyline gate

East Ridge

N
W ← → E
S

1/2 mile

Skyline Blvd.

West Ridge

Joaquin Miller Road
to Oakland

■ Parking
·—·— Best 100 Route
——— Paved Road
▬▬ Freeway
----- Other Roads and Trails
      (bikes may be off limits)

↘ to Oakland   to Lake Chabot ↘

©2000 Fine Edge Productions

parking lot at the Redwood Regional Skyline Gate which is on the right.

Route: From the gate, turn right into the redwoods and onto the West Ridge Trail. Along the way, you have to ignore several beckoning single-tracks that lead down to a creek trail; all of the singletrack here is illegal. Just over 1.0 mile from the gate, the West Ridge Trail seemingly ends at a second parking lot. Shoot straight across and you can see where it continues on the other end.

Right away, you get to test your technical prowess with a section of gnarled, twisty, tall tree roots on the trail. They look kind of like a large primeval nest. At that same point, the

left bank of the trail drops off, so you can't really go around them.

Once you've crossed the roots, the trail winds up and through the forest, leading out of the redwoods and to the next adventure, the rock slabs. The rock is shaped almost like giant, off-kilter stairs and the traction is better than you think it would be. Head on down and keep in mind that the last "step" is kind of tall; beginners should lay off the front brake while more advanced riders should raise their front wheels to smooth out the landing.

From this point, the trail levels and gets dusty for the next 1.0 mile or so. Then the trail veers off to the right and starts to slope downhill.

The grade is gentle at first, leading to a wide turn after which it pitches into a loose and steep straight-away. At the bottom, the trail levels as you wind out of the forest and into a grass clearing. Follow the path through and around the picnic area.

The dirt briefly becomes a paved path as you bear left onto the connector to East Ridge, at 6.0 miles. (Heading straight on West Ridge leads you out of the park to Lake Chabot, a little over 2.0 miles away.) At the sign for East Ridge, the dirt begins again and so does a short, nasty climb.

At the top, there's a brief level spot before the trail pitches uphill again, this time for about 1.0 mile. There are periodic level spots in the climb that make it bearable. There are also great views of the surrounding parklands in between the trees.

Rider enjoying some of Redwood Regional Park's level singletrack

Right around 7.0 miles, you reach the redwoods and the end of relentless climbing. From here, the trail rolls along the canyon wall back to the parking lot.

18 Tilden Park/Wildcat Loop

Distance: 13.3 miles
Difficulty: Moderate, mildly technical
Elevation: 600' gain/loss
Ride Type: Loop on fire roads
Season: Spring through fall
Map: Olmsted & Bros. Rambler's Guide to the Trails of the East Bay Hills (North Section). The East Bay Regional Park District makes a free brochure and trail map available at the park or by calling 510-562-PARK.
Comments: Water is available at the trailhead. The clay-like soil turns into a quagmire in the rain; in the event of spring rains, let it dry out for several days before attempting to ride here.

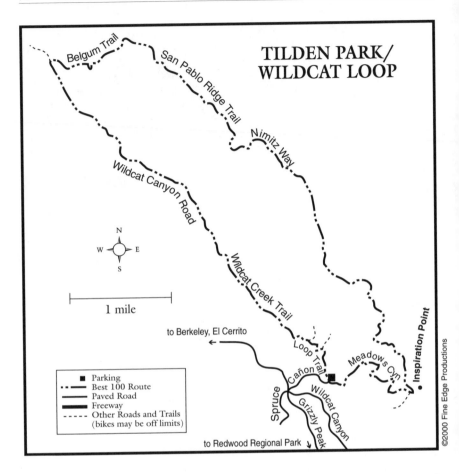

TILDEN PARK/WILDCAT LOOP

Highlights: Tilden, one of the East Bay's oldest parks, is often mentioned in the same breath as Redwood Regional Park. Nestled in the Berkeley hills, this particular loop stretches north beyond the boundaries of Tilden and into adjacent Wildcat Canyon Regional Park. The ride is akin to the Lake Chabot Loop—rolling fire roads through forests of live oak and eucalyptus, a portion of paved bike path, and a climb thrown in for good measure.

There are two features that make this ride a crowd-pleaser; first, it's relatively easy, and second, you can catch a glimpse of the Hayward Fault.

The loop takes you past an unused road and parking lot, abandoned as a result of the damage wrought by the road's placement literally right on top of the active fault. What Californian doesn't secretly fancy herself (or himself) a junior seismologist?

Getting There: From the Bay Bridge, take 80 north (Berkeley/Richmond) to the University Avenue exit. From University, turn left onto Martin Luther King Drive. Follow MLK for about a mile and turn right onto Marin Avenue. About a half-mile up Marin, turn left onto Spruce. Follow Spruce to the intersection at the Spruce Gate with Grizzly Peak, Wildcat Canyon and Cañon Drive. Make a left onto Cañon Drive. Take the first right onto Central Park Drive and left on Lone Oak Road to the Lone Oak parking lot and trailhead.

Route: From the parking lot, head up through the picnic area to the Loop Trail. This quickly leads to Jewell Lake, a popular stop for walkers and bikers. At the lake, bear right onto the Wildcat Creek Trail. This part of the loop is fairly level, leading out of Tilden Park and into Wildcat Canyon. Once inside the Wildcat boundary, the trail rolls very gently to the cracked abandoned road. Welcome to earthquake country.

Past the damaged road, the trail rolls pleasantly to the intersection with the Belgum Trail at about 5.0 miles. Hang a right onto Belgum and start climbing. This trail takes you out of the canyon and up to the views. Within 1.0 mile, you emerge from the trees to the ridge line and the San Pablo Ridge Trail. Bear right and follow San Pablo along the ridge.

There are a couple of nasty little climbs along the way that reward you with views of the Bay to one side and Mount Diablo to the other. With a final descent, the trail joins paved Nimitz Way at 7.5 miles. This path continues rolling along the ridge to Inspiration Point where you turn right, and back onto dirt, on the Curran Trail.

At the next intersection, which comes up quickly, turn right again, onto the Meadows Canyon Trail. Meadows Canyon takes you on a loose washboarded 1.5-mile downhill that ends back at the parking lot.

19 Briones Regional Park/ Short Loop

Distance: 5.7 miles
Difficulty: Moderately strenuous, mildly technical
Elevation: 800' gain/loss
Ride Type: Loop on sometimes narrow fire roads and doubletrack
Season: Spring through fall
Map: Briones Valley. The East Bay Regional Park District makes a free brochure and trail map available at the park or by calling 510-562-PARK.
Comments: Water is available at the staging area. Cattle regularly graze here; please close all gates behind you.

Highlights: Once a local secret, Briones Regional Park has become one of the East Bay's best known parks for cycling. These days it is a popular race venue. Tucked away in a remote corner of Contra Costa County, Briones is a virtual wonderland of winding trails, breathtaking views, miles of rolling woodlands and wild downhills.

At Briones, a smorgasbord of trails awaits you, leading up from the forests in the Bear Creek Canyon and the Alhambra Valley to grassland ridges and peaks. Although the singletrack is illegal for bikes, there's

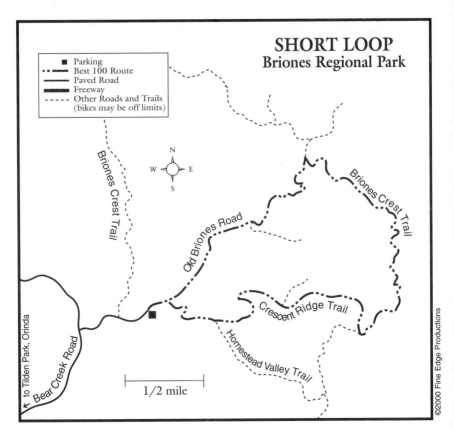

nearly 40 miles of legal fire roads and doubletrack, ranging from short and easy valley forays to day-long adventures filled with thigh-burning climbs and hair-raising downhills.

This particular ride is reserved for the downhill aficionados: a relatively easy climb followed by a twisting, screaming descent that can feel, at times, like a freefall along a loose and dusty fire road with the occasional rock outcropping.

Getting There: From the Bay Bridge, take 580 east to Highway 24 (Walnut Creek). Past the Caldecott Tunnel, take the Orinda exit and turn left onto Camino Pablo. From Camino Pablo, turn right onto Bear Creek Road. The Briones Park Bear Creek Staging Area is on the right, about 4.5 miles up the road. There's a $3.50 day-use fee during the summer and on weekends.

Route: Starting at the gate at the upper parking lot, head up the paved road. The pavement ends around the first turn at a fork where you bear left onto the Old Briones Road Trail. It looks like you're about to climb up into a yucky ol' dry-grass wasteland until you round the first turn. Personally, it reminds me of the Yosemite Valley, sans the big rocks. Whatever impression you get, you find yourself winding around a tree-studded meadow, complete with a

View from Briones Crest.

Stuart/Jensen

creek. The climb starts out very subtly, giving your journey an all-around pleasant beginning.

Just past the corral, turn left at the intersection with the Valley Trail to stay on Old Briones. The climb gets a little tougher, interspersed with a couple of short descents, as you roll your way up to the ridge. As the valley starts to fall away, you can see the San Pablo Reservoir behind you.

At the next trail junction at 1.7 miles, turn right onto the Briones Crest Trail toward Briones Peak. The trail is fairly level at this point and for the next 1.0 mile or so. Between the trees, you can catch glimpses of the surrounding hillsides and Mount Diablo.

At the fork with Table Top and Spengler trails, make a hard right to stay on the Briones Crest Trail. At this point, the roller coaster begins in earnest. The trail heads in an overall downhill direction in a series of sweeping descents followed by sometimes steep climbs.

The trail ends at a cattle gate. Turn right past the gate; this continues to be the Briones Crest Trail. Within 0.5 mile, you see another gate on the right. Turn in here to experience a killer downhill—the often steep, but totally cool Crescent Ridge Trail.

The first hundred feet or so is level, but once the downhill starts it's like a carnival ride. Most of the turns are completely blind so keep your speed in control at all times; you may be greeted by a herd of cows grazing their way across the trail or a couple of startled equestrians.

At about 4.0 miles, at the top of a short climb, the trail levels briefly before pitching down through a very steep granite outcropping. Just wanted to warn you.

The grade eases to almost level at about 4.5 miles at the junction with the Yerba Buena Trail. From here, you can see your valley destination, but you can't see the trail that awaits around the turn. Keep going straight down Crescent Ridge; be prepared for a steep and bumpy ride. The rest of the downhill is a steep, loose and severely hoof-rutted straight-away

down to the meadow.

The trail ends at the Homestead Valley Trail; turn right and follow Homestead Valley across the meadow and through the gate for a last descent to a seasonal water crossing. After a short climb, the trail ends at the junction with the trailhead of the Old Briones Trail. Bear left back onto the paved road to head back to the parking lot.

20 Briones Crest Loop

Distance: 8 miles
Difficulty: Moderately strenuous, mildly technical
Elevation: 800' gain/loss
Ride Type: Loop on sometimes narrow fire roads and doubletrack
Season: Spring through fall
Map: Briones Valley. The East Bay Regional Park District produces a free map of the park available at the park or by calling 510-562-PARK.
Comments: Water is available at the staging area; please close cattle gates behind you.

Highlights: This loop is the most popular ride at Briones Regional Park and a great way to acquaint yourself with the type of trails that the park has to offer. The loop follows the Briones Crest Trail as it rolls around the central portion of the park, through dense forests of live oak and fruit trees, the John Muir Nature Area, past mountain lagoons and back down to the Homestead Valley meadow and Bear Creek. This trail is less taxing than the previous loop; although there are a couple of brief steep climbs and descents, it's suitable for most riders.

Getting There: See the directions for the previous ride.

Route: Beginning at the lower parking lot, go through the gate for the Briones Crest and Deer Creek trails, making the first right onto the Briones Crest Trail. The trail meanders gently up through the trees to the ridge line. At 1.6 miles, you come to an intersection with the Santos Trail; bear left to stay on Briones Crest.

Just past the 2.0-mile mark, you enter the John Muir Nature Area. From this point, the next 2.5 miles roll along the ridge, in and out of the trees and through sweeping turns. Again, be on the lookout for roving herds of grazing cows.

At 3.2 miles, the trail takes you between the two Sindicich Lagoons.

The trail may get a little more populated here by horses and bikes, as this is a convergence point between the northern and southern park entrances.

Past the lagoons, bear right briefly onto Old Briones Road, then make the first left back onto Briones Crest. This section takes you past the park's highest point, Briones Peak (1,483'). On a clear day, you have expansive views of Mount Diablo and the Diablo Valley to the Bay.

At the next trail junction, make a hard right to stay on Briones Crest. The trail hugs the canyon wall as you begin to lose elevation. The trail rolls a little steeper back into the trees, followed by a steepish climb and ending at a cattle gate. Turn right past the gate to stay on Briones Crest. The trail widens for 0.5 mile, giving you glimpses of civilization beyond the trees to your left before turning back toward the park and heading down.

The trail ends at a fork at 6.2 miles. Turn right toward the meadow and onto the Homestead Valley Trail. Just past the next cattle gate, the trail rolls briefly but steeply down to Bear Creek, then back up again to the junction with Old Briones Road. Turn left and follow the trail as it leads out of the park and into the upper parking lot. Cut across the lot to the lower lot and your car.

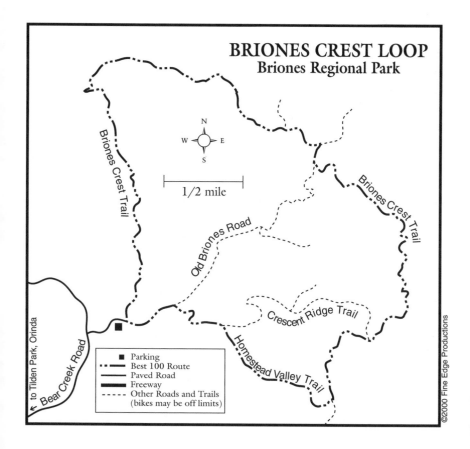

BRIONES CREST LOOP
Briones Regional Park

1/2 mile

Briones Crest Trail

Briones Crest Trail

Old Briones Road

Crescent Ridge Trail

Homestead Valley Trail

to Tilden Park, Orinda

Bear Creek Road

■ Parking
▪▪▪ Best 100 Route
── Paved Road
▬ Freeway
- - - Other Roads and Trails
      (bikes may be off limits)

©2000 Fine Edge Productions

21 Mount Diablo/Wall Point Loop

Distance: 9.5 miles
Difficulty: Strenuous, mildly technical, seasonal water crossings
Elevation: 1,300' gain/loss
Ride Type: Loop on fire roads and singletrack
Season: Late winter through fall
Maps: Diablo, Clayton. (The Mount Diablo Interpretive Assoc. publishes an excellent Trail Map of Mount Diablo State Park and Adjacent Parklands, $5 and worth it at park headquarters.)
Comments: It gets very hot here; carry extra water (available at the trailhead).

Highlights: The feather in the East Bay's cap, the icing on its cake, the heart and soul of the East Bay mountain biking world is Mount Diablo. With a summit elevation of 3,849 feet, Mount Diablo is the tallest mountain in the Bay Area, visible from all corners.

Speaking of views, this mountain has some jaw-droppers. On a clear day, you can get a clean look at Yosemite's Half Dome. At closer range is the Diablo Valley, Sonoma Valley, the Santa Cruz Mountains, Mount Tamalpais and the Marin Headlands.

If it's trails you want, Mount Diablo has them, too. Lots of them. All of the mountain's fire roads are legal, with the added bonus of three singletrack segments. The trails range from almost-easy to forget-it-and-push, and they twist and turn and wind and roll all over the mountain.

While each of the available trails seems to be somebody's favorite, the following rides are known and loved by many. This particular loop is a popular race site, with a couple of challenging climbs and long, sweeping descents. The loop leads through forests of live oak, across a couple of creeks, and up to a chaparral-covered ridge before turning back toward the trees and through the Diablo Ranch.

Getting There: From the Bay Bridge, take eastbound 580 to 24 (Walnut Creek). Follow 24 to the 680 split, taking 680 south (Dublin/ Sacramento). Next, take the Diablo Road exit and turn right at the light. At the intersection of Diablo and El Cerro roads, turn right again, staying on Diablo Road. Turn left onto Green Valley Road and follow to the end at a dirt parking lot and the Macedo Ranch trailhead.

Route: The ride begins with a granny-gear climb up the Wall Point Road trail. You come immediately to a fork where you bear right to stay on Wall Point. Around the next bend, the grade eases and begins to roll through forests of live oak. The first descent leads through a seasonal water crossing followed by a semi-steep climb.

At the bottom of the next descent, turn left and go through another seasonal creek onto Stage Road for a brief level section. At the pond, turn right onto Burma Road. At the top of the first short but steep climb, turn right to stay on Burma.

The trail levels at this point and crosses the paved North Gate Road. Bear right at the fork on the other side of the road and climb up and past two-humped Camel Rock. Bear left at the next intersection to stay on Burma. Again, the climb eases for a brief respite.

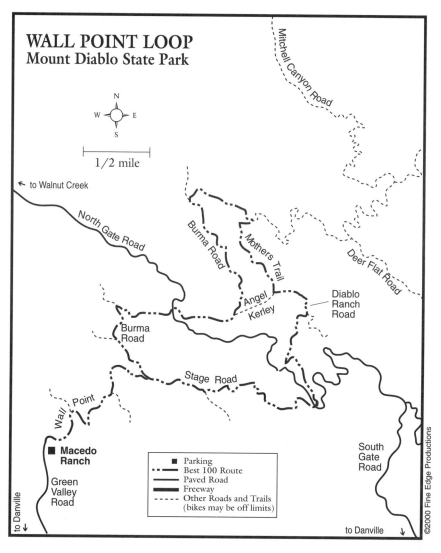

WALL POINT LOOP
Mount Diablo State Park

1/2 mile

← to Walnut Creek

North Gate Road

Mitchell Canyon Road

Burma Road

Mothers Trail

Deer Flat Road

Angel Kerley

Diablo Ranch Road

Burma Road

Stage Road

Wall Point

■ **Macedo Ranch**

Green Valley Road

to Danville ↓

South Gate Road

to Danville ↓

■ Parking
•─•─• Best 100 Route
──── Paved Road
▬▬▬ Freeway
- - - - Other Roads and Trails
(bikes may be off limits)

©2000 Fine Edge Productions

At a fork at the bottom of a short descent, turn right (still on Burma Road) and do a little more climbing. At about 4.7 miles, you reach one of the park's three legal singletracks, Mother's Trail. Hang a right and enjoy it as it leads down, then around, ending in a short rise at Angel Kerley Road. Turn left onto Angel Kerley and then make the first right onto Diablo Ranch Road.

Diablo Ranch starts with a steep downhill that levels past the switchback, then rolls back across the road and through the actual Diablo Ranch. At the ranch, head west back onto Stage Road for a fast fire road descent to the junction with Wall Point. Bear left to connect with Wall Point, endure the last climb, and then it's all downhill back to the trailhead.

22 Mount Diablo/Devils Elbow to Mitchell Canyon

Distance: 12.3 miles
Difficulty: Strenuous, moderately technical
Elevation: 2,800' gain/loss
Ride Type: Loop on singletrack and fire roads
Season: Spring through fall
Map: Clayton. (The Mount Diablo Interpretive Association publishes an excellent Trail Map of the park and adjacent parklands—$5 (and worth it) at park headquarters.)
Comments: Carry extra water; water is available at the half-way point.

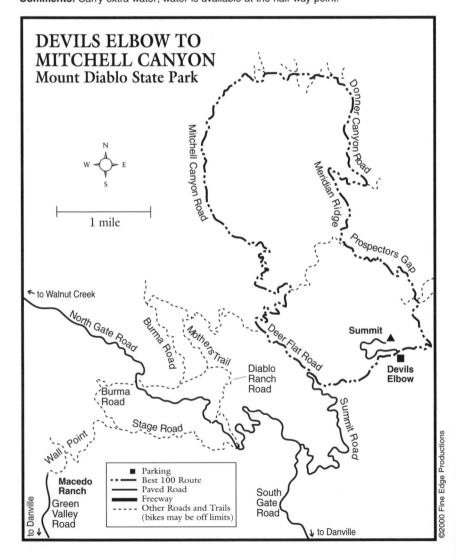

DEVILS ELBOW TO
MITCHELL CANYON
Mount Diablo State Park

1 mile

to Walnut Creek

Mitchell Canyon Road

Donner Canyon Road

Meridian Ridge

Prospectors Gap

North Gate Road

Burma Road

Mothers Trail

Deer Flat Road

Summit

Devils Elbow

Diablo Ranch Road

Burma Road

Summit Road

Stage Road

Wall Point

Macedo Ranch

Green Valley Road

to Danville

South Gate Road

to Danville

■ Parking
∙∙∙▬∙∙∙ Best 100 Route
——— Paved Road
▬▬▬ Freeway
‑ ‑ ‑ ‑ Other Roads and Trails
(bikes may be off limits)

©2000 Fine Edge Productions

Highlights: This ride begins just a few hundred feet from Mount Diablo's summit, affording some amazing views. It begins with a thrilling downhill, the terrain changing from high scrub to forest to a rocky canyon before climbing back up along a creek. Some parts of this ride may be a bit too hair-raising for some folks, but experienced riders will relish it.

Getting There: From the Bay Bridge, take eastbound 580 to 24 (Walnut Creek). Follow 24 to the 680 split, and take 680 south (Dublin/Sacramento). Take the Diablo Road exit, turning left at the light. Follow Diablo Road to Mt. Diablo Scenic Boulevard and turn left. This becomes South Gate Road as you pass through the park gates. Follow the road about 4 miles to the ranger station. Bear right onto Summit Road. Park at the Devils Elbow turnout/trailhead, about 2 miles up.

Route: From the Devils Elbow trailhead, the ride starts off with a bang, beginning with a loose and rocky singletrack downhill. Some might call it devilish! Hope you like steep descents; in the first 1.0 mile, you lose just under 1,000 feet.

Follow the singletrack to the somewhat confusing trail junction with three fire roads and an illegal singletrack. The singletrack is on your left and the other two fire roads on your right. Head straight onto the Prospectors Gap fire road for another gravity lesson. The trail starts off steeply, then smoothes out past the switchback and the crossing of Donner Creek.

After a brief spell of level trail, turn right onto Meridian Ridge Road and lose some more elevation. Past a hairpin turn at Meridian Point,

there's a short climb up to the next trail junction. Turn left here onto the Donner Canyon Road for the last rolling descent along Donner Creek.

At 4.5 miles, turn left onto an unnamed fire road, heading toward the Clayton entrance of the park. At the ranger station, turn left on Mitchell Canyon Road, which begins as a relatively easy climb along Mitchell Creek. At 6.5 miles, it steepens sharply, and you begin the arduous task of regaining all that lost elevation. Periodic level spots generally appear when you start thinking your heart will jump out of your throat.

At about 9 miles, the trail levels as it approaches Deer Flat Picnic Area. At the fork, turn right onto Deer Flat Creek Trail, a rolling fire road that levels off as it contours around the mountain to Juniper Campground. There you follow the paved footpath to Summit Road, where you go left to return to Devils Elbow parking area.

Mt. Diablo's oaks dwarf a rider.

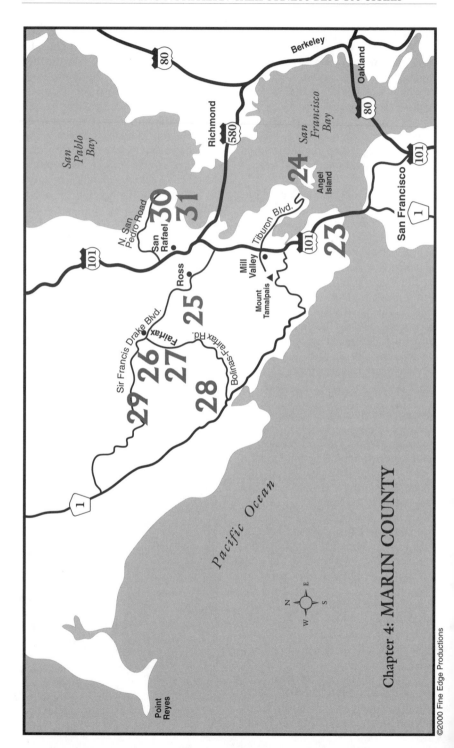

Chapter 4: MARIN COUNTY

CHAPTER 4

Marin County

by Robin Stuart

Marin is probably Northern California's most famous mountain biking county, the cradle of knobby civilization. In the early Seventies, a group of friends got together to play around on their balloon-tire Schwinn cruisers, taking to the trails of Mount Tamalpais (affectionately known as Mt. Tam). Guys with names like Breeze, Fisher, Kelly, Ritchey and Cunningham. Tinkers all, they reinvented the bicycle, piece by piece, their dreams and ideas culminating in the lightweight works of art we now ride.

The trails in this chapter take you through mountain biking history. They also take you through some of the state's most beautiful open space and park lands, lush with redwoods, pine and madrone. Riding here, you understand why John Muir fell in love with the place, and why the region continues to draw artists, dreamers and mountain bikers in droves.

It must be noted, however, that trouble has been brewing here for some time now. From the get-go, hikers and equestrians have been waging a battle against mountain-bike access. So far, they have successfully closed off dozens of trails to us and persuaded the powers-that-be to establish a universal speed limit on the remaining trails.

Since the first edition of this book, things have gotten worse. Local harassment of cyclists has ranged from planting dangerous booby-traps on trails to ticketing them—while on their bikes or in their cars—for anything from not stopping at stop signs to having their cars keyed or tail lights smashed. Our advice is not to park right at area trailheads. Instead, select a very public place, such as a shopping center parking lot, and ride to the trailhead.

If you live here, you owe it to yourself and your fellow mountain bikers to contact the Bicycle Trails Council of Marin at 415-488-1665. If nothing else, at least add your name to the growing number of riders lobbying to challenge trail closures, present and future. Visitors, once they have seen the great riding available and the sorry state of trail closures, may want to get involved, too.

As for the other problem, if you are caught exceeding the rather low speed limit of 15 mph, you may be slapped with a fine of $200! This rule is most stringently enforced on Mt. Tam, by way of radar guns and road blocks. The interesting part about both of these methods is that they are completely contestable; if you fight the ticket, you will probably win.

How? By instituting a "street" rule. If enforcing a speed limit, the rangers have to follow the law as it applies to automobiles. Radar guns are inadmissible as evidence in California courts; road blocks constitute entrapment and any evidence gathered by entrapment is also inadmissible. So, unless the ranger tags you by following you in a vehicle, or can prove your speed by some other legal means, the ticket is no good.

Riders who have fought tickets have also discovered that rangers, like police, aren't really good about keeping their court dates. No ranger, no witness, no crime. Just thought you might want to know.

23 Headlands Loop

Distance: 6.7 miles
Difficulty: Moderate, not technical
Elevation: 1,000' gain/loss
Ride Type: Loop on fire roads
Season: Year-round
Map: Olmsted & Bros. Rambler's Guide to the Trails of Mt. Tamalpais and the Marin Headlands
Comments: The trails get very muddy after rains; give them time to dry out. No water available.

Highlights: The Marin Headlands are legendary—open grassland hills overlooking the San Francisco Bay in the shadow of Mount Tamalpais. This ride is a hit with beginners and the proficient alike, thanks (in no small part) to its breathtaking views.

Wildlife watchers will also enjoy Hawk Hill, located centrally within the loop. It's one of the best places in the country to spot soaring hawks, eagles and other birds of prey. Apparently, they don't like to fly over large bodies of water, so they congregate here while they get their nerve up to cross the bay.

Getting There: From San Francisco, take Highway 101 north across the Golden Gate Bridge to the Highway 1/Stinson Beach turnoff. Bear left onto Highway 1, and then take the Tennessee Valley Road exit. The parking lot is at the end of Tennessee Valley Road.

Route: Begin the ride by heading up the gently-sloping Old Marincello Trail. The trail winds around as it levels, hooking up with the Bobcat Trail. Continue ahead on Bobcat. At about 2.5 miles, you come to a fork as you turn toward the ocean. Bear right to stay on Bobcat and don't forget to look around; the views are pretty great.

The next part is everyone's favorite; the road gently descends for

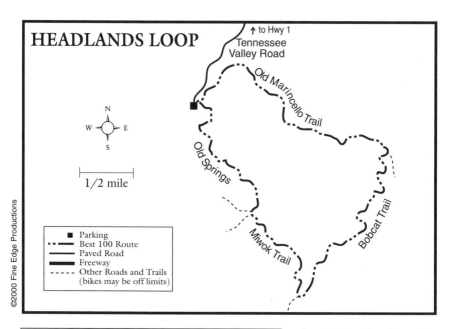

HEADLANDS LOOP

↑ to Hwy 1
Tennessee
Valley Road

Old Marincello Trail

N
W ◆ E
S

1/2 mile

Old Springs

Miwok Trail

Bobcat Trail

■ Parking
·-·- Best 100 Route
——— Paved Road
▬▬▬ Freeway
- - - Other Roads and Trails
    (bikes may be off limits)

©2000 Fine Edge Productions

Stuart/Jensen

View from the famous Marin headlands.

about 2.0 miles from the ridge to the Gerbode Valley. At the bottom, you follow a creek for about 0.5 mile before crossing it.

On the other side of the creek, the trail seemingly ends at an intersection with the Miwok Trail. At one time, this portion of the Miwok was illegal, but it was widened to accommodate bikes. Turn right onto Miwok for a gentle climb.

As you approach the ridge line, you come to an intersection with Chaparral and Wolf Ridge trails; turn right and stay on Miwok until you see a fire road on your left. This is Old Springs Road. Turn left and follow Old Springs as it rolls back up, past the stables and to the parking lot.

24 Angel Island Double Loop

Distance: 10.3 miles
Difficulty: Moderate, not technical
Elevation: 500' gain/loss
Ride Type: Loop on fire roads and doubletrack
Season: Year-round
Map: Available for $1 at the Ayala Cove dock.
Comments: Dress in layers; the temperature varies, sometimes wildly, as you make your way around the island. Restrooms and water are available along the way. A snack bar and full deli at Ayala Cove offer sandwiches, drinks (including beer and wine), and a variety of trail-mix-type snacks. Mountain bike rentals are also available. (Marins, what else!)

Highlights: When was the last time you got to ride your bike around an island? Angel Island State Park is the largest of the San Francisco Bay islands, comprised of 750 acres of grassland, forests and beaches. Its size and location contributed to its long and sometimes checkered history.

The island's earliest known use was as a favorite hunting and fishing spot for the Miwok Indians, the original Marin natives. In 1775, the Spanish explorer, Juan Manuel de Ayala, dropped anchor in what is now Ayala Cove while he and his men developed the first-ever maps of the region. It was Ayala who named the island, "Isla de Los Angeles," adhering to

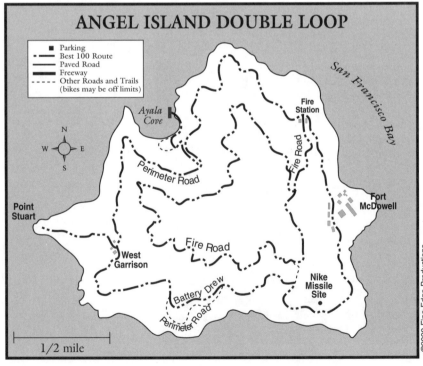

ANGEL ISLAND DOUBLE LOOP

San Francisco Bay

Legend:
■ Parking
▪▪ Best 100 Route
— Paved Road
▬ Freeway
- - - Other Roads and Trails
(bikes may be off limits)

Ayala Cove
Fire Station
Fire Road
Fort McDowell
N W E S
Perimeter Road
Point Stuart
West Garrison
Fire Road
Battery Drew
Nike Missile Site
Perimeter Road

1/2 mile

©2000 Fine Edge Productions

Stuart/Jensen

The Angel Island Double Loop provides numerous waterfront views.

the tradition of Catholic explorers who named their "discoveries" for the nearest religious celebration.

In the early 1800s, the island was the site of Russian sea otter hunting expeditions. In 1814, the British sailing ship, H.M.S. *Raccoon* was beached at Ayala Cove for repairs, becoming the namesake for the deepwater channel between Tiburon and Angel Island, Raccoon Strait.

After a land grant dispute, the federal government declared ownership of the island in 1859, at which time the military took up its long residency. At differing times, the island served as a Civil War defense post, a training and staging area for campaigns against West Coast Indian tribes, a quarantine station to isolate troops exposed to contagious diseases during overseas actions, and a World War I prison for "enemy aliens" arrested on ships harbored on the West Coast.

Angel Island's most infamous incarnation was as the Immigration Sta-

tion which opened in 1910. Although popularly referred to as the Ellis Island of the West, the detention center was actually used to dissuade and exclude new arrivals, most of whom were Chinese immigrants. (A museum at China Cove depicts this less-than-angelic bit of Angel Island history.) The Immigration Station was abandoned in 1940, shortly before the Chinese Exclusion Acts were repealed by the federal government.

Efforts to make the island a state park began in the late 1940s, led by local conservationist Caroline Livermore. Success was hard-won, and it came piecemeal. During this time, a Nike missile-launching facility operated on the south side of the island. In 1963, the missile site was de-activated, and the entire island became state park land.

For those interested in delving into Angel Island's history in more detail, there is a large Visitor's Center located behind the picnic grounds at Ayala

Cove and the above-mentioned museum at China Cove. The ride takes you past and through the remains of the abandoned military outposts.

On the lighter side, you also wander through forests of oak, eucalyptus, pine and fir and along a high ledge of Mount Livermore, named in honor of Caroline Livermore's efforts.

Getting There: This is a ride where getting there really is part of the fun. (Unless you really like boats, I wouldn't say it's "half the fun," more like a third.) Angel Island is only accessible by boat—private craft or the ferry from San Francisco, Vallejo or Tiburon. Located one mile southwest of the Tiburon harbor, the shortest boat ride is on the Tiburon ferry—about 15 minutes from dock to dock.

From the Golden Gate Bridge, follow 101 north to the Tiburon Blvd./E. Blithedale exit. Bear right onto Tiburon Boulevard, following it through Belvedere and into Tiburon. At about 4.5 miles, you reach a turnaround at the marina; park in the lot off the north side of the turnaround ($5). From the parking lot, turn right onto Tiburon Boulevard and bear left onto Main Street. The ferry leaves from 21 Main Street; a sign will direct you through the corridor out to the wooden dock.

The ferry is $5 roundtrip, plus $1 for your bike. The money is collected as you board. Keep your ticket; you need to show it to return.

Route: From the Ayala Cove dock, head up the paved path to the right, past the snack bar, and turn left toward the Visitor's Center. You see a sign for the bike path pointing left, directly across the road from the center. The pavement turns to dirt and gravel immediately.

Just past the second switchback, you come to a paved crossroads; head across, bearing right and up onto Perimeter Road. The trail winds around and rolls through eucalyptus, bay and madrone. Throughout the ride, you are accompanied by great views of the Bay Area on your right.

The pavement is interspersed with dirt and gravel all along Perimeter Road. On the first dirt stretch, at about 1.7 miles, you see the West Garrison on the right. Turn off here, following the trail between the buildings and toward a legal singletrack which leads steeply up to Point Stuart. From a clearing at the top of the trail, you get a great view of the San Francisco skyline and have a good little descent back to the main road. It's definitely worth the side trip.

Come back down the singletrack the way you went up, and continue on Perimeter Road to a fork with the Battery Drew Trail. Veer left up Battery Drew. This steepish climb takes you through a forest of oak and eucalyptus, past a small outcropping of serpentine rocks. At the top of the climb, there's a clearing which looks down on lower Perimeter Road and out to the bay.

The reason I've led you up this way is for the long, fast descent back to Perimeter Road. It's a straight shot down along a slightly loose surface. At the bottom, veer left and continue on Perimeter.

At 3.1 miles, you reach the second crossroads. Turn right, back onto pavement, to continue on Perimeter Road. At 3.4 miles, you pedal past the Nike missile site. This mileage mark also signifies a long, paved descent back to dirt. Technically, you are supposed to walk your bike down the pavement.

Back on the dirt, there's a little washboard followed by smooth dirt and gravel leading to the next historical point of interest: the East Garrison and Fort McDowell. Follow the road as it curves around and between the abandoned military buildings.

Just past the fort area, back on pavement again, you see the park fire station. At 4.5 miles, make the sharp left turn up into the driveway on the right side of the fire house. Within 50 feet, it goes back to gravel, becoming the Fire Road. With the exception of this one tricky turn, the rest of the Fire Road is well signed.

The Fire Road gets a little steep as you pedal up; it's not that hard, but, compared to the rest of the ride, it's a little startling. At a big fork at 4.8 miles, bear right for a last little burst of steepness. Welcome to the amazing loop-within-a-loop.

At the top of the short climb, the road narrows and winds around the mountain along a doubletrack ledge. The next few miles of the ride are an unexpected delight, given the tame quality of the Perimeter Road outer loop. The doubletrack is dry and rocky, clinging to the edge of the mountain amid pine trees and manzanita. The trail is mostly level, leading subtly to its highest point, 100 feet below the mountain's summit. The views are, as one might expect, spectacular.

At about 7.5 miles, the scenery changes from reddish-clay high country to a grassy pine forest. The trail surface goes from slightly loose and rocky to smooth hardpack as it begins to descend.

At 7.8 miles, you are back at the second paved crossroads. Stay left, crossing the pavement, and then shoot straight onto the dirt again, following the signs for the Fire Road. The doubletrack trail continues to wind around through the pine, leading to a fun downhill. The scenery should start looking familiar as you find yourself back at the fork behind the fire station, this time coming down the other side. Head straight out through the buildings to Perimeter Road.

Turn left and follow Perimeter as it rolls its way back to the very first crossroads. Make a very sharp right turn back onto the dirt switchback trail. At the Visitor's Center, turn right to get back to the dock.

25 Hoo Koo E Koo to Phoenix Lake

Distance: 12 miles
Difficulty: Strenuous, some technical sections
Elevation: 1,300' gain/loss
Ride Type: One-way shuttle on fire roads with short loop option
Season: Year-round
Map: Olmsted & Bros. Rambler's Guide to the Trails of Mt. Tamalpais and the Marin Headlands
Comments: Water is available at the Lake Lagunitas picnic area.

Highlights: This ride is a local favorite, a way to get away from the throngs on Mt. Tam. The trails are crowd-pleasers, containing everything—famous names, steep climbs, steep descents, rocky technical sections, lakes, trees, wildflowers—everything but legal singletrack.

The Hoo Koo E Koo trail is one of the most famous on the mountain, probably because people like saying "Hoo Koo E Koo." The trail was named for the Native Americans who inhabited the area at the base of Mt. Tam. Knobby pioneer Gary Fisher, in turn, has named one of his bike models the Hoo Koo E Koo.

This ride also contains a section of the Eldridge Grade, another well-known and beloved trail (Marin Mountain Bikes makes a model by this name), made famous by our fat-tire forefathers.

Getting There: This ride begins at the Old Railroad Grade trailhead and

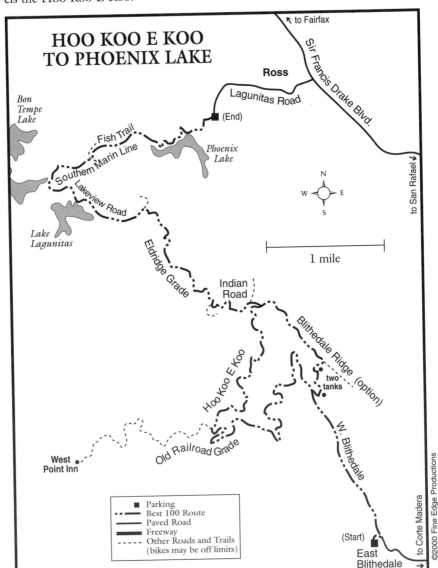

HOO KOO E KOO TO PHOENIX LAKE

ends at Green Park in the town of Ross. To get a return vehicle to the parking lot at Green Park, take 101 north to the San Anselmo/Sir Francis Drake exit, bear left and take Sir Francis Drake west. Follow Sir Francis Drake to Ross and turn left onto Lagunitas Road. The park is at the end of Lagunitas Road.

To get to the Old Railroad Grade trailhead from the Golden Gate Bridge, follow 101 north to the East Blithedale/Tiburon Boulevard exit. Bear left onto East Blithedale and follow it to the heart of Mill Valley, the Mill Valley common. The area resembles a town square with shops and restaurants and several small parking lots around the square. Park here as there is no parking to speak of at the gates of Mt. Tam.

Route: From the Mill Valley common, pedal up West Blithedale Avenue, a narrow and slightly winding paved road, to its end at the park gate. Go over the little bridge and start up the Old Railroad Grade. The trail meanders along in a series of switchbacks at about the same grade for its entire length. You wander through stands of oak, bay and madrone and along exposed and rocky ridges. Almost 4.0 miles up Old Railroad, past the paved section along the top of Summit Avenue and past the three switchbacks, turn right onto Hoo Koo E Koo.

Hoo Koo E Koo winds and rolls its way down along a rocky and sometimes hairy fire road. If it has rained recently, expect the trail to be even rockier and a little rutty. Hoo Koo E Koo, the legal part of it, anyway, ends at Blithedale Ridge.

Those of you continuing on the main route should turn left here (for a short loop possibility see Option 1

below) and mentally prepare yourself for a very steep climb. Thankfully, it's also very short. At the top of the climb, the trail dead ends at Indian Road. Hang a left here. The Blithedale Ridge climb puts things in perspective, making everything else seem pretty easy, including this climb up to the next trail intersection.

Indian Road ends at Eldridge Grade Trail, where you bear right. Eldridge is fairly level at this point, rolling for the next mile or so and briefly climbing before heading back down.

At about 8.3 miles, the trail forks; veer left onto Lakeview Road. This smooth and level fire road takes you past Lake Lagunitas and through a picnic area. When you see the small paved road, turn right and follow it briefly. Make the first right onto the paved footpath, Southern Marin Line. This slopes kind of steeply downhill.

Pretty quickly, you see a fire road turnoff on your left. Veer left here, onto the Fish Trail, not to be confused with Fish Gulch, an illegal singletrack which branches off of the Fish Trail. This is a fun but very steep and rocky descent that leads down to Phoenix Lake. At Shaver Grade Trail, cross the trail to a final short descent and follow the north lake shore route out to the parking lot.

Option 1: If you can't arrange a shuttle or want a slightly shorter loop, you can turn right at the Hoo Koo E Koo/Blithedale Ridge junction for another mile or so of rocky and rolling downhill. Again, the more it rains, the rockier the terrain as water washes the dirt away. This has been dubbed "The Roller Coaster" by locals who have been known to finish this loop and head back up to do it again.

On this option, at about 8.4 miles total, you see an unnamed fire road come up on your right; turn onto it. Locals refer to this trail as "Two Tanks;" you see why as you make your way down the trail past two water tanks. The trail winds between the water tanks and loosely switchbacks its way down to the Old Railroad Grade. At the Old Railroad Grade, turn right to have another go at the Roller Coaster. Turn left to get back out on West Blithedale. This option makes for a 10-mile loop. Of course, the hard core can do the loop and go back up to Blithedale and continue to Phoenix Lake for a very strenuous 22-mile ride.

26 Pine Mountain to Repack

Distance: 4.2 miles
Difficulty: Strenuous, very technical
Elevation: 1,200' gain/loss
Ride Type: One-way shuttle on sometimes narrow fire roads
Season: Year-round
Map: Olmsted & Bros. Rambler's Guide to the Trails of Mt. Tamalpais and the Marin Headlands
Comments: No water available, bring all you will need.

Highlights: It may be short, but it's memorable. Slightly northwest of Mt. Tam, the Pine Mountain Ridge area is for advanced riders looking to explore Marin's more sinister side. The going is steep, loose and rocky—and a whole lot of fun.

This particular ride is probably the most famous in mountain biking lore. The Repack Trail got its name in 1976 when it was the site of the first-ever downhill bike race. Of course, it wasn't a big race—just the Marin mountain biking pioneers and their friends. They were racing on Schwinn cruisers with coaster brakes. Seems the rear hubs got so hot from the constant coaster braking, the grease melted right out of them. They needed to be repacked, and so the trail got its name.

Nowadays, sane people don't hit high speeds on Repack. It's a treacherous, rocky, and very rutted screamer of a downhill not for the fainthearted.

Nothing is sacred and Repack is no exception. In recent years there have been efforts to close the trail, despite its place in mountain biking history. Such efforts were briefly successful, but at press time the trail was open and legal to ride—thanks to the ruckus caused by area cyclists.

Getting There: The ride starts at the Pine Mountain Road trailhead on the Bolinas-Fairfax Road. To get to the trailhead, take 101 north to the San Anselmo/Sir Francis Drake exit. Bear left and take Sir Francis Drake west, following it to Bolinas-Fairfax Road. Turn left and follow Bolinas-Fairfax Road to the trailhead, about 3 miles up. The trail is on the right and parking on the left. Be sure to park in a turnout. Parking on the road will get you towed.

Park the return vehicle along the end of Cascade Drive at the entrance to the Elliot Nature Preserve. To get

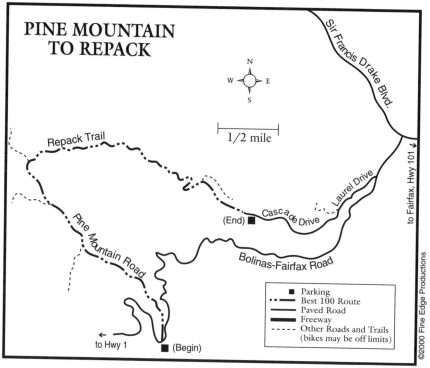

there, follow the directions to Bolinas-Fairfax Road, and turn right onto Laurel Drive. Veer left to Cascade Drive, following Cascade to the end.

Route: From the Pine Mountain Road trailhead, climb up the fire road. The trail is loose and rocky, but not too terribly steep. Follow the trail for 1.7 miles to the Repack Trail. Turn right and get ready for one of the wildest descents ever.

Do not attempt to take this trail at high speeds. The terrain can be unsettling, at best—very loose, very rocky and very rutted. Repack drops for 2.5 steep and twisting miles. At the fork near the bottom, bear right and continue on down to the gate at the end of Cascade Drive.

27 Pine Mountain Loop

Distance: 13 miles
Difficulty: Strenuous, very technical
Elevation: 1,300' gain/loss
Ride Type: Loop on sometimes narrow fire roads
Season: Year-round
Map: Bolinas
Comments: Bring plenty of water as there is none.

Highlights: This ride is almost as famous as Repack; nobody raced here, but it's one of the original mountain bike loops in the area. Those early folks seem to have had a penchant for rocks and loose surfaces. You experience plenty of both on this ride, along with steep climbs and steep descents, making for an interesting afternoon all around.

The loop traverses two ridges and a canyon, where you (literally) run across three creeks. And don't let the name mislead you; like most of the surrounding hills, the ridges are wide-open grassland, affording spectacular views.

Getting There: From the Golden Gate Bridge, follow 101 north to the San Anselmo/Sir Francis Drake exit. Bear left and take Sir Francis Drake west, following it to Bolinas-Fairfax Road. Turn left and follow Bolinas-Fairfax Road to the trailhead, about 3 miles. The trail is on the right and parking is on the left. Be sure to park in a turnout. Parking on the road will get you towed.

You don't have to be a Repack downhiller to enjoy Pine Mountain.

Stuart/Jensen

Route: From the trailhead, start up Pine Mountain Road. The climb isn't too bad except for one brief, steep section. Just past the top of that climb, turn left at the second fork to stay on Pine Mountain Road.

Now the climbing gets nasty. The first mile is the worst—very loose, very rocky and very steep. The good news is that once you've made it,

you're at the highest point in the ride, the Pine Mountain summit. Enjoy the panoramic view while you let your heart rate fall back to an acceptable level.

Now the fun begins. The next section is a long roller coaster ride which ends with a sharp descent to a trail fork and Kent Lake. Turn right at the fork and wind your way through the canyon and across the creeks, subtly climbing. The switchback at the third creek is your signal to start gearing down; the gradual climb gets decidedly steep as you

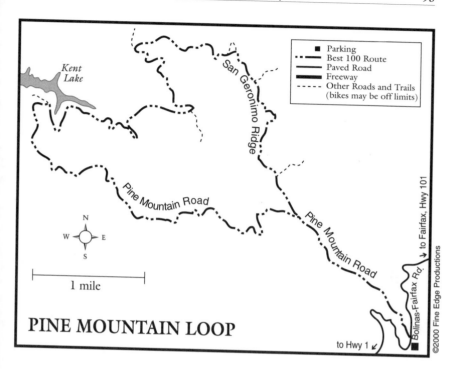

PINE MOUNTAIN LOOP

Kent Lake

San Geronimo Ridge

Pine Mountain Road

Pine Mountain Road

Bolinas-Fairfax Rd.

to Fairfax, Hwy 101

to Hwy 1

©2000 Fine Edge Productions

1 mile

■ Parking
Best 100 Route
Paved Road
Freeway
Other Roads and Trails
(bikes may be off limits)

make your way back up to the ridge.

Up on the ridge, you come to a crossroads near the summit of Green Hill at about 8.5 miles. Turn right and continue climbing, at a less taxing grade now, toward San Geronimo Ridge. Within a mile, you reach another fork. This is a private property boundary. Make a hard right onto San Geronimo Ridge Road and head up for the last bit of climbing.

At about 10.5 miles, the trail once again becomes a roller coaster. San Geronimo Ridge Road ends at Pine Mountain Road. Bear left for the descent leading back to the trailhead.

28 Bolinas Ridge

Distance: 22.5 miles
Difficulty: Very strenuous, mildly technical
Elevation: 1,100' gain/loss
Ride Type: Out-and-back on fire roads and doubletrack
Season: Spring through fall
Maps: Bolinas, San Geronimo
Comments: It can get very hot and dry during the summer months, carry extra water (none is available); fire danger sometimes closes the trail; rideable in the winter if you don't mind a lot of mud; please close cattle gates behind you.

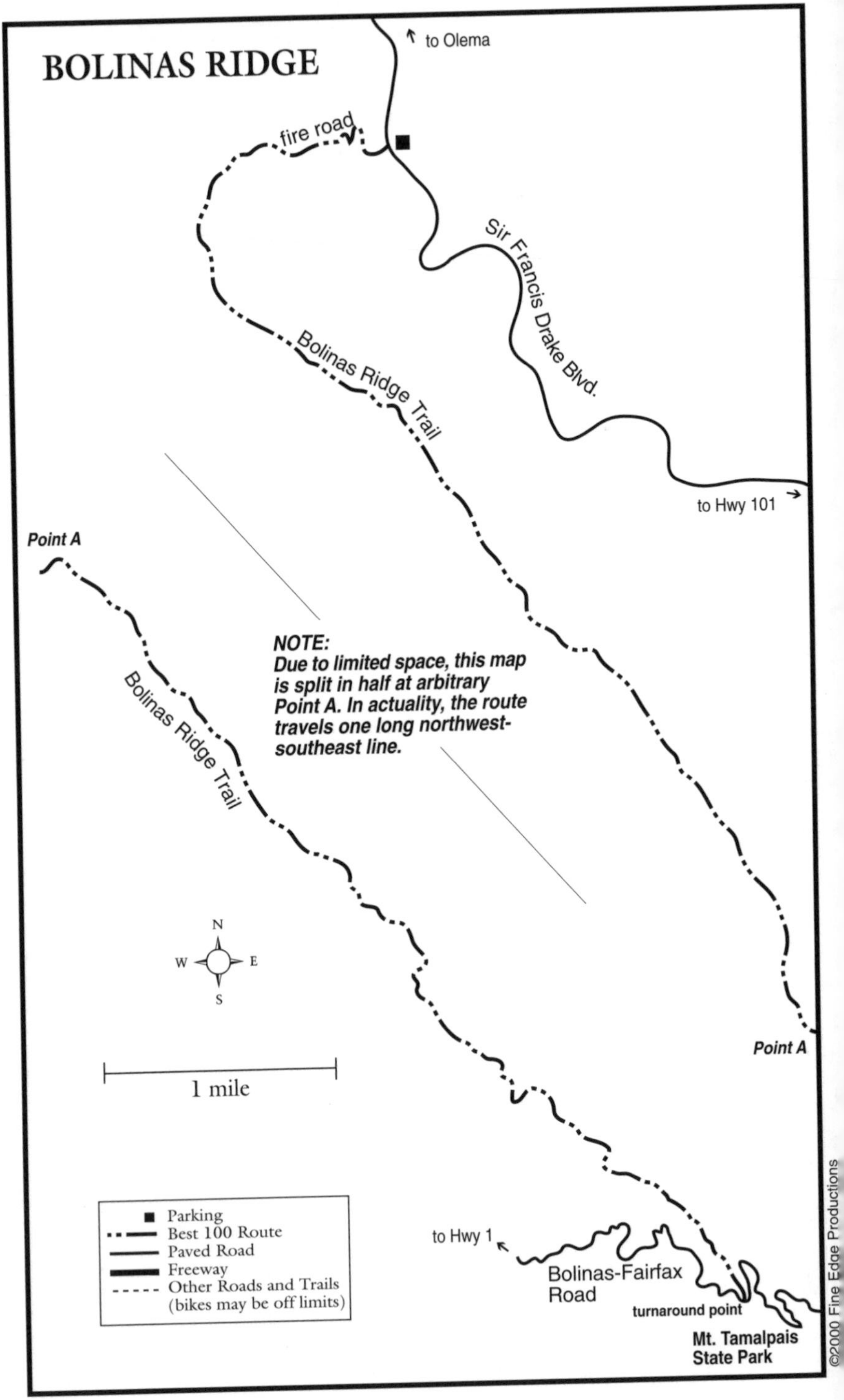

BOLINAS RIDGE

↑ to Olema

fire road

Sir Francis Drake Blvd.

Bolinas Ridge Trail

to Hwy 101 →

Point A

Bolinas Ridge Trail

NOTE:
Due to limited space, this map
is split in half at arbitrary
Point A. In actuality, the route
travels one long northwest-
southeast line.

N
W — E
S

1 mile

Point A

to Hwy 1 ←

Bolinas-Fairfax
Road

turnaround point

**Mt. Tamalpais
State Park**

■ Parking
Best 100 Route
Paved Road
Freeway
Other Roads and Trails
(bikes may be off limits)

©2000 Fine Edge Productions

Highlights: Part of the Golden Gate National Recreation Area, this ride has just about everything a person needs to be happy: cool redwoods, wide open grasslands, great views, neat rocks, long climbs doing double duty as long, sweeping downhills, and a little bit of technical stuff (some tree roots, some rocks). There's enough to hold your interest but not so much that you're demoralized if you ain't exactly Hans Rey.

The trail is on land that's part cattle ranch, part parkland, and the line of demarcation couldn't be more obvious if it had a sign; past the last cattle gate, the madrones close in and the redwoods suddenly spring up around you. From the grassy slopes of the cowfeteria, you get great views of Tomales Bay; from the highest points in the forest, you look down through the trees to the Pacific Ocean.

This ride can be done as a one-way shuttle that's suitable for beginners. But then you miss half the fun.

Getting There: From the Golden Gate Bridge, take 101 north to the San Anselmo/Sir Francis Drake exit. Bear left and take Sir Francis Drake west, following it to the trailhead, about 20 miles. When you see the sign that says *Olema 1 Mile*, the trailhead and parking area are just around the next bend. Park on the wide dirt shoulders on either side of the road.

If you decide to do the ride as a shuttle, you can drop off at the trail's south end near Highway 1. Follow the directions above, but continue on Sir Francis Drake to its end at Highway 1. Turn left. Follow Highway 1 for 10 miles. The first possible left turn is marked only by a wide gate that leads to a single-lane, barely-maintained, paved fire road. There is no sign and if you sneeze you'll miss it. Follow the road for 4 miles to a very small parking turn-out on the right. On the left is the trailhead, marked with a sign but identified only as the Golden Gate National Recreation Area.

Route: From the trail gate, the ride starts off with a short singletrack climb up to the fire road. At the outset, the road is steep, rocky and loose, but the worst of it is over quickly. At the top of the first rise, the trail almost levels briefly before climbing again, this time at a more reasonable grade. This short climb is followed by a brief downhill; it's not much, but you take what downhills you can get.

As the trail heads up again, you reach the first of many cattle gates. Upon passing through it, gear down early. After about 100 feet, the trail rises sharply to the right, through a gnarled, rain-rutted switchback. As an added bonus, in the late summer, the rut becomes sandy, too. Past the rut, the trail heads straight up, marking the first of four very nasty climbs. At the top, you can see Tomales Bay off to the right and tree-dotted parkland rolling below you.

After a too-brief level section comes the second icky climb. Again, it's severely rutted and seasonally loose. This climb is also the longest of the bad ones, about 0.25-mile long. At least you get it over with right away. The good news is, the next bad one is about a mile away.

At the top, the road again levels before rolling in an overall uphill direction. The little downhills are fast and fun, but all too soon, at about 3.5 miles, you reach the third bad climb. It starts off at a bearable grade before suddenly getting steeper and looser toward the top. The trail sur-

A handlebar view of Bolinas Ridge's rolling terrain.

face on this climb is made up of sandy soil and tiny, marble-sized rocks.

Again, the trail plateaus briefly at the top of the hill before rolling toward the last nasty climb. This one is fairly steep but also kind of technical. The trail is rutted and includes rock outcroppings that start halfway up and continue up to the top.

After this climb, the trail levels again. You see a large rock outcropping on the left, in front of a cattle gate, marking the 5.0-mile point. This is a popular break spot. If you do stop here, choose your rest spot carefully—the rock has patches of poison oak growing on and around it.

From here the trail starts to roll with a vengeance. Long descents followed by long climbs lead you out of the open grassland and into the redwoods. Once in the trees and for the next 5 miles, the terrain becomes smooth hardpack with intermittent roots snaking across the trail. You can

really pick up speed in here but be careful; if you're going to see hikers, you see them at this end. Also keep an eye out for bicyclists going in the other direction.

At about 10.0 miles, you start to climb out of the redwoods toward the top of the ridge line. Out in the open for a bit, a final descent leads past a great view of Bolinas to the right and Pine Mountain Ridge to the left. The last 0.5 mile is a climb back into the redwoods to the west entrance of Mount Tamalpais State Park on Bolinas-Fairfax Road.

If you're doing the ride as a one-way shuttle, this is the starting point. For those of us going all the way, this is the turnaround. Head back the way you came for a rollicking good time. Going in this direction, the ride is mostly downhill. Although there are a couple of climbs, there's nothing nasty. As I said earlier, while you are in the forest, keep your speed in check and watch for hikers and bikes.

The redwood roller coaster is over way too soon, leading to the free-for-all back through the grazing area. Remember those four steep climbs?

Guess what you get to do. Back at the big rock, the last 5 miles are basically a series of long, fast and furious descents back to the trailhead.

29 Samuel P. Taylor State Park/ Barnabe Peak Loop

Distance: 6.9 miles
Difficulty: Moderately strenuous, mildly technical
Elevation: 1,250' gain/loss
Ride Type: Loop on sometimes narrow fire roads
Season: Year-round
Map: Available at ranger kiosk for 75 cents.
Comments: Water and restrooms are available in the campground areas. Let the trails dry out for a few days following rain.

Highlights: This is a great date ride. If you happen to be involved with your riding partner and you're looking for a romantic ride, this is it. While you may encounter a few technical challenges, mostly of the mud and tree root variety, the bulk of the ride traverses smooth trails in a drop-dead gorgeous forest of redwood and madrone.

The Samuel P. Taylor State Park encompasses 2,882 acres of redwood canyons and rocky grassland ridges. The property once belonged to Samuel Taylor, a late nineteenth-century entrepreneur who purchased the land with the help of a modest gold strike. He built a paper mill on the property, but rather than use the trees on his land, Taylor instituted a process which utilized scrap paper and rags gathered from other sources. Among his customers were the San Francisco newspapers.

At another site in the canyon, Taylor operated a less successful venture, a blasting powder mill. A huge explosion ended his dream of becoming a major player in the black powder business.

In 1874, a railroad was built through the canyon. Our enterprising friend Mr. Taylor built a hotel next to the rail line and opened Camp Taylor, one of the first recreational camping areas in the United States.

Getting There: From the Golden Gate Bridge, follow 101 north to the San Anselmo/Sir Francis Drake exit. Bear left and take Sir Francis Drake west. Follow it about 16 miles to the park entrance. The entrance and parking lot are on the left. Day-use parking is $5.

Route: From the ranger's kiosk, head down into the campground area on the paved path, following the signs for the Lower Campground. The path ends at the paved Bike and Horse Trail. Turn left and follow it to the gate at the end. The dirt Hiking and Riding Trail starts once you're through the gate.

The trail follows Papermill Creek through a forest of towering redwoods with lots of ferns and moss-covered rocks. Very shortly, you cross

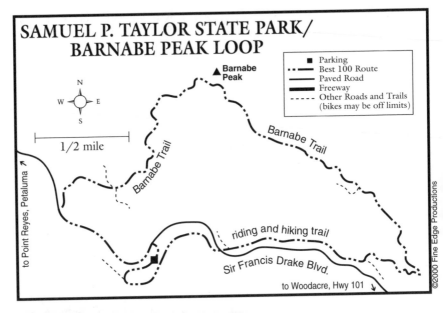

SAMUEL P. TAYLOR STATE PARK/ BARNABE PEAK LOOP

■ Parking
▪▪▪ Best 100 Route
Barnabe Peak
▬ Paved Road
▬ Freeway
▪▪▪ Other Roads and Trails
(bikes may be off limits)

1/2 mile

Barnabe Trail

Barnabe Trail

riding and hiking trail

Sir Francis Drake Blvd.

to Point Reyes, Petaluma

to Woodacre, Hwy 101

©2000 Fine Edge Productions

On the way to Barnabe Peak.

Stuart/Jensen

the creek and the road on a wooden bridge which takes you to the Irving Group Picnic Area. The well-signed trail picks up on the left side of the clearing. You can't miss it.

The trail continues to follow the creek, although now slightly above it. At about 2.0 miles, make the first left onto the Barnabe Trail. Barnabe starts with a steep but short climb, then winds somewhat steeply away from the canyon and up through redwood and madrone. The grade eases considerably after this.

As the climb continues toward Barnabe Peak (1,466'), you emerge from the forest onto the ridge line, with great views of Inverness Ridge and Point Reyes. As you approach the peak, the trail rolls a little bit before heading back down into the forest.

The remainder of the Barnabe Trail is a 2.5-mile winding, redwood-filled frolic back down to Sir Francis Drake Boulevard. Turn left onto Sir Francis Drake. The park entrance and parking lot are about 0.25 mile up. Fortunately, the road provides an ample shoulder and the drivers out here are pretty used to sharing the road with bikes.

30 China Camp State Park/ Bay View Loop

Distance: 4.7 miles
Difficulty: Moderate, slightly technical
Elevation: 800' gain/loss
Ride Type: Loop on singletrack with a little fire road
Season: Year-round
Map: Available for free at the ranger kiosk
Comments: Water and restrooms are available in the parking lot and in campground areas. Because the park sits on the shore of San Pablo Bay, wet weather turns the trails to goo.

Highlights: China Camp is one of the last places in the county where the singletrack is legal (except for one short trail on the bay side that leads to a bird sanctuary). And it's a good thing, too, because more than half of the trails here are singletrack.

China Camp State Park got its name in the late 1800s when it was a Chinese shrimping village. The villagers were fishermen from the Kwangtung Province in China, mostly immigrants seeking to escape racial discrimination in San Francisco. The people supported themselves by exporting shrimp to Hawaii, China and Japan. In 1906, the village provided refuge for thousands of Chinese whose homes were destroyed in the earthquake and fire in San Francisco.

The land remained privately owned until the state purchased it in 1977. Besides the parkland, China Camp is also a wetland sanctuary.

While the park is fairly small, only 1,476 acres, the trails are a blast to ride. The singletrack and fire roads wind through forests of manzanita,

bay, live oak and madrone, and through grassy clearings. Most people spend the day and ride both this loop and the following loop, with a scenic lunch break in between.

Getting There: From the Golden Gate Bridge, follow 101 north to the N. San Pedro Road exit. Take N. San Pedro Road east and follow it to the campground entrance and parking lot. The entrance is on the right, 3 miles up. Day-use parking on weekends and holidays is $3.

Route: From the parking lot, follow the fire road on the right side of the restrooms around the back of Back Ranch Meadows to a 3-way fork. Go straight onto the Bay View Trail which quickly becomes a singletrack. The Bay View Trail rolls, winds and climbs up above the campground through the trees and along a narrow ledge before heading up to a clearing just below a ridge.

At the clearing, turn left onto the Back Ranch Meadows Fire Trail and

to Hwy 101

BAY VIEW LOOP
China Camp State Park

North San Pedro Road

to San Rafael

Shoreline Trail

Miwok Fire Trail

Shoreline Trail

Back Ranch

to Ranger Station

Bay View Trail

N
W E
S

Bay View Trail

Ridge Fire Trail

■ Parking
▪▪▪ Best 100 Route
— Paved Road
--- Other Roads and Trails (bikes may be off limits)

1/4 mile

©2000 Fine Edge Productions

make a quick right back onto the Bay View singletrack. This part of Bay View is mostly level, with intermittent rolling as it hugs the mountain's curves.

At the next fire road intersection, at about 2.8 miles, turn left onto the Ridge Fire Trail. This part of the Ridge Trail can get pretty rutted although it is graded periodically. It starts off as a gradual downhill that

leads to a junction with the Miwok Fire Trail. Go straight onto Miwok (Ridge veers off to the right) for a steep and loose downhill. (If it's muddy, it may be slippery.)

At the bottom of the descent, make a hard left turn onto the Shoreline Trail. This starts as a level and smooth fire road that leads to a day-use picnic area. Follow the trail around the back side of the picnic

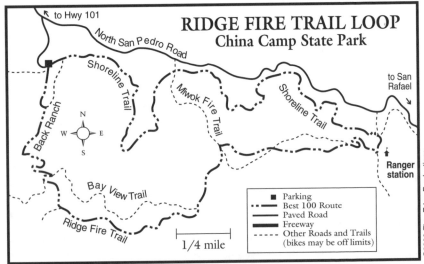

to Hwy 101

RIDGE FIRE TRAIL LOOP
China Camp State Park

North San Pedro Road

Shoreline Trail

Miwok Fire Trail

Shoreline Trail

to San Rafael

Back Ranch

N
W E
S

Bay View Trail

Ranger station

Ridge Fire Trail

■ Parking
▪▪▪ Best 100 Route
— Paved Road
▬ Freeway
--- Other Roads and Trails (bikes may be off limits)

1/4 mile

©2000 Fine Edge Productions

area, where the trail becomes a single-track again. It leads to the back wall of a canyon before heading out toward a wetland meadow and around a small hill. The trail ends back at the campground parking lot.

31 Ridge Fire Trail Loop

Distance: 5.6 miles
Difficulty: Moderate, slightly technical
Elevation: 900' gain/loss
Ride Type: Loop on fire roads and singletrack
Season: Year-round
Map: Available free at ranger kiosk
Comments: Water and restrooms available in the parking lot and at campground areas. Trails may be gooey after rains.

Highlights: This loop takes you from San Pablo Bay to a ridge overlooking San Francisco Bay. This time, there are some fire roads mixed in with the singletrack.

Getting There: Follow the directions for the previous ride.

Route: From the parking lot, follow the fire road on the left side of the restrooms to its end at Back Ranch Meadows Fire Trail. Head up the Back Ranch trail, which gets a little on the steep side when you're in the switchback sections. The trail crosses the Bay View Trail before ending at the Ridge Fire Trail.

Turn left onto Ridge, which rolls along the top of the ridge behind the trees. From here, you get a nice view of the San Francisco skyline and the Golden Gate Bridge.

At about 1.5 miles, you come to another intersection with the Bay View singletrack on the left and an unnamed fire road to the right. Continue straight through toward the Miwok Fire Trail. Within 0.5 mile, continue straight past the Ridge Fire Trail turnoff, briefly following the Miwok Trail.

As the trail starts to pitch down-hill, you see a singletrack trailhead on the right. Turn right onto the single-track to enjoy the handiwork of your compatriots; this unnamed 0.75-mile stretch of roller coaster was built by mountain bikers.

At about 2.8 miles, you once again intersect with the Ridge Fire Trail. Go across to pick up the single-track on the other side. The trail starts to head down; there are three fun switchbacks before a descent into the ranger service area.

Turn left down the road to catch the Shoreline Trail, which comes up quickly on your left. Turn left onto Shoreline and follow it as it snakes its way along the grassy slopes overlooking the bay.

At just under 4.5 miles, Shoreline drops down onto the Miwok Fire Trail. Turn left and immediately bear right to stay on Shoreline. Follow the fire road to the day-use area. Follow the trail to the back side of the picnic area where the trail becomes single-track again. The trail winds along the canyon before heading back out to the meadow, ending back at the parking lot on the other side of the hill.

Chapter 5:

WINE AND LAKE COUNTRY

©2000 Fine Edge Productions

CHAPTER 5

Wine & Lake Country

by Robin Stuart

Just above the Marin County line lies a land of vineyards and farms, pine forests and redwoods, state parks and (happy sigh) legal singletrack. When folks in the Bay Area say they are "going to the country," it's a safe bet they are headed up here. Although the 1990s real estate boom has pushed the northern border of the "Bay Area region" well into Sonoma County, once you get past Santa Rosa you notice that people move a little slower and they're quicker to smile and say hello. It may only be an hour away from San Francisco, but it seems like light years.

Aside from the trails and the tranquillity, this area has another well-known feature. Located in the heart of the county is the world-famous California Wine Country. Most of the wineries have tasting rooms and some offer tours of their facilities. A bike is a great way to get around since many of the wineries are located along winding country roads and auto traffic can get pretty congested, especially on weekends. A word of advice for those who want their wine-tasting trip to be a pleasant experience: don't drink the whole glass. Take a sip, swish it around your mouth, then pour the rest out. No one will think you're rude or silly; au contraire, you'll look like a pro. Plus, you get the flavor without the headache.

To the west of the Wine Country, the more coastal region gets increasingly rugged and wooded. To the east, more open oak- and pine-covered ranges rise up to dominate the landscape before giving way to the expanse of the Central Valley. From some of the higher points in the following rides, you'll even be able to see Mount Shasta and Mount Lassen to the north and northeast on very clear days.

Thanks to smatterings of maple and black oak here and there, the North Bay counties featured in this chapter display the classic colors of fall. Nothing as vivid as New England, of course, but hey, it beats California's usual brown. Winters are typically very wet in these parts, but the reward is warm sunshine and spectacular displays of wildflowers in the spring. The summer temperatures get surprisingly high, so coastal dwellers are advised to plan for early morning playtimes and to bring twice as much water as they think they will need. As for those of us who think the term "hotter than hell" is a selling point, bring lots of water and bask—or is it bake?—in it.

32 Annadel State Park/ Short Loop to Lake Ilsanjo

Distance: 10 miles
Difficulty: Strenuous, technical (very technical in spots)
Elevation: 1,100' gain/loss
Ride Type: Loop on sometimes narrow fire roads
Season: Year-round
Map: Available for $1 from a vending machine in front of the park office.
Comments: The only water available is in front of the ranger station; it gets very hot in the summer so bring as much water as you can carry. Restrooms are strategically placed at locations throughout the park. Speed limit of 15 mph.

Highlights: You haven't truly "done" the Wine Country until you have rolled your tire tread upon the trails of Annadel State Park. This is definitely not a place for beginners. The terrain at Annadel is most often described as "really rocky," but that doesn't quite tell the whole story. The trails vary between loose and bumpy to "you call that a trail?" The rocks here come in all shapes and sizes and in all stages of exposure—from lurking just below the surface, to felt but not seen, to quarry conditions. If you

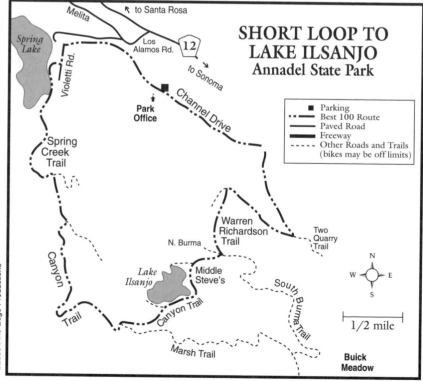

SHORT LOOP TO LAKE ILSANJO
Annadel State Park

to Santa Rosa
Melita
Spring Lake
Violetti Rd.
Los Alamos Rd.
12
to Sonoma
Park Office
Channel Drive

Parking
Best 100 Route
Paved Road
Freeway
Other Roads and Trails (bikes may be off limits)

Spring Creek Trail

Warren Richardson Trail
N. Burma
Two Quarry Trail

Canyon Trail
Lake Ilsanjo
Middle Steve's
South Burma Trail

N
W — E
S

1/2 mile

Canyon Trail
Marsh Trail

Buick Meadow

©2000 Fine Edge Productions

Stuart/Jensen

Lake Ilsanjo

want to practice your technical skills, this is certainly the place.

Not surprisingly, the history of Annadel State Park is linked closely to its geology. Long ago it was considered an important source of obsidian by the Native Americans who inhabited the region. The hard, shiny obsidian was used to make tools and weapons that were hot-ticket items for trade among the Northern California tribes (think titanium and you get an idea of its appeal). With the Spanish settlement in 1770 came a stint of agricultural use until the land was included in a Mexican grant. The first quarrying operations began in 1880.

At the turn of the century, the land was held by two families, the Wymores and the Hutchinsons. They continued the quarrying business, churning out cobblestone which was used in the original Bay Area building efforts as well as the rebuilding of San Francisco after the 1906 earthquake. The park is named for Annie Hutchin-

son, the granddaughter of one of the owners. The area was known as "Annie's Dell" and the name stuck.

With the advent of the automobile came the demise of the cobblestone business. The land changed hands in the 1930s, reverting back to agricultural use and obsidian mining, which continued through the 1960s. The state purchased the property in 1971.

At 5,000 acres, Annadel contains 35 miles of legal fire roads with some legal singletrack. The trails are all well-signed (trails not marked or named have been developed illegally) and fairly easy to follow. The following rides are the most popular loops around the park, bypassing a couple of the ridiculously technical single-track sections. Obviously, these only scratch the surface of the many riding possibilities here.

Getting There: From San Francisco, take 101 north to the Sebastopol/ Sonoma Highway 12 turnoff. Bear right, taking Sonoma East. Follow the signs through downtown Santa Rosa to stay on Highway 12. Turn right on Los Alamos Road, bearing left at the fork with Melita. Just before crossing the second bridge, turn left onto Channel Drive. Follow the signs to the Annadel State Park entrance. You can park along Channel Drive by the park office or continue to the parking lot at the end of the road. There is a $2 parking fee.

Route: Starting from the park office, go west on Channel Drive as if you were leaving the park. Within a mile, you come to Violetti Road; a left turn followed by a quick right takes you into the Spring Lake Park entrance. Follow the path to the left along the shoreline of Spring Lake, which ends at the Oak Knolls Picnic Area and the Annadel gate. Inside the gate, follow the Spring Creek Trail, a fire road that winds along Spring Creek. Just past the 3-mile point, you cross a bridge.

Turn right on the other side of the bridge to stay on Spring Creek. Within 0.5 mile, you see another bridge on your right. Turn here and cross the bridge onto Canyon Trail fire road.

Canyon Trail climbs steadily and, at times, steeply along a wall overlooking forests of Douglas fir and oak, and Spring Creek and Lake Ilsanjo. Unless it has rained recently, this trail is a little bumpy and a little loose, but not terribly rocky. At about 5.1 miles, you reach a fork with the Marsh Trail. Bear left to stay on Canyon Trail.

This stretch of Canyon leads, at long last, downhill to Lake Ilsanjo. After a short rise just past the junction with Marsh, the trail veers fairly gently down to the lake. The lakeshore area is a popular rest stop, particularly in the summer (swimming is allowed and, on some days, is a must). Follow Canyon along the south side of the lake to an intersection with Middle Steve's Trail. To the right is an illegal singletrack portion of Middle Steve's.

On the way to Ledson Marsh.

Stuart/Jensen

Turn left onto Middle Steve's fire road to continue around the lake.

Middle Steve's ends at the Warren Richardson Trail (named for a local cattle rancher and founder of the Sonoma County Trail Blazers). Turn right onto Richardson, following it as it plunges steeply and roughly away from the lake. Within 0.5 mile, you come to a fork with South Burma. Make a hard left to continue the steep and rocky descent along Warren Richardson. Another fork pops up right away, this time with North Burma. Bear right, staying on Richardson as you descend into the redwoods and fir.

The trail seems to end in a redwood grove, but make a hard right and continue the raucous downhill on Warren Richardson. If your arms are tired from the rocky pounding, consider this: this trail is the smoothest of the downhills to Channel Drive. At 8.0 miles, the trail intersects the Two Quarry Trail. Make a hairpin left turn to stay on Warren Richardson. The rest of the descent is relatively smooth and gentle to the parking lot at the end of Channel Drive. Go through the parking lot and head down Channel, back to the park office and the starting point.

33 Annadel State Park/ Long Loop to Ledson Marsh

Distance: 16.3 miles
Difficulty: Strenuous, technical (very technical in spots)
Elevation: 1,300' gain/loss
Ride Type: Loop on sometimes narrow fire roads
Season: Year-round
Map: Available for $1 from a vending machine in front of the park office.
Comments: The only water available is in front of the ranger station; it gets very hot in the summer so bring as much water as you can carry. Restrooms are available along the way. Speed limit of 15 mph.

Highlights: This loop incorporates much of the previous ride's short loop, bypassing Lake Ilsanjo in favor of the high ridge a few hundred feet below the summit of Bennett Mountain, the park's highest peak. The route leads around Ledson Marsh on the park's east side, through meadows and forests, and along terrain that is comparatively smooth and darned near level.

Getting There: See the directions for the previous ride.

Route: The beginning of this ride is identical to the short loop. From the park office, follow Channel Drive out of the park to Violetti Road. Turn left on Violetti, making the first right into the Spring Lake Park. Follow the path at the lake's shore as it leads left, taking you to the Annadel gate. Inside the gate, follow the Spring Creek fire road which runs parallel to Spring Creek. Cross the first bridge, make a sharp right turn, and continue to follow the creek to the second bridge. Turn right, cross the bridge, and climb up the Canyon Trail.

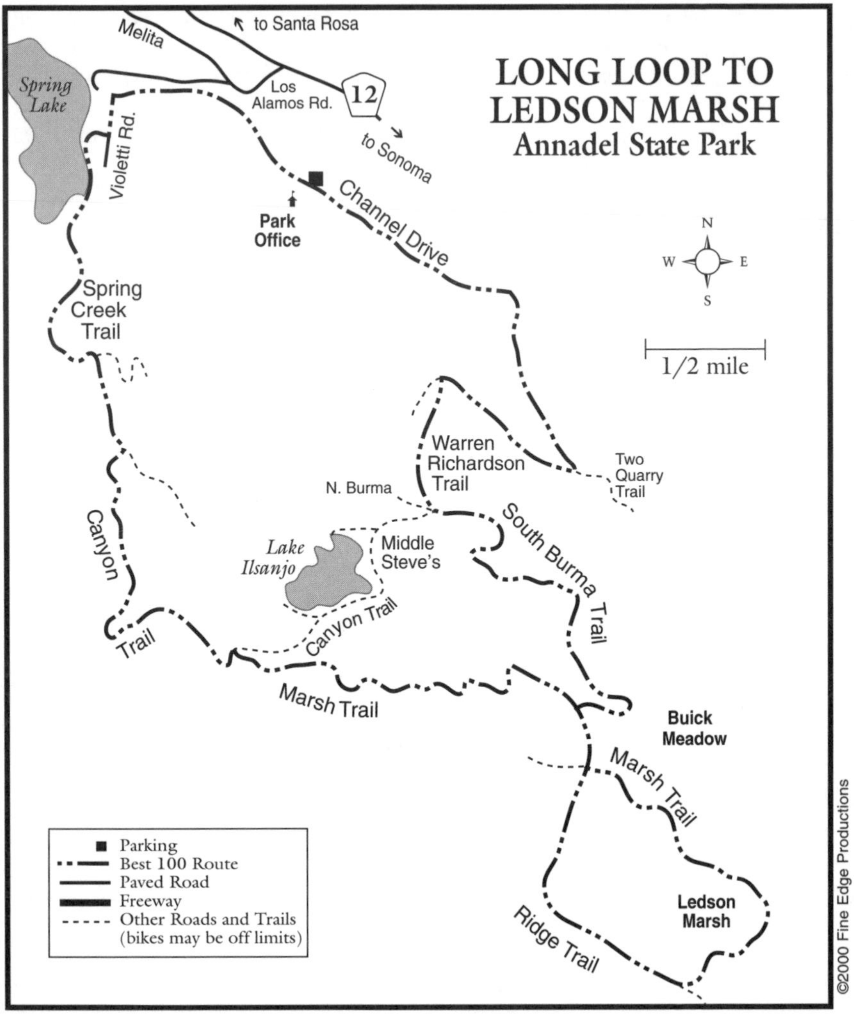

LONG LOOP TO
LEDSON MARSH
Annadel State Park

Upon reaching the fork with the Marsh Trail, bear right this time onto the Marsh Trail and continue climbing. The trail starts off on the steep side, easing at the top of the first short rise to a manageable grade. The terrain is, of course, peppered with rocks as you move in and out of stands of oaks and redwoods, with a seasonal water crossing about halfway up the ridge.

At about 5.7 miles, you reach a fork with the illegal Upper Steve's singletrack. Turn left to continue fol-

lowing the Marsh Trail. Just around the bend from the intersection, the trail levels as you move between the mountain peaks through Buick Meadow. At the next fork, at 6.5 miles, bear right onto the Ridge Trail. The first half of Ridge is a relatively easy climb to the park's southern boundary. At the top of the climb, you see the trail marker for the top of Upper Steve's. Stay left and follow Ridge as it rolls along—you guessed it—Annadel's high ridge.

Just under 8.0 miles, you come to another fork. This time, it's with the top of the Marsh Trail. Turn left onto Marsh and let the fun begin. The trail starts by descending gently to Ledson Marsh. Although there aren't as many rocks around this area, the trail does get pretty rutted. As you make your way down, you see several trails going off to the right. Stay left, following Marsh as it winds around Ledson Marsh, back to Buick Meadow.

Just past the junction with Ridge Trail, you retrace your steps for a brief stretch until you reach the trail marker for the South Burma Trail. You see it at about 11.1 miles. Turn right onto South Burma which winds through Buick Meadow to a scenic overlook with views of the coast. Just past the overlook, you come to another trail intersection; turn left to stay on South Burma. Now the trail returns to typical Annadel terrain, descending steeply at times; it's definitely bumpier.

At approximately 13.1 miles, South Burma ends at the Warren Richardson Trail. Hang a right and follow Warren Richardson into the redwoods and over the rocks, back down to the parking lot at Channel Drive. Go through the parking lot and down Channel Drive to return to the park office.

34 Sugarloaf Ridge State Park/ Bald Mountain Loop

Distance: 6.5 miles
Difficulty: Strenuous, mildly technical
Elevation: 1,500' gain/loss
Ride Type: Loop on fire roads and pavement
Season: Year-round
Map: Available for $1 at the Visitor Center or the ranger kiosk.
Comments: Water is available at the Visitor Center and campgrounds. There's a $5 parking fee (a permit is required to park anywhere on the mountain). Speed limit is 15 mph.

Highlights: Sugarloaf Ridge State Park is so close to Annadel State Park that it's often overlooked. Or else people are scared off by the initial climb. That's too bad because Sugarloaf is another of the little gems of Sonoma County. Not only is it generally less crowded than its more famous neighbor, but it's also well-suited to those not up for Annadel's technical challenges.

Sugarloaf got its name from the shape of the mountains within its 2,700 acres. In the late 1800s, sugar was packaged in cone-shaped "loaves" and grocers would break off pieces of the loaf for individual sale. The mountains in and around the park look decidedly conical, resembling those early sugar loaves.

The land was the long-time home of the Wappo Indians. They fought Spanish settlement only to relinquish their land later to American settlers after back-to-back disease epidemics greatly reduced their numbers in the 1830s. Attempts were made to farm the rocky terrain until the state bought the property in 1920. Plans to dam Sonoma Creek were abandoned thanks to the outcry of local property owners. The land was used as a camping and picnic area, and as a Boy Scout camp, until 1942, when it was leased for cattle grazing. Sugarloaf Ridge became a state park in 1964.

Although the first couple of miles of this loop are paved, don't let that deter you. The descent from the summit of Bald Mountain is a roller coaster on loose and rocky fire roads through forests of maple, pine, live oak, madrone and redwood. Runoff from winter rains (and occasional snow) creates a seasonal network of creeks (i.e., water crossings) that feed into Sonoma Creek, which runs along the southern portion of the park.

Getting There: From San Francisco, take 101 north to the Sebastopol/Sonoma Highway 12 turnoff. Bear right, taking Sonoma East. Follow the signs through downtown Santa Rosa to stay on Highway 12. Turn left on Adobe Canyon Road which ends at the park entrance.

Route: From the parking lot, backtrack about 50 yards to the paved Stern Trail, almost directly across the road from the ranger kiosk. Turn right onto Stern, following it to paved Bald Mountain Trail. Bald Mountain Trail takes you all the way up to the mountain's summit at 2,729 feet, which you reach at 2.8 miles. The trail has a few fairly steep sections, but when you get to the top, you'll (hopefully) think it was worth it. The views from Bald Mountain are spectacular, reaching from San Francisco all the way to the Sierras, overlooking the Wine Country valleys and nearby Mount St. Helena.

The good news is, it's all downhill

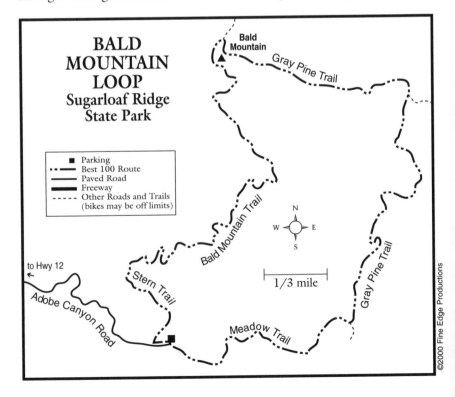

Tackling the climb to Bald Mountain.

from here. Okay, mostly. From the summit of Bald Mountain, head down onto the dirt (at last) Gray Pine Trail. Gray Pine descends rapidly (900 feet in just over a mile), with a couple of short uphill sections, to a fork with Brushy Peaks Trail. Stay right to continue the rolling descent on Gray Pine. This section of Gray Pine has a tendency to get a bit rutted from both runoff and horses' hooves. In the dry summer months, it can be loose.

At about 4.7 miles, the trail flanks a seasonal branch of Sonoma Creek, as it runs down into the valley, shortly before crossing the main creek. In winter months, this crossing can be a little tricky, particularly in heavy rain years. Normally, though, it's no big deal.

Gray Pine ends at the Meadow Trail at about 5.3 miles. Turn right onto Meadow for an easy spin along the creek to the campgrounds. Just inside the campground gate, turn left onto the paved service road and follow it back to the parking lot.

35 Robert Louis Stevenson Memorial State Park/The Peaks

Distance: 13 miles
Difficulty: Moderately strenuous, not technical
Elevation: 2,000' gain/loss
Ride Type: Out-and-back on fire roads
Season: Year-round
Maps: Detert Reservoir, Mount St. Helena
Comments: No water is available; bring plenty, especially in the summer when it can get very hot.

THE PEAKS
Robert Louis Stevenson
Memorial Park

North Peak

to Middletown

N
W E
S

South Peak

1/2 mile

©2000 Fine Edge Productions

- Parking
-·-·- Best 100 Route
——— Paved Road
▬▬▬ Freeway
----- Other Roads and Trails
(bikes may be off limits)

29

to Calistoga ↓

Highlights: Robert Louis Stevenson Memorial State Park is really more like an open space. There's no park headquarters, no rangers and no services. It is a beautiful spot located about halfway up Mount St. Helena, overlooking the Napa Valley. The park is named for poet/novelist Stevenson, who briefly made his home here following his marriage to Fanny Osbourne. The remains of their honeymoon cabin can be found a short hike off the main road (no bikes allowed on the hiking trail).

Although the park encompasses over 1,000 acres, the Peaks route is the only developed multi-use trail. But it's a fun one—semi-steep climbs followed by fast descents with some awesome views along the way. The trail winds its way up and between Mt. St. Helena's North and South peaks, both of which offer far-reaching views from San Francisco to Mount Shasta.

Getting There: From San Francisco, head for Napa Valley by going north on Highway 101 to the Black Point Forest/Highway 37 turnoff. Stay left and follow 37 to Highway 121. Turn left onto 121, bearing east (right) at the fork with 116. About 2 miles later, bear right as Highway 12 joins 121. In about 8 miles, at the intersection with Highway 29, turn left onto 29, which passes through the heart of the Wine Country.

Robert Louis Stevenson is about 35 miles up Highway 29, between Calistoga and Middletown. When you see the trail gate on the left, park along the road (there are wide shoulders on both sides).

Route: This trail is pretty straightforward and easy to follow. From the gate, head up the fire road and into the forest. Bear left at the first fork, at about 0.7 mile. At 1.5 miles, you see the sign and the hiking trail heading down to the Stevenson cabin. Past this point, the trail rolls a little, but steadily climbs up and out of the pine toward exposed rocky grassland dotted with madrone.

The going gets a little steeper as you wind around three wide switchbacks and out into a clearing. From this point, the terrain is a little bit looser with easily avoided ruts (as long as it hasn't rained recently). Alongside the trail, rock outcroppings and madrone decorate the hillside.

At about 3.5 miles, the trail levels out as it leads to the South Peak turnoff, about 0.5 mile ahead. Turn left at the turnoff for a bit of a steep climb up to the South Peak summit (4,003'). The views up here are pretty nice, stretching as far south as San Francisco and, on clear days, beyond. To the east, you can see the Sierras, and to the north, you can make out Mount Shasta (you'll be getting a better view in a few miles).

Head back down to the main fire road, turning left to continue on to North Peak. Along this stretch, the climbing is relieved by a short rolling section. Accompanying you are views of the ocean to your left and Lake Berryessa to the right. At about 6 miles, you come to another fork; follow the sign and veer left for the final steep ascent to North Peak.

Slightly taller than South Peak, North Peak (4,343') offers fabulous views. From here, you can add a better view of Mount Shasta and, slightly east of it, Mount Lassen to your list of sights. After an appropriate amount of gawking time, go back the way you came, enjoying the well-deserved downhill ride to the car.

36 Boggs Mountain Loop

Distance: 12.4 miles
Difficulty: Moderately strenuous, mildly technical
Elevation: 900' gain/loss
Ride Type: Loop on singletrack and fire roads
Season: Year-round
Map: Available free from the forestry office
Comments: Drinking water is not available. Deer hunting is permitted here in August and September. Either wear a lot of safety orange and make a lot of noise or save this ride for a less hazardous time.

Highlights: The Boggs Mountain Demonstration State Forest is a special place for mountain bikers. All of the trails, including approximately 15 miles of buff singletrack, are 100 percent legal. In fact, the singletrack was built with mountain bikes in mind. The men and women of the Califor-

Oak-lined singletrack at Boggs Mountain.

nia Department of Forestry and Fire Protection ride these trails to stay in tip-top shape. To celebrate their efforts (both in building the trails and protecting the forest surrounding them), this loop takes place almost entirely on singletrack.

Boggs Mountain is named after Henry C. Boggs, the timber baron who originally owned the land in 1879. His son operated two sawmills on the northeast side of the mountain between 1880 and 1885. The land subsequently changed hands several times. It was used primarily for timber and cattle grazing until 1949 when the state bought the property. At the time, all economically viable timber had been cut and hauled out of the area. The state used the 3,500 acres to experiment with forestry and demonstrate the productive and economic possibilities of a forest; hence the name, Demonstration State For-

est. Lest you think the area is barren, the once clear-cut land is now replete with ponderosa and sugar pine, Douglas fir and black oak.

Fortunately for us, one of the management objectives is to promote the forest's full recreational value, maintaining a delicate balance with its other uses as a wildlife habitat and watershed, while it continues to supply trees for wood-based products. Camping and hunting are both permitted, and the trail system is "limited" to non-motorized vehicles, specifically including mountain bikes in its trail uses. The local community knows a good thing when it sees one; charitable organizations from nearby Cobb get together with the Boggs Mountain Forest officials to host an annual mountain bike race here to raise money for the Cobb Community Center. Now, if other land managers would just pay attention . . .

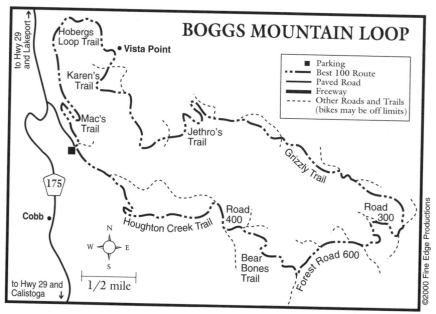

BOGGS MOUNTAIN LOOP

to Hwy 29 and Lakeport →

Hobergs Loop Trail

• **Vista Point**

Karen's Trail

Mac's Trail

Jethro's Trail

Grizzly Trail

175

Cobb •

Houghton Creek Trail

Road 400

Road 300

N
W — E
S

Bear Bones Trail

Forest Road 600

to Hwy 29 and Calistoga ↓

1/2 mile

■ Parking
Best 100 Route
Paved Road
Freeway
Other Roads and Trails
(bikes may be off limits)

©2000 Fine Edge Productions

Getting There: Boggs Mountain lies in the hilly country between Napa Valley and Clear Lake. From San Francisco, take Highway 101 north to the Black Point Forest/Highway 37 turnoff. Stay left, following 37 to Highway 121. Turn left onto 121, bearing east (right) at the fork with 116. About 2 miles later, bear right as Highway 12 joins 121 (there are signs listing the highway as both).

In about 8 miles, at the intersection with Highway 29, turn left onto 29, which passes through the heart of the Wine Country. Follow 29 for about 45 miles to Middletown. At the light in Middletown, turn left onto 175. Boggs Mountain is off 175 just past the town of Cobb. Follow the signs for the State Fire Station (there is a sign for Boggs Mountain once you're on the Forest Road) to the parking area at the heliport and forestry office.

Route: The trail begins just past the heliport and forestry office on Forest

Road 210. Turn left immediately onto the singletrack Mac's Trail. After a couple of steep switchback climbs, Mac's levels for a bit before making a quick descent to a fork in the trail. Stay left, following Hobergs Loop Trail which climbs steeply up through the pine trees. At the ridge line, the trail levels and briefly dips down to a vista point overlooking the Napa Valley.

Past the vista point, the trail begins to climb again, more gently this time. About halfway up the rise, you come to an intersection with a fire road. Cross the road and pick up the trail on the other side. This section of singletrack is Karen's Trail. Karen's continues climbing up an easy grade, ending with a short descent back at the fire road. Turn right onto the fire road, heading up and over a small hill. Within 100 feet or so, the fire road peters out and becomes a singletrack as it descends back into the trees.

Just past the 4-mile point, you come to another fire road. Shoot straight across it onto Jethro's Trail, a fun switchbacking downhill that ends at Forest Road 300 and Mill Creek. Turn right onto the fire road, which continues to head downhill. Almost immediately, you see a singletrack turnoff on the right. You can stay on the fire road or take the singletrack; they're roughly the same distance and rejoin again in about 0.25 mile. I recommend the singletrack.

So, veer off to the right, heading up a short rise that levels to an easy pedal and leads back to the fire road. At the intersection, go straight across the fire road onto the next singletrack, the Grizzly Trail. Grizzly descends, steeply at times, through a forest of black oak. At about 6.7 miles, you reach the next short fire road section, Forest Road 100. Turn right onto the fire road, splash through a seasonal water crossing, and bear right at the next fork, back onto singletrack.

This stretch of trail rolls and climbs back up to the pine trees, ending at another junction with Forest Road 100. Turn right and quickly make another right onto Forest Road

300. After a short, steep climb. the trail levels as it approaches the next fork. Veer left onto Forest Road 600, staying left through the next mini-fork. The fire road meanders its way up past a couple of tempting singletrack turnoffs. You pass in and out of the trees as the trail rolls a bit before the last big push up to the crossroads.

At about 9.1 miles, you find yourself at the intersection of Forest Roads 600, 610 and the Bear Bones singletrack. Make a sharp, hairpin right turn onto the Bear Bones Trail. The trail begins with a rolling section, then becomes a fast and twisting downhill. It's over too soon, ending at Forest Road 400. Hang a left here, followed by a right turn onto the paved main road. Don't worry, you'll be off the pavement in a jiffy.

At 10.5 miles, turn left onto the first singletrack you see, Houghton Creek Trail. Aptly named, the trail follows Houghton Creek for about a mile before crossing it. After some tight switchbacks, the trail straightens and levels, leading back to the main road and the parking area.

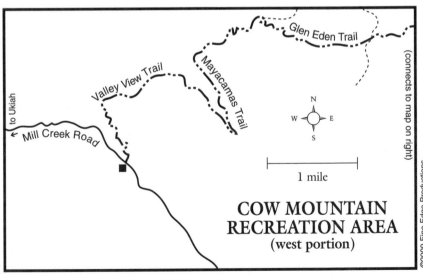

COW MOUNTAIN
RECREATION AREA
(west portion)

©2000 Fine Edge Productions

37 Cow Mountain Recreation Area

Distance: 37 miles or 18.5 miles
Difficulty: Strenuous, mildly technical
Elevation: 4,400' gain/loss
Ride Type: Out-and-back or one-way shuttle on fire roads
Season: Spring through fall
Map: Available free from the Bureau of Land Management, (707) 468-4000
Comments: Water is available at the Mayacamas trailhead and at points along the Glen Eden Trail. It can get very hot here in the summer months.

Highlights: The Cow Mountain Recreation Area is a 50,000-acre site due west of Clear Lake. While technically not a part of the North Bay/Sonoma area, it's close to Sonoma County's north boundary and a playground this size just had to be brought to your attention! There are over 150 miles (!) of trails included in this land, ranging from short and scenic to rough and tumble.

Named after the longhorn cattle that once roamed wild over this range, the recreation area is, for governing purposes, delineated as North and South Cow Mountain. The majority of the trails, and approximately two-thirds of the property, are found in the South Cow Mountain area, open to all, including 4WD vehicles and motorcycles. The trails here are steep, rough and rugged, providing endless hours of fun and amusement.

The northern third, North Cow Mountain, has a handful of trails that are restricted to non-motorized vehicles and provide slightly gentler (and quieter) forms of entertainment. The trails here traverse ridges and meadows and follow seasonal creeks and streams. Fishing and camping are

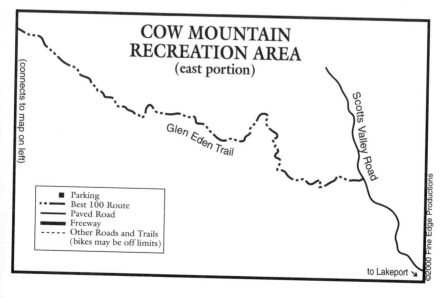

COW MOUNTAIN
RECREATION AREA
(east portion)

(connects to map on left)

Glen Eden Trail

Scotts Valley Road

- ■ Parking
- ▪▪▪ Best 100 Route
- —— Paved Road
- ▬▬ Freeway
- ---- Other Roads and Trails
  (bikes may be off limits)

to Lakeport ↘

©2000 Fine Edge Productions

popular in this area, as well as hunting (every place has its drawbacks).

Because of the area's size, wildlife is abundant here. Beyond the usual Northern California animals such as coyote, deer, fox and rabbits, some of the grander and more exotic species hang out here, too, namely black bears and mountain lions. More than likely, you won't see the big guys but, for the sake of your own safety and that of the animals, wear a whistle around your neck. I've found whistles to be extremely effective when encountering wildlife bigger than a German shepherd. Not only will a couple of short, shrill blasts alert anyone within earshot that you're there and possibly in trouble, it frightens away most animals. (Did you know that bears can jump? Pretty high, too, considering their girth.)

While there are obviously an abundance of trails and combinations in the area, the following route, one of the most popular, is set forth here as an introduction to Cow Mountain. It runs across the North Cow Mountain Recreation Area from the west boundary to the east boundary. It can be done as an 18.5-mile one-way shuttle or a 37-mile out-and-back. Of course, on the out-and-back you can turn around whenever you've had enough.

Getting There: From San Francisco, go north on 101 to Ukiah and take the Talmadge (Ukiah) exit. Take Talmadge Road east to East Side Road, then make the first left onto Mill Creek Road. The trailhead gate is on the left about 4 miles up Mill Creek Road. Park in dirt turnouts on either side of the road.

For one-way shuttlers, the second vehicle should continue on Mill Creek Road and follow it through the South Cow Mountain area to Scott Creek Road. Bear left onto Scott Creek and follow it to Riggs Road, just past the U-Wanna Campground (I didn't name it, folks). Turn left on Riggs, which quickly ends at Scotts Valley Road. Turn left onto Scotts Valley and park at Kelly's Kamp, about 8 miles up.

Route: From the trail gate, follow the Valley View Trail as it climbs up along a grassland ridge. The trail starts as a series of switchbacks that takes some of the sting out of the climb. At the end of the first 1.5 miles, the grade eases considerably while the trail straightens out. From this point, the rest of Valley View rolls to its end at a junction with dirt Mendo Rock Road and the Mayacamas Trail (at the Willow Creek Recreation Site).

Turn left onto Mayacamas which crosses Willow Creek and then follows its bank. A long downhill section leads to the north fork of Mill Creek. The trail turns to follow Mill Creek through a forest of pine and oak. Mayacamas rolls along the bank of the creek, through a seasonal water crossing, and up to a fork with the Glen Eden Trail at about 7.5 miles.

The fun is temporarily over as you turn right onto Glen Eden. Glen Eden climbs steeply up a short rise, about 0.5 mile. As you move away from the creeks, the scenery gets a little less green, opening up to grassland dotted with oak.

At the top of the first rise, the fun is back. The trail becomes a roller coaster that continues for the next 10.5 miles. Glen Eden rolls and turns, up ridges and down again, with great views of Clear Lake in front of you and the Mayacamas Range behind you. At about 12 miles, you cross the seasonal Scotts Creek in the Goat Rock Recreation Site. There are a few more trees here; when you make your way up to the next ridge, the grass and chaparral once again take over.

At approximately 15.7 miles, just past a water refill point, you enter private property. The remainder of the trail is a rolling downhill to the BLM gate (and another water refill point) on Scotts Valley Road. This is the end of the line for one-way shut-tlers. Those riding the whole distance turn around here and go back the way they came.

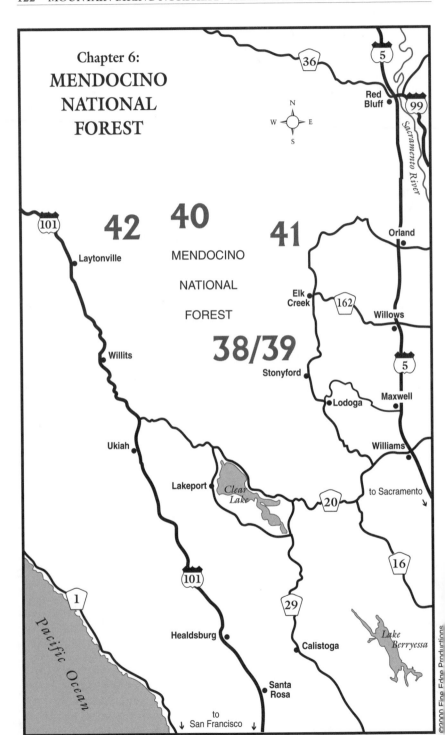

Chapter 6:

MENDOCINO NATIONAL FOREST

Mendocino National Forest

by Robin Stuart

The Mendocino National Forest is one of the largest and most diverse recreation areas in Northern California. Stretching 65 miles from its north boundary of Trinity National Forest to the southern boundary of Clear Lake, and 35 miles across, the forest treats visitors to everything from arid balds to densely-forested lakes and streams with conifer treetops straining to touch the sky. It's also the only National Forest in California not crossed by a paved road or highway. If you want to get away from it all, this is the place.

Visionary land managers originally set aside the property in 1907. Since that time, archaeological expeditions have uncovered evidence of at least five different groups of Native American inhabitants—the Yuki, Nomlaki Wintu, Patwin Wintu, Eastern Pomo and Northeastern Pomo. No doubt each was attracted to the bountiful hunting and agricultural opportunities. Approximately 300 species, including California black bear, bobcat, mountain lion, black-tailed deer, osprey, wild boar and wild turkey, still call this land home.

Prior to its designation as a forest reserve, sawmills and copper mines operated here in the latter part of the 19th century. During World War II, the government temporarily re-examined the mining possibilities by conducting exploratory digs in search of manganese and chrome. The businesses that thrived here well into the twentieth century, however, were centered around the natural hot springs found in various spots around the forest. At the southern end of the forest, near Bartlett Flats, you can find remains of three hotels, mineral baths, and a mineral water bottling plant.

Although the following rides are touted by local riders, including the forest rangers, the entire forest begs to be explored. Hundreds of miles of fire roads and trails wind through, over and around areas bearing such colorful names as The Slides, Impassable Rock, Poison Glade and Elephant Hill. Because of the forest's size, camping is the best option. Campgrounds are accessible by car, although it will need a bath when you get home.

When planning a trip to the Mendocino National Forest, maps are essential. The Forest Supervisor's office is in Willows, just off Interstate 5. The forest is also micro-managed by four ranger districts, with two offices on the east side, Stonyford and Corning, and two offices on the west side, Covelo and Upper Lake. You can call ahead for maps by mail. (See Agencies and Visitor Centers in the Appendix.) You should also call ahead when planning early spring or late fall rides to make sure the trails are open. This is high country; it may only be three hours north of San Francisco, but it snows here. Riding is discouraged following heavy rains or snow melt.

One more advisory—most of the forest is open to off-road vehicles and is particularly popular with motorcyclists. Because of that, trails are generally well-marked. The downside is that summer weekends attract a lot of traffic. Another reason to call ahead is to make sure you're not planning a get-away the same weekend as a scheduled motorcycle enduro event.

38 South End Loop

Distance: 24.5 miles
Difficulty: Very strenuous, somewhat technical
Elevation: 4,000' gain/loss; 5,500' high point
Ride Type: Loop on service roads
Season: Spring through fall
Maps: Fouts Springs. Pamphlet showing map sections available free through district ranger offices; map of entire forest available for $4.
Comments: Unless you do this ride during high camping season (late spring through early fall in most parts of the forest), drinking water is only sporadically available. Bring plenty to avoid the panic associated with the dry sound of a shut-down water main.

Highlights: This ride, perhaps the area's most popular, is not for the faint of heart and lung. The starting elevation is about 1,500 feet. It climbs to 4,000 feet, and reaches a high mark around 5,500 feet before dropping back to 1,500 feet. Along the way, you ride through dense oak and pine forests and pass by Letts Lake, a popular fishing and swimming area. The roads are well-marked, if not always well maintained. Particularly in early spring, watch for fallen trees and overgrown trails. Be careful when choosing a line on the left-hand side of the road—remember you're sharing the road with motorcycles and the occasional car.

Getting There: From the Bay Area, take 80 East to the 505 cutoff past Vacaville. Take 505 to its end at Interstate 5 North. From I-5, take the Maxwell exit and head west. You probably won't notice a sign, but you're on Sites Road. Go 9 miles to a fork at Lodoga Road; turn right. Approximately 15 miles later, in the

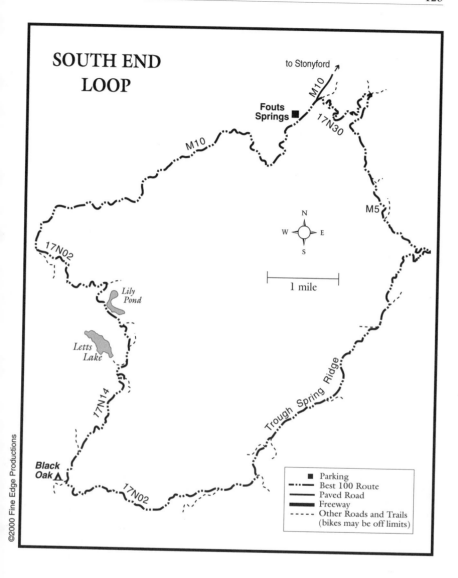

SOUTH END
LOOP

to Stonyford

M10

Fouts
Springs ■

17N30

M10

M5

N
W—E
S

|———| 1 mile

17N02

Lily
Pond

Letts
Lake

17N14

Trough Spring Ridge

Black
Oak ▲

17N02

■ Parking
·-··-··- Best 100 Route
——— Paved Road
▬▬▬ Freeway
- - - - Other Roads and Trails
(bikes may be off limits)

©2000 Fine Edge Productions

very small town of Lodoga, turn right and cross the bridge to continue on Lodoga/ Stonyford Road. Eight miles later, you reach a stop sign in Stonyford. Turn left at the stop and turn left again, two blocks later, onto Fouts Spring Road/M10. Continue on M10 for approximately 9 miles to the Davis Flats/Fouts Springs Staging Area.

From Sacramento, take Interstate 5 North to the Maxwell exit and follow the directions above. From points north (Red Bluff, Redding), take Interstate 5 South to the Maxwell exit and follow the directions above. From Chico, take Highway 32 west to Interstate 5 South and proceed to the Maxwell exit.

Route: From the Fouts Springs Staging Area, turn right and head back out onto the M10 toward Deafy Glade. The road winds uphill, sometimes steeply. The good news is that the steepest sections are short. Although you may be sharing the road with the occasional car, they won't be moving very quickly through here. It's very windy and there seems to be a rule that the tightest point of every bend is also the narrowest.

The pavement, such as it is, peters out after a couple of miles. The final remnants of blacktop disappear completely as you approach the Deafy Glade turnout at about 4 miles. The road becomes more of a classic fire road, replete with large jutting rocks, as you continue the rolling but persistent climb.

At 5.8 miles, turn left onto Forest Road 17N02 toward Letts Lake.

Almost immediately, you find yourself at a fork. Stay right to continue toward Letts Lake. The road gets dusty and narrow as you wind your way toward the lake. The campgrounds appears at approximately 8.5 miles. This is the time to replenish your water supply, make use of the facilities, or take a dip in Letts Lake. The turnoff to the right leads to the lake's shore in less than half a mile. But we're here to ride, right?

Continuing past the Letts Lake campgrounds, bear right onto Forest Road 17N14. The climb becomes more steady at this point and the road becomes more of a trail. Between the rough trail conditions and Mother Nature's attempts to reclaim the areas cleared for vehicles, at times it seems downright singletracky.

The trail starts to level as you approach Black Oak Campground

Heading into the forest for the weekend.

Fragnoli

around 9.2 miles. At the junction with 17N02, turn left. The trail widens again and rolls happily along Trough Spring Ridge. Settle back and enjoy yourself, the worst of the climbs are over.

The ride along the downward-sloping ridge is pretty much a straight shot until a set of tight switchback at 19 miles. Stay with 17N02, now also known as M5, until 17N30 crosses at 23 miles. Turn left and wind your way back down to M10 and the staging area.

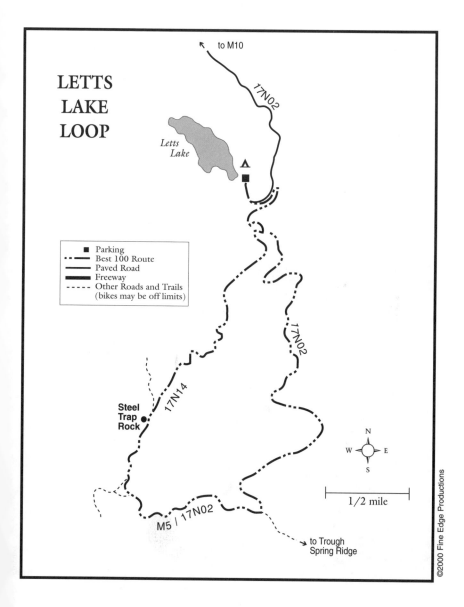

LETTS LAKE LOOP

to M10

17N02

Letts Lake

■ Parking
·—·— Best 100 Route
——— Paved Road
▬▬▬ Freeway
----- Other Roads and Trails
       (bikes may be off limits)

17N02

Steel Trap Rock

17N14

N
W ✦ E
S

1/2 mile

M5 / 17N02

to Trough Spring Ridge

©2000 Fine Edge Productions

39 Letts Lake Loop

Distance: 7.5 miles
Difficulty: Easy, not technical
Elevation: 1,000' gain/loss; 5,500' high point
Ride Type: Loop on service roads
Season: Spring through fall
Maps: Fouts Springs. Pamphlet showing map sections available free through district ranger offices; map of entire forest available for $4.
Comments: Drinking water and restroom facilities are seasonally available at the Letts Lake campgrounds.

Highlights: This ride presents an ideal opportunity for families to combine camping with mountain biking. It's not difficult unless you're unaccustomed to elevations over 4,000 feet. Although you gain a hair over 1,000 feet during the ride, you hardly notice it. The route takes you through classic California mountain terrain—a little dusty, a little rocky, cluttered with a variety of conifers, great and small. There's not much that's prettier than afternoon sunlight filtering through the pine boughs, spotlighting air ferns rising from the red dirt at the base of neighboring trees.

Getting There: Follow the directions for the previous ride, continuing on M10 for 5.8 miles past the Fouts Springs staging area. Turn left on 17N02 and follow the signs for Letts Lake. Park in the Letts Lake Campground day-use lot.

Route: From the parking lot, turn left and head back out to the intersection with 17N02 and turn right. The road rolls on a gentle uphill slope. At the fork with 17N14 at 0.5 mile, bear left. Don't worry, you'll see that fork again soon enough.

Stay on 17N02, rolling past a trail spur on the left at 1.2 miles. The trail rolls a lit-

Fragnoli

Well-marked trails are a big help.

tle more level for a bit before an easy coast of a downhill brings you to a seasonal creek crossing at 2.8 miles. The creek is generally dry by late fall.

The road ends at 3.2 miles. Turn right onto M5 (also known as 17N02). After a brief burst of uphill, the road levels, then rolls pleasantly again. At 4.5 miles, turn right onto 17N14 for the last bit of climbing. At the top, at 5.2 miles, you've reached the highest point of the ride at Steel Trap Rock (5,457 feet). It's all downhill from here. Coast on down to the fork with 17N02 at 6.7 miles, veering left to head back to the campground.

40 Anthony Peak/ Buck Rock

Distance: 8.5 miles
Difficulty: Strenuous, somewhat technical
Elevation: 950' gain/loss; elevation ranges from 6,000' to 7,000'
Ride Type: Out-and-back on jeep trail
Season: Spring through fall
Maps: Mendocino Pass, Buck Rock. Pamphlet showing map sections available free through district ranger offices; map of entire forest available for $4.
Comments: Either bring your own water or stop at a full-service campground along the way. Once you're on the trail, there are no facilities.

Highlights: This ride is unusual in that it's quite possibly the easiest ride in this book to follow and one of the hardest trails to reach. The views alone are worth the effort. Again, I recommend a camp-and-bike combo to make the most of the journey.

Getting There: From I-5, about 18 miles south of Red Bluff, take the

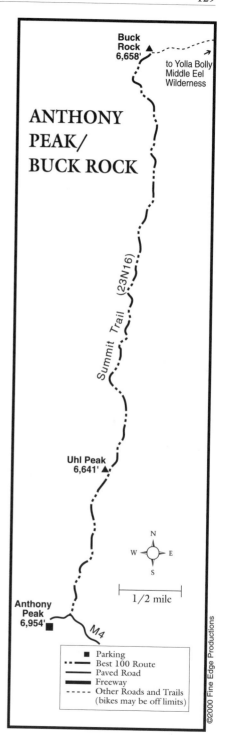

ANTHONY PEAK/ BUCK ROCK

Buck Rock 6,658'

to Yolla Bolly Middle Eel Wilderness

Summit Trail (23N16)

Uhl Peak 6,641'

Anthony Peak 6,954'

M4

N
W — E
S

1/2 mile

■ Parking
▪▪▪ Best 100 Route
— Paved Road
▬ Freeway
---- Other Roads and Trails (bikes may be off limits)

©2000 Fine Edge Productions

Corning exit and head west on Corning Road. In the town of Paskenta, bear left at the fork onto the M4 recreation road into the forest. The pavement gives way to dirt just past the Salt Creek Conservation Camp. Stay on M4 as it twists and winds through a variety of campgrounds and recreation areas. Just past Sugar Springs, take the first left and follow the signs for Covelo. Approximately one mile past the Brewer Oak Campground, turn right and follow the signs to Anthony Peak.

Route: As I said, this ride is easy to follow. From 6,954-foot Anthony Peak, named for a group of 19th-century sheep-herding brothers, turn left onto 23N16, more commonly known as the Summit Trail. There are no more turns except 180 degrees to return.

The Summit Trail is a fire road, at times more of a doubletrack, popular with four-wheel drives, motorcycles and bikes. As you can glean from the name, the trail follows the ridge lines leading from peak to peak to peak. It's popular because it's a dirt roller coaster, chock full of the rocky goodness you expect from mountaintop riding. From each of the high points, notably Uhl Peak (6,641') and Buck Rock (6,658'), the views are breathtaking—and not just because you're at high elevation. Forest rangers, the literature, and most people suggest catching your breath and soaking in the view at Buck Rock, about 4.2 miles from Anthony Peak, before turning around.

If you're in good shape and you're up for even steeper rollers, the jeep trail continues on for another 4.5 miles. About 6 miles in, you drop a little deeper into the canyons. The fun is over for motorized vehicles and bikes at the boundary of the Yolla Bolly Middle Eel Wilderness. Turn around and go back the way you came.

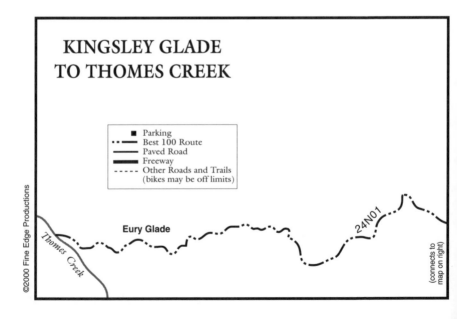

KINGSLEY GLADE
TO THOMES CREEK

41 Kingsley Glade to Thomes Creek

Distance: 16 miles
Difficulty: Moderate, not technical
Elevation: 2,200' gain/loss
Ride Type: Out-and-back on service roads
Season: Spring through fall
Maps: Ball Mountain, Log Spring. Pamphlet showing map sections available free through district rangers' offices; map of entire forest available for $4.
Comments: Water and facilities seasonally available at campgrounds.

Highlights: Another good camp-and-bike opportunity, this ride takes you through several campgrounds and dense conifer woods before depositing you on the shores of Thomes Creek. Fairly easy to follow, this is another of the Mendocino Forest's no-turn rides. It just sort of seems like you're turning a couple of times.

Getting There: From I-5, about 18 miles south of Red Bluff, take the Corning exit and head west on Corning Road. In the town of Paskenta, turn right on Toomes Road which becomes the M2/Forest Road 23N01. Continue for approximately 18 miles to the end of the pavement and turn left onto Forest Road 24N01. Follow 24N01 approximately 4 miles to Kingsley Glade Campground.

Route: From the campground, turn right back onto 24N01. The further you go on the road, the less it seems like a road. At the 1.5-mile point, bear left to stay on 24N01 as you wind around Kingsley Glade and make the gradual descent toward Straight Arrow Camp.

Several roads converge at 2.7 miles. Make a sharp left to stay on 24N01. It's a little confusing, but well marked. Continue the casual downhill through Sugarfoot Glade (an optional starting point for a shorter, easier

ride). As you happily hum along, remember that which you descend

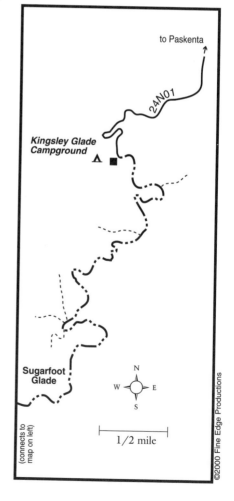

you shall climb on the way back. Just a little reality check for you.

The trail gets a little more interesting around 6 miles. It's steeper, rockier and less traveled as you ride through Eury Glade, which marks the beginning of the final descent. It's a steep and fun 2-mile frolic down to Thomes Creek. In the middle of the summer, it's a good idea to stop for a soak in the creek before facing the uphill return.

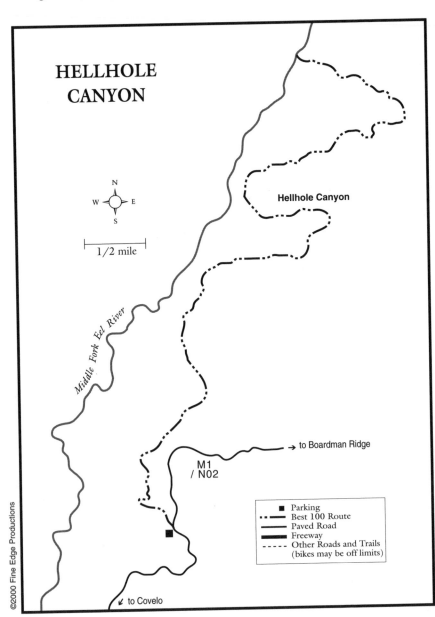

HELLHOLE CANYON

N
W — E
S

|—— 1/2 mile ——|

Middle Fork Eel River

Hellhole Canyon

→ to Boardman Ridge

M1
/ N02

■   Parking
∙∙∙—   Best 100 Route
—   Paved Road
▬   Freeway
- - -   Other Roads and Trails
        (bikes may be off limits)

↙ to Covelo

42 Hellhole Canyon

Distance: 14 miles
Difficulty: Strenuous, technical
Elevation: 1,800' gain/loss
Ride Type: Out-and-back on singletrack
Season: Summer and fall
Maps: Newhouse Ridge, Leech Lake Mountain. Pamphlet showing map sections available free through district ranger offices; map of entire forest available for $4.
Comments: No water or facilities are available.

Highlights: This is one of the few singletracks in the Mendocino National Forest where you're more likely to encounter hikers and equestrians than motorcycles. The rocky trail hugs the side of a wooded ridge before winding down, rather steeply at times, to the Middle Fork of the Eel River. Despite the intriguing name, you never ride in Hellhole Canyon, although you do cross its mouth.

Getting There: This trail is nearer to the forest's western boundary and is therefore more easily accessed via Highway 101. From 101, about 12 miles north of Willits, take the Highway 162 turnoff. Follow 162 through Covelo to the Eel River Work Center. Turn left onto Forest Road N02 (also signed as M1 at the beginning). Follow N02 for approximately 4 miles to the trailhead, located in a turnout on the left side of the road. The only sign is a post with a hiker symbol.

Route: This trail, like Anthony Peak, is very easy to follow as there are no turns. But unlike Anthony Peak, you don't have to contend with high elevations (it stays below 3.000 feet), which is a good thing since there are plenty of steep ups and downs.

The singletrack begins with a predominantly level ride through the pine and oak forest. A short dip in the trail leads you through Buck Creek at 0.7 mile. Ignore the trail spur on the right (which leads back up to the service road) and make the short steep climb away from the creek.

At 1.5 miles, go straight across the fire road. The trail crossing is followed by a downhill which ends in a seasonal creek crossing. The immediate steep climb gives way to a kinder, gentler climb that leads away from the river. A tight switchback signals a steep climb followed by an equally steep descent back toward the river. You get close enough to see the river before the trail turns away again for a last steepish climb back up into the trees. Once again, a switchback is your signal. At 5.8 miles, you start the last long drop to the end of the trail at the bank of the Eel River.

Catch your breath, have a nosh, then head back the way you came.

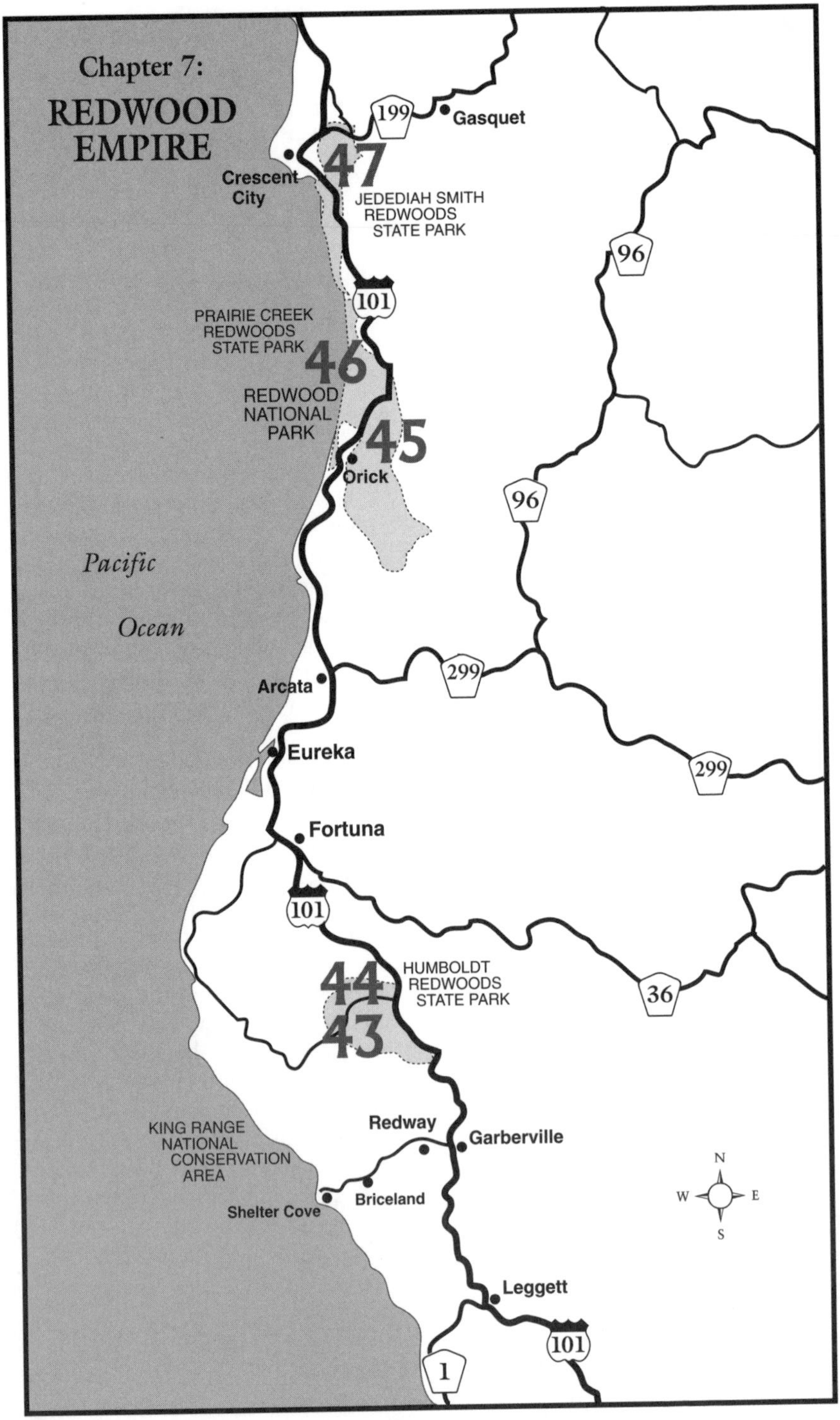

Chapter 7:

REDWOOD EMPIRE

199 Gasquet

47

Crescent City

JEDEDIAH SMITH REDWOODS STATE PARK

96

101

PRAIRIE CREEK REDWOODS STATE PARK

46

REDWOOD NATIONAL PARK

45

Orick

96

Pacific

Ocean

Arcata

299

Eureka

299

Fortuna

101

44

HUMBOLDT REDWOODS STATE PARK

43

36

Redway   Garberville

KING RANGE NATIONAL CONSERVATION AREA

Briceland

Shelter Cove

N
W   E
S

Leggett

1   101

Redwood Empire

by Delaine Fragnoli

We could tell you that the redwoods are among the oldest and largest living things on earth. We could tell you that an old-growth redwood forest is a rare and beautiful ecosystem. So rare and beautiful, in fact, that Redwood National Park and the surrounding California state parks have been declared a World Heritage Site and an International Biosphere Reserve by the United Nations.

We could pull out the overused superlatives that still don't convey the reality of these trees and forests. Words like majestic, towering, noble, venerable, awe-inspiring. Phrases such as "it's like being in a cathedral."

Fact is, even then we wouldn't come close to describing these marvels. The best we can do is urge you to go see them for yourself. See them on a mountain bike. Go and be awed.

While mountain bike opportunities in the national and state parks are limited (partly because of heavy use, partly because of unsuitable terrain and soil types, and partly because of politics), a mountain bike remains a great way to explore the redwoods. The biking you can do is both scenic and fun. Moist, tacky soil carpeted with pine needles provides great traction. Any hills you have to climb—they tend to be short and steep—are amply rewarded by forest views and ocean panoramas.

Along the fabled Humboldt coast, the best riding is in Humboldt Redwoods State Park with over 100 miles of trails, many of which are open to bikes. Access is off of Highway 101. The largest town in this area is to the north, but several smaller communities dot the 101.

Redwood National Park, Prairie Creek Redwoods State Park, Del Norte Coast Redwoods State Park and Jedediah Smith Redwoods State Park form an emerald ribbon along California's northernmost coast. With the exception of Del Norte, each of these parks offers one substantial loop for mountain bikers.

Crescent City in the north and Eureka in the south are the largest jumping-off spots for exploring the area, although several smaller towns along the coast offer services to travelers. Access is easy via Highway 101 and the Newton Drury Parkway, which bisects Redwood National and Prairie Creek parks.

An area no longer covered in this chapter but still of interest to mountain bikers is the Smith River National Recreation Area. Bordering the eastern side of Jedediah Smith State Park, Smith River offers longer backcountry trips on old logging roads and toll roads. Besides a rich mining history, the area is home to some of the eastern-most coastal redwoods as well as many other tree species, including four types of cedar.

As part of the Six Rivers National Forest, the area used to be managed primarily for logging, so you can see evidence of clear-cutting in some spots. As a relatively new recreation area (it was established in 1990), the area is still developing its recreational potential. Plans for more campgrounds and efforts to map routes and trails are in the works, and NRA personnel are eager to help. Check with rangers for the latest trail information and road conditions.

Trails Illustrated makes a Redwood National Park/North Coast State Parks/Smith River NRA topo map. This is the single map to get if you plan on exploring the whole area. To order, call (800) 962-1643. The map does not cover the Humboldt area.

43 Humboldt Redwoods State Park/ Grasshopper Peak

Distance: 17.5 miles
Difficulty: Very strenuous, mildly technical
Elevation: 3,100' gain/loss
Ride Type: Loop on dirt roads , little bit of pavement
Season: Year-round; tends to be wet in winter and spring, foggy in summer, best (warm and dry) in fall
Map: Park map available at Visitor Center for $1
Comments: Bikes are not allowed on hiking trails. Stay on fire roads. Consult the park map for details. Watch for poison oak. Water available at campgrounds or treat at trail camps.

Highlights: There are lots of reasons to visit Humboldt Redwoods State Park. Altogether, 17,000 of the park's 51,000 acres are old-growth. The term old-growth refers not just to the size and age of the trees, but to the whole forest ecosystem. An old-growth forest houses young and old trees, snags, and a rich carpet of mosses and ferns.

Humboldt is also home to the Rockefeller Forest, the largest tract of undisturbed old-growth coastal redwoods in the world, as well as the Giant Tree, the world-champion coast redwood. The world champion status is based upon the tree's height, circumference and crown size.

The park encompasses the entire Bull Creek watershed. Most of the available bike routes are in the Bull Creek area. Like much of the park, this area was acquired with financial support from the Save-the-Redwoods League. Founded in 1917, the League has been accumulating private funds and using them to purchase redwood forests since 1921.

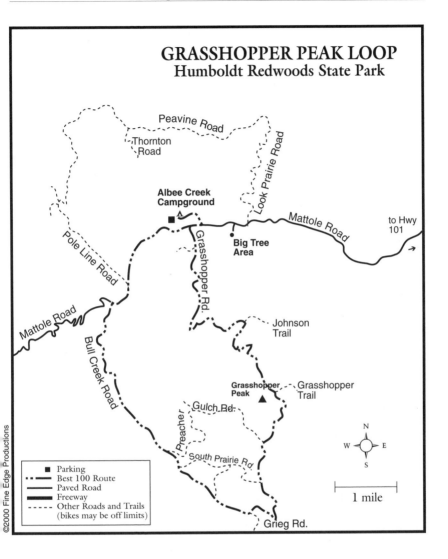

GRASSHOPPER PEAK LOOP
Humboldt Redwoods State Park

Long before the League took an interest in the area, the Sinkyone Indians inhabited the land. Hunters and gatherers who lived on salmon and tanoak acorns, the Sinkyone used parts of the redwood trees for housing, basket-making and canoes.

Gold miners passed through the area during the nineteenth century, and Northwestern Pacific Railroad built the Redwood Highway in 1922. Then full-scale logging and tourism took over until the League intervened.

This particular loop, one of the best, highest, and most difficult climbs along the coast, takes you to Grasshopper Peak (3,379') and back along Bull Creek. The climb may be arduous, but the descent is fun and your surroundings are green and lush beyond imagining.

Getting There: The park is located north of Garberville and 30 miles south of Eureka on Highway 101. The Bull Creek area is off of Mattole Road, about 10 miles north of the Visitor Center. The Grasshopper Peak trailhead is on the south side of Mattole, half a mile west of the Albee Creek Campground entrance. Note that Mattole Road is referred to as Bull Creek Flats Road in some park publications.

Route: From the trailhead, head south and up on Grasshopper Road. Might as well put it in your granny gear from the get-go. This climb takes no prisoners as it ascends over 3,000 feet in 7 miles. Take it slow and enjoy your surroundings.

You have to go around a locked gate very early on. About 0.5 mile later, Squaw Creek Ridge Road takes off to your right. Stay on Grasshopper Road.

About halfway up, at a right-hand switchback, the Johnson Trail (no bikes) comes in from your left. This is a pretty spot to take a break, drink some water and rest your legs.

Just before 7 miles, when you approach Grasshopper Trail Camp on your left, your work is almost done. The Grasshopper Trail takes off from here, but it is closed to bikes. Grasshopper Peak itself and a fire lookout are on your right. The lookout reportedly makes a great sunset-watching spot for those of you with romantic notions in your heads and lights for your bikes. No matter what time of day, the views are great.

Now your work is over and you get to descend. Continue on Grasshopper Road down the backside of the peak. When you pass Preacher Gulch Road at 8.5 miles, you will already have descended 800 feet. Drop 500 feet more and pass South Prairie Road at 9.5 miles. At 10.5 miles, Grasshopper Road ends at Grieg Road.

About 0.3 mile and

A great ride to keep cool in summer's heat.

Jason Houston

500 feet of elevation loss later, steep Grieg Road dead-ends at Bull Creek Road. Go right to continue your descent. Around 11.8 miles, you pass South Prairie Road again. You pass Preacher Gulch Road and the Bull Creek Trail Camp at 12.8 miles.

From here, Bull Creek Road parallels Bull Creek for 3.5 miles, all the way back down to paved Mattole Road. A right turn onto the pavement takes you back to the trailhead and Albee Creek Campground.

44 Humboldt Redwoods State Park/ Peavine Ridge Road

Distance: 16.5 miles
Difficulty: Moderately strenuous, mildly technical
Elevation: 2,200' gain/loss
Ride Type: Loop on dirt roads and pavement
Season: Year-round; tends to be wet in winter and spring, foggy in summer, best (warm and dry) in fall
Map: Park map available at Visitor Center for $1
Comments: Bikes are not allowed on hiking trails. Stay on fire roads. Consult the park map for details. Watch for poison oak. Water available at campgrounds or treat at trail camps.

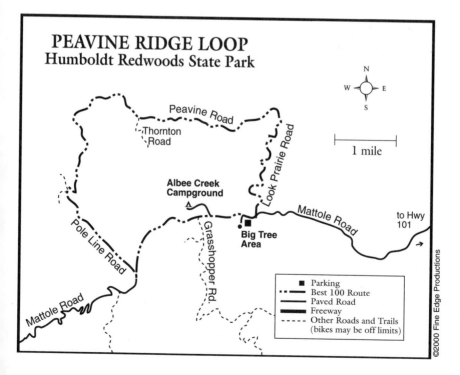

©2000 Fine Edge Productions

Highlights: Although this ride starts with a steep climb, it is easier than the previous ride. The 7-mile stretch along Peavine Ridge is lovely, generally rolling terrain. The ride's greatest appeal, however, is that it takes you through plenty of old-growth forest.

Getting There: The turnoff for this ride, Mattole Road, is located 25 miles north of Garberville and 30 miles south of Eureka on Highway 101. The start of this ride, the Look Prairie Road trailhead, is a quarter-mile east of the Big Tree Area on the north side of Mattole Road. Note that Mattole Road is referred to as Bull Creek Flats Road in some park publications.

Route: Head north up Look Prairie Road. You have to go around a gate almost immediately. From here, you do most of your climbing in the first 4 miles. As you near the top of the climb, go around another gate. Soon after, Look Prairie ends at Peavine Ridge Road.

Head west, left. The road rolls along the ridge until it seems to end at Thornton Road, which drops off to your left. Go right to stay on Peavine. Soon the road begins to descend gradually on its way to Pole Line Road.

You have another gate to go around. Just after it, Pole Line Road takes off to your left (south), dropping 1,300 feet in 3 miles. Take Pole Line to its end at Mattole Road (there's another gate just before it reaches the pavement).

A left turn and 3 miles of easy spinning takes you back to the trailhead.

45 Redwood National Park/ Holter Ridge Loop

Distance: 19.5 miles
Difficulty: Moderately strenuous, not technical
Elevation: 2,100' gain/loss
Ride Type: Loop on dirt, gravel and paved roads
Season: Year-round; wet in winter and spring, crowded and foggy in summer, best (warm and dry) in fall
Maps: Redwood National Park puts out a brochure and trail map available at any Visitor Center; the Redwood Natural History Association produces a Trail Guide with map, suggested routes and mileages; Trails Illustrated Redwood National Park.
Comments: Information and maps of the surrounding state parks can be obtained from the National Park's Visitor Information Center.

Highlights: This is the only legal mountain bike loop in Redwood National Park. The route climbs through old-growth and second-growth forest, crossing two streams on its way. While the old logging roads and pavement return do not require a lot of mountain biking skill, the climbing is steep in parts and the scenery is awe-inspiring. Riders without the endurance or desire to do the entire loop can do Lost Man Creek Trail as an out-and-back venture.

Getting There: The ride begins at Lost Man Creek picnic area inside

Redwood National Park. To get there, head north from the town of Orick for 3 miles on Highway 101. Turn right onto gravel Lost Man Creek Road. (If you reach the Prairie Creek Visitor Center, you've gone too far.) Follow it for 2 miles to the picnic area.

From Crescent City, take Highway 101 south about 25 miles to the Newton B. Drury Scenic Parkway. Take the Parkway until it rejoins the highway. Continue 2 miles and go left on Lost Man Creek Road for 2 more miles to the picnic area.

Route: Begin by following lush, rock-studded Lost Man Creek. You cross two bridges in the first mile and another one soon after. The beauty of the creek and the climb that awaits you are enough to make even the heartiest rider want to linger.

Tear yourself away and prepare to sweat—you climb almost 1,000 feet

in a mile! The grade eases just a bit, then climbs another 250 feet abruptly before mellowing out. You still go up until, at just under 4.0 miles, you reach a trail junction.

Head right onto Holter Ridge Road which follows the park's eastern boundary. Like most ridge routes, this is an up-and-down affair. You keep gaining altitude, but the climbing isn't steep or unpleasant. As you near the 9.5-mile mark, you top out at 2,250 feet and head down to paved Bald Hills Road.

A right onto Bald Hills (if you want, you can go straight and head out to the Redwood Creek Overlook) takes you onto flat, even slightly descending terrain and gives your legs a chance to rest. Partway down, around 13.5 miles, look for the Lady Bird Johnson Grove (named for the former First Lady) on your right at the apex of a hairpin turn.

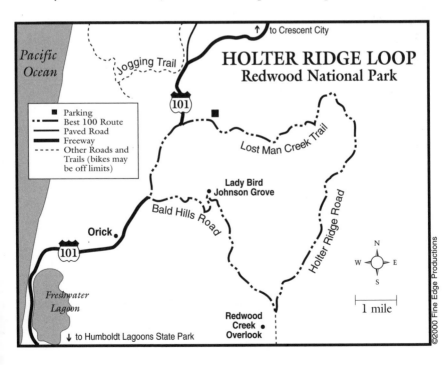

Park your bike in the parking area (bikes aren't allowed on the trail) and walk the self-guided Nature Loop Trail (informational pamphlets available at the trailhead) through mature redwood forest. From here, you also get a view of the Lost Man Creek drainage—the one you worked so hard to get out of!

Back on your bike, be prepared for a steep downhill (various sources estimate the grade at 15-17 percent!)

as you plunge over 1,000 feet in less than 2 miles. Be careful! This section of road sees quite a bit of traffic from people venturing up and down from Lady Bird's Grove.

At 15.5 miles, your descent ends at Newton Drury Parkway. Go right and pedal the pavement for just over 2.0 miles. A right onto Lost Man Creek Road and 2.0 more miles of spinning bring you back to your car.

46 Prairie Creek Redwoods State Park/Gold Bluffs Loop

Distance: 19 miles
Difficulty: Moderate, mildly technical
Elevation: 900' gain/loss
Ride Type: Loop on dirt and gravel roads, singletrack, pavement
Season: Year-round; winter and spring are wet, summer is crowded and foggy fall is best (warm and dry).
Maps: Redwood National Park puts out a brochure and trail map available at any Visitor Center; the Redwood Natural History Association produces a Trail Guide with map, suggested routes and mileages; Trails Illustrated Redwood National Park.
Comments: Information and maps of Redwood National Park and the surrounding state parks can be obtained from the National Park's Visitor Information Center.

Highlights: The only legal mountain bike route in Prairie Creek Redwoods State Park, this lovely circuit begins on pavement but soon takes you into tall trees, through coastal prairies, past herds of Roosevelt elk, along pristine Gold Bluffs Beach and through second-growth forest. If that's not enough, you have several stream crossings, short sections of sand, and a few logs and rocks for a bit of technical challenge. This is probably the most enjoyable mountain biking in the redwood parks.

The loop can also be done in reverse, the only advantage to this is that you won't have to cross the park's main thoroughfare. The route

is more fun the way it's described here. This way, most of the climbing is on pavement and most of the descending is on dirt.

Getting There: From Orick, go north on Highway 101 about 7 miles to the Prairie Creek Visitor Center, which is on your left (beach side).

If you're coming from Crescent City, head south on Highway 101 for 25 miles. Take the Newton B. Drury Scenic Parkway for just over 8 miles to the Prairie Creek Visitor Center on your right (beach side). There is a $5 state park day-use fee. Additional parking can be found at the adjacent campground.

Route: Begin by going back out to the Drury Parkway. Be careful of the traffic! Cross it and head north (left turn). This is mostly uphill for just over 6.0 miles, but the climb is gradual and you do have a shoulder to ride on. Try to ignore the cars and enjoy your surroundings.

Be on the lookout for the Ossagon Trail on your left, across the parkway. The trail, which leads to Carruthers Cove Trail, Butler Creek, and the Coastal Trail, heads steeply up an embankment from the parkway. You'll probably lose all momentum crossing the parkway and, as a result, may have to walk your bike up this section.

Once over the embankment, a 0.5-mile downhill takes you into birch forest and to Ossagon Creek. Dismount and carry your bike on the stairs and across the bridge. On the other side, the trail remains level for awhile as it crosses a small prairie, a spot that the Yurok Indians used to call home.

Soon you head down steeply and back into the trees. Watch your speed here and stay in control. Some hikers have complained about cyclists "flying" down this trail.

The trail crosses Ossagon Creek again and continues another 0.5 mile to a trail junction at about 8.0 miles. Hang a left and head south. You're

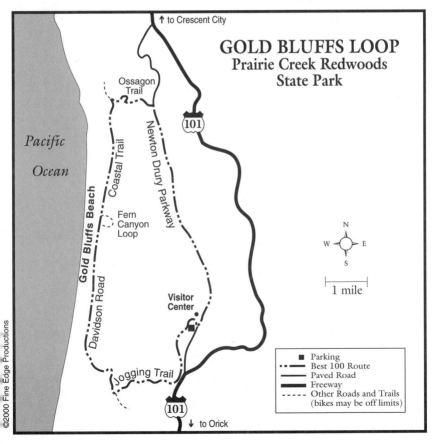

↑ to Crescent City

GOLD BLUFFS LOOP
Prairie Creek Redwoods
State Park

Ossagon Trail

Pacific

Ocean

Coastal Trail

Newton Drury Parkway

Gold Bluffs Beach

Fern Canyon Loop

Davidson Road

Visitor Center

Jogging Trail

101

101

↓ to Orick

N
W — E
S

1 mile

■ Parking
∙−∙− Best 100 Route
— Paved Road
▬ Freeway
---- Other Roads and Trails
  (bikes may be off limits)

©2000 Fine Edge Productions

Jason Houston

Enjoy the level cruise.

now on the Coastal Trail. Soon you splash through Butler Creek and then pass Butler Creek Trail on your left.

The singletrack leads out of the woods and onto a wide expanse of beach and grass called a coastal prairie. You soon come to a Y where one branch goes through the prairie and the other along the bluffs. Pick your trail; they soon rejoin. Then they split again. You may have to pick your trail according to where the elk are.

It seems that forests full of big trees demand at least one big mammal to inhabit them. This is a favorite area for the park's herd of Roosevelt elk, which feed in prairie areas but like the shade of the forest. The animals can grow to over 1,000 pounds and have impressive antlers that reach their largest proportions in the late summer and fall.

At 10.5 miles or so (depending on which trail you took through the prairie), the Coastal Trail crosses Fern Creek and arrives at Fern Canyon, complete with picnic area and off-limits-to-bikes Fern Canyon Trail. If you have the time, hike this beautiful trail; it's less than a mile and leads to a 50-foot-deep canyon festooned with giant ferns and graced by a small waterfall.

Continuing the bike loop from Fern Canyon, the trail widens and turns into gravel Davidson Road. Be careful, Davidson is open to motor vehicles. It's easy riding along this relatively-smooth road. You splash through two more creek crossings on your way toward the Jogging Trail (yes, that's the official name).

At about 15.0 miles, start looking for the Jogging Trail which takes off on your left. Originally a logging road, the 4-mile trail heads into second-growth forest. They may be second growth, but these skyscraper trees still impress. The route is clearly marked with yellow signs with a jogger icon.

The trail crosses Wolf Creek Bridge before emerging at campsite 48 in the Prairie Creek Campground. Make your way through the campground and back to your car at the Visitor Center, approximately 19.0 miles.

47 Jedediah Smith Redwoods State Park/Howland Hill Road

Distance: 12.5 miles
Difficulty: Easy, not technical
Elevation: 750' gain/loss
Ride Type: Out-and-back on degenerating asphalt and gravel road
Season: Year-round; wet in winter and spring, crowded and foggy in summer, best (warm and dry) in fall
Maps: Redwood National Park puts out a brochure and trail map available at any Visitor Center; the Redwood Natural History Association produces a Trail Guide with map, suggested routes and mileages; Trails Illustrated Redwood National Park.
Comments: Information and maps of Redwood National Park and the surrounding state parks can be obtained from the National Park's Visitor Information Center.

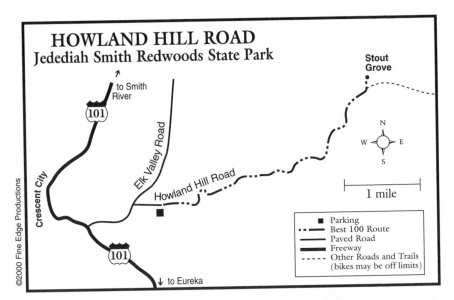

Highlights: In an area of limited mountain bike routes, Jedediah Smith Redwoods State Park is the most limited. The paved and gravel Howland Hill Road is virtually the only option for the fat-tire crowd. (You can ride unpaved Walker Road as well, but Howland Hills is the more scenic route.) While the mountain biking itself isn't challenging and the gawking tourists sharing the narrow road can be annoying, the route's virtue is its scenery—eye-popping, jaw-dropping scenery.

The road takes you through some incredibly large, old redwoods, depositing you at Stout Grove, home of the densest stand of redwoods on the coast. This old-growth grove was donated to the state by the Stout family, hence the name. The most spectacular specimen in

Time for a snack.

Fragnoli

the already spectacular grove is the Stout Tree, the largest redwood in the park.

The route is of historical interest, too, as it was originally the Crescent City and Yreka Turnpike, a stage road that connected mining camps in California with their counterparts over the border in Oregon.

Getting There: From Crescent City, head south on Highway 101 to Elk Valley Road; turn left. Howland Hill Road is on your right, 1 mile up. Park along the road. This trip can easily be shortened by driving farther up the road and parking in any turnout.

Route: This is a very straightforward route, allowing you to marvel at your surroundings rather than study a map. Simply head up Howland Hill Road. You get

Feeling small?

a nice, easy 0.8-mile warm-up before the road begins to climb. It enters the state park and soon turns to dirt and gravel. Your climb is over at 1.8 miles.

Enjoy the level cruise from here to Stout Grove as you pass through one magnificent grove after another. You may want to stop at Mill Creek bridge and enjoy the view. At 6.0 miles, bear left onto the road to Stout Grove. Follow it to the parking area.

Leave your bike here and walk the half-mile Stout Grove Trail. Visit the Stout Tree and try to absorb its immensity—both its age and its size. Then turn your puny, insignificant self around and head back the way you came.

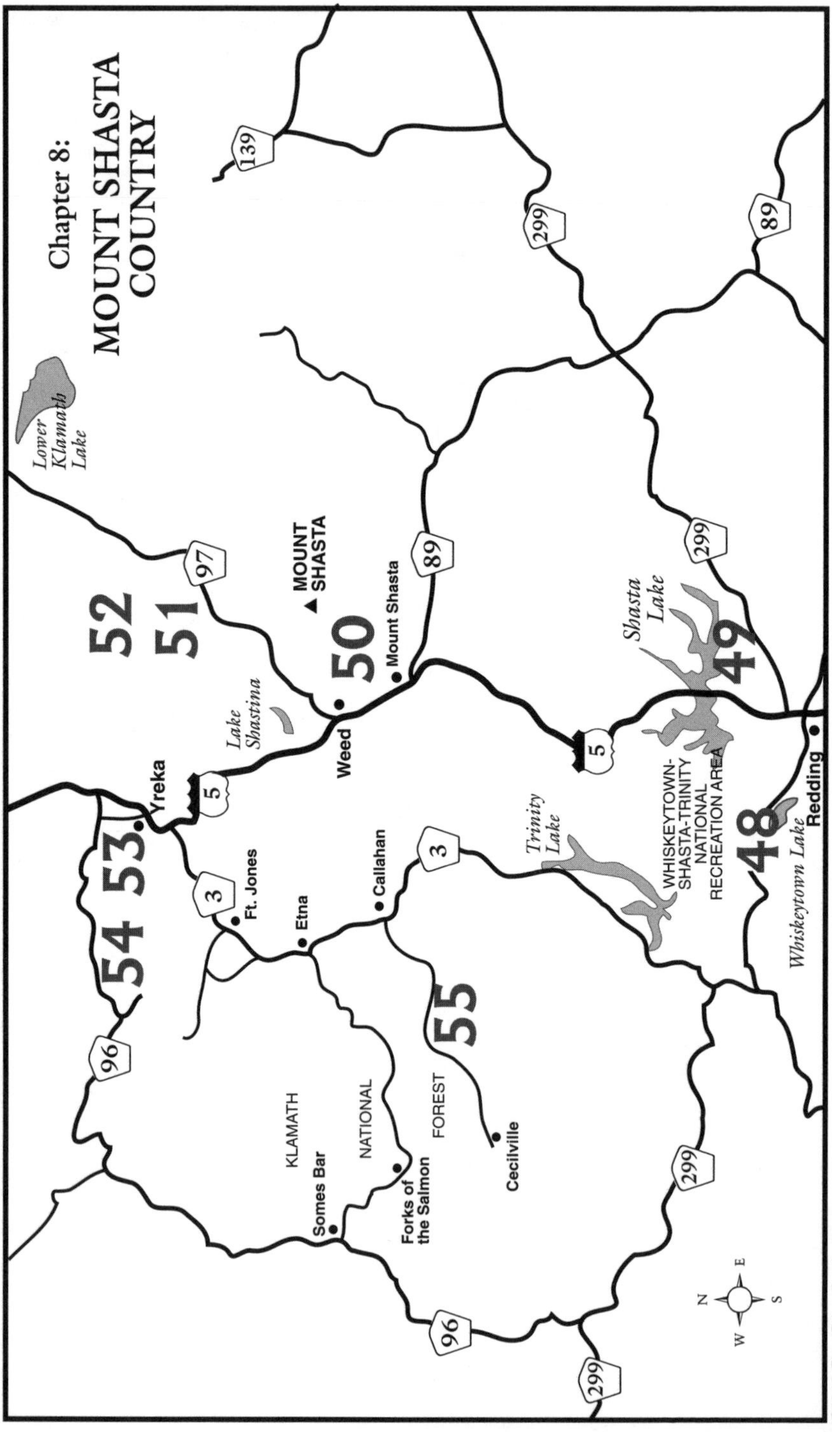

Chapter 8:
MOUNT SHASTA
COUNTRY

Lower
Klamath
Lake

139

299

89

97

▲ MOUNT
SHASTA

89

299

52
51

Lake
Shastina

• 50
• Mount Shasta

Shasta
Lake

299

49

Weed

5

Yreka

5

WHISKEYTOWN-
SHASTA-TRINITY
NATIONAL
RECREATION AREA

48

Redding •

54 53

3

Ft. Jones

Etna •

Callahan •

3

Trinity
Lake

Whiskeytown Lake

96

55

KLAMATH

NATIONAL

FOREST

Ceciliville •

299

Somes Bar •

Forks of
the Salmon •

N
W——E
S

96

299

©2000 Fine Edge Productions

Mount Shasta Country

by Delaine Fragnoli

Dominated by the towering bulwark of Mt. Shasta (14,162'), the northernmost reaches of California offer the mountain biker rugged and remote terrain. Solitude is easy to come by and the views go on forever. The terrain can be challenging as dirt roads plunge into and out of major river drainages. All-day epic rides and hill climbs are par for the course.

It's no wonder that some of the earliest mountain bikers hailed from this area. The first official mountain bike race, the Whiskeytown Downhill, originated here in 1981. Nearly 40 miles long, the "downhill" featured almost 1,500 feet of climbing and over 3,000 feet of descending near Whiskeytown Lake. By 1986, the event was so popular it attracted over 500 riders. But its popularity was its demise. The area couldn't handle that many racers and it went the way of Suntour components. The promoter of the event, Gary Larson, still runs a bike shop, Chain Gang (530-223-3400), in the area and is a fount of local knowledge. One of the very first mountain bikes, designed and built by fat-tire pioneer and Hall of Fame member Jeff Lindsay, bore the model name Whiskeytown Downhill.

Today the most popular riding area is still the Whiskeytown-Shasta-Trinity National Recreation Area just north of Redding (all services). Trails, many of them singletracks which follow 19th-century water ditches, trace the four lakes (Trinity, Lewiston, Shasta and Whiskeytown) formed by the modern plumbing of Shasta Dam. Even when the lakes are crowded with houseboats, the trails remain relatively uncrowded.

The natural landmark of this area is, of course, Mt. Shasta (14,162'). Although you can't ride on the mountain, you can ride all around it in the Shasta-Trinity National Forest. Most routes in the forest are on dirt roads and jeep tracks. The nearby Mt. Shasta Ski Park offers lift-served mountain biking and special events. (See the appendix for more details on services.) About 60 miles north of Redding, Mt. Shasta City makes the best base for exploring Mt. Shasta; you can ride right from town—but be prepared to climb. There are a couple of bike shops in town, including The Fifth Season.

Even farther north, the Klamath National Forest provides true backcountry bicycling. If you like seclusion and want to feel like you're in the middle of nowhere, this is the place for you. Located between the coast ranges and the Cascades, the Klamath houses the Marble, Salmon, Scott Bar and Siskiyou mountain ranges. The Forest's four National Wild and Scenic Rivers are among the largest in the state. These rivers and steep, high mountain ranges make quite a playground, with awesome white-water rafting, over 1000 miles of trails, picnicking and camping, and outstanding fishing and hunting.

Local mountain bikers retain the sport's original ethos; they're laid-back and not as interested in shredding gnarly singletrack as they are in exploring beautiful areas by bike. Not that they dislike singletrack, but there's not that much around, except the off-limits-to-bikes Pacific Crest Trail. Most of the riding is on fire roads (some 3,000 miles worth) that climb to vista points and fire lookouts. Other roads parallel several of the major waterways, so cool swimming holes are never far away. A few legal singletracks and rough doubletracks provide technical challenges for the more advanced rider. The only hazards you need watch out for are logging trucks and hunters during hunting season.

Access to the Klamath is fairly easy via Interstate 5, which intersects the Forest. Once off the interstate, however, you can expect narrow roads which climb and dip, wind and curve. There's no getting anywhere fast in this terrain. The jumping-off spot for exploring the area is Yreka, a full-service town which houses two notable facilities for visitors: Klamath Forest Headquarters and the Phoenix Nest Brewery. Visit the one before you ride for maps and information, the other after you ride for good food and locally brewed hops. If you need a bike shop, try Shasta Valley Bikes (530-842-7701) on Miner Street.

48 Oak Bottom/Boulder Creek

Distance: 14.5 miles
Difficulty: Moderate; somewhat technical in spots
Elevation: 1,100' gain/loss
Ride Type: Loop on pavement, gravel roads and singletrack
Season: Year-round; cooler temperatures and nice color make fall especially nice
Maps: French Gulch, Whiskeytown
Comments: Alternate parking, restrooms, water and picnic tables can all be found at Carr Powerhouse.

Highlights: Along with Shasta Lake, Whiskeytown Lake is a focal point for recreational activities in the Whiskeytown-Shasta National Recreation Area. Plenty of campgrounds, water sports, abandoned mines, and miles of dirt roads and trails make Whiskeytown a great vacation spot for a weekend or a week.

Just one of several available mountain bike routes, this ride along Boulder Creek offers something for both beginning and more advanced riders. The ride is highlighted by views of Whiskeytown Lake, half a dozen stream crossings, a trip to a waterfall, and two sections of singletrack. The proximity to water—

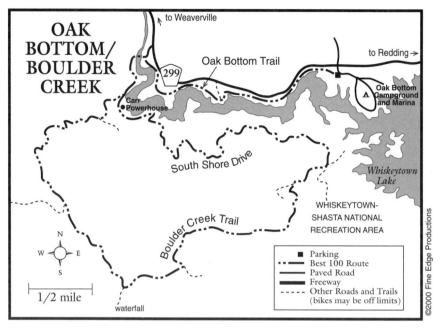

OAK BOTTOM/ BOULDER CREEK

to Weaverville

Oak Bottom Trail

to Redding →

299

Carr Powerhouse

Oak Bottom Campground and Marina

South Shore Drive

Whiskeytown Lake

Boulder Creek Trail

WHISKEYTOWN-SHASTA NATIONAL RECREATION AREA

N W E S

1/2 mile

waterfall

■ Parking
·—·—· Best 100 Route
——— Paved Road
▬▬▬ Freeway
- - - - Other Roads and Trails
(bikes may be off limits)

©2000 Fine Edge Productions

Beginning of Boulder Creek Trail.

except on the opening climb—makes it a cool ride in the summer months.

Getting There: From Interstate 5 in Redding, go west on Highway 299 for 13.5 miles. Turn left at the Oak Bottom Marina and Campground turn-off. Look to your right for a dirt parking area and trailhead. This is the best spot to park, but space is limited. You can also park at the marina or near the campground . If you're camping at Oak Bottom, just ride from there.

Route: Head west down the trail from the dirt parking pullout. Although officially designated the Water Ditch Trail, this oak- and manzanita-lined singletrack is locally known as Oak Bottom Trail. It makes a nice outing by itself for beginners and provides a much needed warm-up for more experienced riders doing the full loop. It would be hard to get lost here since the trail in sandwiched between Highway 299 to your right and the lake to your left.

Almost immediately the trail splits, with cyclists routed to the right and hikers routed to the left. At 1.5 miles, you reach a pump house, set of stairs and a gate. Walk or ride over and around these obstacles. Just beyond, a dirt road takes off to your right. It leads to camping spots. Zig to your left and then zag to your right to get back onto the trail.

At 2.0 miles the trail turns into a paved road. Follow this road west to paved South Shore Drive and go left. Take the dirt and gravel road on your right at 3.0 miles. Prepare to suffer. This is the ride's major climb. It starts out steep and gets steeper. But it doesn't go on for too long—and the rest of the ride makes it well worth the effort.

Soon you come to a fork in the road. Head right and pass through a gate. Continue climbing through a forest of madrone, oak, maple and pine until you top out at 4.8 miles. This is a good place to regroup, catch your breath and take in the view.

Enjoy a brief but well-deserved downhill section. At 5.0 miles, take the Boulder Creek Trail (marked by a brown post) to your left. The trail is actually more of a doubletrack at this point. After a steep uphill, you begin your descent to Boulder Creek, which

Waterfall at Boulder Creek.

you cross for the first time at 6.0 miles.

On the other side of the creek, a foot trail (signed as being built and maintained by boy scouts) leads to a series of waterfalls and swimming holes. Time to stash the bikes and cool off. This makes an especially nice rest stop on a hot summer day.

Back on your bike, downshift and prepare for a steep uphill pitch. After that, the trail heads downhill, getting steeper and rockier (there's a reason it's called *Boulder* Creek). Don't get going too fast because there is a left-hand switchback at the end of a long straightway.

You head into a smooth, bermy section before encountering more rocks and a series of stream crossings. Most of these are rideable—depending on the time of year and water level. During higher water, watch out for hidden boulders that can and will take you down. At points the trail seems to end at or in the stream. Keep looking and you can make out other riders' tracks. Stay on the trail as it narrows, avoiding an unappetizing road uphill to the left.

There's one final fast, smooth section of trail before you reach a gate. Go around the gate and drop onto dirt South Shore Drive. Go left. You have one more climb here, but it is a

One of the many stream crossings along Boulder Creek.

bit shorter and much easier that the first climb. You top out at 10.3 miles. Begin a fast, wide-open descent. Watch your speed—the road is open to vehicles.

As you near the Carr Powerhouse, the road turns to pavement. Bypass the Carr Powerhouse parking lot (restrooms and water should you need them). Continue on the pavement past the first dirt road you climbed, now on your left. Catch the paved road on your right which leads to the Oak Bottom Trail and the ride start.

49 Clikapudi Trail

Distance: 7.5 miles
Difficulty: Moderate, mildly technical
Elevation: Rolling, there are no major climbs
Ride Type: Loop on singletrack
Season: Year-round; summer can be crowded
Map: Bella Vista (trail not shown)
Comments: Nearest services are in Redding, 15 miles away. Restrooms and water are available at the Jones Valley boat ramp. Watch for poison oak along the creek.

Highlights: Of the three hiking trails in the Shasta Lake area that are open to mountain bikes, this one is the longest and most interesting. (The other two trails, Bailey Cove and Packers Bay, barely amount to 6 miles together.) Besides being almost all singletrack, the loop features a few

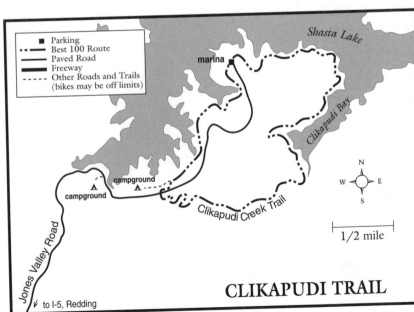

CLIKAPUDI TRAIL

View of Mount Shasta (14,162') and Shastina (12,330')

steep downhills with fun switchbacks. You follow the shore of Shasta Lake and Clikapudi Creek (the route can be muddy in spring) as you make your way through oak, madrone and Douglas fir. The stream crossings and a dip in the lake make the route a fun choice even when summer temperatures break the 100-degree mark.

You also pass an archeological site where a Wintu Indian village is being excavated. In fact, *Clikapudi* comes from the Wintu word *klukapusa*, which means "a fight" or "to fight." No, this ride won't hurt you! The name comes from a battle between the Wintus and some local traders.

Getting There: From Redding, take Interstate 5 north to the Oasis Road exit and head east. Follow the road signs to Old Oregon Trail, Bear Mountain Road and Jones Valley. Proceed to the end of the road (Jones Valley Road at this point) and park in the Jones Valley Marina lot ($5 parking fee).

Route: Although it is possible to ride this loop in the opposite direction, this clockwise version lets you go down the steepest stuff, and thus tests your downhill abilities. There are two trailheads. You want the signed one in the northeast corner of the parking lot. The trailhead at the other end of the lot is marked by two wooden posts. This is where you will exit the trail to finish the loop.

The trail's first 4 miles are pretty level with a few short ups and downs as it follows the shoreline of Shasta Lake that curves into Clikapudi Bay. As you near the end of Clikapudi Bay, you cross a small stream. The single-track continues straight across on the other side. Soon you come to an intersection with an access road that leads to the Wintu village site. Stay right and continue on the trail.

The trail follows Clikapudi Creek for a while before heading upward. At least the trail surface is smooth, and you get a view of the lake from the top. On the other side of this hill, a nice little series of switchbacks awaits you. Don't dab in the corners! I warned you that they were coming up.

The switchbacks deposit you on a paved road. Go right and look for the trail, which continues on the other side of the road just a few yards away. Head down to a T in the road. The left fork goes to the lower Jones Valley campground. Make the sharp right switchback to stay on the main single-track. This is the ride's easiest-to-miss turn.

For the next mile, the trail contours along the lakeside at a gentle grade. There are several access points to the lake's shoreline if you want to go for a swim—a welcome opportunity in the scorching summer months. Follow the trail to its end at the southwest corner of the parking lot.

50 Mount Shasta Loop

Distance: 65 miles
Difficulty: Epic 4WD road is technical; see Options for shorter, easier possibilities.
Elevation: 3,200' gain/loss
Ride Type: Loop on pavement, dirt roads, 4WD tracks and gravel
Season: May through October; can be hot in mid-summer
Maps: City of Mount Shasta, McCloud, Elk Springs, Ash Creek Butte, Mount Shasta, The Whaleback, Juniper Flat, Hotlum
Comments: You must be self-sufficient on this ride. Take plenty of clothing as temperatures and weather conditions can change a lot throughout the day, no matter what time of year you ride. Pack a good supply of food and water, and don't forget your tools. Carry a good map or maps, treat all water taken from streams, and allow plenty of time. Nearest services are in the towns of Mt. Shasta and Weed.

Highlights: Mount Shasta's network of logging roads offers lots of possibilities, although much of the surrounding forest has been logged extensively (expect logging trucks on this ride). The area's hiking trails tend to be very sandy and, therefore, not a heck of a lot of fun to ride. Since 14,162-foot Mount Shasta is a designated wilderness area, you cannot bike on the mountain itself. This route, however, will provide great views of the mountain and allow you a good look at the area's fascinating geology. Plus, I think it's cool to be able to circle one of California's defining natural landmarks by bike. How many people do you know who can brag that they rode all the way around a major mountain?

Although epic in length, the route can be completed in one long day by strong riders. Less-conditioned riders may cut the route short by devising a shuttle (see the Shuttle Options at the end of the Route description). The roughest terrain and most difficult route finding occur from Military Pass Road to Black Butte. These sections can be avoided, however, if you run out of time and/or energy (see the Options). Other than the length, the opening climb and the rougher section mentioned above, the route is not as challenging or as technical as you might think, making it a good choice for fit roadies looking for some off-road exploring.

You see a great variety of terrain and vegetation as you make your way around monolithic Mount Shasta. The mountain's east side has several streams and is wetter. As you head north, you move into high desert sage and juniper. At the ride's summit at Military Pass, you have views of the enormous rock formation, The Whaleback, to the north. On the north side you pass through a volcanic landscape of lava flows. To the south, you can see the mountain's glaciated north faces. Two distinct formations, Cinder Cone and Black Butte, mark the route's western side.

Spring is a good time to ride since you'll be treated to wildflowers. Although the route can be a little muddy, that's better than the sand

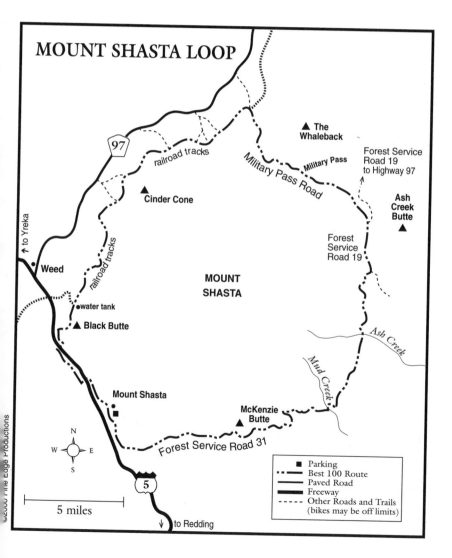

you get by the end of the summer. Fall color is nice, you won't see a soul, and if you ride a few days after a rain, the soil will be packed down. Most of the year, expect gravel, sand and washboard.

Getting There: Start in the town of Mt. Shasta.

Route: Make your way to Mt. Shasta Boulevard and head south. Go left on Old McCloud Road. The Alpine Lodge is on one corner and the sheriff's station on another. Mileages are from this corner.

You begin with a steep pavement climb; in fact, this is the toughest climb in the whole ride. At 1.4 miles the road turns into Forest Service Road 31 (signed). The pavement is not as good here and there is no center line. Cross railroad tracks at 2.4 miles. Stay on the pavement. At 3.9 miles the pavement becomes more broken.

Several dirt Forest Service roads shoot to the left and right. Ignore all of them and stay on Road 31.

At 5.5 miles, pass a sign for Bear Springs I Plantation. Here you have a good view of Mount Shasta—courtesy of the logging folks. At 6.1 miles, you T into a paved road signed 88/31. Go left. At 6.3 miles, head straight onto dirt and gravel Forest Service Road 31. The paved road (numbered Road 89 named Ski Park Highway) curves left and continues climbing to the Mount Shasta Ski Park.

Road 31 passes through a clearcut area. The terrain is relatively flat or gradually uphill. This is pretty easy going, but the road is open to motor vehicles and it can turn to washboard.

At the Y-intersection at 9.8 miles, stay right on Road 31. Soon there's another road to the right. Stay on Road 31, which is broken pavement here. You lose any views of Mount Shasta until about 11 miles, at which

View of Mount Shasta from the loop.

The distinctive cone of Black Butte, 6,325'.

point you start a mostly downhill section. At 12 miles you pass through a clearing. "Squaw Road" (according to a handpainted sign) is to the left. Stay on Road 31.

At the Y-intersection at 12.7 miles, continue right, still on Road 31 (signed). Roll through a logged area and, at 14.1 miles, make the first of several stream crossings. You hit another creek crossing a mile later and begin a gradual uphill. Thanks to more clear-cuts, you have views of Mount Shasta to your left.

At 18 miles pass a sign for Clear Creek Trailhead. Almost immediately you reach a four-way intersection. Go straight on signed Road 31. Left leads to the Mount Shasta Wilderness (bikes prohibited), while the right fork is signed 41N15. Head downhill through Sierra Pacific land, where a sign informs you that the company has been "treefarming" here since 1989.

At 20 miles, cross a creek and head up to a Y-intersection at 20.2 miles. Stay right on Road 31. At 21.6 miles, Road 31 crosses another road. Go straight to stay on 31. Almost immediately, 21.8 miles, Road 31 Ys into another road. Veer left and then cross yet another stream. Soon thereafter, 22.1 miles, you reach an intersection. Go straight on Road 31. Note that these streams are the last dependable water sources. *Treat all water.*

Two miles later you come to a T-intersection with a bona fide stop sign. Road 31 ends here at Forest Service Road 19. Go left on Road 19. Ash Creek Butte is the big hill in front of you at this intersection. Immediately bypass a road to the left to stay on Road 19 toward Highway 97 (signed). At 26.1 miles, you pass a road sign. Road 19 can be a real washboard in this section.

At 28 miles, go left onto dirt Military Pass Road. This intersection can be easy to miss. Military Pass Road is opposite a brown road sign for Highways 89 and 97. It is marked by a brown post with the Forest Service symbol, but is not named or numbered. *Note*: For a shorter ride involving a shuttle or to avoid the more difficult 4WD and railroad track section, please see Shuttle Options at the end of the Route description.

For the main route, take this left onto Military Pass Road and make the very gradual climb to Military Pass (6,000'). It can get sandy along here, but persevere—the sandy sections don't last forever. Frankly, I found this section a welcome relief from the rattling washboard of Road 19.

At 28.4 miles, veer right to stay on Military Pass Road (signed). Then pass a sign calling this Road 43N19. Stay on 43N19. You have a good view of Mount Shasta, which has been obscured for awhile. At 31.2 miles there's a road junction and sign. Continue straight toward Highway 97, 7 miles away. Enjoy the downhill.

At 32.8 miles, pass a sign that says you are entering the Deer Mountain/Whaleback Road Management Area. The Whaleback is the enormous mountain looming over your right shoulder. At the big intersection at 33.7 miles, go left on Andesite Mining Road (signed). There's also a big recreation fee sign here and a Northgate Trailhead sign.

Now listen up. You do not want to miss the next turn or you could get hopelessly lost. From the big intersection, climb 0.7 mile (34.4 miles total) on Andesite Mining Road to a Y-intersection. Go right on signed 42N34 for a fun downhill complete with good views of Mount Shasta. The road soon narrows as manzanita crowds its edges.

At the T-intersection at 36.4 miles, go right. The road soon degenerates into a steep, rocky 4WD track. At 37.3 miles, veer right to keep going downhill. Last time I was here there was red flagging to follow—but don't count on it, it could be gone by the time you read this. At 39.4 miles veer right to continue downward. There are a ton

of 4WD tracks throughout this area. When in doubt, keep heading to the right and downhill.

At 40 miles you reach railroad tracks. Here you have a decision to make. If you don't mind a lot of pavement, you can continue straight out to Highway 97 and take it toward Weed, 11 miles away. (See Highway 97/Weed Option below.)

More adventurous spirits can turn left and follow the railroad tracks. There is no established road here so you ride on gravel—for almost 15 miles. It's not as bad as it sounds. The gravel is actually pretty well packed. Plus, you don't have to worry about the vehicle traffic you have to contend with on Highway 97. There are several bail-out points —dirt access roads that take you out to Highway 97 if you decide you've had enough. (See Railroad Tracks Option below.)

Highway 97/Weed Option: From the railroad tracks, continue on the dirt road to Highway 97. (This road hits the highway just before a 4,000 foot elevation sign, if you want to try to arrange a shuttle.) Go left on Highway 97 for a mostly-downhill cruise into Weed, reached at about 51 miles. Food, drink and even a bike shop (Mt. Shasta Bicycling Adventures, 9404 N. Old Stage Rd., 530-938-3002) can be found in Weed.

Go left (a sign indicates South 97) at the flashing red light in town. Bypass the on-ramps to Interstate 5 and go under the freeway. Turn right on College Avenue (signed) at 51.6. About 2.4 miles later, College Ts into North Old Stage Road. Go left. Cross railroad tracks at 57.3 miles. Continue straight at the stop sign at Deetz Road at 58.1 miles. At 60.4 miles, North Old Stage Road turns into

Beginning of the climb to Military Pass, 6,000'.

Abrams Lake Road; go straight. At 61 miles, Abrams Lake Road Ts into Spring Hill Road. Go right. At 62.2 miles, make a left onto Mt. Shasta Boulevard to return to your starting point.

Railroad Tracks Option: From the intersection of the dirt road and the railroad tracks, go left to follow the tracks. At 45 miles you come to a high railroad trestle. Cross it. This may be disconcerting for some of you and you may elect to ride down into the valley and back up.

Continue to follow the tracks as they loop southward. As you near the 55-mile point, be on the lookout for a big black water tank on the opposite side of the tracks. (This is at the Black Butte siding yard.) Cross the tracks here. Soon you see a dirt road on the left. Take it and make the first right

onto a graded dirt road. This road leads to pavement. Go left.

Take the pavement along the west flank of Black Butte, the black, double-peaked mountain to your left. This road takes you under Interstate 5. After crossing under the freeway, turn left onto Summit Drive. Go left 0.3 mile later on Abrams Lake Road and cross I-5 again. Abrams Lake Road intersects Spring Hill Drive 1.3 mile later. Go right and follow Spring Hill Road to Mt. Shasta Boulevard. Turn left and head into the town of Mount Shasta.

Shuttle Option 1: Avoid the steep opening climb by driving to or having someone drop you off at the junction of paved Forest Service Road 88/Ski Park Highway and dirt Forest Service Road 31 at 6.3 miles. See the beginning of the Route section for details.

Shuttle Option 2: Leave a vehicle or have someone pick you up in Weed. To get to Weed on your bike, bail off the main route onto Highway 97 via Forest Service Road 19 or the Andesite Logging Road. See the Route section for details. Either way, when you get to Highway 97, go left (south) to Weed.

Shuttle Option 3: Leave a vehicle or have someone pick you up along Highway 97. A good spot would be where Forest Service Road 19 (signed Military Pass Road) comes out onto Highway 97. To do this, follow the ride directions until the junction of Road 19 and Military Pass Road. Continue on Road 19 (signed) toward Highway 97.

Shuttle Option 4: Combine Shuttle Option 1 with either Shuttle Option 2 or 3.

51 Herd Peak Lookout Loop

Distance: 21 miles
Difficulty: Moderately strenuous, mildly technical, optional doubletrack descent is more technical
Elevation: 2,300' gain/loss, 7,071' high point
Ride Type: Loop on dirt roads
Season: Spring, summer, fall; check snow levels in spring
Maps: Grass Lake, The Whaleback, Solomons Temple
Comments: Nearest services are in Weed. CalTrans has a rest stop 2 miles north of the starting point on Highway 97 with restrooms, water, picnic tables and a phone.

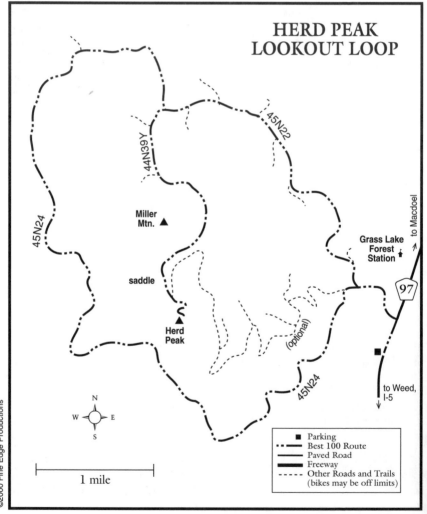

HERD PEAK
LOOKOUT LOOP

45N22

44N39Y

45N24

Miller
Mtn. ▲

saddle

Herd
Peak ▲

Grass Lake
Forest
Station

97

to Macdoel

(optional)

45N24

to Weed,
I-5

N
W ⬥ E
S

1 mile

■ Parking
■·■· Best 100 Route
── Paved Road
▬▬ Freeway
---- Other Roads and Trails
(bikes may be off limits)

©2000 Fine Edge Productions

Highlights: In an area with great lookouts and wonderful views, Herd Peak in the Klamath National Forest may offer the most spectacular vista, particularly of Mount Shasta. One Forest Service publication gushes that the panorama from Herd Peak lookout is a "visual feast . . . one of the finest vista points in Siskiyou County." It's hard to take such hyperbole on faith, so make the pilgrimage and see for yourself.

Getting There: From the town of Weed, take Highway 97 northeast for about 20 miles. Park at the Mount Shasta overlook on the northwest side of the highway just south of Grass Lake Summit.

Route: Cross the highway and head north (left) on it for .25 mile. Look for a dirt turnout on the left side of the highway just past the 5,000 foot elevation sign. This is the start of 45N22. Again cross the highway and

Stairs leading to lookout, Herd Peak.

head up 45N22. About 0.7 mile later you come to a Y-intersection. 45N22

View of Mount Shasta from Herd Peak lookout.

Fragnoli

Sign at the top of Herd Peak.

continues to the right toward Miller Mountain (signed). The left fork is 45N24. There is no number sign on it, but a very faded sign indicates that it leads to Davis Gulch. Go left on 45N24. At 1.1 miles, avoid the rough doubletrack to the right. This road is the optional return route. For now, stay on 45N24.

The next 6 miles contour along the west side of Miller Mountain, offering sweeping views into Shasta Valley. Most of the climb is pretty moderate and the trail surface a little rocky. At 4.7 miles pass through an open gate. Ignore the doubletrack on the left. Several doubletracks shoot off the main route in the next few miles. Most of them pitch up or down very steeply. Avoid them and stay on the main road.

At 7.9 miles, fork left. There was a cairn here the last time I was through. Begin a moderate downhill. Pass a

gate at 9.5 miles, cross a creek, and reach a T-intersection at 9.6 miles. Go right here and climb to another T-intersection at 10.3 miles. Go right again, climbing pretty steeply. At the four way intersection at 10.8 miles, make yet another right. Continue climbing moderately for another 1.2 miles (12 miles total).

Here a sign indicates that Herd Peak Lookout is 4 miles to the right (don't despair, it's really less than 3 miles away) and that 45N22 lies to the left. Go right on 44N39Y and finish the climb to the lookout, reached at 14.8 miles. The last .75 mile gets steep and rocky, and the final 100 yards pretty brutal.

If your quivering quads can handle it, climb the four flights of stairs to the lookout for the best view in the county. The panorama includes stunning Mount Shasta, Shasta Valley, the Eddy peaks, Butte Valley, and more. The only direction you have no view of is behind you to the north. The lookout is manned in the summer months and you're welcome to visit from 9:30 a.m. to 6:00 p.m.

When you're ready to leave, you can head down 44N39Y the way you came to where it ends, 17.8 miles. Go right on 45N22 and take it back to the junction with 45N24 at 19.8 miles. This is a fast, fun downhill. Go left to the highway, then right on highway back to the vista point.

For a more demanding descent, look for a very rough doubletrack dropping off the east face of Herd Peak just before you get to a small saddle. At the top, it's closer to a singletrack than a doubletrack. Steep and bumpy, it descends in a series of switchbacks to 45N24. Several other roads traverse the eastern flank of Herd Peak. Stay on the one that pitches downward.

52 Ball Mountain Loop

Distance: 11.8 miles
Difficulty: Moderate, mildly technical
Elevation: 1,900' gain/loss, 7,780' high point
Ride Type: Loop on dirt roads
Season: Spring, summer, fall; check snow levels as late as June
Map: Panther Rock
Comments: Nearest services are in Weed. Water and toilets are available at the campground.

Highlights: If you have time for just one ride in this area, do the previous ride, Herd Peak Lookout Loop. It's more accessible and provides an even better view. But if you have time to spend a weekend camping, the more remote Ball Mountain route should be next on your list. The starting point, Martin Dairy Campground, is a peaceful, high mountain campground on the Little Shasta River. The lush meadow is shaded by pines and separated from private property on one side by a quaint split-rail fence.

The route is mostly on an unmaintained dirt road that is closed to 4WD traffic, so expect lots of peace and quiet. Also expect to see wildlife—deer, bear and eagles—as you pass through high-elevation, old-growth fir forests on the ascent of Ball Mountain, where you get good views of the Shasta Valley and Mount Shasta as well as the Butte Valley.

Getting There: From Weed, drive approximately 28.5 miles northeast on Highway 97 to Forest Service Road 70 (signed and with a smaller sign for Martin Dairy Campground, 13 miles) near Mt. Hebron Summit. Road 70 is a paved road on the left.

Take Road 70 for 3 miles to a Y-intersection. Go right (signed: *Martin Dairy Campground, 10 miles*) to stay on Road 70, which turns to dirt and gravel. At the four-way intersection 3.6 miles later, go straight to stay on Road 70, which is paved for a section past this

Fragnoli

Lookout atop Ball Mountain, 7,780'.

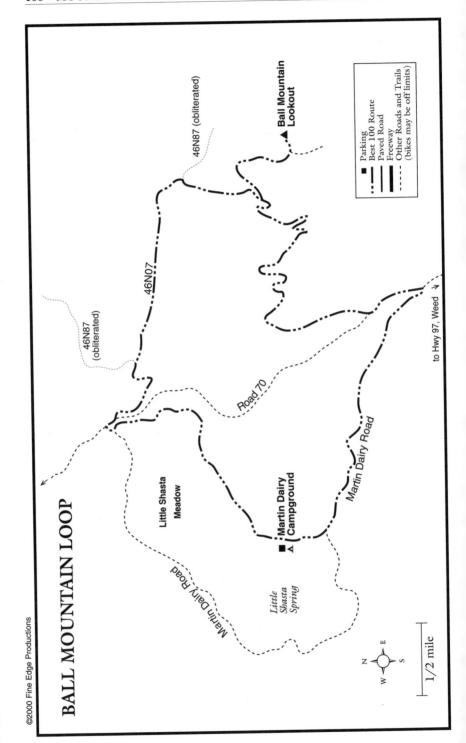

BALL MOUNTAIN LOOP

©2000 Fine Edge Productions

Ball Mountain Lookout

46N87 (obliterated)

46N07

46N87 (obliterated)

to Hwy 97, Weed

Road 70

Little Shasta Meadow

Martin Dairy Road

Martin Dairy Road

Martin Dairy Campground

Little Shasta Spring

Parking
Best 100 Route
Paved Road
Freeway
Other Roads and Trails
(bikes may be off limits)

1/2 mile

N
W E
S

Fragnoli

View of Yreka from Humbug Road.

point. Cross a cattleguard 3 miles later and continue another 1.3 miles to a Y-intersection. Go left at the sign: *Martin Dairy Campground, 2 miles.* (Road 70 continues to the right.) Cross a bridge 1.5 miles later. Bypass the horse camp on the right and continue .25 mile to a sign for Martin Dairy Campground. Go right to the campground. Although the sign says it's a mile, it's only 0.3 mile.

Route: Continue north/northwest through the campground on the road you took into the campground. It climbs moderately for 1.9 miles to Road 70. Go right on Road 70 (signed). Shortly after that go left onto dirt road 46N07. At 2.7 miles you reach an intersection. A *Road Closed* sign and gate block what was once 46N87 to the left. In the first edition of this book, that was the designated route. The road has been obliterated, so the route now continues to the right up 46N07.

Climb 46N07 to a T-intersection at 4.1 miles. The road coming in from

the left is the top remnant of 46N87. Go right to continue the climb to Ball Mountain. At 4.6 miles, go left for the final grunt up to the lookout. There may be a closed gate you have to go around just past this last intersection. At 5.4 miles you're at the top.

From the lookout you have tremendous views, especially toward Mount Shasta in the south. Try to catch your breath—you're at 7,780 feet—before you begin your descent.

Now you backtrack down to the last intersection you passed on the way up. Go left to drop off the west face of Ball Mountain. You have about a 5.5-mile downhill run on dirt road back to Martin Dairy campground.

The dirt descent is steep, dropping almost 1,000 feet in about 3 miles. When the dirt road ends at Road 70 (9.1 miles), go left. Soon after, at 9.5 miles, make a hard right onto Martin Dairy Road to complete your loop. This is the road you took into the campground. It's downhill most of the way to the campground, reached at 11.8 miles.

53 Gunsight Peak Loop

Distance: 20 miles
Difficulty: Moderately strenuous, somewhat technical
Elevation: 3,300' gain/loss, 6,100' high point
Ride Type: Loop on dirt roads and rough doubletrack
Season: Spring, summer, fall
Maps: Badger Mountain, McKinley Mountain, Indian Creek Baldy, Yreka
Comments: Nearest services are in Yreka, 3 miles away. Carry plenty of water.

Highlights: Yeah, so you have to climb some on this ride. It's worth it. On the way up you get fine views to the south, including Mount Shasta, and the climb is broken up. You have to climb some at the beginning of the ride and some at the end. Once you top out at Gunsight Peak, you get 10 miles of downhill nirvana, including 7 miles of fun and challenging doubletrack. This is gold country as well, and the area is dotted with mine sites.

It's also the site of the annual Humbug Hurry-Up, one of the last great epic loop courses, that attracts over 400 competitors. If you're here in July, give Dave Rawlings and Team One Speed a call at 530-842-7701 for more information. But be prepared to really climb—the long course features a 13-mile hill. Because of the wealth of riding in the area, Rawlings has considered organizing a 100-mile ride which he would name the Humbug Hurry On and On and On.

Getting There: From central Yreka, head west on Miner Street. Turn right onto Gold and then left on

View from climb to Gunsight Peak.

Fragnoli

Fragnoli

View to the north from ridge between Mahogany Point and Gunsight Peak.

North. Take North to Humbug Road and go right. Follow Humbug for 3.8 miles (it turns into a dirt road) to the Four Corners saddle. Park off the road here. Note that masochistic climbers who want to add another 1,800-foot climb to the ride can pedal from town.

Route: From the intersection, head southwest on Road 45N28. Get into a comfortable gear for the long but very manageable climb. The road is a graded, maintained road so traction isn't a problem as you gain about 1,700 feet in the next 6 miles.

Take in the views to the south. Along here you can see Yreka behind you, Shasta Valley and Mount Shasta to the south, and the Humbug Creek drainage to the north.

You ride along the flank of several peaks in these first 7 miles, some of which have radio facilities on them. You pass a group of towers at 1.4 miles. When you reach Mahogany Point with its radio towers, it's worth

stopping to soak in the view. To do so, at 4.4 miles detour right up to the towers, reached at 4.8 miles. It's a steep drop back to 45N28 at 5.1 miles.

From here, it's roughly another 2 miles to Gunsight Peak. You get a

Fragnoli

Mahogany Point

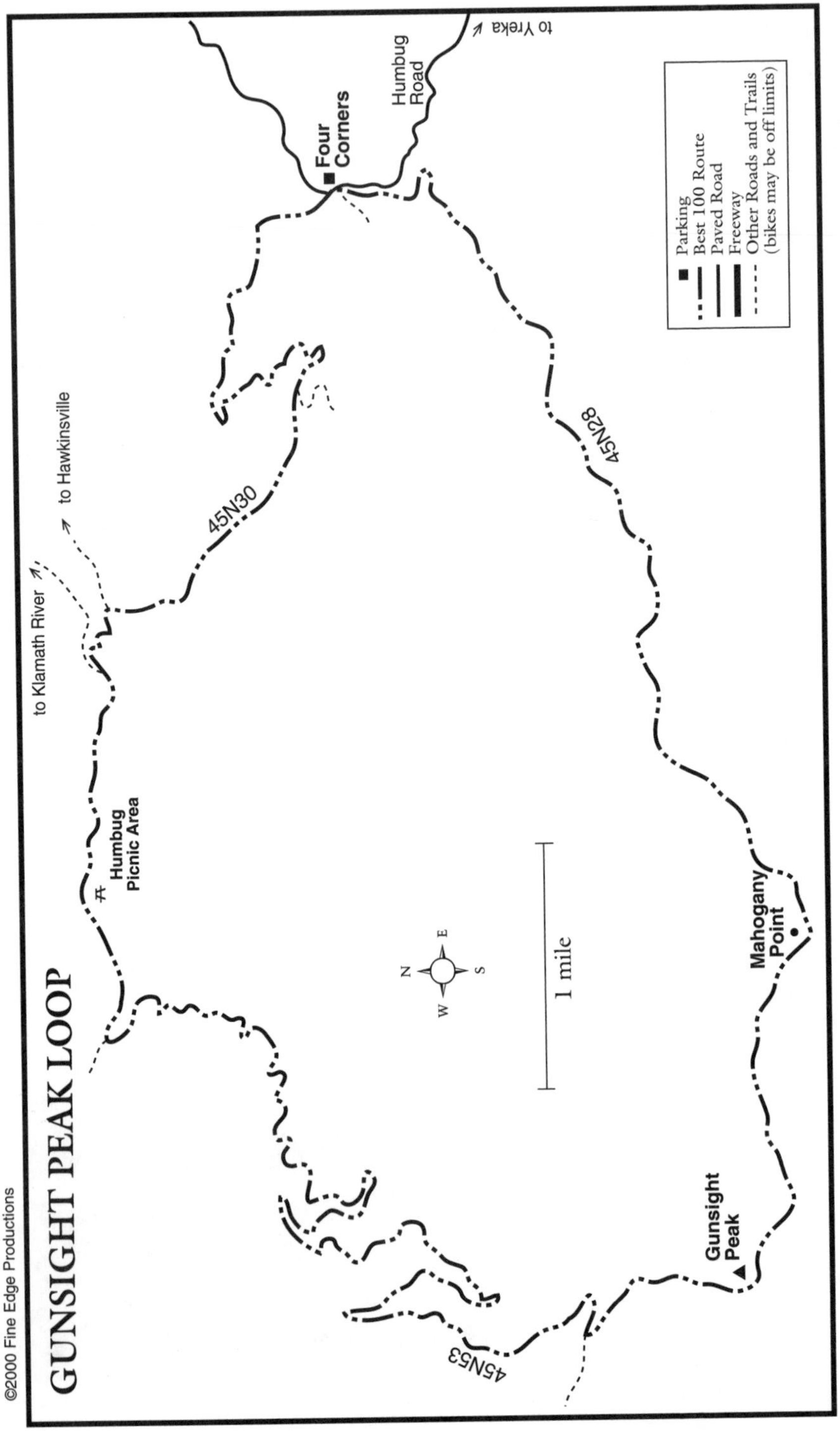

©2000 Fine Edge Productions

GUNSIGHT PEAK LOOP

to Yreka

Four Corners

Humbug Road

to Hawkinsville

45N30

to Klamath River

Humbug Picnic Area

45N28

Mahogany Point

Gunsight Peak

45N53

N E S W

1 mile

Legend

■ Parking

Best 100 Route

Paved Road

Freeway

Other Roads and Trails (bikes may be off limits)

brief descent before climbing again. You reach Gunsight Peak at 7 miles. At the peak, the road swings north and starts to descend. At 7.9 miles, you reach an intersection with 45N53 (signed). Make the sharp right onto 45N53. This is Sucker Creek Road. Don't worry, you won't be a sucker for taking this route.

This rough doubletrack drops almost 3,300 feet in 7 miles, so be careful. It's easy to get up speed here. Loose rocks and steep dropoffs are the main hazards and can send you sliding and cartwheeling.

Once you're down to Humbug Creek, you cross the creek at 14.5 miles and go right at 14.6 miles. The doubletrack turns into a graded road here and follows the creek for a couple of miles past Humbug picnic area. This is easy pedaling until you reach a bridge at 16.2 miles. Just beyond the bridge, at 16.3 miles, avoid the road on the right. But at 16.5 miles take the road (45N30) to the right. (Straight is signed 45N39.)

This is where things get painful. Now you have to climb out of the creek drainage and back up to the Four Corners intersection. Get in your granny gear and suffer up a 1,500-foot climb (in about 4 miles). Hey, that downhill was fun, wasn't it? Keep telling yourself that as you grunt and groan your way back to your car.

54 Upper Klamath River

Distance: 19 miles
Difficulty: Easy, not technical
Elevation: Rolling, negligible gain/loss
Ride Type: One way on dirt road with car shuttle, or an out-and-back of whatever length you desire
Season: Year-round; spring brings wildflowers and fall brings color
Maps: Badger Mountain, McKinley Mountain, Hawkinsville
Comments: The town of Klamath River has a gas station and convenience store. There are also several lodges in the area.

Highlights: On this quiet, peaceful ride you parallel the upper reaches of the Klamath River and Highway 96. The road is largely shaded by oaks and pines, and lined in many spots with berry patches. You can see remnants of the area's past in the form of old dredger piles and abandoned cabins. You're also likely to catch sight of deer, muskrats, turtles, eagles, osprey and great blue herons. Make this an all-day affair. Bring along a picnic lunch—there are many suitable spots to stop and kick back. The route is a good choice for novice riders, families or those wanting to spin out some easy cruising miles. The steepest, rockiest sections are at the ride's midpoint, so you can ride out and back from either end. I think the eastern end is the nicest—you're closer to the river and the road is more secluded.

Getting There: From Yreka (pronounced Y-reka), head north on Highway 3/263 (Main Street in town) for 9 miles to Highway 96 (right after you cross the Klamath

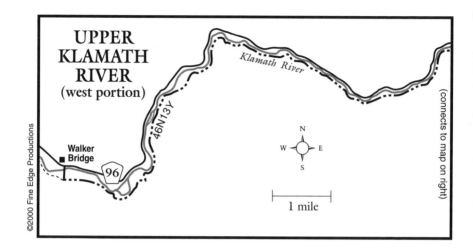

River) and make a hard left (west) onto the signed Klamath River Highway. About 1.8 miles later, you come to picturesque Ash Creek Bridge, built in 1901. There's a little parking spot on the opposite side of the highway from the bridge. This is where you start your ride. But first, if you're going to shuttle, you need to drop your return vehicle at Walker Bridge, 18 miles farther down Highway 96. Park off the road in both places.

Route: Cross the Klamath River on wooden-planked Ash Creek Bridge and hang a right onto 46N13Y. This graded, well-maintained dirt road parallels the Klamath River as it makes

Ash Creek Bridge at ride start.

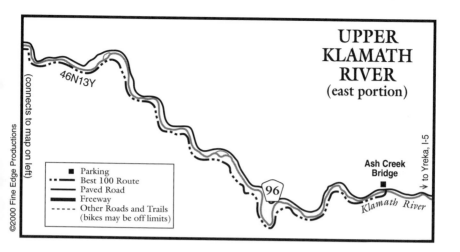

UPPER
KLAMATH
RIVER
(east portion)

46N13Y

(connects to map on left)

©2000 Fine Edge Productions

■ Parking
- - ■ - - Best 100 Route
         Paved Road
         Freeway
- - - - Other Roads and Trails
         (bikes may be off limits)

Ash Creek
Bridge

↓ to Yreka, I-5

96

Klamath River

its way downstream. Although the road is open to vehicles, most auto tourists take Highway 96, so you won't encounter much traffic. The river itself sees a lot of use from rafters and fishermen.

The road rolls along, but never steeply and never uphill or downhill for long as it follows the river's undulating course. At times you ride right beside the river, and at times you climb briefly onto bluffs for more of an overview of the area. But you're never far from the sight and sound of the river. Stay hugging the river and you can't get lost.

In spots there is some broken pavement, but it never lasts for long. There is a surprising amount of private property between the road and the river as well as on the other side of the road. Most of it is vigorously signed. Don't trespass to access the river.

Around the 9-mile mark, the road climbs more, is tighter, windier, rockier and less well maintained. If this is too much for you to handle, you can always retrace your steps. You're well above the river here but soon drop back down.

You know you're near the end of

the ride when you pass the Eagle Nest Golf Course around mile 17. At the road fork at the golf course, go right. At 18.5 miles, although the road continues to follow the river downstream, you veer right to cross Walker Bridge. Continue out to Highway 96, reached at 19 miles.

View of Klamath River from Road 46N13Y.

Fragnoli

55 Carter Meadows Loop

Distance: 11 miles
Difficulty: Moderate, somewhat technical
Elevation: Gain/loss 1,600', high point 6,200'
Ride Type: Loop on dirt roads, singletrack and pavement
Season: Spring, summer, fall
Map: Deadman Peak
Comments: No services nearby. Water and toilets are available at Trail Creek campground.

Highlights: Among the prettiest areas of the Klamath National Forest, Carter Meadows is crisscrossed by old logging roads and trails. Like most meadows, it's nicest in spring when the wildflowers bloom. It's also wettest in spring. In the summer it's relatively cool. It's quiet and beautiful no matter when you visit.

This route circles Carter Meadows, following the South Fork of the Salmon River—which isn't much more than a stream at this point— much of the way. A section of single-track and an old logging road offer some technical challenge, too.

Trail Creek campground makes a good base camp for checking out this remote area. It's worth spending a

weekend here, as there are miles of roads and trails to explore by foot or by knobby.

Getting There: From central Yreka, take Highway 3 south toward Fort Jones. Stay on Highway 3 for 43 miles to Callahan. From Callahan, take the Callahan-Cecilville highway west for 12 miles to the Carter Meadows Summit. There's a Pacific Crest Trail sign just before the summit. You can park in the unmarked dirt pullout at the crest, but I prefer to park at Trail Creek campground, 5 miles farther down the highway on the south side of the road. (Do NOT take the Carter Meadows Trailheads turnoff less than a mile down from

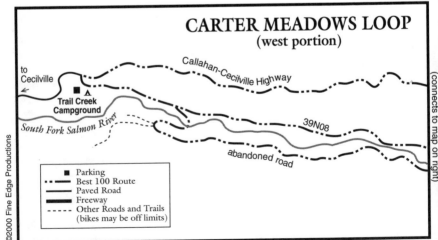

CARTER MEADOWS LOOP
(west portion)

the summit.) This way you get the 5-mile pavement climb over with at the beginning of the ride.

Route: Leave the campground and head back out to the highway. Turn right (east) and begin the 1,300-foot climb to the summit. As pavement climbs go, this one isn't too bad. It's steep enough, but traffic is minimal. Look on it as a good way to warm up and to earn the singletrack that's coming up.

At 5 miles you reach Carter Meadows summit. There is a dirt pullout on the right. A doubletrack goes uphill to a small parking area and a helipad. To the right of the doubletrack, the signed PCT (closed to bikes) heads into the trees. To the right of the PCT is an unsigned singletrack. This is the trail you want. Don't get on the PCT by mistake.

Pacific Crest Trail at Carter Meadows Summit.

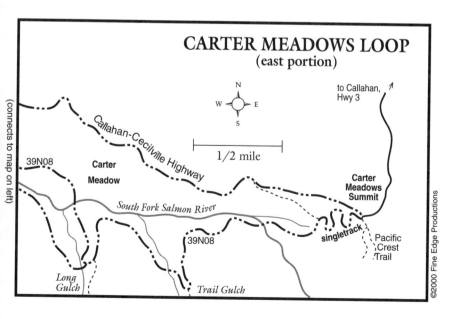

©2000 Fine Edge Productions

Fragnoli

Bike-legal singletrack at Carter Meadows Summit

head at Long Gulch (signed), you have a decision to make. You can swing right to continue on 39N08 or you can pick up an old abandoned road on the other side of the gulch.

Option 1: Road 39N08 leads directly back to Trail Creek campground in 3.5 miles. This is an easy downhill cruise.

Option 2: Although tougher, mainly because the trail surface is rougher, the abandoned route is more secluded. It is also harder to find and to follow. Every year it degenerates more. You're on your own if you pick this option. Two helpful hints to keep you oriented: Road 39N08 follows the north side of the South Fork and the abandoned road follows the south side. If you reach the Trinity Alps Wilderness boundary, you're too far south.

As you near Trail Creek campground, two roads come in from the left, one immediately after the other. You switchback to the right, cross the South Fork on a wooden bridge and rejoin 39N08. A left turn on 39N08 will take you to the campground.

Option 3: I recommend this route for the adventurous rider. Instead of climbing to Carter Meadows Summit on the highway and descending Road 39N08, climb 39N08 to the highway.

The singletrack drops steeply through the trees to Carter Meadow where there are several campgrounds and trailheads. Follow the trail through this area until, about a mile from the summit, it runs into a graded dirt road (39N08). Go left. (A right turn would lead back up to the highway.)

Descend 1.7 miles to Trail Gulch (signed). Continue descending another mile to Long Gulch. Note that some older Forest Service publications mistakenly reverse Long Gulch and Trail Gulch. Long Gulch is downstream (west) of Trail Gulch. Just before a stream crossing at the trail-

At the highway, go right for 0.8 mile to the summit. Take the singletrack back down to 39N08. Follow 39N08 downhill for 2.7 miles to Long Gulch where you can pick up the abandoned road back to the campground.

South Fork Salmon River from bridge in Trail Creek campground.

Fragnoli

Chapter 9:
FEATHER RIVER COUNTRY

©2000 Fine Edge Productions

CHAPTER 9

Feather River Country

by Delaine Fragnoli

Flowing from the northern reaches of the Sierra Nevada, the Feather River drains a huge swath of land on its way to California's great Sacramento Valley where the linchpin of the California Water Project, Oroville Dam, harnesses its power for energy and its water for agriculture. Where does all the water for the Sacramento Valley come from? You're looking at it when you ride around the heavily-engineered waterworks associated with the dam.

The stats on the dam are impressive. Completed in 1968, it stands 770 feet high and is 6,920 feet across the top, making it the tallest and one of the largest earthen dams in the country. Mine tailings (this was previously big mining country) were used to construct the dam. Beneath the dam, an enormous cavern houses six power generation units. These units, along with those from other related power plants, produce more than 2.8 billion kilowatt-hours of power annually. Created by the dam, Lake Oroville has a surface area of 24 square miles with a shoreline of 167 miles and boasts the best bass fishing in the state (according to *Bassmaster* magazine). Lake Oroville is hugely popular with the boating set, leaving the trails in the surrounding State Recreation Area to hikers, horseback riders and cyclists.

Lake Oroville is worth a weekend of riding itself and makes the best starting point for exploring the Feather River's upper reaches. The Plumas National Forest houses most of the drainage, encompassing much of Plumas County's public land. Between the national forest, Pacific Gas and Electric and railroad lands, some 91 percent of the county's land is public. What that means for mountain bikers is miles and miles of dirt roads, logging roads, 4WD tracks and trails. The area's smaller dams have created numerous man-made reservoirs and lakes, many of which provide world-class fishing and function as recreational centers in the forest. They make great base camps for cyclists who can find days of riding around Bucks Lake and Lake Davis, among others. Virtually all of the forest's roads and trails are open to bikes, with the exception of the Pacific Crest Trail, the Bucks Lake Wilderness, and a few other assorted trails. The Forest Service prints a series of route sheets (available from ranger stations) describing recommended mountain bike rides. A couple of these are included in this chapter.

Access from Oroville is via Highway 70, recently designated a National Scenic Byway. A twisty two-lane built in the 1930s, the highway follows the river, taking you over a slew of bridges, including two famous sets of double bridges (one for the highway and one for the railroad), and through three historic tunnels. Despite the cluster of dams and powerhouses plugging the route (mostly for flood control and energy needs), the Feather River retains much of its turbulent nature. The Middle Fork is a National Wild and Scenic River and the dramatic terrain features blade-thin ridge lines, dramatic canyons cut by rivers and streams, and several waterfalls, including the impressive Feather Falls.

Note that there are few reliable facilities once you leave Oroville until you reach Quincy, the Plumas County seat. There are no dedicated bike shops to speak of outside of Oroville. Your best bet in Oroville is Greenline Cycles, 530-533-7885. Quincy has several hotels and restaurants to choose from. Try Morning Thunder for pre-ride carbo loading.

Lassen National Forest borders the Plumas National Forest on the north. Straddling the northern reaches of the Sierra Nevada and the southern flanks of the Cascade Mountains, its varied topography includes volcanic lava flows (Lassen Volcanic National Park sits in the middle of the Forest), dry oak-covered hills in the east, and high peaks and deep canyons in the south. Lake Almanor and the town of Chester make the best home base for adventuring here. Seek out backcountry guru and Mountain Bike Hall of Fame member

Fragnoli

Double bridges, one for the highway, one for the railroad, at Tobin

Chuck "Bodfish" Elliot at Bodfish Bicycles & Quiet Mountain Sports (530-258-2338) for trail information. Any attempt to document the riding would pale in comparison with his encyclopedic knowledge.

Located in the middle of the great Sacramento Valley, Chico makes a great jumping-off spot for visiting Lassen National Forest. Chico itself is a laid-back town with an aura of Northern California hipness. It's also home to several fringe-of-the-bike-industry types (that's said as a compliment). Jeff Lindsay, maker of Mountain Goat bicycles, Bob Seals, inventor of the Cool Tool, and the self-proclaimed retro-grouches of Retro Tec, all call Chico home. Pleasant most of the year, the area can get sweltering hot in the summer months. That's when local cyclists head to the hills.

56 Chico/Upper Bidwell Park

Distance: 11.5 miles
Difficulty: Moderately strenuous, technical
Elevation: 900' gain/loss
Ride Type: Loop on dirt road, singletrack and pavement
Season: Year-round; can get hot in summer
Maps: Richardson Springs, Paradise West. Trail map of Chico and Bidwell Park can be obtained by calling the City of Chico at 530-895-4972.
Comments: Helmets are required in the Upper Park except on pavement (?!). Bicycles are prohibited in the Caper Acres area. Do not ride right after a rain. Water and restrooms available in the lower park.

Highlights: A very bike-friendly city (*Bicycling* magazine has named it one of the nation's best bicycling cities), Chico has plenty of bike paths. The easily accessible Bidwell Park is the town's mountain biking center, par- ticularly Upper Bidwell Park. Centered around Chico Creek, Lower Bidwell Park has a maze of mostly unmarked trails which are fun to explore. But most riders head up Upper Bidwell's North Rim Trail,

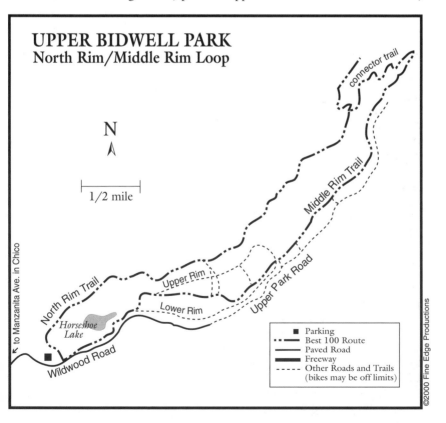

UPPER BIDWELL PARK
North Rim/Middle Rim Loop

N

1/2 mile

to Manzanita Ave. in Chico

North Rim Trail

Upper Rim

Lower Rim

Horseshoe Lake

Wildwood Road

Middle Rim Trail

connector trail

Upper Park Road

■ Parking
Best 100 Route
Paved Road
Freeway
Other Roads and Trails
(bikes may be off limits)

©2000 Fine Edge Productions

which gives you great views of the Central Valley. To the east, you can see the Sierra Nevada. In the spring and summer, swimming holes along the Lower Rim Trail provide much needed relief from the heat. You can extend this ride by biking from Chico to the park or by dropping into Lower Bidwell on the way out or back.

The 2,400-acre park gets its name from Annie Bidwell, widow of General John Bidwell, Chico's founder. Annie Bidwell donated the land to the city but, ironically, died destitute. The whole park is about 10 miles long and contains swimming pools, picnic areas and a variety of other recreational facilities. It's a great place to spend a leisurely day or get a quick and rewarding workout.

Getting There: From the town of Chico, ride your bike or drive northeast on South Park Drive. Bear left at the Y onto Centennial Avenue and quickly hang a left onto Manzanita Avenue. Take the first right, Wildwood Road, for 1 mile. There's a trail sign for North Rim on the left side of the road. Park in the dirt lot on the left side of the road.

Route: Many options are possible here. A series of parallel trails with connectors are open to bikes: North Rim Trail, Upper Rim Trail, Middle Rim Trail, Lower Rim Trail and the Upper Park Road. The following is just one possibility. If you're not sure if a trail is open to bikes, watch for trail symbols painted on rocks.

From the parking area, go around the gate and start climbing the rough doubletrack. There are lots of offshoots; stay on the main trail. At first the wide trail is rough, having been cut from volcanic basalt, as it climbs up the ridge. Climbing on this rough,

rocky stuff is what earns this ride its moderately strenuous rating. If you crash in these sharp rocks, you will bleed. The fire road smoothes out as you ascend into a pine forest and later it begins to narrow. The pitch is moderate as you make your way to the park's northeastern corner.

At about 3 miles there is a great overlook to the right at the Y, marked by a rock formation and an oak tree. It makes a good spot to watch circling raptors. At 4 miles, a connector trail drops off to your right, but you keep on North Rim. Loop around a big fallen tree. There are more rocks and more climbing as the trail narrows. Watch for rattlesnakes; I saw no fewer than three rattlers while riding here one May. At 4.5 miles the trail ends on a plateau. From here you have those views I mentioned earlier. I have spotted foxes, mountain lions and turkey vultures from this viewpoint. Gawk for a while before backtracking.

Go around the fallen tree and down a rocky pitch. Less than 0.5 mile from the overlook, look for the connector trail on your left. You might have seen this on the way up, but it is easy to miss. There is no sign, but there is a wooden post on which someone has written *Bikes OK*.

Take this singletrack down to the Middle Rim Trail. It is steep, especially at first, and throws up some technical, rocky switchbacks to challenge you. These are interspersed with blissfully-smooth sections. As the trail traverses the hillside, it seems to be going in the wrong direction to loop back, but then it switches back one more time and drops near a streambed. There are some short, steep, rocky ups and downs as the trail drops into and climbs out of several gullies—major poison oak alert!

Erosion can be a bit of a problem along here so be careful, especially in the switchbacks.

At the Y, go left to the main dirt road and then go right onto the road. Several trails take off from the Middle Rim. Most of the ones which take off to your left connect with the Lower Rim Trail, while the ones which go to your right lead up to the Upper Rim Trail. Stay on the dirt road for an easy downhill cruise. You pass Salmon Hole, a diversion dam and some dirt parking areas, all on the left. When you reach Bear Hole,

also on the left, it's worth stopping for a swim.

When you're done, continue down the dirt road. Look for a trail on your right. It's not signed, but it passes between two wooden posts. It offers more rocky and steep ups and downs and some rolling terrain before ending at Horseshoe Lake. If you don't want to take the trail, you can stay on the dirt road to Horseshoe Lake. At the lake, go out to the pavement. There's a bike lane/path. Take the pavement back to the parking area where you started.

57 Lake Oroville Bike Route

Distance: 41 miles; can be broken into much shorter sections
Difficulty: Strenuous in its entirety; can be broken into much easier sections
Elevation: Low point 174', high point 901'; elevation gain/loss 727'
Ride Type: Loop on singletrack, dirt/gravel roads and pavement
Season: Year round; can be brutally hot with little shade in the summer months; spring and fall best
Map: Free from local bike shops (try Greenline Cycles on Oro Dam Blvd.) or in visitor's guide
Comments: Water and restrooms are available at Lake Oroville State Recreation Area, Thermalito Forebay Recreation Area North, Thermalito Forebay Recreation Area South, and Bedrock Park.

Highlights: The Oroville Bicycle Trail (OBT) leads you across one of the world's largest and tallest earthen dams (Oroville Dam), reveals scenic views of Table Mountain, the Sacramento Valley, the Sutter Buttes (the world's smallest mountain range) and the dam's many forebays and afterbays. You have plenty of opportunity for bird watching and other wildlife viewing as the route also passes through the Oroville State Wildlife Area. Administered by California Department of Fish and Game, the 11,000-acre area provides a year-round or seasonal home to 171 spe-

cies of birds and has an outstanding heron and egret rookery, active from February to June.

The recreation area around the dam has become a popular race site, hosting an event usually held in May. Unfortunately, some of the trails used for the races are not open for biking during the rest of the year. The OBT does, however, include some of these trails.

Doing the whole OBT is quite an undertaking. I did it; it was. Avid dirt heads will find the eastern sections (east of Highway 70) near the dam the most interesting. Families, nature

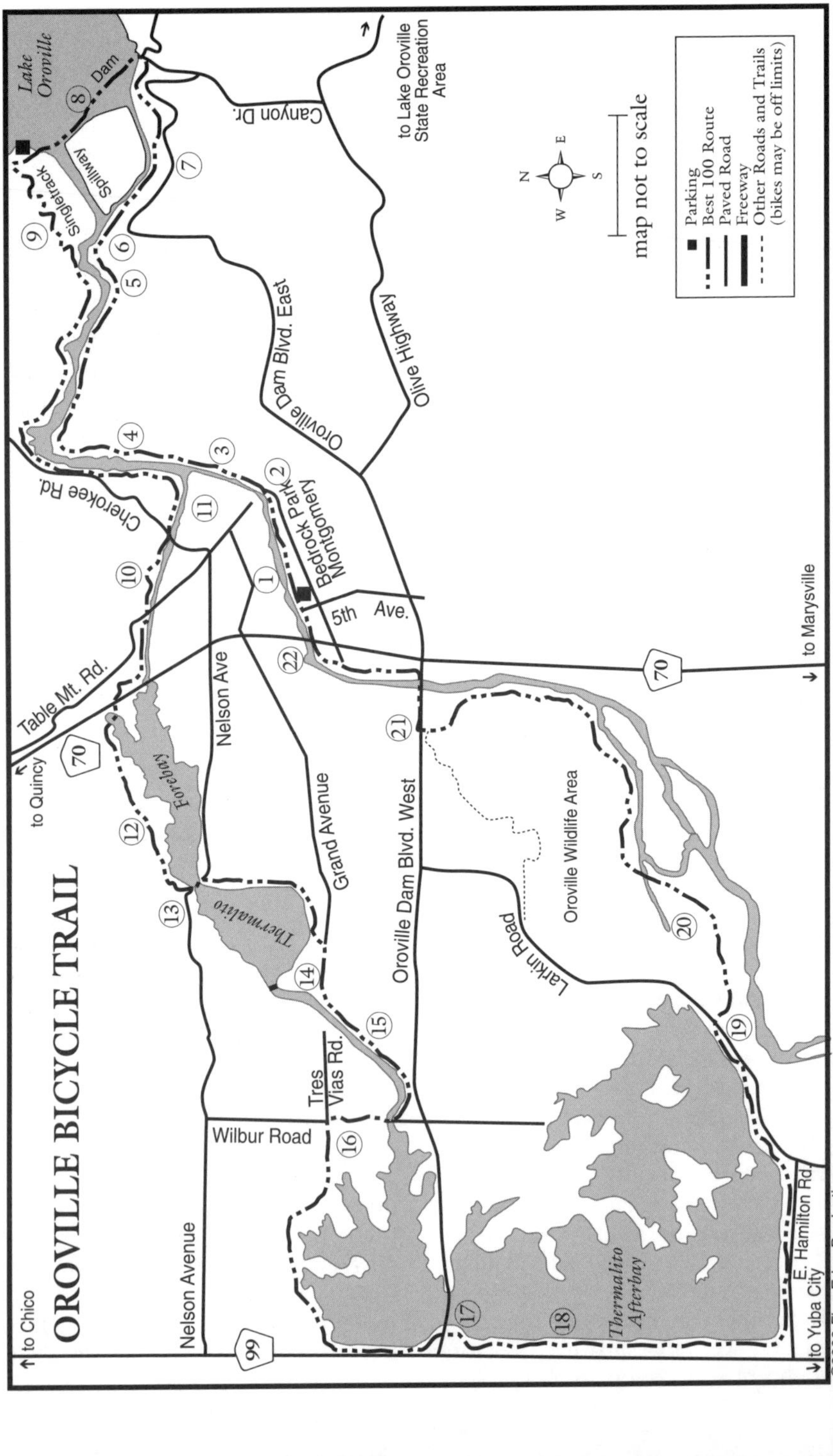

OROVILLE BICYCLE TRAIL

Lake Oroville

Dam

Spillway

Singletrack

Canyon Dr.

to Lake Oroville State Recreation Area

map not to scale

- ■ Parking
- ·—·· Best 100 Route
- ——— Paved Road
- ——— Freeway
- ----- Other Roads and Trails
  (bikes may be off limits)

N
W E
S

Oroville Dam Blvd. East

Olive Highway

to Marysville

Cherokee Rd.

Table Mt. Rd.

to Quincy

Bedrock Park

Montgomery

5th Ave.

Nelson Ave

Grand Avenue

Oroville Dam Blvd. West

Larkin Road

Oroville Wildlife Area

Forebay

Thermalito

Tres Vias Rd.

Wilbur Road

Nelson Avenue

to Chico

Thermalito Afterbay

E. Hamilton Rd

to Yuba City

©2000 Fine Edge Productions

Fragnoli

View of Table Mountain from Nelson Avenue bridge.

lovers, and the less-conditioned will appreciate the minimal elevation and paved or smooth dirt surfaces of the western section (west of Highway 70) of the loop. Most of the paved sections are on bike paths, protected from traffic.

Getting There: Those staying in Oroville and those interested in the western section of the OBT would do well to start at Bedrock Park in the city of Oroville. From Highway 70, go east on Oroville Dam Blvd. Go north on 5th Ave. past Montgomery Street to the park, along the banks of the Feather River.

Those camping at the state recreation area may want to start at the dam. The disadvantage to this is that you will end your ride with a roughly 3-mile climb back up to the dam. From Olive Highway (Highway 162), turn north onto Canyon Drive (signed *To Oroville Dam Spillway Ramp.*) Follow the signs to the dam

and recreation area. Once in the recreation area, cross over the dam, following the signs to the spillway ramp. Park in the big gravel parking lot for the spillway ramp. The OBT starts at the dead-end circle you pass as you make the final right-hand turn toward the parking lot. There is a day-use fee for the recreation area, waived if you've already paid to camp.

I recommend camping at Loafer Creek. It's a big campground but can be virtually deserted during the week in the fall. The oak-shaded sites feature nearby hot showers, restrooms and laundry tubs.

Route: I am not going to give you a mile-by-mile, blow-by-blow account of the OBT because: one, we would be here all day; two, the route is generally very well marked. Look for brown posts with yellow directional arrows, brown posts with yellow section numbers (the route is divided into sections which are NOT related

Fragnoli

Trail sign at Thermalito Forebay, Table Mountain in background.

to mileage), brown posts with yellow tips, and yellow circles with a bicycle in the middle. I will, however, offer some suggestions and some description of the various sections of trail.

First off, a little orientation. The OBT is designed as a counter-clockwise loop, and this is the preferred way to ride it. From Bedrock Park eastward to the dam is uphill. From the dam down to Highway 70 is mostly downhill. The western section from Highway 70 to Highway 99 and back is basically level. The best cut-off or bail-out point is an L-shaped section of trail (section 11) between Table Mountain Blvd. and Cherokee Road. Those coming down from the dam can use it to loop back up, cutting out the paved sections of the route, while those not interested in the elevation gain and technical challenges of riding near the dam can use it to cut off the easternmost portion of the OBT. Once you head into the westernmost portion of the route (sections 15 through 20), you are

committed. There are no good bail-out options. Going back on Oroville Dam Blvd. would be unpleasant, and any other road options would be just as long and probably more arduous than the OBT. Once you leave the Thermalito Forebay Recreation Area South (section 15), there are no facilities on the route—not even any shade—until you return to town (section 21).

Now for more details on the various trail sections. For ease of reference, I will start at section 1 which starts at Bedrock Park.

Sections 1–4: Take the riverfront paved bike path east from Bedrock Park. Continue on the bike path until it forks. Go right uphill. A metal post here has a yellow stripe and #1 painted on it. Make a hard right at the top, switchbacking until you're going in the opposite direction. Follow the gravel out to a paved road and go left. You're riding along the backside of some businesses here. Go left at the first intersection onto Montgomery. Go uphill to the light at Washington. On the far corner, diagonally across, there's a sign for the Feather River Visitors Center. This is where you want to go. Drop down the rough asphalt back to the river. Railroad tracks soon appear to your right. The pavement is blocked at a powerhouse or some such facility. Look for a singletrack going uphill on your right. It climbs steeply but soon tops out. You are above the tracks but paralleling them. Eventually the singletrack drops down to the tracks. Ride alongside them in the rocks, then cross them to pick up a gravel road on the right side of the tracks. Follow the gravel road to a tunnel which is just long enough and curved enough for you to need a light. A flashlight will do, but you absolutely need some kind of light.

Sections 5–8: Avoid the multi-use trail without a brown and yellow post on your right. A little later there is a singletrack with the OBT's brown and yellow post on the right. Take it up and down and out to a gravel road. There's a whole bunch of crisscrossing gravel roads here. Look for the one with the OBT post. It leads to a major gravel road. Go right and climb around a left-hand switchback. This gravel road runs into pavement. Go right to an intersection and then left at the intersection. Follow signs back to the dam/spillway ramp. From here you have about a 3-mile climb to the dam.

Sections 9–10: Starts at a dead-end circle just before the final right-hand turn to the spillway ramp. It's marked by a yellow bicycle circle, and consists of gravel road and singletrack marked with brown posts with directional arrows. Then you're mostly on gravel

road. You pass through a cattle gate and cross a bridge. You cross some pavement and then go through a chainlink "tunnel." Cross a road and zigzag across two wooden bridges. Cross Table Mountain Road. Cross another bridge. Zigzag some more; your route is gated and fenced in most directions. Go left on pavement, cross Highway 70 and enter Thermalito Forebay Recreation Area north, a nice rest stop.

Sections 12–14: From the picnic area, continue around the forebay. Go left to cross the Nelson Ave. bridge. Pick up the trail on the right on other side of the bridge. There is a good view of Table Mountain from the bridge. About 1.5 mile later you reach a boat ramp and picnic area with port-a-potties at the Thermalito Forebay Recreation Area South. This is your last good rest stop for almost 20 miles! From here the trail goes left on pavement.

Sections 15–19: Go right on Wilbur Road for roughly 0.5 mile and then left on Tres Vias, following signs. Tres Vias dead-ends at a gate. Go through, following signs. Other routes are clearly marked *No Bikes.* Begin looping around Thermalito Afterbay. This section of the trail feels the most remote and desolate. The trail curves south, paralleling Highway 99. Cross Highway 162 (Oro Dam Blvd. West) and pick up the trail on the other side. You begin what felt to me like an interminable paved section sandwiched between the highway and the afterbay. The trail is paved here and elevated. The trail eventually bends eastward. About 6 miles south of Highway 162, watch for a sign indicating that you turn right and cross Larkin

Road. Enter the Oroville Wildlife Area and follow the yellow signs to the left back onto a gravel road.

Sections 20–22: You are on dirt and gravel roads for about 5 miles through the wildlife area. The road can get washboarded at times. There is one confusing three-way intersection just beyond a sandy wash. Take the gravel road uphill. You eventually come out on Highway 162 (Oro Dam Blvd.) You go right and cross the Feather River on a bridge on the highway. The OBT resumes on the other side of the bridge along the opposite side of the river (the river was to your right, now it's on the left) before you reach Highway 70. From here the OBT heads north before bending east under Highway 70. Here at River Bend Park, the trail turns into a paved bike path. It's less than a mile back to Bedrock Park.

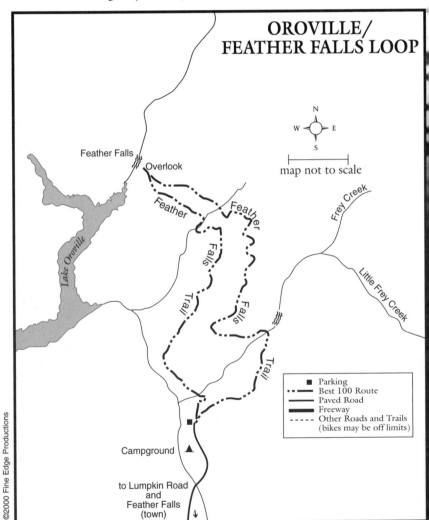

©2000 Fine Edge Productions

58 Oroville/Feather Falls Loop

Distance: 8 miles
Difficulty: Moderately strenuous, somewhat technical
Elevation: 2,400' gain/loss
Ride Type: Loop on singletrack
Season: April through October; the falls are most spectacular in spring
Maps: Brush Creek, Forbestown; Plumas National Forest (return loop not shown on any maps)
Comments: Nearest services are in Oroville. The town of Feather Falls has a restaurant and a store. There is no water but there are port-a-potties at the trailhead.

Highlights: One of the biggest attractions in Plumas National Forest, Feather Falls is the nation's sixth tallest waterfall, dropping 640 feet. The Feather Falls Trail leads to a dramatic overlook; the materials for the observation platform had to be helicoptered in. You can definitely get vertigo up here. The falls cascade into the granite-lined Middle Fork of the Feather River, this portion of which is a protected Wild and Scenic River, one of the first such designated rivers.

Since the first edition of this book was published, the Forest Service has completed a new trail which allows for an all-singletrack loop to the falls and back. Previously you had to ride out and back. Although the loop is relatively short—8 miles—it packs a wallop, not just in terms of scenery but also in elevation loss and gain. It's no walk in the park for beginners. Even if you find yourself pushing your bike, the views make it all worthwhile.

Getting There: Take State Route 162 east from Oroville to Forbestown Road, about 8 miles. Go right on Forbestown. Five miles later, take a left (signed) onto Lumpkin Road

Trailhead for Feather Falls Loop.

Fragnoli

toward the town of Feather Falls. The road gets narrow, steep and twisty in spots. On the outskirts of town, 11.2 miles from the turn, there's a sign for Feather Falls, directing you to go north on a paved road. The road ends at the trailhead, which is at the far end of the campground parking lot.

Route: From the far end of the parking lot, take the paved trail. It shortly turns to dirt. The trail is wide and smooth here. You pass a hiking trail sign that says: *9 mile loop; Allow 4 or 5 hours; Carry plenty of water.* Although the sign indicates it is a 9-mile loop, my mileage was closer to 8 miles for the whole loop. Next you pass a trail register.

At 0.3 mile, take the trail to the left. The trail really starts descending from

Fragnoli

Part of Feather Falls, 6th tallest falls in the country.

here. At 0.5 mile you hit the first of three wide, rideable switchbacks. Cross a creek at 1.1 mile. Last time I was here the bridge was out; it may have been repaired by the time you visit. Beyond the creek the trail gets rougher, with intermittent technical rock outcroppings, including several steep, technical uphill pitches.

Begin climbing in earnest. You pass a 3-mile marker and, right after, a wooden bench, then come to a trail intersection. A wooden sign indicates that the loop trail goes right and that the direction you came from is the more difficult route. A separate brown sign directs you to the falls straight ahead.

To visit the falls, go straight up the steep hill and around a left-hand switchback. Make your way, if you can, up the broken chunks of concrete (how they got out here I'll never know) to a vista point overlooking the Middle Fork of the Feather River. We ditched our bikes here and hiked the rest of the way to the falls. From the vista point the trail goes up, then levels before dropping steeply to the Feather Falls viewing platform. Last time I was here the platform was roped off because some of the platform beams had rotted away. Regardless, you have stunning views of the cascading falls and the churning Feather River.

When you've had enough scenic splendor, backtrack to the 3-mile trail intersection. Go left to continue around the loop. The first section of trail is smooth and gradual, blissfully downhill. Alas, it soon begins climbing more than it descends—but there are some swoopy, fun downhill sections. Overall this climb is much more manageable than the earlier climbing. The trail stays wide and smooth most of the way back. You cross a couple of creeks, some with brand new bridges, as you roll through a beautiful forest with some great oaks, manzanita trees (not bushes!), pines, cool rock formations and, of course, reams of poison oak.

Soon you are back at the very first trail intersection. Continue straight ahead back to the parking lot.

Feather Falls: near the mid-point of the single track loop.

59 Quincy/Bucks Lake Singletrack

Distance: 5 miles
Difficulty: Easy, mildly technical in spots; may have to portage across creek
Elevation: 5,200' to 5,520'
Ride Type: Loop on singletrack and a tad of pavement
Season: June through October
Maps: Bucks Lake NE and NW; Plumas National Forest; trail is relatively new and not shown on most maps
Comments: Water can be found at White Horse Campground.

Highlights: Although the Plumas National Forest is generally short on singletrack (if only non-Wilderness sections of the PCT were open to bikes), this route takes in a tasty morsel of trail near the popular-for-fishing Bucks Lake. Removed from the hustle and bustle immediately around the lake, this loop consists of two trails, Summit Trail and Bucks

Fragnoli

Hunter's blind in meadow along the Summit Trail.

Creek Trail, and follows Bucks Creek for much of its route, passing through woods and meadows on its way. It's easy to keep oriented here: Bucks Creek parallels Bucks Lake Road. Summit Trail runs along the south bank of Bucks Creek, while Bucks Creek Trail parallels the north bank of the creek, sandwiched between the creek and the road.

Getting There: From Oroville, take Oro Dam Blvd. Turn right at Olive Highway which becomes the Oroville-Quincy Road (this is the old Wells Fargo Stage route), due to be paved during 2000. Continue 35 miles northeast to Bucks Lake Rd. Continue on Bucks Lake Rd. past the lake to the well-signed Bucks Summit. There is a restroom and large parking area here, largely for snowmobile staging during the

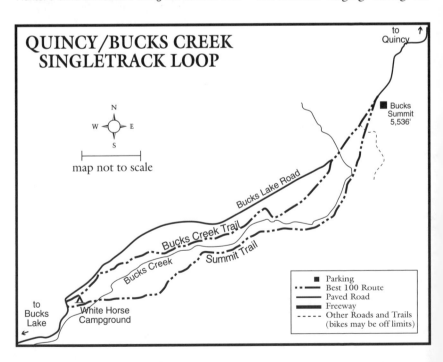

QUINCY/BUCKS CREEK SINGLETRACK LOOP

to Quincy

N
W — E
S

map not to scale

Bucks Summit
5,536'

Bucks Lake Road

Bucks Creek Trail

Bucks Creek

Summit Trail

to Bucks Lake

White Horse Campground

■ Parking
-·-·- Best 100 Route
——— Paved Road
▬▬▬ Freeway
- - - - Other Roads and Trails
(bikes may be off limits)

winter months. Park here.

From Quincy, take Bucks Lake Rd. (Main Street in town) west for 14 miles to Bucks Summit.

If you're camping at White Horse Campground, you can start there.

Route: From the summit, head down toward Bucks Lake (west) on Bucks Lake Road. There is a trailhead for the PCT (closed to bikes) just past the summit on the left. It is marked by a big brown recreation board. It is not, however, signed as the PCT; it is marked by a brown Adopt-a-Trail sign. Do NOT take this trail by mistake.

Continue 0.25 mile past the PCT and look for the Summit Trail, also on your left. It is clearly signed, with a big brown sign, as a ski and mountain bike trail. Take this trail as it heads downhill and into the trees.

Trailhead for the well-marked Summit Trail/Bucks Creek trails.

If you're new to singletrack, don't worry; this is probably the steepest section of trail on the whole ride. You soon cross a dirt road. The trail continues on the other side. The trail is well signed throughout, marked by blue arrows (for cross-country skiers) and white bike signs up in the trees.

The trail is great fun as it rolls mostly downhill through meadows, some with elevated trail sections to keep you out of the mud. As you can imagine, the area sparkles with wildflowers in the early summer.

As you near Bucks Lake Road, you have to cross Bucks Creek, which can be a portage in the spring. Once on the other side, continue out to paved Bucks Lake Rd. and go right. Immediately go right again onto Bucks Creek Trail—look for the blue and white signs up in the trees. You're basically doing a tight U-turn from one trail onto the road and onto the other trail. There is a big Bucks Creek Trailhead sign and small parking area on the opposite side of Bucks Lake Rd. This is NOT the trail you want; it leads into a wilderness area.

Follow Bucks Creek Trail through Whitehorse Campground. Pick up the trail near the far end of the campground at campsite 13. There are no signs or arrows here. Look for tree blazes near the picnic table for site 13. Cross the creek on a big fallen tree.

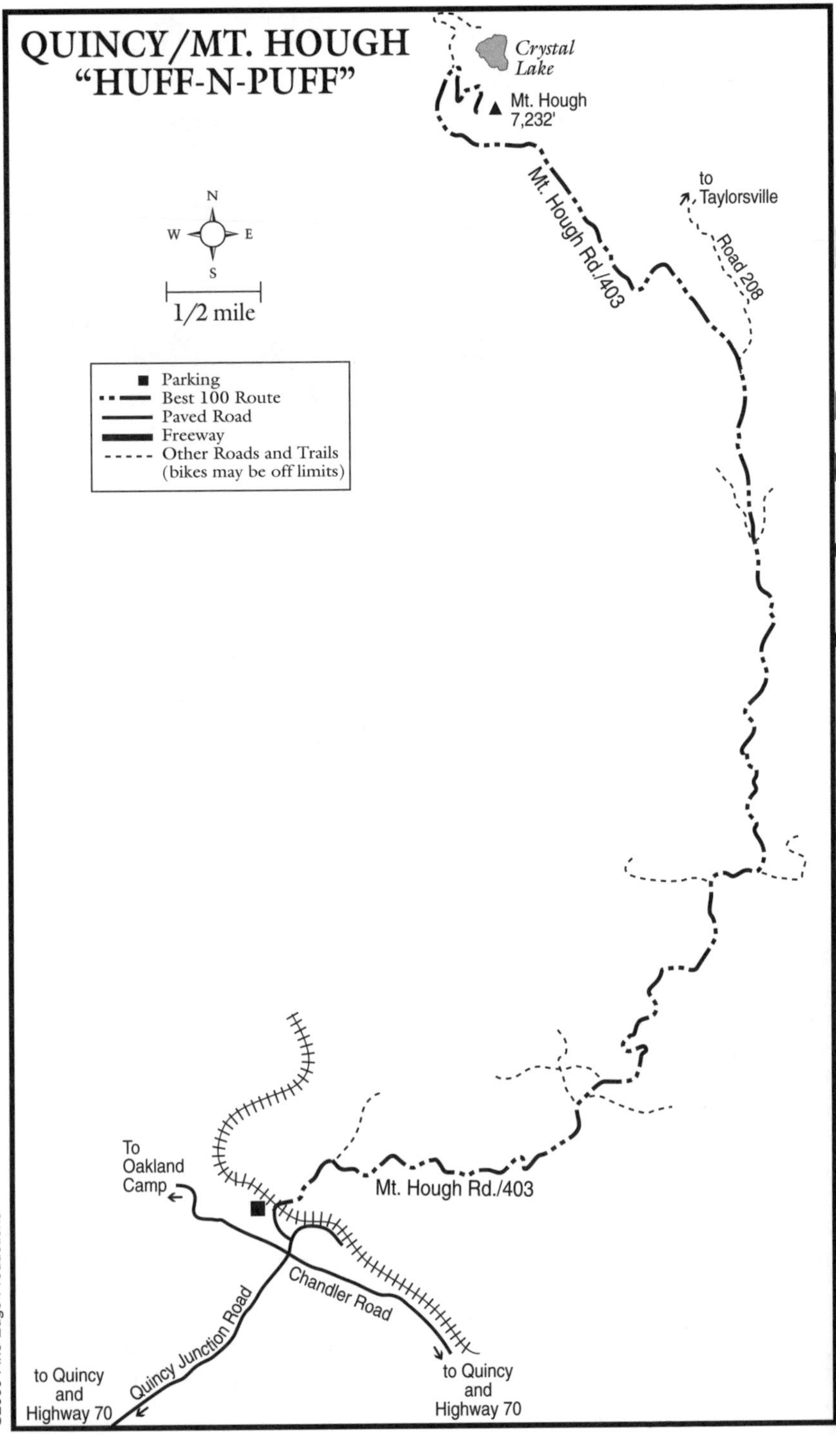

QUINCY/MT. HOUGH
"HUFF-N-PUFF"

Crystal
Lake

▲ Mt. Hough
7,232'

Mt. Hough Rd./403

to
Taylorsville

Road 208

N
W — E
S

1/2 mile

■ Parking
Best 100 Route
Paved Road
Freeway
Other Roads and Trails
(bikes may be off limits)

To
Oakland
Camp ←

Mt. Hough Rd./403

Quincy Junction Road

Chandler Road

to Quincy
and
Highway 70

to Quincy
and
Highway 70

©2000 Fine Edge Productions

From here the trail climbs, regaining elevation on the way back to the summit. Some of the gains come in short, steep pitches. This section of trail is more exposed and rockier than the Summit Trail. The trail parallels Bucks Lake Road, getting quite close at points. About 0.5 mile from the campground there is a pullout from the road on your left with wooden vehicle stops. Continue straight.

The trail soon pops out onto Bucks Lake Road. Go right and take the road back up to the summit.

60 Quincy/Mt. Hough "Huff-n-Puff"

Distance: 20 miles
Difficulty: Abusive, mildly technical
Elevation: 3,528' low point, 7,232' high point; 3,704' gain/loss
Ride Type: Out-and-back on dirt roads
Season: June through October
Maps: Quincy, Spring Garden, Taylorsville, Crescent Mills
Comments: Take everything you need (food, water, extra clothing, oxygen tank, spare pair of quadriceps) with you.

Author puffing atop Mt. Hough.

Highlights: One of northern California's great hill climbs, this savage route contains everything that excites mountain goats and makes the rest of us ask "why?" You get a long, steep 10-mile climb which gets rougher and steeper as you go, plenty of elevation gain to put you into the real suck-wind altitudes, solitude, fabulous views (no less an expert than Bodfish calls the view from Hough "one of the best in the Northern Sierra"), and a neat lookout structure at the summit. Of course, topping out confers bragging rights and a sense of satisfaction as well. At one time there was a local "race" (more like a survival fest) to the top called "Huff-n-Puff," but it has died out because, as one local put it, "It was just too painful for most of us." If unmitigated

Fragnoli

View of Indian Valley from Mt. Hough.

suffering is your thing, this is your ride.

Getting There: From the only stop light on Highway 70 in Quincy (at the high school and across from Safeway), turn onto Quincy Junction Rd. Continue on Quincy Junction past its intersection with Chandler Rd. Go left at the very first intersection (not signed) past Chandler Rd. Park off the side of the road near the railroad tracks.

Route: Mileages are from the railroad tracks. Cross the tracks and head up the dirt and gravel road on the other side. Prepare to sacrifice a lung to the climbing god Pulmones. The Mt. Hough Road looks benign enough from here, but it starts climbing and switchbacking almost immediately, yielding views of Quincy. Lucky for your soon-to-be-oxygen-deprived brain, the route is easy to follow. Stay on the main gravel road past lots of small, un-signed side roads. For much of the way the road squirms from one

side of Grizzly Ridge to the other, providing more views of Quincy and the American Valley to your left and Indian Valley to your right.

At 1.2 miles, the grade levels a bit and the climbing eases somewhat—it's all relative. Continue past the spur road to the right at 1.4 miles. At the intersection with 25N14 at 2.2 miles, stay straight on signed Road 403 (Mt. Hough Rd.). The road climbs more steeply here. but then levels out at 3.8 miles, just before a signed Y-intersection. Road 403 goes to the right while 25N73 goes left. Stay right on 403.

You come to another Y-intersection at 4.2 miles. To the left is a sign: *Mt. Hough, 5 miles, Road 403.* To the right: *King Solomon Saddle, 8 miles, 25N07.* Go left toward Mt. Hough. Because of the sign, you might think you're already halfway to Mt. Hough. You're not. It's closer to 6 miles, not 5 miles. For your own mental health, ignore the mileages on the road signs—they tend to be cruelly optimistic.

The road begins to roll. If that sounds like some kind of relief from the grade you've been battling, think again. Some of the uphill pitches are very steep. From 5.6 miles to 6.2 miles you get a bona fide downhill. There are several side roads; stay on the main road. While the descent provides a bit of a breather, I can never truly enjoy such downhills. To me they're "negative elevation," elevation I've struggled to gain which I am now relinquishing and will have to regain. There's no such thing as a free lunch on a climb like this.

At 7.1 miles you come to a big Y-junction. Road 403 is signed to the left. A knocked down sign on the right indicates Road 208. Continue left on 403. I found the last 3 miles to the lookout to be especially trying. The pitch continues to get steeper and the trail surface

Crystal Lake (foreground) and Indian Valley (background) from Mt. Hough

View from Mt. Hough (Mt. Lassen in the distance).

rockier. During the last mile you're basically riding on scree at the steepest grade yet. Not only does traction become a problem, but you're also really feeling the elevation at this point. Yes, you will huff and puff. Somewhere along here I actually whimpered out loud.

At 9.6 miles there is an unsigned road on your right. One hundred feet farther, go right at the fork to climb one final super steep pitch. Once up this unnecessary bit of malice, veer right to the lookout at 10 miles.

From the summit, you can see the American Valley to the south/southwest, the Indian Valley and town of Taylorsville to the north/northeast, and Lake Almanor and Mt. Lassen to the north. If the climb hasn't already, the view will take your breath away. Be sure to walk to the northern edge of the flat area around the lookout. Directly below you is Crystal Lake, a tiny jewel of an alpine lake circled by granite. In a word, gorgeous.

Follow the same route back down to the railroad tracks where, if you're smart, you will have a bottle of Advil waiting for you in your car. Ten miles of bone-rattling descent should complete your debilitation. Any body part not sore at this point is probably numb. Give it some time. But, hey, only the tough climb Mt. Hough, and you did it.

61 Lake Davis Loop

Distance: 18.5 miles
Difficulty: Easy, not technical
Elevation: 5,800'
Ride Type: Loop on pavement and dirt roads
Season: Spring through fall
Maps: Grizzly Valley, Crocker Mountain; Plumas National Forest
Comments: Facilities are at campgrounds around Lake Davis. The nearest town is Portola, 7 miles away.

Highlights: One of the Feather River's northernmost bits of plumbing, Lake Davis makes the perfect base for a weekend of camping, fishing and riding. The surrounding State Game Refuge and lake offer good bird and wildlife viewing. There's something here for just about everyone in the family. Formed by the Grizzly Valley Dam in the 1950s, the lake was named for conservationist and dam proponent, Lester T. Davis.

Although you wouldn't know it to look at the lake's placid surface, it has had a turbulent recent history. In the early 90s, state officials discovered a non-native fish, the northern pike, in the lake. Afraid that the fish, known for its hearty appetite for other fish, would move downstream and decimate native fish species all the way to Lake Oroville, the state Department of Fish and Game (DFG) decided to poison the lake to eradicate the pike. Local opposition (the lake provides drinking water to the nearby town of Portola) mushroomed from concern to outright protest as the department arrogantly proceeded with its plan. The poisoning was a complete disaster: it failed to eradicate the pike; the poison took much longer than DFG predicted to dissipate, leaving the city without drinking water; and the local tourist economy, heavily dependent on revenues from fishermen, was devastated. Although the city of Portola and Plumas County eventually received a $9 million settlement from the state and DFG has restocked the lake, Portola and its residents have yet to recover from the debacle.

When you visit, try to spread a little money around town. There are several motels to choose from as well as some good restaurants. I like the Station Cafe in town for a pre-ride breakfast, while the Log Cabin on Highway 70 serves copious amounts of food at reasonable prices—sure to replenish your glycogen stores after riding.

Getting There: From Highway 70 in Portola, go north on West Street. There's a brown sign indicating Lake Davis Recreation Area just before the turn. Continue on West St. as it climbs toward Lake Davis and changes names to Lake Davis Rd. You reach the dam at 7 miles. Park near the information kiosk. If you are camping at one of the Forest Service campgrounds on the east side of the lake, you can ride from there.

Route: I prefer a counterclockwise loop of the lake. That way you climb on pavement and descend on dirt, which can get quite washboarded at times.

From the dam, continue east along the lake's south shore to the junction with County Road 112 (Beckwourth-Taylorsville Road), 0.5

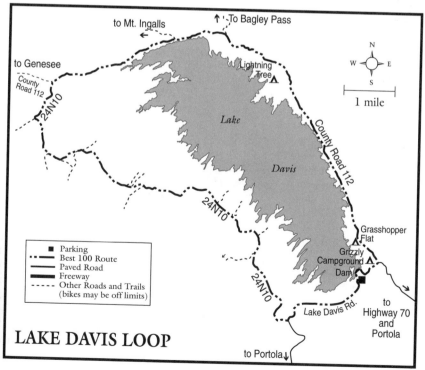

LAKE DAVIS LOOP

Fragnoli

View of Lake Davis from Smith Peak.

mile. Go left. Road 112 rolls along, climbing and descending gradually on its way past the lake's three campgrounds: Grizzly, Grasshopper Flat and Lightning Tree. The road turns from pavement to dirt/gravel just past Lightning Tree.

About 1.8 miles past Lightning Tree, ignore the dirt road to your right. It climbs a steep 500 feet to Bagley Pass. Continue around the lake, bypassing another dirt road on your right a mile later. It climbs toward Mt. Ingalls, a much more epic undertaking.

You have on-and-off views of the lake throughout these first few miles. As you round the north end of the lake, however, you lose those views. Don't be disappointed; they're soon replaced by lovely meadow views, particularly nice in spring.

At 8.6 miles, turn left onto Forest Road 24N10. Several spurs and 4WD roads branch off to the right and left. Stay on the main road as it rolls along, losing more elevation than it gains. This side of the lake is less developed, with no campgrounds or facilities, giving it a more "out there" feel. At times the road can turn to washboard, but otherwise it is an easy cruise.

At 16.7 miles, 24N10 ends at paved Lake Davis Road, the road you drove in on. Go left for 1.7 miles back to the dam and your car.

Trail sign on loop around Lake Davis.

62 Lake Davis/Smith Peak Lookout

Distance: 15.5 miles
Difficulty: Moderately strenuous, mildly technical
Elevation: 5,800' low point, 7,693' high point; 1,900' gain/loss
Ride Type: Out-and-back on dirt roads
Season: June through October
Maps: Crocker Mountain, Grizzly Valley, Blairsden, Portola; Plumas National Forest
Comments: Facilities are at campgrounds around Lake Davis. The nearest town is Portola, 7 miles away. There's an outhouse at the lookout.

Highlights: This route features a relatively short and not-too-difficult climb (for the area) with great scenic payback. The view from Smith Peak Lookout takes in Mt. Ingalls, Mt. Lassen, Lake Davis, the town of Portola, the Sierra Valley and the Sierra Buttes. The lookout itself is classic Sierra, perched atop a bare, craggy granite outcropping of rock.

Getting There: From Highway 70 in Portola, go north on West St. There's a brown sign indicating Lake Davis Recreation Area just before the turn.

Continue on West St. as it climbs toward Lake Davis and changes names to Lake Davis Rd. You reach the dam at 7 miles. Park here near the information kiosk. If you are camping at one of the Forest Service campgrounds on the east side of the lake, you can ride from there. Head south and west from the dam to begin, or combine the previous ride with this one by looping around the lake to the north.

Route: From the dam, backtrack west along Lake Davis Road for 1.7 miles. Turn right at the Camp 5/Boat Ramp

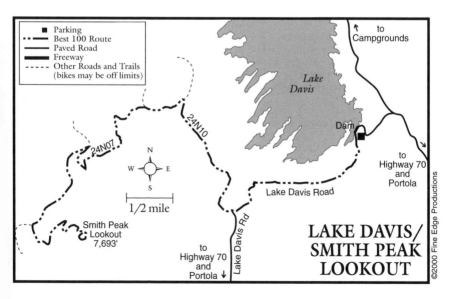

Fragnoli

View of Portola (town) and Beckwourth Peak from Smith Peak Lookout

sign onto Forest Service Road 24N10. Avoid spurs to the left and right and stay on the main gravel road. Although it is pretty level, it can get washboarded. At 3.3 miles, go left on 24N07 and begin climbing. Around 3.7 miles you start climbing in earnest. The climb gets steeper in places, but offers brief, flatter spots where you can catch your breath. The trail surface is mostly smooth with some rock and gravel, and you are generally shaded by fir and pine.

At 4.5 miles, bypass spur roads 24N07B on the right and 24N07C on the left. Half a mile later, 5 miles total, you go around a big right-hand switchback. There's an arrow in a tree on the right. Soon thereafter, 5.2 miles, you pass through a more open area which provides views of the lake. Continue around a steep, rocky left-hand switchback.

At 5.8 miles go straight past Road 23N88. At 6.5 miles go left, signed as 1 mile to Smith Peak Lookout. (The right branch leads to Willow Creek Road.) Don't believe it; it's closer to 1.5 miles to the top. The climb grows steeper and the road rockier the closer you get. You reach the gate to the lookout at 7.7 miles. Push or hammer the last bit to the lookout itself if you want, or you can park your bike at the gate. The lookout is manned in the summer months.

Enjoy the view. To the north are Mt. Ingalls and Mt. Lassen. To the east, you can see all of Lake Davis (you'll probably see a number of boats out on the lake), to the southeast, the expansive Sierra Valley and the Sierra Buttes, and to the south, the town of Portola. The distinctive mountain to the south of town is Beckwourth Peak, named for Jim

Fragnoli

Smith Peak Lookout.

Beckwourth who discovered the lowest pass, Beckwourth Pass (5,228'), into the Sierra Nevada. The emigrant trail he pioneered (yes, the Beckwourth Trail) followed Grizzly Creek and Valley, now under the water of Lake Davis.

When you're done gawking, return the way you came. When you get back to 24N10 you can return the same way to the dam, or you could do the previous loop in reverse for extra miles around the lake.

63 Bizz Johnson Trail

Distance: 25.4 miles, 29.9 miles if you ride from the town of Westwood
Difficulty: Easy, not technical
Elevation: Begin 5,500', end 4,200'
Ride Type: One way on dirt roads and trail, some pavement; can be done as an overnight trip; can be shortened by accessing the trail at any of six trailheads; all options require a car shuttle unless you want to ride out and back
Season: May to September; check snow levels in April and October
Map: The route is very well signed with numbered interpretive stops along the way. Get a free brochure, trail map and interpretive guide from the BLM office in Susanville or the Lassen National Forest, Eagle Lake Ranger District.
Comments: If you want to make this a multi-day trip, there is a 3-day limit between trailheads. You must camp at least 1 mile from trailheads. You need a campfire permit and seasonal fire restrictions apply.

Highlights: The Bizz Johnson Trail is a poster child for the Rails-To-Trails Conservancy and the Bureau of Land Management. The first successful rails-to-trails conversion on BLM lands, the route is co-managed with the Lassen National Forest (16 miles of the trail are on National Forest lands). Named for the congressman who helped secure the right-of-way, the trail follows the old Fernley and Lassen line of the Southern Pacific Railroad.

The mellow 3-percent grade

BIZZ JOHNSON TRAIL
(west portion)

to Hwy 89

44

(connects to map on right)

Westwood
Junction

Goumaz

LASSEN
NATIONAL
FOREST

■ Parking
·–·–· Best 100 Route
——— Paved Road
▬▬▬ Freeway
– – – – Other Roads and Trails
        (bikes may be off limits)

N
⋀

⊢——— 1 mile ———⊣

©2000 Fine Edge Productions

Mason Station
Trailhead
■

↓ to Westwood

means you can ride the trail from Westwood to Susanville or vice versa. Riding it west to east (i.e., starting in Westwood) allows for a virtually all-downhill ride—and that's the route described below. Along the way you

Train at world famous Keddie Wye in the canyon.

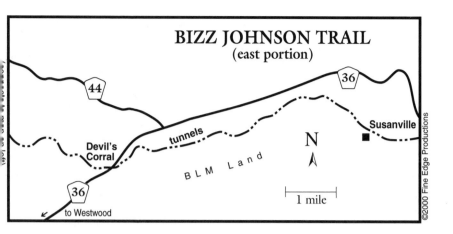

BIZZ JOHNSON TRAIL
(east portion)

44

36

tunnels

Devil's
Corral

Susanville

N

BLM Land

1 mile

36

to Westwood

©2000 Fine Edge Productions

drop from ponderosa pine forest to high desert landscape.

In addition to the route's historic interest, it travels the beautiful and rugged Susan River Canyon for 18 of its 25 miles. You cross the river 11 times on planked bridges and trestles as you make your way along this natural boundary between the Cascades to the north and the Sierra to the south. For an added thrill there are two unlighted tunnels to maneuver through.

Getting There: Leave one car at the Hobo Camp trailhead and picnic area just outside the town of Susanville (at the end of South Street) or in Susanville itself. (If you're riding from Susanville, you can access the trail at the south end of Lassen Street or Miller Road.)

From Susanville, drive the second car west on Highway 36 toward Westwood. Turn right on County Road A-21 just before you reach Westwood. Go 3 miles to County Road 101 and turn right again. The well-signed trailhead at Mason Station is a quarter-mile down Road 101 on your left.

If you're staying in Westwood,

you can ride from town to the trailhead by taking Ash Street (County Road A-21) north. Follow the signs out of old town. Cross Highway 36 and continue for 3 miles to dirt Road 101 on the right. The trail is signed before this turn. Mason Station is a quarter-mile down Road 101 on your left. This will add 4.5 miles to your total.

Route: From the back of Mason Station parking area, take the connector trail 0.25 mile to the Bizz Johnson Trail. Go right. That's about all the trail directions you need to follow this well-signed route. There are some 32 signed interpretive stops along the way. Be sure to get a copy of the "I remember when" brochure from the BLM or Lassen National Forest so you know what you're looking at.

It's 7.5 miles to Westwood Junction, the next trailhead. Along the way you ride through pine forests, which include some old-growth pines, and catch views of Pegleg Mountain to the northeast. You have nice views of the Susan River as you make your way to Goumaz Station (campground), located 12.7 miles into the ride.

Fragnoli

Trailhead sign for Bizz Johnson rail trail.

The scenery gets more and more beautiful as you continue. You can see the Diamond Range, the northernmost range of the Sierra Nevada. You cross a trestle before reaching Devil's Corral at 18.9 miles. From here, it's 6.5 miles into Susanville. This last segment is where you find the tunnels. If you find riding through the darkness disconcerting, there are trails which skirt each tunnel.

This trail should be taken at a leisurely pace. Pack a picnic lunch to enjoy along the way. Those of you who like to fish or swim may do so in the Susan River.

Chapter 10:
LAKE TAHOE

CHAPTER 10

Lake Tahoe

by R. W. Miskimins and Carol Bonser

Among Northern California's rightly celebrated landscapes, none is more spectacular than Lake Tahoe. Surrounded by the granite ruggedness of the Sierra Nevada, Lake Tahoe beckons, a turquoise jewel. While the lake itself is the focal point for much of the area's recreation, it's not the only place for awesome mountain biking.

The surrounding foothills and mountains are filled with alpine lakes and meadows, pine forests and aspen groves. You'll also find remnants of Tahoe's rich mining past as well as historic routes such as the Old Emigrant Trail (traversed by the ill-fated Donner party).

The riding is rigorous for its elevation (up to 10,000'), elevation gain, and sometimes technical terrain. But whatever sweat you pour out, your efforts will be well rewarded—often with epic panoramic views. Don't worry, we've included some easier rides in addition to classics such as The Great Flume Ride and Tahoe to Truckee.

The rides traverse the Tahoe National Forest, parts of the Toiyabe National Forest, and the Lake Tahoe Basin Management Unit. The area is dotted with campgrounds, while Tahoe itself has a wide of range of hotels, restaurants and services for those of you planning an extended vacation.

From the foothills on the western slope of the Sierra Nevada, eastward to the high country of the Lake Tahoe Basin, and southeast to the Toiyabe Forest along the Nevada border, the areas described in this chapter provide some of the most extensive, varied and beautiful mountain bike riding in the country. Located just four hours east of the San Francisco Bay Area and two hours east of Sacramento, this area offers challenging riding and gorgeous scenery.

You can begin your rides in the foothills of the Sierra in late autumn and winter on dirt logging roads that wind through oak and pine forests. As spring and summer temperatures rise, you can work your way eastward to the higher elevations, riding on jeep roads and trails that take you to the very edge of four Wilderness Areas—Granite Chief, Desolation Valley, Mokelumne and the Carson Iceberg. (Enjoy the views, but don't ride in the Wilderness Areas. Bikes are prohibited.) In June, July and August, you can still enjoy fields of flowers that you saw at lower elevations in April and May and find relief from lowland temperatures.

If you choose the right time to visit, the foothills will be full of pink dogwoods or brilliant yellow big-leaf maples. In autumn, aspen in the high country and on the eastern slopes of Hope Valley and Markleeville range from shades of yellow to gold and bright orange. And we haven't forgotten Lake Tahoe itself; we've included rides that let you see just how big and beautiful the lake really is.

Over the past decade, the Lake Tahoe area has become one of the most popular destinations for mountain biking in the entire western United States—and for good reason. For updated trail conditions and campground information, call El Dorado National Forest, Lake Tahoe Basin Management Unit or Toiyabe National Forest. (See *Agencies, Visitor Centers and Mountain Bike Clubs* in the Appendix.)

64 Hole In The Ground

Distance: 17.5 miles
Difficulty: Strenuous—you are at elevation here; technical
Elevation: 1,600' gain/loss; 8,040' high point
Ride Type: Loop on singletrack, dirt road and pavement
Season: June through October
Maps: Norden, Independence Lake, Soda Springs, Webber Peak (trail is new and is not shown on most maps); Sowarwe-Werher produces a Hole In The Ground Trail topo.
Comments: Nearest services are at Soda Springs. There are restrooms at the rest stop just east of Boreal Ridge Ski Area on Interstate 80, but no "unattended parking" is allowed here. In other words, you can't park here to do the ride. En route, there are restrooms and water at the Donner Summit/PCT trailhead (signed) 0.4 mile east of Boreal Ridge Ski Area.

Highlights: One of the newest trails in the area, the Hole In The Ground singletrack has quickly become one of the most popular trails for riders from Sacramento (the Folsom-Auburn Trail Riders Action Coalition has adopted the trail) to Reno and beyond. Rightly so, since it serves up technical trail riding, ridge running, scenic vistas and high-alpine lakes. It's so nice it almost makes you forget about all the sections of the Pacific Crest Trail in the area where you can't ride. The Forest Service even recommends that equestrians take the PCT and stay off the first 3 miles of the Hole in the Ground Trail, leaving it to mostly mountain bikers.

Because of length and elevation, the route is a tough one. But intermediate riders can certainly enjoy it—pace yourself, pack plenty of food and water, and plan for an all-day outing.

Getting There: The ride begins near Soda Springs, about 13 miles west of Truckee. From Truckee, take Interstate 80 west to the Soda Springs exit. Go right (north) on Old Donner Pass Road and right (east) again almost immediately on the paved road that leads to the fire station. Pass the fire station and continue 0.3 mile to the parking area. This is actually the trailhead for the Lower Lola Montez Lake

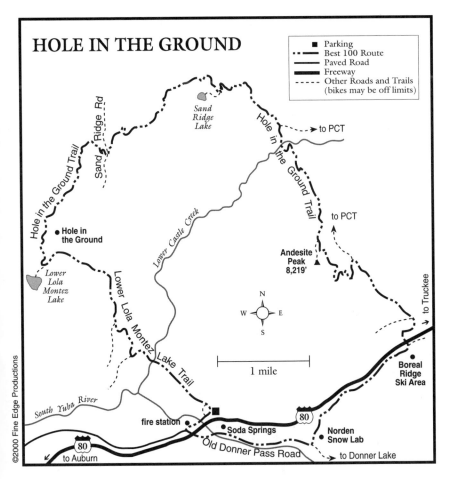

HOLE IN THE GROUND

■	Parking
▪·─·─·	Best 100 Route
───	Paved Road
▬▬▬	Freeway
-----	Other Roads and Trails (bikes may be off limits)

Sand Ridge Rd

Sand Ridge Lake

Hole in the Ground Trail

to PCT

Hole in the Ground Trail

to PCT

● Hole in the Ground

Lower Castle Creek

Andesite Peak 8,219'

Lower Lola Montez Lake

Lower Lola Montez Lake Trail

to Truckee

N
W ⊕ E
S

1 mile

Boreal Ridge Ski Area

South Yuba River

fire station

● Soda Springs

80

Norden Snow Lab

Old Donner Pass Road

to Donner Lake

80
to Auburn

©2000 Fine Edge Productions

Trail. You will finish your ride by coming down this trail.

It's also possible to do the loop from Boreal Ridge Ski Area, 4 miles east of Soda Springs on I-80. But I prefer to start at Soda Springs. Starting at Soda Springs lets you get the pavement portion of the ride over with early and, more important in my mind, gives you a better warm-up before the steep climb to Andesite Peak.

Route: From the trailhead parking area, backtrack past the fire station. Turn left on Old Donner Pass Rd. and pass under the freeway. Continue 1.5 miles on Old Donner Pass Rd. to the USDA Norden Snow Lab. Go left here onto a dirt road. Follow it for 2 miles as it climbs to Boreal Ridge Ski Area. The road turns to pavement as you near the ski resort. Follow the paved road under the freeway, re-crossing to the north side of I-80.

Climb the paved road, which turns to dirt at 4.2 miles. Ignore the dirt road on the left soon thereafter. Continue climbing. At 5.3 miles you reach a trail sign for the Hole in the Ground Trail on the left. There's a parking area here for the PCT (closed to bikes) as well. Go left onto the trail and prepare for the ride's biggest climb. It's a steep, switchbacked one, climbing almost 500 feet in a mile up the eastern slope of Andesite Peak (8,219') to Andesite Ridge. As you climb you are surrounded by old-growth forest. At 6.3 miles a trail to Andesite Peak goes to the left if you're so inclined.

From this junction, you lose almost all the elevation you've gained in the next 1.5 miles. Gravel and several switchbacks conspire to make this a slip-and-slide affair, then the trail levels and rolls on its way down to Castle Creek, reached at 7.9 miles.

Make the 0.3-mile climb to Sand Ridge Trail junction at 8.2 miles. Go left. Continue climbing and then descending gradually for the next 1.5 miles. The trail passes through open forest and crosses several small meadows—the trail is elevated here but can still get muddy. Keep climbing to the Sand Ridge Lake junction, a short spur road off to your left at 9.7 miles. I didn't go to the lake, but the Forest Service makes the sidetrip sound worthwhile, describing the lake as "a lovely, yet fragile high elevation lake which makes an ideal lunch spot." If you do go, the Forest Service asks that you please park your bike on the trail to avoid damaging the lakeshore.

Back at Sand Ridge Lake junction, the trail contours along the north side of Sand Ridge. As ridge riding usually implies, there are quite a few little ups and downs along here. At 10.9 miles you begin descending, and at 11.9 miles you cross dirt Sand Ridge Road. Continue downhill to a creek. Parallel it, then cross it, then parallel it again on the other side. You cross a side creek as you near Lower Lola Montez Lake. A trail to the lake goes to the right at 14 miles.

Enjoy another 0.5 mile of trail—you're on the Lower Lola Montez Lake Trail now. At 14.5 miles it joins a dirt road. At 15.4 miles, veer left off the road and back onto the trail. Prepare for a steep half-mile drop. At 16 miles the trail Ts into another dirt road. Go left. Drop to and cross Lower Castle Creek, a tributary of the South Yuba River. Climb out of the creek and continue toward I-80 on the dirt road. At the power pole at 17.2 miles, go left. A trail leads 0.25 mile to the parking area above the fire station.

Paved trail near Lake Tahoe

Miskimins

65 Old Emigrant Trail to Donner Peak

Distance: 18.5 miles
Difficulty: Strenuous, technical
Elevation: 5,940' to 7,840'
Ride Type: Out-and-back on jeep roads and singletrack
Season: June through October; fall is particularly scenic
Maps: Norden and Truckee
Comments: Water and restrooms are available at Donner Memorial State Park. Late in the summer you may not reach water again for 12 miles (Cold Creek). Be sure to filter or treat all water you take from streams.

Highlights: A scenic high-country ride, this route features a fun downhill on singletrack and old jeep roads. Some people may have to walk a few short sections of the uphill, but never for very long. A good ride for enjoying fall colors, this ride follows a section of the Old Emigrant Trail, which was first marked in 1924.

The whole Donner Summit area is rich in California history. Everywhere you ride, you will be reminded of the early pioneers who traveled through here on their journeys to the west. Monuments are dedicated to the tragic journey of the Donner Party, which tried to cross the Sierra during the winter of 1846–47, and to the amazing tunnel dug by hand through the mountains to complete the Central Pacific Railroad. If you enjoy history, be sure to visit the museum at the entrance to Donner Memorial State Park.

Like much of the area along Interstate 80, there is a great deal of private land in the vicinity. New gates, No Trespassing signs and No mountain bikes signs have begun to show up, closing off routes to the public. The Pacific Crest Trail also crosses through this area and it is closed to mountain bikes. This ride goes through private land, but it is open to the public.

A new 22-mile trail, the Donner Lake Rim Trail, is currently under construction in the area. At press time only a few miles had been completed. Check with rangers for the latest information when you visit.

Getting There: This ride starts and ends at Donner Memorial State Park located just off Interstate 80 on the shore of Donner Lake. From Tahoe City, go north on Highway 89 to Interstate 80. Head left (west) on 80 to Donner State Park, on your left.

Route: From Donner Memorial State Park, ride west through the park along the shore of Donner Lake. At 1.4 miles, go around the two gates that mark the western boundary of the park, and continue riding west on South Shore Drive. Turn left on Lakeview Canyon Road at 2.7 miles. It is hard to find, but if you look carefully you can see a brown Forest Service sign, *Lakeview Canyon*, almost hidden in a patch of overgrown bushes. The road starts off steep, then eases up the rest of the way into the canyon. At 3.4 miles stay right on the main road and continue climbing. At 3.8 miles go left and finish the climb up to the railroad tracks. (The right turn also goes to the tracks, but the left is more direct.)

When you reach the railroad

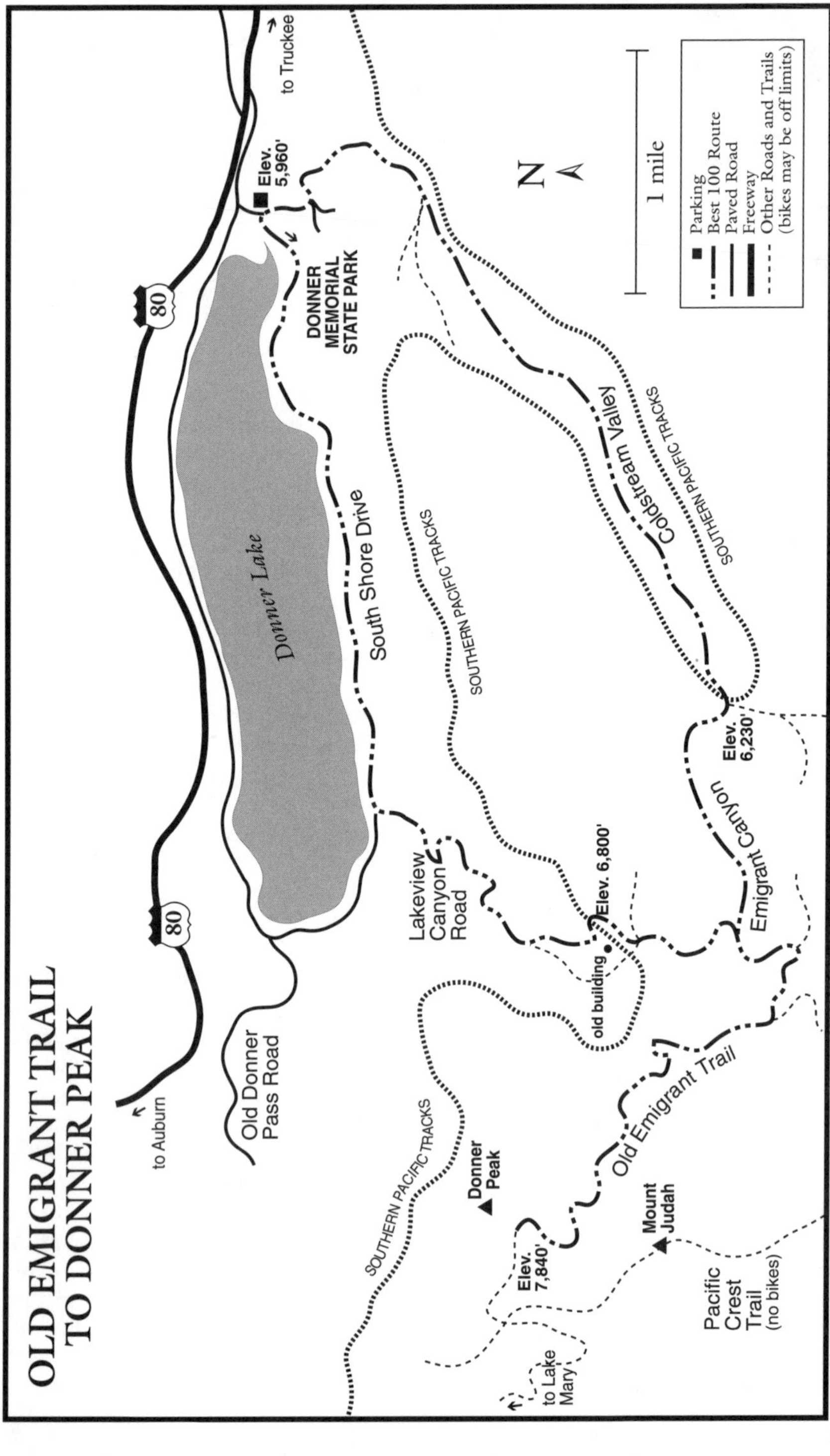

OLD EMIGRANT TRAIL TO DONNER PEAK

to Truckee

Elev. 5,960'

DONNER MEMORIAL STATE PARK

80

Donner Lake

South Shore Drive

Copstream Valley

SOUTHERN PACIFIC TRACKS

SOUTHERN PACIFIC TRACKS

Lakeview Canyon Road

Elev. 6,800'

old building

Elev. 6,230'

Emigrant Canyon

80

to Auburn

Old Donner Pass Road

SOUTHERN PACIFIC TRACKS

Donner Peak

Elev. 7,840'

Old Emigrant Trail

Mount Judah

Pacific Crest Trail (no bikes)

to Lake Mary

N

1 mile

Parking
Best 100 Route
Paved Road
Freeway
Other Roads and Trails (bikes may be off limits)

©2000 Fine Edge Productions

tracks, 4.2 miles, turn right on the road that follows along the tracks. At 4.8 miles, as the railroad tracks begin to curve into Lakeview Canyon, look across the tracks for the power lines. Ride a short distance past the lines and then carefully cross the tracks. Look for a trail that goes up the hill next to the remains of an old building. Follow this trail to the top of the saddle. (It becomes a road on the way up.) After 5.0 miles, you reach the top from which you can see Squaw Peak and the mountains of Granite Chief Wilderness to the south.

Turn right on Old Emigrant Trail at 5.4 miles. The road is very rocky at first, but smoothes out as you begin the climb up Emigrant Canyon. Old Emigrant Trail is very well marked with a variety of older and newer signs. At 6.2 miles, when you reach a small round meadow on your right, the road forks in several directions. Take the road that goes straight ahead, just to the left of the meadow. It turns into a trail, and you should still be following the old trail signs. In the next section there may be short uphills that some people will walk, but if the traction is good, the uphill is all rideable.

You reach a saddle at the base of Mount Judah at 7.6 miles and the trail again becomes a narrow road. The steep parts of the climb are over, and the road gradually climbs the rest of the way to Donner Peak. At 8.9 miles, Old Emigrant Trail reaches the saddle behind Donner Peak. Look for the monument with a sign: *Emigrant Trail Truckee River Route—Highest Point on the Truckee Route—Elevation 7,850 ft.* From here there is a trail to the top of Donner Peak (8,019'). Hike up to the top, enjoy the view, and prepare for the fun downhill ahead! When you are rested, follow your tracks back down to the intersection where you first got onto Old Emigrant Trail.

At 12.4 miles, when you reach the intersection, continue straight ahead on Old Emigrant Trail. Stay right at 13.4 miles and ride across Emigrant Creek. When the road ends at just under 14 miles, turn left and ride up to the railroad tracks. Cross when it is

Hundreds of cyclists flock to Tahoe's singletrack.

safe and continue on the main road through Coldstream Valley. Stay to the left when you reach the ponds. After you leave Coldstream Valley, 17.4 miles, you arrive at a gate that may be open or closed. Go around the gate and continue. If you are stay-ing in the park, you can enter the campground on the trail next to the split rail fence ahead. If you parked at the entrance, continue riding out the paved road, turn left by the gas sta-tions on Donner Pass Road, and ride back to your car.

66 The Great Flume Ride

Distance: 13.75 miles; 23-mile loop option
Difficulty: Intermediate, technical in places
Elevation: Start, 6,990'; low point, 6,295'; high point, 8,150'
Ride Type: Usually a shuttle, loop possible; mostly dirt road and singletrack
Season: June through October
Maps: Glenbrook, Marlette Lake; Fine Edge Productions' North Lake Tahoe Basin Recreation Topo Map
Comments: Water and restrooms are available at the picnic area at Spooner Lake.

Highlights: The Great Flume Ride is one of the true "classic" Tahoe rides, a technical ride with magnificent views the entire way. It has received considerable national attention and was labeled one of Western America's Top Ten routes. It has been pictured and described in virtually every national mountain biking magazine. It certainly ranks as the most popular off-pavement ride among the hundreds of possibilities in the Lake Tahoe area.

The ride is not technically diffi-cult, but does require basic mountain biking skills to assure safety. If you are a beginner or are afraid of heights, do not attempt the second portion of this ride (the Flume Trail itself), where you must cycle a narrow trail, sometimes alongside a steep drop-off, for over 4 miles. The first portion of the ride is the climb to Marlette Lake, an elevation gain of 1,200 feet. This part is best suited to intermediate or advanced riders.

Getting There: From South Lake Tahoe, drive northeast on U.S. 50 about 12 miles past the casinos and turn left onto Nevada State Highway 28. Continue north for about 0.5 mile before turning right into Spooner Lake State Park.

From the north shore of Lake Tahoe, take Nevada State Highway 28 south from Incline Village. Just before the junction of Highway 28 and U.S. 50, turn left into the state park. There is a parking fee which is used to maintain the park's trails.

Depending on enthusiasm, stami-na, skill, and vehicle availability, there are different ways to approach this ride. Described below is the basic Spooner to Sand Harbor route (via Highway 28). This route follows Ser-vice Road 504 (North Canyon Road) from Spooner Lake to Marlette Lake, then the Flume Trail from Marlette Lake to Tunnel Creek Road, and fin-ishes by descending Tunnel Creek

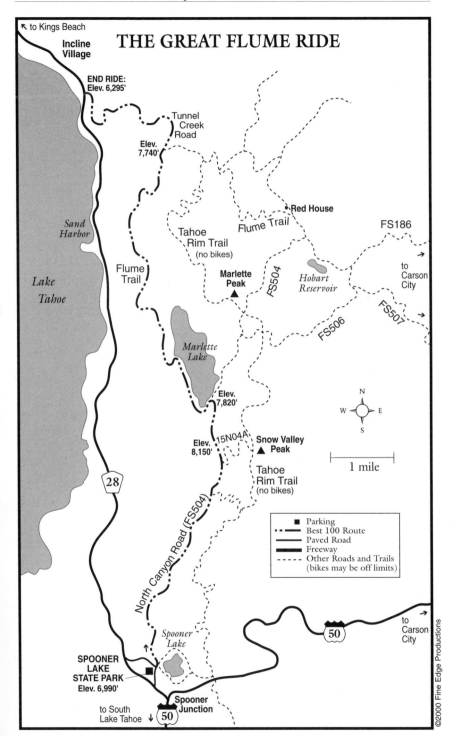

THE GREAT FLUME RIDE

to Kings Beach

Incline Village

END RIDE:
Elev. 6,295'

Tunnel Creek Road

Elev. 7,740'

Red House

Flume Trail

FS186

Sand Harbor

Tahoe Rim Trail
(no bikes)

Flume Trail

Marlette Peak ▲

FS504

Hobart Reservoir

to Carson City

Lake Tahoe

FS506

FS507

Marlette Lake

Elev. 7,820'

Elev. 8,150'

15N04A

Snow Valley Peak ▲

N
W ⊹ E
S

1 mile

Tahoe Rim Trail
(no bikes)

28

North Canyon Road (FS504)

■ Parking
▪▪▪ Best 100 Route
— Paved Road
▬▬ Freeway
- - - Other Roads and Trails
(bikes may be off limits)

Spooner Lake

50

to Carson City

SPOONER LAKE STATE PARK
Elev. 6,990'

Spooner Junction

to South Lake Tahoe ↓ 50

©2000 Fine Edge Productions

Fragnoli

Beginning of Flume Trail at Marlette Lake.

Fragnoli

Technical section near the beginning of the Flume Trail.

Road back down to Highway 28 between Sand Harbor and Incline Village. This approach to the Great Flume Ride involves leaving a car in the Sand Harbor area to shuttle people and bikes back to Spooner Lake State Park.

Route: Begin the Great Flume Ride by cycling east from the parking lot toward Spooner Lake and turn left (north) up North Canyon Road toward Marlette Lake (follow the signs). You then begin the long climb to the ridge just before Marlette Lake, an elevation gain of just over 1,200 feet. As with many climbs, this one gets steeper as you go. At 2.8 miles you reach the first of the backcountry campgrounds. Continue straight ahead.

At 3.9 miles you pass a

right turn to Snow Valley Peak (9,214'). A trip to the peak is not long (about 1.5 miles one way), but involves over 1,000 feet of elevation gain on a rough and rocky jeep trail (for strong riders only). If you choose to take this side trip, you will encounter a breathtaking, world-class view. Its breadth is so remarkable only a panorama camera would have any possibility of capturing it on film. The view of Lake Tahoe from Snow Valley Peak is as good as it gets. The north-south singletrack you encounter up high on the mountain is the Tahoe Rim Trail and is closed to mountain bikes.

If you're not interested in this detour, continue ahead on the main road to Marlette Lake (the climbing is almost over). You crest the ridge and start downhill at 4.2 miles. When you reach the lake at 5 miles, consider a break and a little exploring time.

When you are ready to press on, turn left and ride around to the west side of the lake. The road ends by the dam at 6.2 miles. Look off to the left end of the dam (southeast) for the sign for the Flume Trail. (Early in the riding season the beginning of the trail can actually be under water.) Ride or walk the steep and rocky little section of trail across Marlette Creek and around a bend, and you will be on the Flume Trail.

The Flume Trail is a narrow, 4.5-mile singletrack following the ridge to the north about 1,500 vertical feet above Lake Tahoe. If you are not a confident, experienced mountain biker or are frightened by heights, you should turn around and head back to Spooner Lake. In fact, the most popular option for the Great Flume Ride is to ride from Spooner Lake to Marlette Lake and back. This is a scenic, relatively easy 10-mile out-and-back, suitable to hardy beginners and better.

The Flume Trail follows the route of an old wooden flume that carried

View of Lake Tahoe from Flume Trail

View of Lake Tahoe from the Flume Trail.

water and logs to Virginia City, Nevada, during the Comstock silver mining boom. Now about 125 years later, there are still a few pieces of the flume along the trail and some of the pipes that replaced the original wooden structure.

Ride the Flume Trail carefully; slow down or stop often to enjoy the fantastic view of the Lake Tahoe Basin. You should consider bringing a camera along for this ride. There are great photo opportunities—you can get pictures of cyclists riding through the trees or alongside white granite walls with beautiful Lake Tahoe and the surrounding mountains as the backdrop.

At 10.6 miles from Spooner Lake State Park, the Flume Trail ends as you intersect Tunnel Creek Road. Bear left and begin the sometimes steep, sometimes sandy, and sometimes washboarded 3-mile descent to Highway 28 at Hidden Beach. Exercise caution on this downhill; ride in control at all times.

When you reach the pavement at 13.75 miles, turn left to head toward Sand Harbor or right to Incline Village to find your shuttle car. Where Tunnel Creek Road intersects Highway 28, you are 9 narrow, heavily-trafficked highway miles north of the Spooner Lake State Park parking lot.

Option: When riders reach Tunnel Creek Road at the end of the Flume Trail, many prefer to turn right and make a big loop east, then south, around Marlette Peak. This would make a 23-mile loop. If you choose this route, you do considerably more climbing.

To make this loop ride, turn right from the end of the Flume Trail and climb to the top of the ridge. At 11.1 miles, continue straight at the Twin Lakes Road and watch for another section of the Flume Trail to your right at 11.8 miles. If you miss this right turn, continue ahead and take the next main road turning right. Either route takes you past the Red House, an old flume tender's home built in 1910.

Follow the Flume Trail as it contours around the east side of the Carson Range. Watch out for downed trees. Some of them you can ride over, others you can ride under, and some you may have to portage around.

At 14.2 miles, your trail ends at a small diversion dam. Walk across the dam, up to the main road, and turn right. About a half-mile later, 14.7 miles, turn right on Forest Service Road 504 (North Canyon Road). It soon crosses Franktown Creek and you begin a hot, exposed 1-mile climb with nearly 1,000 feet of elevation gain. At 15.9 miles you reach the top. Continue on out the ridge.

At 16.3 miles the road forks.

Although it may seem like it is time to go downhill, continue straight ahead. After a bit more ridge riding, the road quickly descends to Marlette Lake. At 19 miles you are back at Marlette Lake and have completed the loop part of the ride. Turn left at the intersection and follow the signs back to Spooner Summit.

After a short—but steep—climb, it's time for 4 miles of downhill. This section can get quite wild—sand seems to be in all the turns. Be sure to watch out for hikers, horseback riders and other cyclists. Stay on the right side of the road and control your speed at all times. Upon returning to Spooner Lake, you will have finished 23 miles of some of the best pedaling on dirt that America has to offer.

67 South Camp Peak Loop

Distance: 16.5 miles
Difficulty: Strenuous intermediate-to-advanced ride
Elevation: 2,200' gain/loss
Ride Type: Loop on 4WD roads
Season: Mid-May through October
Map: Glenbrook (Nevada)
Comments: Water at Logan House Creek—treat!

Highlights: The South Camp Loop takes you through several large aspen groves, making this a fantastic fall color ride. The most scenic time to do the ride is probably just after the first freeze, some time in mid-October, when the aspens turn from shiny green to bright yellow and orange. If you choose to ride in the fall, be prepared for that first snowfall of the season. Dress in layers, carry tights and a windbreaker.

Getting There: From South Lake Tahoe, continue east on U.S. 50 past

the casinos and on up the east shore of Lake Tahoe. Stay on U.S. 50 to Spooner Junction where Highway 28 intersects with 50. Look on the southeast side of the road for the highway maintenance station and turn in here. Park out of the way near the maintenance station. Please be aware that the nearby section of the Tahoe Rim Trail (and the route from the Spooner Lake area to Genoa Peak) is closed to mountain bikes. The Forest Service has made that closure because Genoa Peak Road is nearby and basically covers the same territory.

Scenic Sierras near South Camp Peak Loop.

Route: Consider riding back and forth on the flats along the highway before starting. Try to stretch and loosen up a bit because this ride goes up right away. After loosening up, ride out the road behind the maintenance station—Genoa Peak Road. At 0.9 mile, stay right on Genoa Peak Road (road to left climbs to the top of White Hill and dead-ends). 0.6 mile farther on, the loop begins and ends. This ride can be done in either direction with good ups and downs either way. These directions continue clockwise. Stay left on the road marked 14N32. At the intersection at

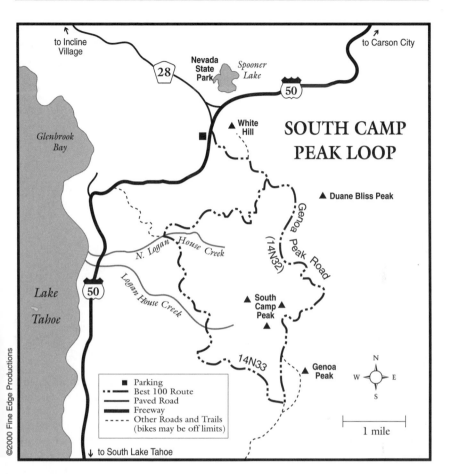

1.8 miles, you may want to go left a short distance to the overlook where the mountains drop straight down to the Carson Valley. After taking a look, continue right on 14N32.

The road continues to climb gradually at first, then the road surface turns to loose rock and gets much steeper. If it's not too torn up and you have the determination, it's all rideable, though you may choose to walk certain sections. When you reach the switchback, the climb is almost over. 0.8 mile: You top out on the ridge of South Camp Peak, 8,700 feet. South Camp Peak is a large plateau with three peaks rising up from the flat.

Continue left on the main road. Then it's time for the downhill to begin. 1.5 miles: This is the southernmost point of the ride; go right to follow the loop. If you continue straight ahead, the road leads to Kingsbury Grade (4 miles of dirt, then 2 miles of pavement). If you start to climb again you missed this turn.

2.8 miles: You reach Logan House Creek, a small creek in a shady aspen grove. This creek was the only creek on this ride still running in September during the drought of 1988. Be sure to filter or treat all water. Continue on for some more winding downhill with lots of waterbars. 1.8

miles: You cross North Logan House Creek (dry by the end of summer). Turn right to finish the loop. The last climb snakes through a meadow, then winds its way back up to the top of the ridge. The next section contours around Montreal Canyon and then climbs to the top. At 2.5 miles, stay right on the main road. It is 0.4 mile back to the intersection of Genoa Peak Road. Go left and enjoy the last downhill back to your car.

68 Mr. Toad's Wild Ride

Distance: 13 miles one way or 22-mile loop
Difficulty: Advanced, technical
Elevation: Start at 7,320'; low point 6,340'; high point 8,820'
Ride Type: Shuttle or loop on trail and pavement
Season: June through October
Maps: Freel Peak, South Lake Tahoe; Fine Edge Productions' South Lake Tahoe Basin Recreation Topo Map
Comments: Services in Meyers

Highlights: Mr. Toad's Wild Ride draws its colorful name from the exciting descent on the Saxon Creek Trail from Tucker Flat to nearly lake level. It is a relentless downhill run—a drop of nearly 1,500 feet in less than 6 miles. What comes down must first go up, however.

This is definitely not a ride for novices. The climb is not very long (just over 4 miles), but it is narrow, steep, and sometimes extremely rocky and technical. The descent, at anything faster than a crawl, requires good riding skills and good judgment. Almost everyone will walk at least a few places during this ride.

Getting There: From South Lake Tahoe, go west on U.S. 50 to Meyers. Leave one car in Meyers. There are numerous places to park—for example, the Lake Tahoe Basin Interagency Visitors Center. To get to the ride start from Meyers, turn left on Highway 89 and travel south to the Big Meadow Trailhead for the Tahoe Rim Trail. If you are going to make a complete loop (which adds about 9 miles), park in Meyers and pedal the uphill section on Highway 89.

Route: Start this ride at Big Meadow Trailhead (if you pedaled from Meyers, reset your mileage here) by heading north on the Tahoe Rim Trail in the direction of Armstrong Pass and Star Lake. At 0.5 mile, carry your bike across the creek, then continue climbing. The trail is narrow, uphill singletrack with lots of switchbacks and numerous rocks, in a beautiful, wooded, Sierra Nevada setting.

At just over two miles, don't turn right across the bridge over the creek; instead, continue straight ahead. From here the climb gets tougher (steeper, more winding, and rockier). At about 3.5 miles you begin riding along the ridge. You can catch a few glimpses of Lake Tahoe to your left. At 4.25 miles, you reach the summit of the ride (8,820 feet).

You encounter a three-way intersection at just over 4.5 miles. There is a 4x4 post sign indicating that a left

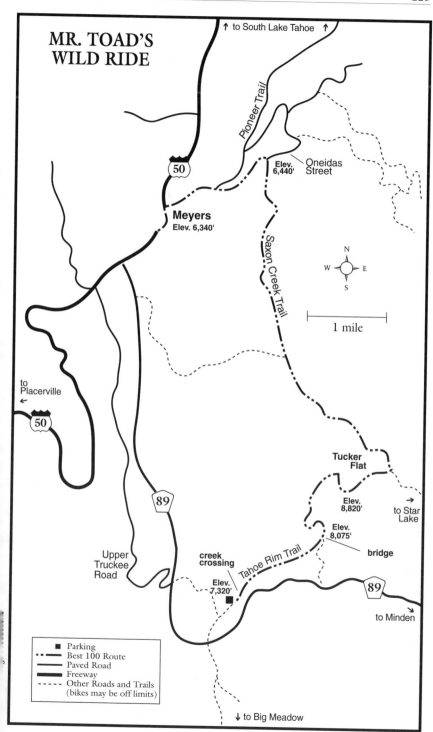

turn puts you on the Saxon Creek Trail. Turn left here and ride through Tucker Flat to begin the rapid descent alongside Saxon Creek. The descent is sometimes steep and sometimes technical, but always fun if you ride in control. There are some corners that are nicely banked for high-speed turning, and most of the trail is getting wider from increased use over the past few years. The last mile or so flattens out and follows an old fire road.

At 10.5 miles you reach Oneidas Street, a narrow, paved, single-lane. Be aware that near the end of the descent there are multiple options for connecting with Oneidas and/or returning to Meyers. You need to go west (or northwest) if you find yourself off the beaten path. Turn left on Oneidas; then at 11.5 miles, turn left on Pioneer Trail. At 12.5 miles, go left on U.S. 50. Less than a mile later, your ride ends in Meyers.

69 Angora Lakes

Distance: 8 miles; 11 miles from Fallen Leaf Campground
Difficulty: Easy, not technical
Elevation: 770' gain/loss, 1,200' from the campground
Ride Type: Out-and-back on pavement and dirt road
Season: June through October
Maps: Echo Lake; Fine Edge Production's South Lake Tahoe Basin Recreation Topo Map
Comments: Water and restrooms at campgrounds in the area

Highlights: This is a fun ride, especially if you are staying in the Fallen Leaf or Camp Richardson areas. You can start right from your campsite. You travel past several lakes and you get some great views without too

One of Lake Tahoe's popular bike paths along the Truckee River

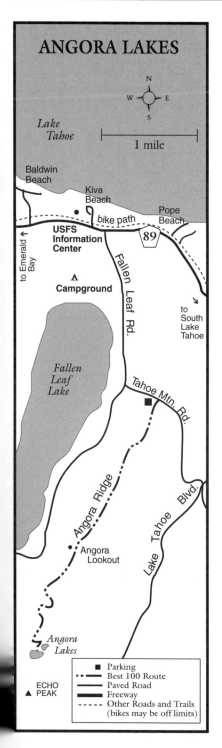

ANGORA LAKES

N
W — E
S

|——————————————|
1 mile

Lake Tahoe

Baldwin Beach

Kiva Beach

bike path

Pope Beach

89

to Emerald Bay

USFS Information Center

Fallen Leaf Rd.

▲ Campground

to South Lake Tahoe

Fallen Leaf Lake

Tahoe Mtn. Rd.

Angora Ridge

Lake Tahoe Blvd.

Angora Lookout

Angora Lakes

ECHO PEAK

■ Parking
▪·▪·▪ Best 100 Route
——— Paved Road
▬▬▬ Freeway
- - - - Other Roads and Trails
(bikes may be off limits)

much climbing.

Getting There: From South Lake Tahoe, go north on Highway 89 along the southwest side of Lake Tahoe to the road to Fallen Leaf Lake (1 mile past Camp Richardson). Turn left and go past Fallen Leaf Campground. At a little over 1.75 miles, turn left on a paved road that goes uphill. After 0.4 mile, turn right on the dirt road. There is parking for several cars along the road just before you turn on Road 1214. If you have a larger group, or want a longer ride, park back by Fallen Leaf Campground.

Route: This is an easy ride to follow; just stay on Angora Ridge Road. (Some sections of the road are paved.) After a bit of a climb (600'), you come out on Angora Ridge with a spectacular view in all directions. At 1.5 miles you reach the old Angora Lookout. Take a topo map with you so you can recognize the surrounding peaks—Mt. Tallac and Angora Peak— then look down on Fallen Leaf Lake and a corner of Lake Tahoe.

When you are ready, continue south toward Angora Lakes. At 3.0 miles the road arrives at a large parking lot and a gate. This is the end of the road for motor vehicles. Check the sign. Hikers, horseback riders and mountain bikes are all still allowed on the trail (an old road) to the lakes. There's plenty of room for everyone, but be sure to watch out for hikers and horseback riders.

The lower lakes are quieter, with most of the hikers heading to the upper lake. If you ride to the upper lake (4.0 miles), be prepared to park your bike. The resort owners have built a log bike rack, complete with locks and chains. Lock your bike, then go to the resort and give them your name and the number of your lock. The idea is to provide a safe place to park bikes and to keep the bikes off the beach area. The resort sells lemonade, ice cream and candy bars and rents small rowboats, so you can take a "cruise" on the lake. Swimming is good here, too.

From here, follow your tracks back to your car. Stay in control at all times and watch out for hikers. Then watch out for vehicles once you reach the road.

70 Barker Pass Loop

Distance: 23 miles
Difficulty: Advanced, with high elevations
Elevation: 6,230' to 8,740'
Ride Type: Loop on dirt roads, 4WD trails and singletrack
Season: June through October
Map: Homewood
Comments: Water available from Barker Creek. Treat all water.

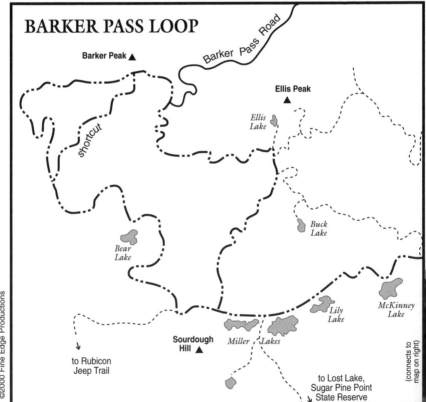

BARKER PASS LOOP

Barker Peak ▲

Barker Pass Road

Ellis Peak ▲

Ellis Lake

shortcut

Buck Lake

Bear Lake

Lily Lake

McKinney Lake

Sourdough Hill ▲

Miller Lakes

to Rubicon Jeep Trail

to Lost Lake, Sugar Pine Point State Reserve

(connects to map on right)

©2000 Fine Edge Productions

Highlights: This ride takes in part of the extremely popular Rubicon Jeep Trail. An incredibly scenic high-country route, the jeep trail travels across the crest along the edge of Desolation Wilderness and ends in the town of Tahoma. This loop is rough and rocky with many granite slabs to ride and many boulder creek crossings.

Getting There: The ride begins near the town of Tahoma on the West Shore of Lake Tahoe. From Highway 89 near Tahoma, go west on McKinney-Rubicon Springs Road, located just south of Chambers Lodge, and follow the signs for McKinney-Rubicon OHV Access. When the road turns to dirt, look for a place to park.

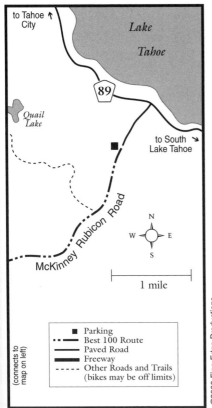

Route: Continue on the McKinney-Rubicon Road on your bike. The road is known for its boulder creek crossings, most of which are dry by August. The boulders are impressive, stacked together by years of 4WD traffic. Riders not used to riding the rocks may think these sections are unrideable, but if you find the right gear (low, but not too low), get up off the saddle and keep the pedals spinning, you can ride through them all.

0.7 mile: Look off to your right for a side road that crosses a bridge. This road leads to Ellis Peak, another ride in the area. Continue straight ahead. 1.3 miles: Continue on the main road to Miller Lakes. (The 4WD road to the right climbs to Buck Lake, then on up to Ellis Peak. We have ridden UP this road once. It climbs 900 feet in 1.2 miles, often through rocky sections. We probably pushed as much as we rode the first part of this road. If you choose to come down this one, use caution. This route is technical in both directions.)

1.2 miles: Off to your left is the first in a series of lakes—McKinney Lake. Next you pass Lily Lake, then Upper and Lower Miller Lakes. This series of lakes is full of lily pads. 2 miles: Just as you pass Lower Miller Lake, you see a road to the left. This road goes to Richardson Lake, Lost Lake and Sugar Pine Point State Park. Continue straight ahead. Just past Upper Miller Lake, another jeep road enters from the right. It is a steep climb to Ellis Peak (Buck Lake Road joins this one). This is one of those roads that's a dream to come down and a definite workout in the uphill direction. This will be your return route. For now continue on past this road.

A half mile farther, the road splits (to the left is the Rubicon Trail that

Riding a sandy singletrack.

Miskimins

then takes you past "Red Cabin Estates," an old cabin in great condition, painted bright red. Continue on the main road that suddenly starts climbing. Like most short cuts, it is steeper, but it's a much quicker route to Barker Pass. If you choose the road up Barker Creek, you will be riding through private land. Be sure to stay on the road; no camping allowed.

2 miles (on the short cut), 3.5 miles (on the main road): Both roads meet at the top of Barker Pass. This is a great spot to enjoy the view in all directions. Take a rest, refuel and get ready for a bit of pushing. When you are ready to go, turn right (east) on Barker Pass Road. 0.5 mile: Just as the road changes from dirt to pavement, look to your right and you'll see the motorcycle/hiking trail. The trail climbs 600 feet in about seven switchbacks, some of which are rideable, but if it hasn't rained in a while the soil will be loose and most people will push the first part. The view from the next stretch of trail is spectacular. To the southwest you can see Loon Lake (the biggest lake) and the rocky terrain of Desolation Valley Wilderness Area. To the northwest are Blackwood Canyon and Lake Tahoe. After some fun, singletrack downhill, the trail begins to climb again toward the top of Ellis Peak. 2 miles: The trail ends at a sign indicating Ellis Lake to the left. A left here takes you to Ellis Lake in 0.4 mile. Go right to continue the loop. 0.3 mile: The road splits.

goes to Rubicon Springs and Loon Lake). Go to the right on the road to Barker Pass. The first mile is all up on a good dirt surface. After climbing to the top of the ridge, you descend toward Bear Lake. Then the road circles the lake and continues. There are roads all through this section—just remember to stay on the main road unless you want to go exploring. At 4.0 miles you leave the lake and climb some more. If you look carefully, you should see where the Pacific Crest Trail (closed to bikes) crosses the road.

0.4 mile farther on, you cross Barker Creek. The main road continues straight ahead, winds around, gradually climbing, then eventually reaches Barker Pass. The jeep road to the right (just after you cross the creek) is a short cut to the top. The jeep road follows Barker Creek, goes along the edge of Barker Meadows,

Continue straight ahead. (This may happen anyway if you are rapidly descending.) The next 3 miles is a fast descent with one rest spot when you reach a large meadow at North Miller Creek. This road drops from 8,200 feet to Miller Meadows at 7,100 feet in three miles—most of the drop in the last 1.5 miles. Be careful. Some of the steep sections are loose and rocky. The road ends at McKinney Road. Turn left and enjoy 5 more miles of downhill back to your car. Watch out for the boulder patches—they actually seem rougher on the way down than on the way up.

71 Miller Lake Loop

Distance: 14 miles
Difficulty: Advanced
Elevation: Start, 6,230'; low point, 6,230'; high point, 7,320'
Ride Type: Loop on pavement, dirt road, and singletrack
Season: June through October
Maps: Meeks Bay, Homewood; Fine Edge Production's North Lake Tahoe Basin Recreation Topo Map
Comments: Water and restrooms at General Creek Campground

Highlights: Miller Lake Loop is best suited to advanced riders. It has about as much variability in riding surface as you will find on any regularly ridden route in the Lake Tahoe Basin. You ride on highways, residential streets, wide dirt thoroughfares, narrow, boulder-strewn 4WD roads, well-groomed, smooth singletrack, and treacherous, rocky, 18-inch-wide paths. Only a little over 3 miles of the ride is on pavement, and most of it is deep in the Sierra forest. This ride is a challenging and scenic mountain biking getaway.

Getting There: Start at General Creek Campground just south of Tahoma, off Highway 89 on the west side of Lake Tahoe. For a small fee, you can park your vehicle in one of the day-use areas.

Route: From the entrance to General Creek Campground, ride through the campground in a northwesterly direction, following the signs to camp spaces 149 and 151. Between these two spaces, about .75 mile from the entrance, ride onto the dirt road headed west. You are on a loop from the campground that is very popular for cyclists and hikers and, when the snow falls, for cross-country skiers as well.

At just over one mile, you come to a large sign reading *Meadows in the Tahoe Basin* where you continue west on the main road. At just over 2.2 miles, the main trail turns left to loop back to the campground. You continue straight ahead onto singletrack. A sign at this point indicates that Lily Pond and Lost Lake lie ahead.

Ride and walk the narrow, sometimes technical, singletrack until a turn at 3 miles. The trail straight ahead goes to Lily Pond and bicycles are not allowed. Turn left, following the signs directing you toward Lost Lake. At 5 miles the trail crosses General Creek. A half-mile later, your trail

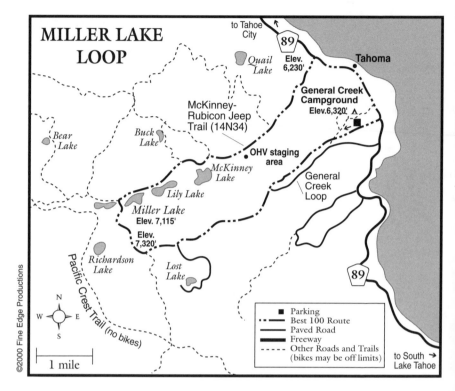

ends at a jeep road T, where you turn right (the left is a dead-end road going to Duck Lake and Lost Lake).

After your right turn at 5.5 miles, you cross the creek again and climb up the ridge. At nearly 6.5 miles, you crest the ridge and start downhill to reach Miller Lake. At 7.2 miles (next to Miller Lake), you come to another T where you turn right on the Rubicon Jeep Trail. Be warned that the Rubicon road has areas of boulders that can give novice cyclists problems. Jeep traffic has packed them tightly together, so most of the boulder fields are rideable if you don't slow down too much.

Ride east and northeast, past Miller, Lily and McKinney lakes, all on your right. At about 10 miles, just after a brief and tricky rocky downhill, you pass an OHV staging area on

your right (with restrooms). At 10.7 miles, you pass a road going across a bridge left (to Quail Lake). Continue ahead on the Rubicon Jeep Trail until you reach pavement at 11.5 miles.

Once on pavement in a residential neighborhood, follow the signs to Highway 89 (Springs Road, Bellevue, McKinney-Rubicon Springs Road). Reaching Highway 89, you've ridden 12.5 miles. Go right (south) through Tahoma. Most of this part of your ride is on a paved bicycle trail paralleling the highway. At 13.75 miles turn into General Creek Campground and head for your car in the parking lot. Arriving back at your car, your total ride without sidetrips has been 14 miles.

Option: An extremely popular ride for beginning mountain bike enthusiasts is the General Creek Campground Loop. Starting from the day-use parking area, ride the route described above to the point where you go onto singletrack (2.25 miles). Instead of going ahead toward Lost Lake, stay on the main trail swinging left and across the bridge. Consider riding on the long wooden ramp just for fun. At 2.5 miles, swing left back onto a wide trail across the bridge. At 3.75

miles turn left, crossing the creek on a big bridge, to end the loop part of this ride at just over 4 miles (at the sign about meadows). Go right to return to your car. When you reach the parking lot, you've completed a total ride of about 5.2 miles. This loop, all on relatively smooth roads and trails, is suited to riders of all levels, with the total elevation gain of only 200 feet.

72 Ward Creek Loop

Distance: 15.5 miles
Difficulty: Intermediate
Elevation: Start, 6,240'; low point, 6,185'; high point, 7,280'
Ride Type: Loop on pavement and dirt
Season: June through October
Maps: Tahoe City; Fine Edge Production's North Lake Tahoe Basin Recreation Topo Map
Comments: Water and restrooms available at William Kent Campground

Highlights: This ride is well-suited to intermediate riders or better. It is only moderately strenuous and not very technical, with about two-thirds of the route on pavement. Beginners with strength and endurance can also do well on this ride.

Getting There: From the Y in Tahoe City (junction of Highways 89 and 28), drive south about .25 mile. Turn right and park at the Truckee River Access Bike Trail Parking. This is a large parking lot to accommodate the hundreds of cyclists who ride in this area every day all summer.

Route: From where you parked, ride your bike out of the parking area (retrace the route you drove in). At just under .25 mile, just before Highway 89, turn right onto the paved bicycle trail that runs alongside the

Lake Tahoe bike rental

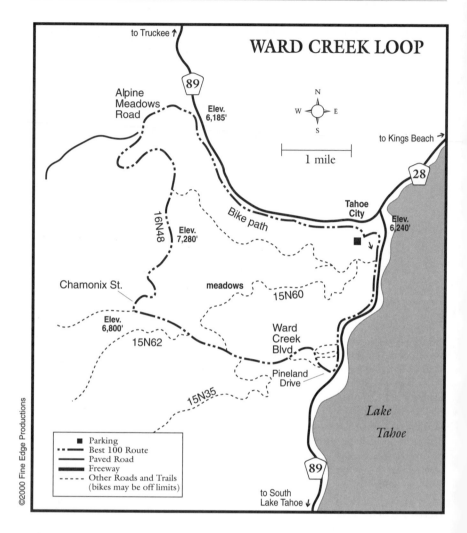

highway. Ride south past William Kent Campground.

At 2.2 miles, turn right onto Pineland Drive (look for two large poles with "Pineland" carved into them). About 0.5 mile later, turn left onto Twin Peaks Drive. A sign at this turn points to Ward Valley. Stay on the main road as the name changes to Ward Creek Boulevard, and later to Courchevel Road (5 miles from where you started).

Turn right onto Chamonix Street

at 5.2 miles. When the pavement ends (just over 5.5 miles), take the dirt road directly ahead. Ride up a short hill, then go right on the main road marked 16N48. At 6.7 miles, after crossing a creek bed, stay on the main trail to the left. After 8 miles of cycling, you can catch some views of the Truckee River below and Lake Tahoe behind you for about a half-mile. The road then swings west through an abandoned ski area. After a brief view down into Alpine Meadows, the descent begins!

The dirt road you've been following ends at a Forest Service gate, 10.2 miles from where you started the ride. Continue down the paved road (Snow Crest). At just over 10.5 miles, turn right onto Alpine Meadows Road. When you reach Highway 89 (11.5 miles), turn right and pick up the paved trail along the south side of the road. Follow this trail back to the Y, turn right, and cycle back to the parking lot for a total mileage of 15.5 miles.

West Lake Bike Path at Tahoe

Option 1: A popular option for the Ward Creek Loop makes it shorter, easier (eliminates most of the climbing) and less of a pavement ride. It requires shuttling cyclists to the start of the dirt at the end of Chamonix Street. This eliminates about 5.5 miles, reducing the total ride mileage to 10 miles. For a second variation that makes an easier and shorter ride (11 miles total), 1.5 miles after you turn left onto Twin Peaks Road, watch for a left turn onto a dirt road called Upper Ward Creek. Follow the main road (there are several turns available for exploration) until the road ends, then turn around and ride back to where you started.

Option 2: Another popular option to the Ward Creek Loop is to add a loop past Paige Meadow, or to ride it as a separate, short (about 10 miles) beginner route. Pick up this loop between the Truckee River Access parking lot and William Kent Campground. Follow the signs to Granlibakken Ski Resort (the turn is about one mile south of the Tahoe City Y). Just before the resort, turn left on Rawhide and stay on it as it turns to dirt. At about 4 miles from the highway, you come to Paige Meadow (a group of several large meadows). Go west through the meadows and head southwest to connect with Ward Creek Blvd. A left turn takes you back to where you started in Tahoe City.

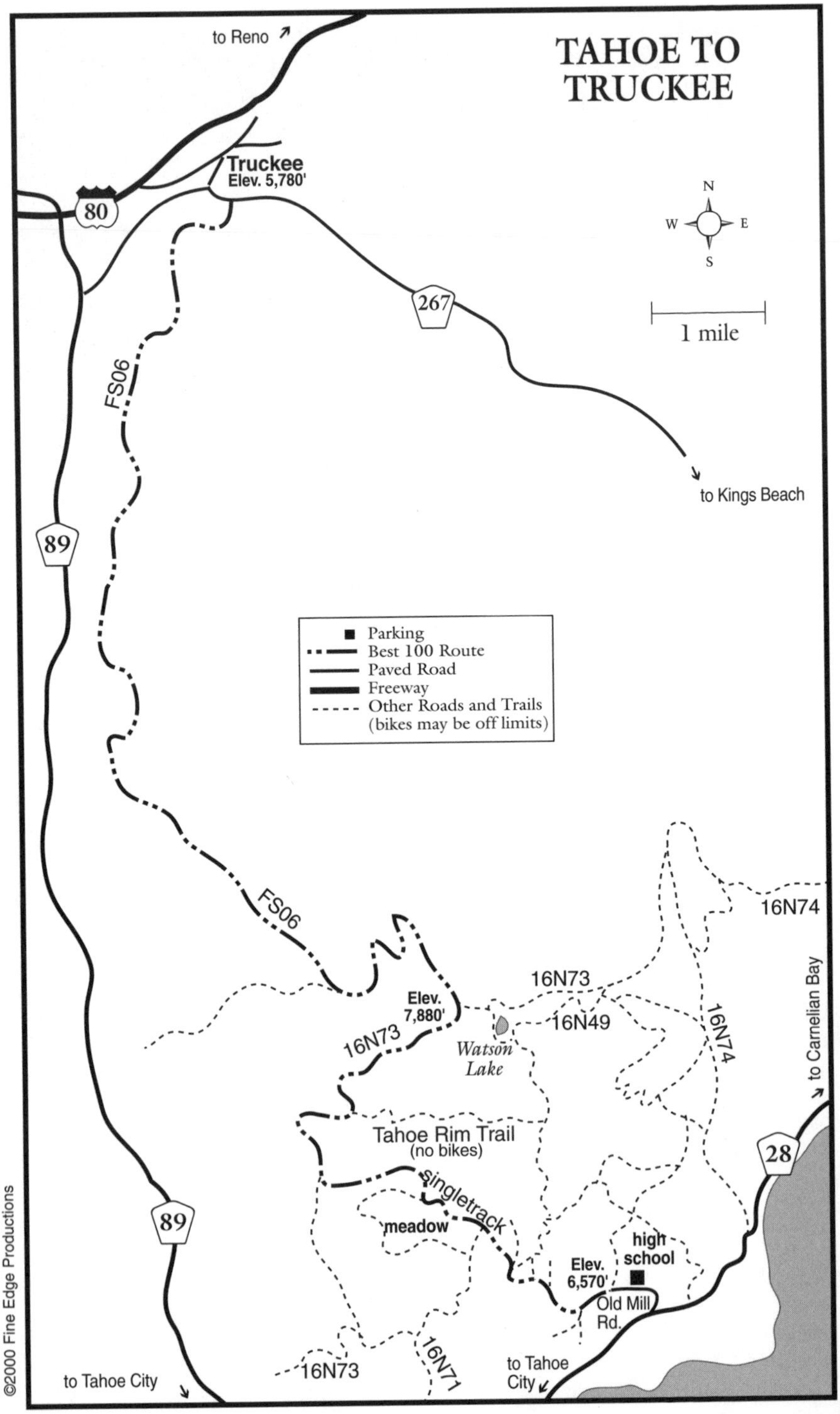

TAHOE TO TRUCKEE

to Reno

Truckee
Elev. 5,780'

80

267

89

FS06

to Kings Beach

N
W   E
S

1 mile

Parking
Best 100 Route
Paved Road
Freeway
Other Roads and Trails
(bikes may be off limits)

FS06

16N74

16N73

Elev.
7,880'

16N73

16N49

Watson
Lake

16N74

Tahoe Rim Trail
(no bikes)

28

singletrack

meadow

Elev.
6,570'

high
school

to Carnelian Bay

89

16N73

16N71

Old Mill
Rd.

to Tahoe
City

to Tahoe City

©2000 Fine Edge Productions

Miskimins

Truckee River Access Bike Trail parking lot

73 Tahoe to Truckee

Distance: 17.5 miles
Difficulty: Intermediate
Elevation: Start, 6,570'; low point, 5,780'; high point, 7,880'
Ride Type: Shuttle with varied riding on pavement, dirt road and singletrack
Season: June through October
Maps: Kings Beach, Tahoe City, Truckee; Fine Edge Production's North Lake Tahoe Basin Recreation Topo Map
Comments: No water along the way

Highlights: Sometimes called the TNT, Tahoe to Truckee is one of the most popular rides in the Lake Tahoe area—due, in part, to its great variety. There are long sections of climbing, flat riding, and descending. Although it is entirely on dirt, the trail surface ranges from wide, well-groomed road to narrow (but not very technical) singletrack to rocky, non-maintained jeep trail. Due to its length, the climbing involved, and a few rough spots here and there, the Tahoe to Truckee route is best suited to inter-

mediate riders. The hardiest mountain bikers approach it as an out-and-back, with a total distance of between 35 and 45 miles, depending on where they start and end and where they turn around. With between 4,000 and 5,000 cumulative feet of climbing, they certainly get plenty of riding for one day.

Getting There: Start at North Lake Tahoe High School in Tahoe City. Please note that locals start this ride from various locations, including a

Historic Truckee

singletrack access from the Highlands Community Center. The simplest route, however, begins at the high school. From the Highway 28/89 junction in Tahoe City, drive or cycle north on Highway 28 (through town). At Old Mill Road (about 2.5 miles), turn left. At 3 miles turn left on Polaris Road at the top of the hill. Continue 0.4 mile farther to the end of the pavement just past the high school. Park your vehicle here out of the way of school traffic. If you ride your bike to this point, you've added a little over 3 miles to the one-way Tahoe to Truckee mileage.

For a shuttle, leave a car at the north end of dirt road FS06 near Truckee. From Truckee, drive south on Highway 267, turn right on Palisades Road (0.5 mile), turn right on Silver Fir Drive (1.5 miles) after Palisades becomes Ponderosa, then turn left onto Thelin Drive (1.75 miles) and find the green gate for Forest Service Road 06 (2 miles) off to your left. Park the shuttle vehicle here.

Route: Most often ridden one way after shuttling a vehicle, this ride offers a delightful tour of the Sierra from Lake Tahoe to the town of Truckee. Beginning just past the pavement at North Lake Tahoe High School, continue ahead on dirt. At just under a quarter of a mile, you pass a sign for Burton Creek State Park. A few hundred feet later (just under a third of a mile), turn right and start up the hill (straight swings left and down through a creek bed).

Just past a yellow sign—*California State Park Property* (0.75 mile)— go left at the fork. At just under 1.2 miles, swing left at a sloppy four-way intersection. (A right turn here can get you back to Highway 28, a few miles east of Old Mill Road.) Continue on the main road about 2.7 miles (just past Antone Meadows on your left), and make a right turn here. You pass the back of a yellow sign on your left and soon start climbing on a delightful singletrack. *Caution*: Traffic on this singletrack is two-way. Watch for oncoming, downhilling cyclists.

At 3.7 miles, the single-track ends at Forest Road 16N73, which turns sharply as you encounter it. Turn right and proceed up the forest road. (A left turn here can loop you back to Tahoe City.) At 4.5 miles, the Tahoe Rim Trail crosses the road you're riding on—continue ahead. At 4.7 miles stay on the main road where another road takes off to the left. You pass a sign facing in the downhill direction which says *Tahoe City, 3 miles*. At 5.8 miles, as the road contours around the north side of the ridge, another road enters from the right. Go straight.

At 6.7 miles you arrive at an intersection with another main road, Forest Service Road 06. If you bear right and uphill you will follow Mt. Watson Road (73) and come out on State Highway 267 at Brockway Summit. To complete the Tahoe to Truckee run, however, bear

Hilly singletrack

left and begin descending—it's mostly downhill the rest of the ride! Stay on the main road (wide and not technical) all the way to Truckee. This is logging country, so there are roads taking off all over the place. The main route is also a snowmobile and cross-country ski route, so you will see orange diamonds and snowmobile signs marking Forest Road 06. You ride along the boundary of Northstar Ski Area, then through a large plantation of trees.

At 11 miles there is a large covered sign on your left for the Robie Equestrian Park—no bikes allowed. Continue ahead on the main road. Forest Service Road 06 ends in Truckee at Thelin Drive, 17.5 miles from North Lake Tahoe High School. Downtown Truckee is two miles away. If you are cycling all the way to Truckee (19.5 miles from North Lake Tahoe High School), follow in reverse the shuttle parking directions in the "Getting There" section. The total distance of the Tahoe to Truckee Ride, if you cycle from downtown Tahoe City to downtown Truckee, is 22.5 miles.

Chapter 11:
GOLD COUNTRY

CHAPTER 11

Gold Country

by Delaine Fragnoli

Mountain bikers can find something better than gold in the Sierra foothills—namely, a motherlode of singletrack—much of it built by and designed for mountain bikers. This chapter may contain the very best of the best; nowhere else in the state can you find such a fine collection of trails, both scenic and out-right fun to ride.

Imagine a world of primeval beauty where the trees reach all the way to the sky, the terrain varies between mellow fire roads and rugged singletrack, and the trail-user conflicts consist of "after you." A perfect world? You bet. And the good news is that it really exists. Just north of Sacramento on Interstate 80 and along Highway 49, nestled below the jaw-dropping beauty of the northern Sierra Nevada mountain range, sit the Sierra foothills.

This region is as rich with California history as the hills once were with gold. In fact, many of the hundreds of miles of trails that exist today were mining routes, blazed by those who heeded the call of the Mother Lode in 1849. Hanging out up here, you encounter far more old than new; original buildings still stand, some lovingly restored and some which never fell into disrepair in the first place. Trains still roar through towns, and open mine shafts yawn from hillsides, deserted for over 100 years.

Through it all, fed by snow and rain runoff from the higher elevations, flows the American River. Its three forks, North, South and Middle, converge just south of Auburn and feed into Folsom Lake in Sacramento. The prime riding area here is the Auburn State Recreation Area (ASRA) where local mountain bicyclists, particularly the Folsom-Auburn Trail Riders Action Coalition (FATRAC), have worked with rangers to create a stellar trail network. If miles of buff singletrack with river views is your thing, look no farther. About the only drawback to riding around Auburn is the blistering summer heat.

You can find everything you need in town, including the very good Auburn Bike Works bike shop (530-885-3861). An excellent resource is Soware-Wer-her's topo map to the ASRA, available at most bike shops and the visitor's bureau.

North of Auburn, at the junction of Highways 49 and 20, Nevada City is another mountain biking hotbed. The Yuba River is to this area what the American River is to Auburn. It is the recreational focal point of the community and offers awesome kayaking and mountain biking. More rugged and rockier than the American, the Yuba serves up picture-perfect swimming holes and plenty of granite slabs for basking in the sun. You don't have to contend with Tahoe's high elevations or Auburn's summer heat here. In fact, many of the trails can be ridden year round.

Nevada City is a bike-friendly place, hosting the Tour of Nevada City, an annual stage race for roadies. It's home to an excellent bike shop, also called the Tour of Nevada City (530-265-2187), and to a unique motel, the Outside Inn (530-265-2233). The Inn offers outdoor-themed rooms, including a Single-track Suite for mountain bikers. Not only are the prices relatively affordable, compared to the ubiquitous and almost-too-cute bed and breakfasts in the area, but the staff can set you up with route sheets (they turned me on to a couple of the rides in this chapter), rentals, guides and just about anything else you might need or want—including a massage right across the street.

Farther north on Highway 49, Downieville has become a mecca for the downhill set. Serious riders flock to the steep, rocky, technical trails which have been featured in virtually every national bicycling magazine. Although downhill shuttles, the area's most popular rides, may sound like an easy way out, they're not. The terrain is rough enough that you will be surprised at how beat up you'll feel, especially if you lack the almost requisite dual-suspension bike. Hill climbers and cross-country riders can enjoy the area as well—there's no reason you *have* to shuttle to the higher elevations. No matter what your proclivities, a good resource to have, if you can find it, is TerraPro's Downieville, California topo map.

Every August, the former mining town hosts a hugely popular race, the Coyote Classic, a 25-mile point-to-point epic as well as the Downieville Downhill, one of the longest downhill races (15 miles) in the world. There is one bike shop/outfitter in town, Downieville Outfit-

Fragnoli

Beginning of the Salmon Falls Trail

ters, which offers shuttles to the most popular trailheads (some of the shuttles are quite long and, consequently, worth the money). Sadly, the area's original tour company, Coyote Adventures, has recently gone out of business. They introduced me to many of the trails and deserve credit for boosting the area's profile. I hope they resurface.

A tip of the hat should also go to Bill Haire, recreation officer for the Downieville District of the Tahoe National Forest. (Most of the Nevada City and Downieville rides are in the forest.) His hard work and openness to the local mountain biking community has helped develop the 300-mile (and growing) network of trails.

74 Salmon Falls Trail

Distance: 18 miles
Difficulty: Moderately strenuous, mildly technical
Elevation: 1,100' gain/loss
Ride Type: Out-and-back on singletrack; shuttle possible
Season: Year-round; winter can be wet and muddy
Maps: Pilot Hill, Clarksville (route not shown on maps)
Comments: Water and toilets available at the turnaround point. Be on the lookout for rattlesnakes, particularly in the summer months.

View of American River from the Salmon Falls Trail.

Highlights: Although its official name is the Darrington Trail, everyone knows and loves this ride as the Salmon Falls Trail, named for the waterfall that feeds into the American River just beyond the trailhead. If rolling (all the elevation gain is in fits and spurts) singletrack through breathtaking scenery sounds like a great way to spend a few hours, this ride is for you.

Not challenging enough, you say? Well, let's toss in a little acrophobia, then. The trail spends its first mile clinging to a wall along the South Fork canyon, giving you a heart-stopping vertical view of the river rushing

50 feet or so below. The only thing between you and it are a lot of rocks and the oddly-placed tree. It's not really that technical—as long as you don't look down.

Getting There: From Sacramento, take Interstate 80 east to the Highway 49 exit, following the signs for 49 through Auburn. At the American River confluence, bear right over the bridge to stay on 49 to the town of Cool. Go 3.3 miles past the stop sign in Cool. Turn right onto Rattlesnake Bar Rd., followed by a quick left onto Salmon Falls Rd. Follow Salmon Falls Road 6 miles to the trailhead and

Fragnoli

Wildflowers and proximity to the American River make this a great spring ride.

parking lots. There are two paid parking areas, one on each side of the road, and a large dirt turnout across the bridge. Parking in a paid area is $2. The parking lot on the left has bathrooms.

Route: The trailhead is located at the south (river) end of the first parking lot on the right side of the road. The trail forks immediately. Either branch will work. The right fork is a steep, rocky, rutted climb while the left is flatter. I like to go out via the right fork and come back on the left.

As you round the first corner and the left side of the trail falls away, you get a spectacular view of the American River's South Fork winding below and ahead of you. The feeling is a little unsettling at first, but you get used to it. The singletrack is actually on the wide side, although rocky in spots. It's not a fire road by any means, but there is room to pass—as long as somebody stops.

After the initial climb, the trail rises and falls along the contour of the canyon wall. The trail follows this pattern for most of its 9 miles, interspersed with cuts into oak woodlands at the plateau level.

At 0.8 mile the trail veers inland. At 1.0 mile, go left and cross the bridge onto doubletrack. Half a mile later, take the singletrack to the right. Just under 2.0 miles, the trail makes the first of innumerable tight curves and switchbacks into and out of small stream crossings; get used to it—getting in and out of these dips constitutes the ride's major technical challenge. I found that carrying a little bit more speed than you really want to into the dips makes getting up the other side easier.

At 2.6 miles, switchback left and up a short pitch. At 3.0 miles cross a dirt road. At 3.3 miles, when the trail veers right, you fork left onto the 4WD path. Just under 4.0 miles you reach the first of two steep climbs and

Fragnoli

Section of Salmon Falls rightly famous singletrack.

descents. In between, the trail forks. Either fork will work, but the less-used left one gets very narrow with nothing to stop you before you hit the water should you slip.

At 4.5 miles go left to cross the stream. On the other side go left again onto singletrack. At 5.1 miles, and again at 5.2 miles, ignore the singletracks heading right. Stay straight. Past the 6-mile mark, after a series of climbs and descents, the trail opens up, smoothes out and generally grows more buff and less technical as it drops toward the river.

There's yet another stream crossing at 7.5 miles. At 7.7 miles the trail joins a dirt road and you

Smooth section of trail beside the American River.

begin one final steep climb. It ramps up very steeply at the end—at least it's short and the road is smooth! You top out at a four-way intersection at 8.2 miles. Go straight. By the way, if you don't need water or bathrooms at Peninsula campground, you can save yourself some anaerobic distress and turn around before this climb and head back the way you came.

At 8.8 miles the road ends at a gate and a paved road. Go around the gate and to the right down to a second gate and paved road. A left here will take you to the huge (100 sites) campground; a right will take you to a picnic table and a port-a-potty. If you need water, you have to head to the campground. Otherwise, the picnic table area makes a good rest stop/turn around point.

Option: You could turn this into a 9-mile one-way ride by arranging for a pickup at Peninsula Campground. To get a second vehicle to the campground, take Rattlesnake Bar Road and follow the signs all the way to the campground. (See Getting There.) It's 9 miles from the intersection of Rattlesnake Bar and Salmon Falls roads to the campground but it feels a lot longer. Be sure to designate a meeting place in the sprawling campground or you could wander around a long time before you find one another.

75 Olmstead Loop

Distance: 9 miles
Difficulty: Moderately strenuous, technical sections
Elevation: 1,100' gain/loss
Ride Type: Loop on fire roads, single- and doubletrack
Season: Year-round; winter can be wet and muddy
Map: Auburn State Recreation Area by Sowarwe-Werher
Comments: No drinking water is available; port-a-potty at trailhead. Be on the lookout for rattlesnakes, particularly in the summer.

Highlights: Cool isn't just a state of being, it's also a small town in the Sierra foothills. And, yes, it is a cool town. Cool proper consists of a small town center where you can take your pet to the Cool Animal Hospital or have some Cool Pizza. Or you can ride a cool trail—the Olmstead Loop (sometimes referred to as the Knickerbocker Loop).

The trail is named in memory of a local mountain bike advocate, Dan Olmstead, who succeeded in gaining access to what was previously a horse trail. (There's still a BIG equestrian presence here—be courteous.) The Olmstead legacy lives on in Dan's wife and son who own Auburn Bike Works in nearby Auburn. For the last several years, the Olmsteads have held an annual February mudfest of a race on this loop. The race and the trail are so popular they have had to limit the number of entrants at the behest of local land managers, who asked that they keep it down to 250. The first year, almost 500 racers showed up.

So what's all the fuss about? Well,

Olmstead Loop.

it's a really fun loop, for one thing. It's got a little bit of everything: a little fire road, a little singletrack, a little doubletrack (and one triple), some rocks, a little steep climbing, a little steep descending, a couple of water crossings. All of these come in one tidy 9-mile package.

Although there aren't any services available at the trailhead, except for the outhouse at the rear of the staging area, the town center is on the other side of the fire station (see directions). Among the possibilities are two restaurants, a deli and a liquor store.

Getting There: From Sacramento, take Interstate 80 to the Highway 49 exit and follow the signs for 49 through Auburn. At the American River confluence, bear right across the bridge and follow the highway south into Cool. Just past the town sign, turn right onto Saint Florian, immediately before the fire station. There's a hard-to-see Auburn State

Recreation Area sign just before the turn. If you reach the town's only stop sign, you've missed the turn. There's a dirt parking lot on the left behind the fire station. There's an information board here. There's also a large equestrian staging area with a port-a-potty

Route: The trail is well-marked and easy to follow. From the parking area, cross Saint Florian to the trailhead. Follow the doubletrack as it heads back out toward the highway then curves around to the left, turning into a fire road as you reach the trees. The fire road rolls along the ridge line for about a mile or so. As you reach the last rise, you can almost hear the click-click-click that tells you the E-ticket ride is about to begin.

Where the trail veers to the left again, it narrows as it pitches steeply, sending you on a rocky slalom-like downhill. The trail snakes its way through a forest of black oak with lots

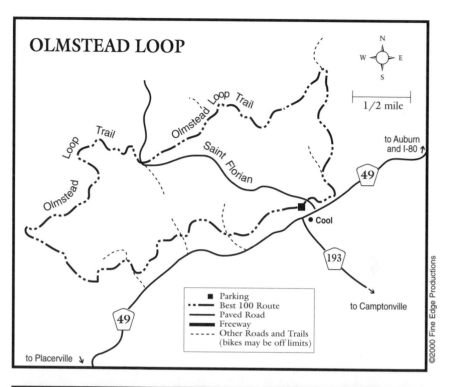

OLMSTEAD LOOP

Olmstead Loop Trail

Loop Trail

Olmstead

Saint Florian

to Auburn and I-80 ↑

49

Cool

193

to Camptonville

N
W — E
S

1/2 mile

■ Parking
∙—∙ Best 100 Route
— Paved Road
▬ Freeway
--- Other Roads and Trails
(bikes may be off limits)

49

to Placerville ↓

©2000 Fine Edge Productions

Cathy Jensen

Enjoying Olmstead's "cool" terrain.

Well-signed start to the Olmstead Loop.

of fast berms, rock jumps and deep sand. At about the time you start to realize that you've been going downhill for a long time, the trail levels and you see how you have to pay for it. Looming in front of you is an exasperatingly steep and sandy climb. Although it's only a half-mile long, this granny-grinder feels like so much more.

At the top of the climb, the trail rolls along the ridge again, a little faster and steeper than before. At about the 4-mile point, the trail again pitches downhill along a steep and rocky singletrack that leads through a creek. On the other side, you begin the steep grind back up. Around the first bend, the trail hugs the side of the mountain, while to your right the canyon falls away just past the trees, giving you a nice view of the American River valley below you.

The trail quickly leads away from the mountain's edge and through a meadow to the first of several cattle gates. From this point, the rest of the climb gets decidedly easier. Within a half-mile, the trail levels, becoming fire road again, as you make your way

Rolling singletrack and oak-dotted hills mark the Olmstead Loop.

past a stand of towering pine at about 4.7 miles. The trail leads along a short rolling section through an orchard, then gives way to doubletrack along grassland hillsides.

The rest of the loop rolls along the exposed hillsides on single- and doubletrack, and for one brief stretch it splits into tripletrack. You come to the last steep climb at about 8 miles. Thankfully, this one is short. At the top, it's all downhill, a little steeply near the bottom, back to the staging area and parking lot.

76 Foresthill Divide Loop Trail

Distance: 11.3 miles
Difficulty: Moderate, only a few mildly technical sections
Elevation: Loses and gains the same 200' umpteen times
Ride Type: Loop on singletrack
Season: Year-round; winter can be wet and muddy
Map: Auburn State Recreation Area by Sowarwe-Werher
Comments: No water or facilities at trailhead; port-a-potty at 5.6-mile point

The clearly signed Foresthill Divide Loop Trail traverses rolling hills shaded by oaks.

Highlights: One of the newest trails in the Auburn State Recreation Area's burgeoning trail system, the Foresthill Divide Loop Trail (FDLT) is pure fun— a singletrack loop that dips and climbs, swoops and rolls, twists and winds. It passes through oaks and manzanita as it wriggles back and forth across the ridge that divides the North and Middle Forks of the American River. This thoughtfully designed and immaculately built trail goes to show that it does make a difference when trails are planned and constructed with mountain biking in mind. Once again, thanks and gratitude should go to FATRAC for their trail-building efforts and to ASRA land man-

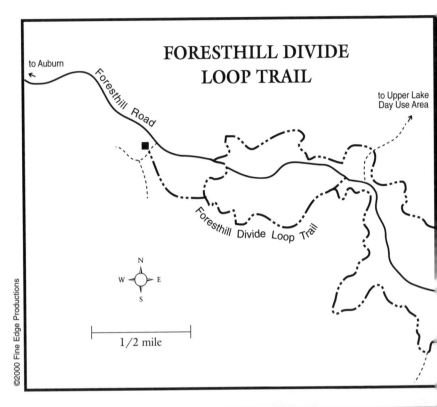

Ho hum, more miles of perfect singletrack. . .

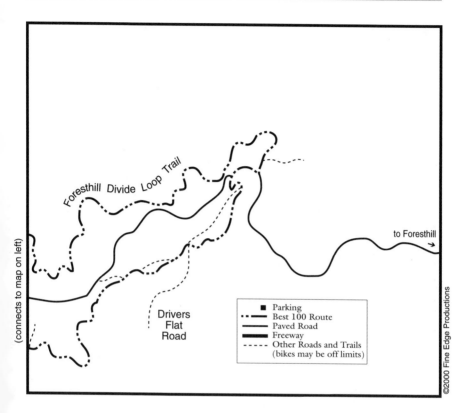

(connects to map on left)

Foresthill Divide Loop Trail

to Foresthill
→

Drivers
Flat
Road

■   Parking
▪▪▪▬ Best 100 Route
▬▬▬ Paved Road
▬▬▬ Freeway
▬ ▬ ▬ Other Roads and Trails
        (bikes may be off limits)

©2000 Fine Edge Productions

agers for their openness to and support of mountain biking. If all areas shared such a great partnership, we'd be in two-wheeled heaven.

Getting There: From Sacramento, take Interstate 80 east to Auburn and exit at Foresthill. Continue on Foresthill Road for just under 5.0 miles. There's a paved parking area on the right. A green horse gate and multi-use trail signs mark the trailhead.

Route: Ignore the doubletrack paralleling the fence line, and head up the trail to an immediate Y-intersection. Fork left and begin a moderate climb to a T-intersection (signed) at 0.6 mile. This is the start of the loop. People ride, hike and bike the loop in both directions; you can loop it either

way, but be alert to other trail users. The following directions are for a clockwise loop.

At the T, go left. Drop down to Foresthill Road. Pass through the horse gate and cross the road. Go left and ride alongside the road. Turn right and pass through another horse gate to pick up the trail. From here you have a short climb followed by a short descent. At 2.3 miles, cross a dirt road (it leads to Upper Lake Day Use Area) and continue on the trail on the other side.

You have a short, sharp climb followed by a longish, swoopy descent. At 4.3 miles the trail drops very close to Foresthill Road. There's a gate and a fence leading to the road on your right. Ignore all this and stay on the trail. Begin one of the ride's more

Vista point along Foresthill Divide.

Oaks and pines provide shade on the hot-in-summer FDLT.

sustained climbs. You top out at 5.1 miles. A tiny singletrack on the right leads to the top of a hill if you want to take a gander.

The trail joins a dirt road at 5.6 miles. Go right. There's a picnic table and port-a-potty here. Pass through a horse gate and parking/ staging area to Foresthill Road. Go right on Foresthill. Cross the road when you see the guardrail on the opposite side of the road end. Exactly where the guardrail ends, 5.8 miles, the singletrack drops down an embankment. Take the singletrack.

It curves left and closely parallels a paved road (Drivers Flat Road) for 0.1 mile. At 5.9 miles the trail makes a sharp (180-degree) left turn onto a gravel road. The gravel road shrinks back to singletrack very shortly.

At 6.4 miles the trail crosses a dirt parking area. Ignore dirt

Drivers Flat Road to the left. You see a paved road, also on the left. Head toward it. At 6.5 miles, take the singletrack just before the paved road on the left. At 6.9 miles the trail comes out onto the paved road. Go left. At 7.0 miles take the singletrack when it veers off the road to the left. At 7.1 the trail joins an old dirt road. At 7.5 miles, once again turn off the dirt road onto singletrack, this time to the right. This all sounds more confusing than it is; the singletrack basically plays touch-and-go with a series of dirt roads. Keep your eyes peeled, look for multi-use trail signs, and you shouldn't have any problems.

At 7.9 miles the trail crosses a wooden bridge. At 8.0 miles zig left onto a dirt road and, at 8.1 miles, zag right off the dirt road and onto singletrack. Begin a sustained but moderate climb to the top of a knoll. You top out at 8.8 miles. From here the trail races downhill toward Foresthill Road. As you near Foresthill Road, 9.8 miles, go left onto a dirt road. When the road makes a 90-degree left at 10.3 miles, go right onto singletrack.

At 10.7 miles you're back at the T-intersection at the beginning of the loop. Go left to head back to the parking area, reached at 11.3 miles.

77 Lake Clementine Loop

Distance: 11.1 miles
Difficulty: Moderately strenuous, mildly technical with a couple of very technical sections
Elevation: 1,800' gain/loss
Ride Type: Loop on fire roads and singletrack
Season: Year-round; winter can be wet and muddy
Map: Auburn State Recreation Area by Sowarwe-Werher
Comments: No drinking water is available along this ride so bring plenty. There's a port-a-potty at the bottom of Stagecoach Road. Be on the lookout for rattlesnakes, particularly in the summer. Summers get very hot and the proximity to water throughout the ride means lots of sun; even if you don't burn easily, slather on the sunblock.

Highlights: The hugely popular Lake Clementine Loop is a must for anyone new to the area. The route follows two different branches of the magnificent American River, the North and Middle Forks. As you make your way along the canyon floors, you see the river at its calmest points. Past Lake Clementine to the north, its rapids are a favorite among rafters from all over.

The route leads down from a high ridge in the town of Auburn to the North Fork canyon, climbs back up and drops down into the Middle Fork Canyon. The ride takes place on mostly smooth, narrow fire roads and singletrack, with a couple of rocky and rutted sections thrown in for good measure. If you ride early enough, the only sound you hear is the river gurgling and rushing by.

Getting There: From Sacramento, take Interstate 80 east to Auburn and exit at Foresthill. Go right (east) onto

Fragnoli

Riding through culvert under Foresthill Road.

Fragnoli

View of the American River from Stagecoach Road.

Foresthill. Make an immediate right at the light onto Lincoln Way. Go 0.5 mile and take a left on Russell, clearly signed before the intersection. The trailhead is half a mile down the road, in a large dirt turnout on the left. Park in the turnout.

If you're coming from the north on Interstate 80, exit at Russell Road. At the stop sign, go right. Go right again to get on Russell Road. At the stop sign, go straight (the cross traffic doesn't have to stop). The trailhead is half a mile down the road, in a large dirt turnout on the left. Park in the turnout.

Route: Starting from the Stagecoach Road trailhead on Russell Road, follow the fire road as it makes its rolling descent to the Old Foresthill Bridge. Overall, the road is smooth and not terribly steep, which is good since you have to climb this at the end of the ride. At

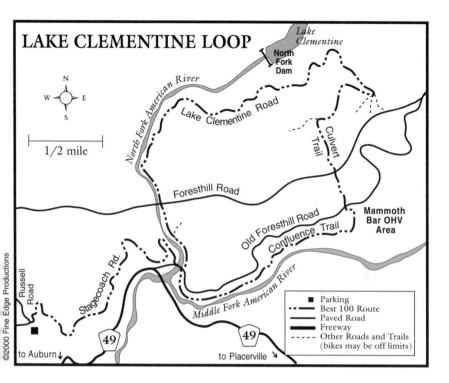

LAKE CLEMENTINE LOOP

Lake Clementine

North Fork Dam

N
W E
S

1/2 mile

North Fork American River

Lake Clementine Road

Culvert Trail

Foresthill Road

Old Foresthill Road

Confluence Trail

Mammoth Bar OHV Area

Russell Road

Stagecoach Rd.

Middle Fork American River

■ Parking
∎·∎· Best 100 Route
—— Paved Road
▬▬ Freeway
----- Other Roads and Trails (bikes may be off limits)

49

49

to Auburn ↓

to Placerville ↘

©2000 Fine Edge Productions

1.8 miles, go right to continue down to the river. At the bottom at 2.0 miles, the road ends at the Old Foresthill Bridge (you can see the new bridge up behind you). Turn left across the old bridge, which is Old Foresthill Road, and cross the river. On the other side of the bridge, turn left onto Lake Clementine Trail, a narrow fire road which rises above the North Fork.

Shortly you come to a fork in the trail. Veer left, following the trail that hugs the river. Keep your eyes peeled for this fork. The trail is just before the fire road starts climbing in earnest. Just past the fork, the trail becomes a singletrack. The singletrack is smooth and scenic, widening to a fire road about a mile later. At this point, the trail climbs a little steeply to the North Fork Dam and Lake Clementine.

At the top of the climb at 3.8 miles, you come to a gate at a paved road. Go right and continue climbing on the road for about 1.5 miles. At about 5.2 miles, you see a bunch of boulders and a gate on your right. Turn right here. Just inside the gate, you have your choice of three trails. Head up the trail to the right, which takes you up and down a little rolling section that turns into a downhill straight-away.

At approximately 5.9 miles, you see a singletrack on the left. Turn onto it and continue descending. The trail ends at a culvert (thus it's official name, Culvert Trail) which leads under Foresthill Road. Head on through and begin the next downhill section. This one gets a little steep and a little rocky, ending at Old Foresthill Road (not to be confused with Foresthill Road) at 6.9 miles.

Cross the road and enter the Mammoth Bar OHV area. At 7.1 miles there's a yellow gate on the right and a bike path sign. Go right and take the bike trail as it continues to head downhill. The fire road narrows to a singletrack that follows the north bank of the Middle Fork of the river. Called the Confluence Trail because it leads to where the North and Middle Forks of the American River join, the singletrack gets rocky and technical in spots, with some short, sharp ups and downs—and considerable exposure at points. Although the view into the Middle Fork canyon will tempt you, keep your eyes on the trail. Toward the end it's mostly downhill, leveling out before ending with a little rise. Keep your speed in check—this stretch is popular with hikers.

The trail ends at the Old Foresthill Bridge at 9 miles. Turn left across the road and the bridge, and turn right onto dirt Stagecoach. Climb up Stagecoach back to the parking lot on Russell Road.

Option: For a shorter loop, you can eliminate the Stagecoach portion of the ride (4 miles worth) by beginning and ending at the junction of Highway 49 and Old Foresthill Road (the American River confluence). Note that parking is limited here.

78 Pioneer Trail

Distance: Anything from 5 to 40 miles
Difficulty: Moderate; mildly technical
Elevation: 2,600' gain/loss maximum (40-mile route); 5,125' high point
Ride Type: Out-and-back on single- and doubletrack; shuttle possible
Season: Spring through fall
Maps: Tahoe National Forest; free route sheet available at the Outside Inn; free map available at the Harmony Ridge Market
Comments: Water and toilets are available at various campgrounds.

Highlights: The Pioneer Trail is actually two trails, Lower and Upper, that flank Highway 20 just inside the boundary of the Tahoe National Forest. The trails were originally developed as horse trails, and a couple of years ago mountain bikers asked permission to use them. The local equestrian group (the Gold Country Trails Council) that maintains the trails said, "Sure, why not?" Makes you wish it was always this easy. Show your appreciation to the horse folks by treating them courteously.

Many sections of the trail follow the Old Emigrant Road, the first wagon road between Nevada City and Bear Valley, used by emigrants and gold miners. The trail consists of singletrack that at times widens to doubletrack that gradually climbs and descends through a dense forest of pine and oak. The trails are very easy to follow; every few trees are marked with a white diamond-shaped sign. The Lower Pioneer is the easiest section and is a good choice for beginners while the Upper Pioneer is more chal-

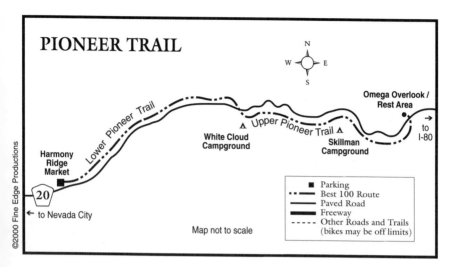

lenging. The hard-core rider can extend the route by starting in Nevada City and/or by continuing on to the Omega Overlook/Rest Stop (water and restrooms) on Highway 20. (See Options in the Route description.) Or you can shuttle any section(s) of the trail.

Getting There: From Interstate 80, take the Highway 49 turnoff and follow it north through Nevada City. Bear east at the 49/20 junction and take Highway 20 about 5 miles past Nevada City. When you see the Five Mile House restaurant (closed) on the right, turn left into the parking lot for the Harmony Ridge Market (park

The Outside Inn in Nevada City offers a Singletrack Suite and a Tour of Nevada City Room, specially designed for cyclists.

Bike shop in Nevada City, named for annual stage race.

near the rear of the lot). The trailhead is on the right side of the market, between two big boulders. Why not show the proprietors that you appreciate their letting you park at the market by picking up a drink or a snack before or after your ride?

Route: From the trailhead, follow the Lower Pioneer singletrack as it parallels the highway. Within the first mile, it veers a little to the left so you won't have to look at the highway the whole time. From that point, the trail meanders through the trees and through several crossroads. Just keep heading straight.

The trail climbs so gradually it almost feels level. This section is also pretty smooth with a few smatterings of small rocks, ruts and tree roots. At about 5 miles, the trail crosses the highway and enters White Cloud Campground, where it becomes the Upper Pioneer Trail. For a 10-mile out-and-back you could turn around here. An historical side note: White Cloud was once a mining camp and then a logging operation. Its name comes from the clouds of white dust that wagon trains kicked up during the dry season.

From the Upper Pioneer trailhead, the trail continues up to the left. This portion of Pioneer is again a virtual straight line, paralleling the highway. However, the trail gets a little more interesting. The singletrack is more consistently narrow and the rocks are a little bigger. Still not too imposing, though.

At 10 miles, you reach Skillman Campground. If you have the time and inclination, it's worth nosing around the campground a bit. The ditch that runs around the campground is one of the water ditches built by the South Yuba Canal Company to supply water to Nevada City.

When you're ready, turn around here and head back the way you came. Going this direction is a lot of fun because, although it's not steep, you do pick up speed. Keep an eye out for horses and have a good time.

Option 1: To extend the ride, you can continue from Skillman Campground to Omega Overlook/Rest Area. The trail continues on the south side of the highway. It crosses two dirt roads before recrossing the highway to the Omega Overlook/ Rest Area. This would make a roughly 15-mile ride one way or 30 miles out and back.

The rest area is named for the Alpha and Omega Diggins, one of the gold country's largest hydraulic mines. The Omega Ditch diverted water from the Yuba River into cliff-side wooden flumes, some hung several hundred feet above the river—an impressive bit of engineering.

Option 2: Another way to extend the ride (5 miles each way) is to ride from/ to Nevada City. The following directions are courtesy of the Outside Inn.

Make your way to Nevada Street and head north until it intersects Highway 20. Cross to the north side of the highway onto Margarita Diggins Road. One block later, just before the turquoise auto shop, turn left onto the paved road leading up to the Nevada Irrigation District (NID) water storage tanks. The gate here may or may not be closed. Make your way through or around the gate. A singletrack trail begins to the right of the water storage tanks and travels along the water ditch. About a mile later, the trail ends at Highway 20. Look across the highway just past the Steep Hill Road sign and you can see the singletrack as it begins again along the water ditch. Cross to the south side of Highway 20 and ride alongside the ditch until it intersects Willow Valley Road. Turn left and ride up Willow Valley Road for one

mile until it intersects Highway 20. Do not cross the highway. Instead, follow the singletrack to the right as it parallels the highway. Cross the highway at Harmony Ridge Market to catch the Lower Pioneer Trail (see the Route description above).

When it comes time to turn around, simply reverse the directions to get back into town. Riding from Nevada City all the way to Omega Overlook/Rest Area and back would make for a burly 40-mile adventure.

Option 3: For an easier ride, you can shuttle between any two points. For a mostly downhill ride, ride from east to west. Obvious pick-up/drop-off points are Harmony Ridge Market, White Cloud Campground, Skillman Campground or Omega Overlook/ Rest Area. The epic downhill shuttle (over 20 miles) would be to drop-off at Omega Overlook/Rest Area (18 miles up Highway 20 from Nevada City) and ride back into town.

South Yuba River

79 Missouri Bar/South Yuba Loop

Distance: 18 miles
Difficulty: Moderately strenuous, technical
Elevation: 2,600' gain/loss
Ride Type: Loop on singletrack and dirt roads
Season: Spring through fall
Maps: North Bloomfield; Tahoe National Forest
Comments: Outhouses at the camps; water at the campground at Malakoff Diggins .
Watch for poison oak along the Missouri Bar and South Yuba trails.

Highlights: This ride has a little bit of everything: lots of great singletrack, including the awesome and scenic South Yuba Trail, a 1,200' descent to the river on the Missouri Bar Trail, epic swimming holes, and a stop at the restored gold-mining town of North Bloomfield and the hydraulic diggings at Malakoff Diggins State Historic Park.

Getting There: From Nevada City, take Highway 49 north 0.25 mile past the intersection with Highway 20. Turn right (north) on North Bloomfield Road. At the top of the hill, fork

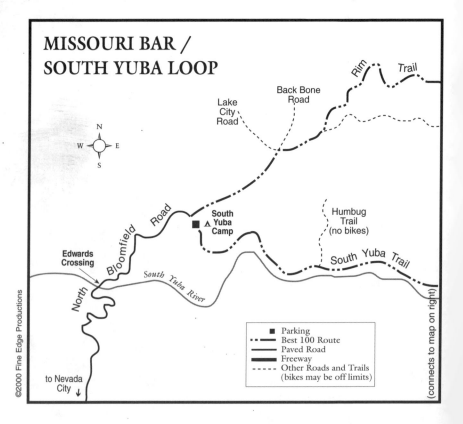

MISSOURI BAR /
SOUTH YUBA LOOP

Rim Trail

Back Bone Road

Lake City Road

N
W E
S

South Yuba Camp

Humbug Trail (no bikes)

Bloomfield Road

Edwards Crossing

North

South Yuba River

South Yuba Trail

■ Parking
- ·- ■ Best 100 Route
——— Paved Road
━━━ Freeway
- - - - Other Roads and Trails
　　　(bikes may be off limits)

to Nevada City ↓

©2000 Fine Edge Productions

(connects to map on right)

right to stay on North Bloomfield. Continue down a steep series of switchbacks for 8.5 miles to the bridge over the South Yuba River at Edwards Crossing. Continue across the bridge. The road turns to dirt here. Take the dirt road for another 2 miles up another hill. At the fork at the top, veer right to stay on North Bloomfield. The road descends and then starts to climb again. As it begins to climb you pass a sign for the South Yuba River Campground. Turn right and then make an immediate left into a parking area.

Sign at Malakoff Diggins State Park.

Fragnoli

Route: Backtrack to North Bloomfield Road, go right and begin climbing. The climb is not too steep and the road is well graded and fairly smooth. At 3 miles keep right at the intersection with Lake City Road. Continue climbing toward Malakoff Diggins SHP and North Bloomfield.

At 4 miles look for a trailhead to the Rim Trail on the left (marked by a small sign). The singletrack Rim Trail loops through Malakoff SHP for 3 miles, emerging at a campground. At the campground, cross the road and pick up the trail (signed toward North Bloomfield). You then descend into the town of North Bloomfield. Several of the structures in this mining town have been restored. It's worth poking around and taking a rest break.

When you're ready to continue, head toward the west end of town and turn onto Relief Hill Road (signed), heading south toward the town of Washington. Cross the wooden bridge and begin a 0.8-mile climb to the easy-to-miss Missouri Bar trailhead on your right. Make this right and then immediately look for the singletrack to your left.

This is where the ride kicks into overdrive. The trail drops—more like

North Bloomfield

Relief Hill Road

to Washington →

Missouri Bar Trail

South Yuba River

(connects to map on left)

©2000 Fine Edge Productions

Map not to scale

Saloon at restored mining town of North Bloomfield.

Hydraulic diggings at Malakoff Diggins State Historic Park

plummets—from 3,480 feet to 2,280 feet (that's 1,200 feet) in just 1.7 miles on its way to the South Yuba River. One Forest Service route sheet describes the trail as passing through a forest of black oak, ponderosa pine, incense cedar and Douglas fir—like you're going to be looking at anything but the trail going down this pitch. Considering disc brakes?

At the bottom, the trail Ts into the South Yuba Trail. You and your brakes may want to cool off here. And why not? Missouri Bar makes the perfect swimming hole. In picking this trail as one of the nation's top swimming hole rides, *BIKE* magazine described Missouri Bar as a "crystal-clear, Olympic swimming pool-size hole, 15 feet deep. There are plenty of rocks and even a sandy beach for hanging out." I defy you not to take a dip on a hot summer afternoon.

Thus refreshed, continue your ride downstream on the South Yuba Trail, a most excellent piece of single-track. Paralleling its namesake river, the trail rolls up and down and in and out of every little river drainage. None of the ups and downs are too steep, but they do add up after awhile. Should you get hot and tired, well, there are several other opportunities to cool off in the always-close-at-hand Yuba.

About 3 miles down the trail, you reach South Yuba Primitive Camp. There are quite a few side trails here. Two bits of advice: keep right at the outhouse and keep heading downstream. The section of trail below the primitive camp is subject to washouts so you might have to portage a cou-

ple of sections, depending on what recent weather and trail work have accomplished.

Just past this section, you cross Humbug Creek and Humbug Trail (closed to bikes), and come to a picnic area—a good stopping point if you need a rest/food/swim break.

Beyond here the trail grows smoother and easier. These last 5 miles go by pretty quickly. When the trail comes out onto a dirt road, turn up the road. About 0.5 mile up the road, look for the singletrack on your left. A sign—*No OHVs*—is your cue. When the trail splits, veer right to climb back to the South Yuba Campground and your waiting vehicle.

Option: More interested in swimming and basking on rocks than riding? Then pedal out and back as far as you want on the South Yuba Trail from the South Yuba Campground.

80 Bullards Bar Loop

Distance: 13 miles or 22 miles
Difficulty: Moderately strenuous, technical in spots
Elevation: 1,700' gain/loss (22-mile loop)
Ride Type: Loop on singletrack, dirt roads and pavement
Season: Year round; winter can be wet and muddy
Maps: Camptonville; TerraPro's Downieville California topo map; Tahoe National Forest
Comments: Water and bathrooms are available at various campgrounds and picnic areas.

Highlights: Try this ride for miles and miles of sweet, rolling singletrack on a very well-marked trail system with inspiring lake (OK, it's a reservoir) views, old-growth forests and great swimming possibilities. Part way between Nevada City and Downieville, it makes a good addition to a trip to either area or a stop between the two. Camp at one of the area

campgrounds and spend a couple of days exploring the whole trail network. It's well worth it. There are enough options to keep everyone from the advanced beginner to the hard-core rider happy. The northeast end of the trail is more technical, cliffy and narrow than the southwest end, which is wider, smoother and not as steep, making the long loop the

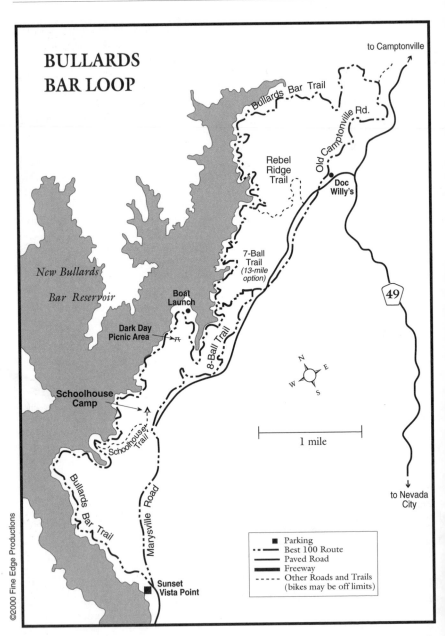

BULLARDS BAR LOOP

to Camptonville

Bullards Bar Trail

Old Camptonville Rd.

Rebel Ridge Trail

Doc Willy's

7-Ball Trail *(13-mile option)*

49

New Bullards Bar Reservoir

Boat Launch

Dark Day Picnic Area

8-Ball Trail

Schoolhouse Camp

Schoolhouse Trail

N
E
W
S

1 mile

Bullards Bar Trail

Marysville Road

to Nevada City

Sunset Vista Point

■ Parking
-·-·- Best 100 Route
——— Paved Road
▬▬▬ Freeway
- - - Other Roads and Trails
(bikes may be off limits)

©2000 Fine Edge Productions

choice for advanced riders and the short loop a good choice for intermediate riders.

Getting There: From Nevada City, drive north on Highway 49 for 21 miles. Turn left on Marysville Road. It is well signed and there is a ranger station here. Continue on Marysville Road for 6 miles and park at the Sunset Vista Point.

Route: From the vista point, turn left onto paved Marysville Road for 1.5 miles to the Schoolhouse Campground (well signed). Turn left. Almost immediately on your right is the trailhead for 8-Ball Trail (signed toward Dark Day picnic area). Go right onto 8-Ball. It closely parallels Marysville Road. At 2.5 miles it crosses the paved road to Dark Day. Continue on the trail on the other side of the road.

The singletrack continues rolling upward for almost another 1.5 miles before reaching a paved road near the Old Scaling Station. Go left on the pavement. Immediately on your left is the 7-Ball trailhead. Those of you interested in the 13-mile loop should take 7-Ball—skip to the Option described below. If you're doing the full 22-mile loop, bypass the 7-Ball Trail and continue out to Marysville Road, reached at 4 miles.

Go left up Marysville Road. Or cross the road and look for a single-

A characteristically well-signed section of Bullards Bar's sweet singletrack.

track that parallels the right side of the road. If you take the pavement, you pass a trailhead on the left in

Bullards Bar Reservoir at low water.

Fragnoli

Trail junction and start of the 8-Ball Trail.

swervy, sweeping single-track and occasional doubletrack drops you to the reservoir's shore. From here you have over 10 miles of rolling singletrack which bobs in and out of the trees, offering intermittent views of the reservoir. Think you can handle that?

At 12.0 miles you pass the bottom of Rebel Ridge Trail; at 14.2 miles you pass the bottom of 7-Ball Trail. (Those who opted for the shorter 13-mile loop can pick up the ride description from here.) Around 16 miles you reach the Dark Day boat launch. Head straight across the pavement and pick up the trail again on the other side. This smidgen of trail then deposits you at Dark Day picnic area. Zig right onto the pavement, then zag left across the parking area to catch the trail again.

At 18.8 miles, bypass the Schoolhouse Trail on your left and continue to follow the reservoir's shore. At 21.4 miles the singletrack fun ends at a paved road. Go left to climb this road back to the vista point where you started.

about a mile. This is the Rebel Ridge Trail, an alternate route down to the reservoir and Bullards Bar Trail. Unless you're getting tired, bypass the trail and continue up Marysville Road toward Highway 49.

At 5.2 miles, turn left onto Jaynes Lane, pass Doc Willy's beer garden and go left up Old Camptonville Road at 5.4 miles. About 0.5 mile later the road turns to dirt. Continue climbing until you top out at 6.8 miles. Keep your eyes peeled as you head down from here. You're looking for the trailhead to Bullards Bar Trail, about 0.3 mile from the crest of the hill on your left (7 miles total).

Turn left down this trail, following signs to Dark Day, and let the fun begin! Nearly 3 miles of fast, jumpy,

13-Mile Option: Follow the route description above until the 7-Ball/8-Ball trail junction. Fork left onto 7-Ball Trail. You drop several hundred feet in just one mile as the trail snakes its way to the reservoir's shore. It ends at the Bullards Bar Trail. Go left and follow Bullards Bar along the shoreline. Pick up the route description above at the 14.2-mile point for details on completing the loop.

81 North Yuba Trail

Distance: 15 miles
Difficulty: Moderate, technical with considerable exposure in spots (the skittish need not apply)
Elevation: 1,000' gain/loss
Ride Type: Loop on singletrack and pavement; out-and-back and shuttle options
Season: Spring through fall
Maps: Goodyears Bar; TerraPro's Downieville California topo map; Tahoe National Forest
Comments: No facilities

Highlights: This technical single-track follows the crashing North Yuba River for 7.5 miles between Rocky Rest campground on the west and the small town of Goodyears Bar on the east. The trail is not really that technical, but it is narrow and exposed in spots, offering serious consequences if you do bobble. Surrounded by old-growth trees, you cross numerous creeks which drain into the North Yuba.

You can ride out-and-back from either point, or loop from either point, using Highway 49. Although a study of topo maps (as well as Forest Service route sheets) shows more elevation gain riding west to east (Rocky Rest to Goodyears Bar), there are so many little ups and downs that it feels to me like six of one and half a dozen of the other . The last time I rode this trail with a couple of girlfriends we had ridden both Downieville Downhill rides (see later in this chapter) the day before and were more than happy to loop back via the highway.

Getting There: From Downieville, take Highway 49 west (toward Nevada City) for 7.5 miles. Turn left into Rocky Rest Campground. Park in the day-use area. This is my favorite campground in the area. It has a secret, very private campsite—the best in the campground. But if I told you where to find it, it wouldn't be very secret then, would it? One hint: look up.

If you want to shuttle the ride or prefer to start at Goodyears Bar, head west from Downieville on Highway 49. Go left (south) on Mountain House Road/County Road 300. Cross the bridge and turn right at the stop sign. Continue .25 mile as the road crosses a creek and turns to dirt. The trailhead is on the right, a parking area is on the left.

Route: From Rocky Rest campground, take the foot bridge over the North Yuba River to catch the trail. The trail goes to the left (upstream), following the south bank of the river. Route finding is easy. Once on the trail, there's really nowhere else to go: to your left, cliffs drop straight to the river (the exposure can be very disconcerting in spots) and to your right, canyon walls rise almost as steeply. Let's just say that if you get "off trail," you have way bigger problems than being lost!

Exposed, rocky ascents and descents with stunning views of the river alternate with cool, tree-shaded ups and downs as the trail winds into and crosses out of the many small drainages which feed into the North Yuba River. Because the trail spends

NORTH YUBA TRAIL

←   to Nevada City

North Yuba River

49

North Yuba Trail

▲■

Rocky Rest Campground

©2000 Fine Edge Productions

(connects to map on right)

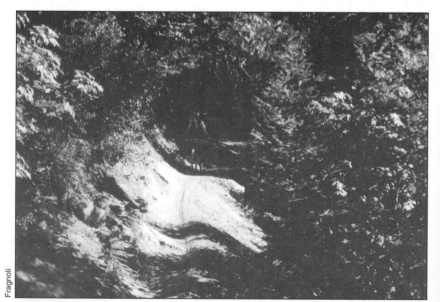

Fragnoli

Singletrack high above the North Yuba River.

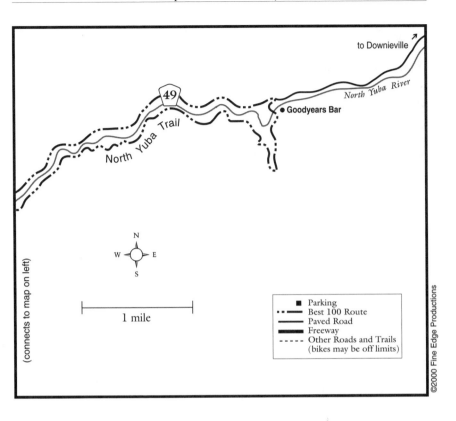

to Downieville

North Yuba River

Goodyears Bar

North Yuba Trail

49

(connects to map on left)

N
W — E
S

1 mile

■ Parking
■ - ■ - Best 100 Route
——— Paved Road
▬▬▬ Freeway
- - - - Other Roads and Trails
        (bikes may be off limits)

©2000 Fine Edge Productions

much time high above the river, there aren't as many swimming opportunities as you might think, although you can always take a quick dip in one of the side streams.

A cautionary tale about local wildlife: while riding here one hot August, my girlfriends and I were plagued by what we refer to as 6-mph gnats—those tiny, annoying little insects that swarm around your face and try to infiltrate every orifice (nose, mouth, eyes, ears) any time you slow to less than 6 mph. Well, the North Yuba gnats are on more performance-enhancing drugs than the Tour de France *peloton*. We had to ride a good 10 mph, even as fast as 12-14 mph (no easy task in this terrain), to drop the pesky beasts. As you can guess,

relief came only on downhill sections. So, don't forget to throw some insect repellent in your pack.

After about 7.5 miles of pitching and bucking, the trail drops around a tight switchback and deposits you on a dirt road. This is Mountain House Road. If you're doing a shuttle, your car should be parked across the road. If you're doing an out-and-back, turn around here. If you want to loop back on the highway, go left and descend toward Goodyears Bar. At the stop sign at the T-intersection, go left again. Cross over the Yuba River and continue out to Highway 49, about 8.5 miles total. Turn left onto the highway. You have roughly 6.5 rolling-to-mostly-downhill miles back to Rocky Rest.

82 Chimney Rock/Empire Creek

Distance: 20 miles
Difficulty: Strenuous, technical
Elevation: 1,500' gain/ 3,800' loss; 6,760' high point
Ride Type: Shuttle on dirt roads and singletrack
Season: Spring through fall
Maps: Downieville, Mt. Fillmore; TerraPro's Downieville California topo map; Tahoe National Forest
Comments: No facilities. Watch for OHVs and car traffic on the road portion of the route. There's a 15-mph speed limit in Downieville. Help keep Downieville a bike-friendly place by adhering to the speed limit and stopping at all stop signs.

Highlights: The work you put into the climb to Chimney Rock is amply rewarded by scenic vistas and the old-growth-choked singletrack through lovely Empire Creek. This route is best done, in my opinion, as a shuttle. However, plenty of people ride it as a loop. Looping it turns it into a very strenuous 28-miler with just over 5,000 feet of climbing. If you are a glutton for this kind of punishment, simply cycle the driving directions below.

Getting There: Leave one car in Downieville. From Downieville go west on Highway 49 for 0.2 mile and turn right on Saddleback Road. Continue up this dirt road for 8 miles to a five-way intersection. Continue straight on Road 25-23-1 (gotta love the Forest Service road numbering system) for another .25 mile, passing the turnoff to Saddleback Lookout on the right. Just past the turnoff is the "Bee Tree," a local landmark. Park off the road here. You'll know

Descent from Chimney Rock.

Fragnoli

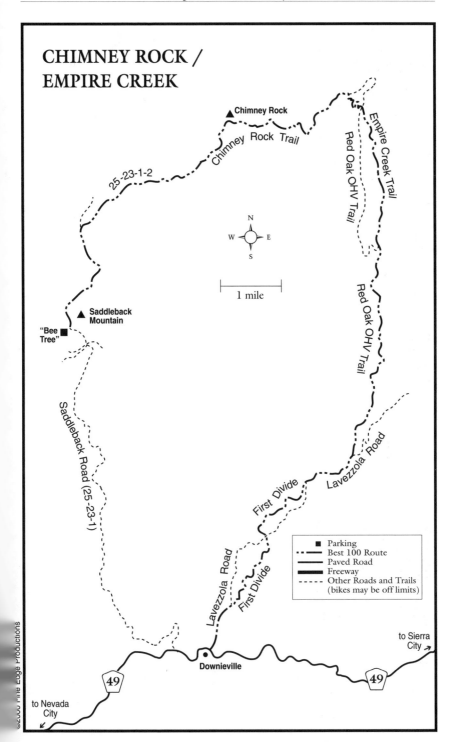

CHIMNEY ROCK / EMPIRE CREEK

▲ Chimney Rock

Chimney Rock Trail

25-23-1-2

Red Oak OHV Trail

Empire Creek Trail

N
W — E
S

1 mile

▲ Saddleback Mountain

"Bee Tree" ■

Red Oak OHV Trail

Saddleback Road (25-23-1)

Lavezzola Road

First Divide

Lavezzola Road

First Divide

■ Parking
·–·– Best 100 Route
—— Paved Road
▬▬ Freeway
----- Other Roads and Trails
(bikes may be off limits)

to Sierra City →

Downieville

(49)   (49)

to Nevada City

Singletrack near Chimney Rock.

the spot by the big tree and the views of Mt. Lassen to the north.

Route: Continue on the road you drove in on. You begin with an immediate downhill. Don't get too excited. It doesn't last for long and you'll soon be climbing quite steeply. At 1 mile, keep right at the intersection and keep climbing. Keep right and keep climbing again at the next intersection at 2 miles. The second right takes you off Saddleback Road (25-23-1) and onto Road 25-23-1-2, which is signed: *Dead End, Road Not Maintained.*

At 2.6 miles go straight, passing the Poker Flat OHV Trail which bears left. Beyond this intersection the road grows steeper and looser. Thanks to the OHVs which frequent the area, the soil can get churned to dust. By August this pitch can be unrideable on a bike. Don't kill yourself trying to clean it; you've still got some climbing to do to reach Chimney Rock.

This is followed by an equally steep and loose descent, a real butt-over-the-rear-wheel, skiddy, surfy lesson in trying to find traction. Try to keep it somewhat in control so you don't blow by the Chimney Rock trailhead. At about 4.2 miles, the trail takes off to the left just as the road makes a tight right.

The Chimney Rock Trail climbs just 400 feet in its 4-mile length, but almost all of the elevation gain comes in the first switchbacked mile. Don't be surprised if the narrow, loose, rocky trail forces you off your bike from time to time.

As you near Chimney Rock, you leave the trees and enter a more open, volcanic landscape of multi-colored spires. While the lack of vegetation confirms the violent geomorphic events that must have occurred here, it also provides great views, especially to the north. It's worth stopping for a break here to try and take it all in.

As you might guess from the name, Chimney Rock (6,698') is a chimney-shaped rock formed as lava explosions cooled. At 25 feet tall and 12 feet in diameter at its base, it's an impressive landmark. It and the section of trail which passes by it look like something you'd expect to encounter in Moab, Utah rather than in the Sierra.

Beyond Chimney Rock, the trail descends briefly before beginning another switchbacked climb. You may really feel the altitude as you make your way to the ride's high point of 6,760 feet between Needle Point and Rattlesnake Peak—more vista points along here. Ignore the rough trail to your right near Needle Point and continue to trail's end at the Empire Creek trailhead (signed), to your right at 8.2 miles. The Red Oak OHV Trail also runs through here. You want the Empire Creek Trail.

This is your payback for the climbing you've been doing. The trail loses 1,940 feet in 2.5 miles as it drops to and then follows Empire Creek. The trail passes under a canopy of old-growth trees and crosses several small streams. After the dry, exposed volcanic landscape around Chimney Rock, this cool, damp, shady trail feels like another world.

The technical singletrack begins with a series of switchbacks interspersed with narrow, rocky, sidehill sections. Great fun for the skilled rider! At 9 miles, the trail crosses over Red Oak OHV Trail and continues on the other side. From here, it's more downhill to and through a meadow—nice wildflower display in the spring.

All too soon, at 10.7 miles, the singletrack ends at Red Oak OHV Trail, more like a road at this point. Go left for a fast and furious 4-mile descent. At 14.7 miles, Red Oak runs into Lavezzola Road. Lavezzola Road used to be the only way back into Downieville. But now those of you who want more singletrack (who doesn't?) can pick up the First Divide Trail, a juicy 3-mile tidbit that's been added to the trail system in the last couple of years.

From the Red Oak/Lavezzola junction, continue downhill on Lavezzola. Keep your speed in check because: one, there is vehicle traffic on this road; and two, you need to keep a look out for the First Divide trailhead. The trailhead is about 1 mile down the road (about 15.7 miles total) on the right, just past a bridge. It starts out on a dirt road alongside Lavezzola Creek, but the singletrack soon takes off to your left.

It descends a bit before climbing back up to Lavezzola Road at about 17 miles. Cross the road and continue onto a dirt road. Note that this trail junction is signed. If you missed the top trailhead, you can pop onto the trail here.

The trail soon narrows into singletrack before spreading into doubletrack for the rest of its course. When the trail ends at Lavezzola Road, go left and continue downhill for a mile into Downieville.

Aspen-lined meadow along Empire Creek Trail.

83 Downieville Downhill

Distance: 14 miles
Difficulty: Moderately strenuous, technical
Elevation: 7,000' to 2,899'; 4,101' loss
Ride Type: One-way downhill on dirt roads and singletrack
Season: June through October
Maps: Gold Lake, Sierra City and Downieville; TerraPro's Downieville California topo map; Tahoe National Forest
Comments: Requires car shuttle. No facilities. Be alert for motorcycles on sections of the route.

Highlights: A visit to the Sierra Buttes area should appear on every mountain bike rider's "must do" list. The Sierra Buttes are gigantic, jagged, rocky pinnacles that push straight up over 2,000 feet from the surrounding forest lands. They can be seen from miles away and form a strong contrast to the more gentle northern Sierra Nevada. The forest land below the Buttes, known as the Lakes Basin Recreation Area, has an incredible amount of area to explore by mountain bike.

The Downieville Downhill (Butcher Ranch, Third Divide and First Divide trails) is definitely a ride to

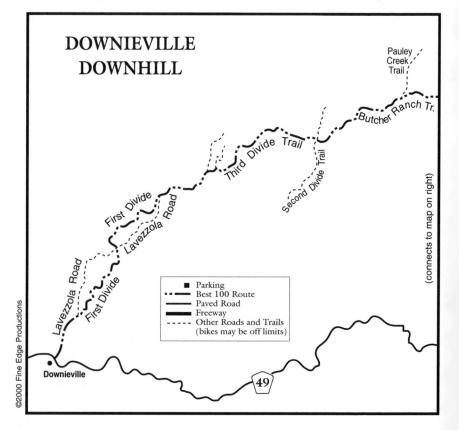

DOWNIEVILLE DOWNHILL

Pauley Creek Trail

Butcher Ranch Tr.

Third Divide Trail

Second Divide Trail

First Divide

Lavezzola Road

Lavezzola Road

First Divide

(connects to map on right)

■ Parking
▪▪▪ Best 100 Route
── Paved Road
━━ Freeway
▪▪▪▪ Other Roads and Trails
(bikes may be off limits)

Downieville

49

©2000 Fine Edge Productions

match these mountains. A long-time race course, the mostly downhill route serves up plenty of technical challenge and has become hugely popular with the downhill crowd. Don't be put off however. It isn't so difficult as to intimidate intermediate riders. Plus it has much else besides gonzo thrills to recommend it. It twists, turns, swerves and drops (OK, there is one quarter-mile climb) along several creeks and through old-growth forest as it makes its way to Downieville.

Getting There: You need to arrange a shuttle or leave a car somewhere near the town of Downieville. There is limited parking in Downieville, so you might find it easier to have someone meet you just outside of town

along Highway 49. (There are good swimming holes on the North Fork of the Yuba River.)

To get to the ride start from Downieville, take Highway 49 east. Pass through Sierra City and continue east on Highway 49 for another 5 miles to the small town of Bassetts Station. At Bassetts, turn north on the Gold Lake Highway. Take the highway for 1.5 miles. Turn left and cross the bridge over Salmon Creek. Continue 0.3 mile and turn right onto Packer Lake Road. Follow it for 2.5 miles to Packer Lake. At the road fork here, go left onto Packer Saddle Road (Forest Road 93). Take this road 2 miles to Packer Saddle and turn left, following the sign for Sierra Buttes Lookout and Pauley Creek. Immedi-

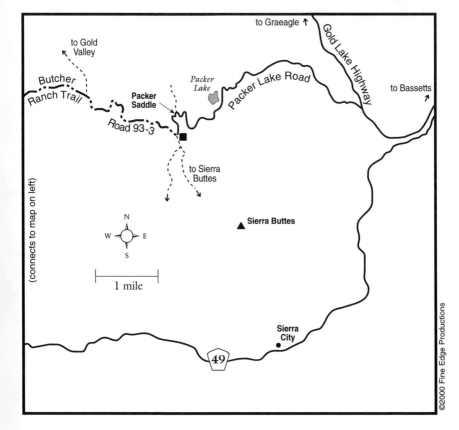

©2000 Fine Edge Productions

ately before the road turns to dirt there is a parking area to the left and a paved road to the right. Park here.

Route: From the dirt parking area, take the paved road (Forest Road 93-3). The road switchbacks downhill. When it splits at 0.5 mile, go right *(Butcher Ranch 1 mile, Pauley Creek 4 miles)* downhill toward Gold Valley. The road turns to dirt beyond here. At 1.2 miles there is another sign directing you to the Butcher Ranch trailhead, and indicating that the road ahead is steep and recommended for 4WD vehicles only. As advertised, the road does get bumpier and rockier from this point on. In another mile, 2.2 miles total, the road curves to the right toward Gold Valley. Keep your speed in check and look for the Butcher Ranch Trail (11E08) to the left in this curve. If you start climbing, you missed the turn.

The trail drops steeply down a rock-infested two-track before crossing a couple of baby-head-laden streams. Making plans for a dual-suspension bike yet? Less than a mile down the trail you come to a Y-intersection. Keep left and you will soon be on singletrack, tracing the contour of Butcher Ranch Creek for 1.5 miles.

At 3.7 miles, Pauley Creek Trail comes in on the right. Go left and continue descending in and out of old-growth forest. The trail follows Pauley Creek for 2 miles, bypassing several waterfalls and pools. At roughly 5.7 miles, the trail crosses Pauley Creek on a wooden foot bridge. The bridge makes a nice regrouping point, and the views up and downstream from the bridge are quite nice.

From the bridge you have the ride's only real climb—about .25 mile to the intersection of the Second Divide and Third Divide trails. Go right uphill onto the Third Divide Trail (11E07). (See the following ride

for a description of the more technical and more exposed Second Divide Trail.) The climb soon ends, about 6.2 miles total.

From here the trail is drier, less technical and rocky, more rolling (always trending downhill)—and fast. For the first time since the ride start, you are not close to water until near trail's end when it parallels and then crosses Lavezzola Creek on a wooden foot bridge. The trail ends shortly thereafter at Lavezzola Road at 8.2 miles. Go left on this dirt road.

At 8.5 miles Red Oak Canyon OHV road joins Lavezzola Road on the right. Continue downhill on Lavezzola Road. Lavezzola Road used to be the only way back into Downieville. But now those of you who want more singletrack (who doesn't?) can pick up the First Divide Trail, a juicy 3-mile tidbit that's been added to the trail system in the last couple of years.

From the Red Oak/Lavezzola junction, continue downhill on Lavezzola. Keep your speed in check because: one, there is vehicle traffic on this road; and two, you need to keep a look out for the First Divide trailhead. The trailhead is about 1 mile down the road (about 9.5 miles total) on the right, just past a bridge. It starts out on a dirt road alongside Lavezzola Creek at the primitive camp, but the singletrack soon takes off to your left.

It descends a bit before climbing back up to Lavezzola Road at about 11 miles. Cross the road and continue onto a dirt road. Note that this trail junction is signed. If you missed the top trailhead, you can pop onto the trail here.

The trail soon narrows into singletrack before spreading into doubletrack for the rest of its course. When the trail ends at paved Lavezzola Road at 12.8 miles, go left and continue downhill for a mile into Downieville.

84 Downieville Downhill II

Distance: 23 miles
Difficulty: Moderately strenuous, technical with exposure in places
Elevation: 7,000' to 2,899'; 4,101' loss
Ride Type: One-way downhill on dirt roads and singletrack
Season: June through October
Maps: TerraPro's Downieville California topo map; Tahoe National Forest
Comments: Requires car shuttle. No facilities. Be alert for motorcycles on sections of the route.

Highlights: This route links Pauley Creek, Second Divide and First Divide trails for a thrilling downhill equal to the previous ride. Once you've experienced both rides, you can mix and match these trails as you please. Second Divide has more exposure than any of the other trails and is definitely not for the inexperienced. Pauley Creek Trail is part of the downhill portion of the Coyote Classic cross-country race course.

Getting There: Follow the directions for the previous ride.

Route: This route begins the same as the previous ride. From the dirt parking area take the paved road (Forest Road 93-3). When it splits at 0.5 mile, go right (*Butcher Ranch 1 mile, Pauley Creek 4 miles*), downhill toward Gold Valley. The road turns to dirt beyond here. At 1.2 miles, there is another sign directing you to the Butcher Ranch trailhead, and indicating that the road ahead is steep and recommended for 4WD vehicles only. As advertised, the road does get bumpier and rockier from this point on. In another mile, 2.2 miles total, the road curves to the right toward Gold Valley. The Butcher Ranch Trail is off to the left at this curve. Bypass it and continue on Road 93-3 toward Gold Valley.

Stay on the main road heading northwest for about 3 miles. Bypass two roads to your left. After a creek

crossing, Gold Valley Road bends to the left. The right turn to the north leads to Summit Lake. There is a trail sign way up in a tree on the left: *Pauley Creek 2 miles.* Continue west on Gold Valley Road into Gold Valley. It is a quick and easy trip through the valley.

At the first intersection, go right. About a mile later the road starts to deteriorate. You bounce through several bouldery switchbacks. Keep your head up because it's easy to miss the next turn. As you come out of the fourth switchback, a doubletrack comes in from the left. Once again there is a trail sign for Pauley Creek high up in a tree. The intersection is also marked by tree stumps. If you find yourself in an aspen grove (not a bad place to be lost), you overshot the turn.

Take this doubletrack to the left. It rolls down through a meadow and across three creeks. At the top of the climb after the third creek crossing, the road goes to the left. Two roads veer off to the right, but you stay left. Continue to follow Pauley Creek downstream on the main road. About 0.5 mile later you reach the official Pauley Creek trailhead, signed *Recommended Parking.*

Say good-bye to the jeep tracks—it's singletrack time now. From the trailhead, the Pauley Creek Trail sweeps steeply through old-growth forest. It is cool, shady and wet down here; you cross several seeps and creeks on the swoopy, swervy trail. Pauley Creek Trail intersects Butcher Ranch Trail at the second wooden bridge. Go downhill to the right.

The trail follows beautiful Pauley Creek for 2 miles, bypassing several lovely waterfalls and inviting pools. The trail crosses Pauley Creek on another wooden bridge (the third one for the whole ride). The bridge makes a nice regrouping point, and the views up and downstream from the bridge are quite nice. From this bridge you have the ride's only real climb—about 0.25 mile to the intersection of the Second Divide and Third Divide trails. You take the Second Divide Trail on the left.

The 4.5-mile Second Divide Trail tends toward the narrow and technical. At times it's loose and sidehilly, other times rocky and exposed, full of hazards with colorful names like Crank Rock—scrape a crank here and you'll take a fast trip into the churning creek below. A quick grab of a tree limb is all that saved my Coyote Adventures guide the first time I rode this trail!

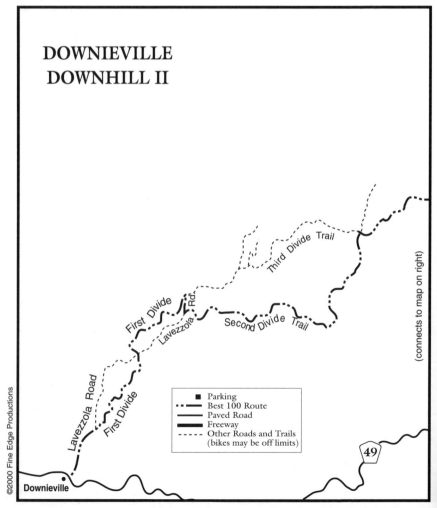

DOWNIEVILLE
DOWNHILL II

Third Divide Trail

(connects to map on right)

First Divide
Lavezzola Rd.
Second Divide Trail

Lavezzola Road

First Divide

■ Parking
Best 100 Route
Paved Road
Freeway
Other Roads and Trails
(bikes may be off limits)

49

©2000 Fine Edge Productions

Downieville

Eventually the trail makes its way up, down and out to Lavezzola Road. Lavezzola Road used to be the only way back into Downieville. But now those of you who want more singletrack (who doesn't?) can pick up the First Divide Trail, a juicy 3-mile tidbit that's been added to the trail system in the last couple of years.

Turn right on Lavezzola Road and descend 0.25 mile to the Lavezzola Creek Bridge. Before crossing the bridge, turn left into the primitive camp area to catch the First Divide Trail. It starts out on a dirt road alongside Lavezzola Creek, but the singletrack soon takes off to your left.

It descends a bit before climbing back up to Lavezzola Road. Cross the road and continue onto a dirt road. Note that this trail junction is signed. If you missed the top trailhead, you can pop onto the trail here.

The trail soon narrows into singletrack before spreading into doubletrack for the rest of its course. When the trail ends at Lavezzola Road, go left and continue downhill for a mile into Downieville.

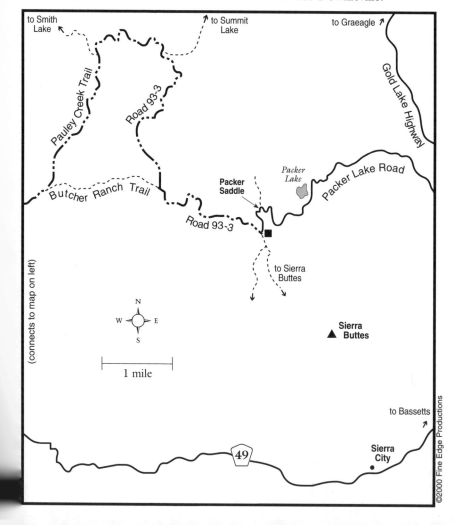

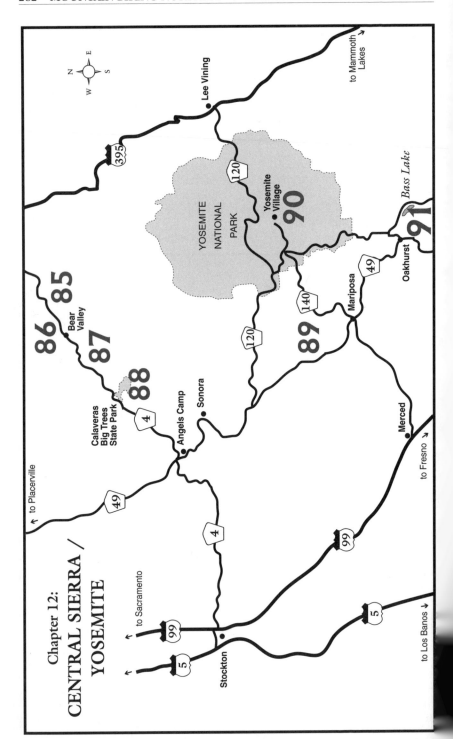

Chapter 12:
CENTRAL SIERRA /
YOSEMITE

CHAPTER 12

Central Sierra/Yosemite

by Delaine Fragnoli

Thanks largely to the images of Ansel Adams, the granite beauty of Yosemite National Park is familiar to those who have never even been to the area. More than other natural landmarks, Half Dome, El Capitan, Sentinel Rock and other Yosemite rock formations have been firmly etched into the American consciousness.

No travel book on California would be complete without a section on Yosemite. While the riding opportunities within the park are limited to paved roads, bike paths and one trail on the valley's floor, bicycling in Yosemite is still something special. Besides the incredible scenery you can see from your saddle, a bike makes the ideal way to get around the valley and to avoid the park's traffic.

To the northwest, Stanislaus National Forest borders the park and offers more off-road opportunities. With the exception of three wilderness areas (Mokelumne, Carson-Iceberg and Emigrant), most of the forest's roads and trails are open to bikes. This is high-alpine country (with correspondingly high elevations), bisected by four major rivers: the Mokelumne in the north, the Stanislaus and Toulumne in the center, and the Merced in the south.

The cross-country ski area at Bear Valley, on Highway 4 east of Stockton, is the forest's biggest draw for mountain bikers. Steep and very rocky, the riding consists mostly of jeep trails and singletrack and is rugged and technical. Even the "easiest" routes prove tough for beginning riders. Experienced riders will have a blast. Even on weekends with races or special events scheduled at the ski area, the trails remain relatively deserted—this is Alpine County, California's least-populated county. Do expect to encounter motorcycles on the jeep tracks. They can really beat the trails to dust by the end of the summer. You can find lodging, dining and a bike shop in Bear Valley Village, or you can camp at numerous campgrounds in the area. Once you leave Stockton, the only other bike shop is in Angels Camp.

Nearby is Calaveras Big Trees State Park, also on Highway 4. Although the park is popular, you can escape the crowds by heading to the less-visited south end. Here you can explore seldom-used fire roads while taking in the grandeur of some of the western Sierra's biggest trees.

On the south side of the Merced River, the Sierra National Forest tucks up against Yosemite's southwest boundary. The town of Oakhurst and nearby Bass Lake are the best places from which to explore this area. You can find everything you need—except a bike shop (the local shop had gone out of business the last time I was through; nearest shops are in Fresno)—in town or at the lake, including an active mountain bike club (Yosemite Sierra Fat Tire Association) and a guide service (Southern Yosemite Mountain Guides).

Although I have only included one ride in the area (Goat Mountain), that is a result of not having the time to document other rides, not because the riding isn't worthy of inclusion. In fact, the climb to Shuteye Peak is one of the very best, most scenic lookout rides I've ever done; the descent features miles of singletrack on a trail known as "007"—more thrills than a James Bond movie. The Nelder Grove ride serves up high-speed doubletrack and a singletrack through a gorgeous grove of sequoias.

You can do both of these rides on a weekend tour with Southern Yosemite Mountain Guides (see the Appendix). I highly recommend the company. Because both rides have some tricky route finding and require longish shuttles, it's well worth the price. Or, you can try to hook up with the mountain bike club. RecTech produces a *Southern Yosemite Adventure Map* with elevation profiles and route information. Contact the Sierra Forest Foundation, P.O. Box 3488, Oakhurst, CA 93644, 559-683-3379, for a copy.

85 Lake Alpine Loop

Distance: 4.8 miles
Difficulty: Moderate, technical in spots
Elevation: 7,400'
Ride Type: Loop on singletrack, 4WD road and pavement
Season: Late spring through fall; check snow levels
Maps: Tamarack, Spicer Meadow; also clearly shown on Lake Alpine Area inset map on the Stanislaus National Forest map
Comments: Parts of this loop, especially near lakeside campgrounds, can be heavily trafficked. Be on your best behavior. Water and bathrooms are available at several picnic areas and campgrounds on or near your route.

Highlights: This high elevation loop features fun singletrack and views of Lake Alpine.

Getting There: From Bear Valley Village take Highway 4 east for 2.6 miles. Look for a turnout on your right immediately past Silvertip Campground and the winter closure gates. A trail sign indicates Osborne Ridge Trailhead. Park here. Parking is limited, but there are other spots to park along Highway 4 if there's not room here.

Route: Begin by crossing Highway 4 and catching a singletrack on the other side. A trail sign calls this trail

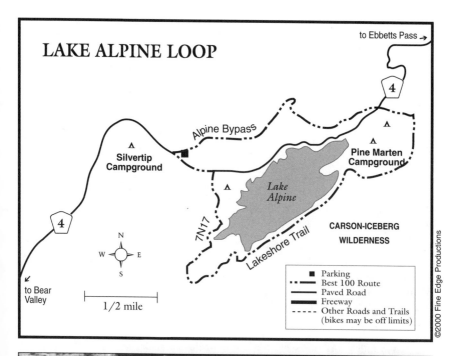

Sign at parking area/ride start.

Alpine Bypass. Generally swoopy and fun with some intermittent technical rocky sections, the trail rolls through the trees. At 0.3 mile you cross a dou-bletrack and continue on the trail on the other side. At 0.9 mile, go right at the intersection with the Tahoe-Yosemite Trail.

Fragnoli

View of Lake Alpine.

At 1.5 miles you intersect another trail. Go right toward Lake Alpine (signed). The other fork is overgrown and uninviting anyway. The trail soon (1.6 miles) deposits you on Highway 4. Cross it and take the paved road on the other side. Immediately on your right are restrooms should you need them.

The road soon crosses a creek. At 1.8 miles, take the signed road on the right toward Pine Marten campground. At 1.9 miles go around a big *Road Closed* sign and a gate onto a dirt road. At 2.0 take the trail cutting off to your right. This is the Lakeshore Trail. At 2.2 miles go straight. (A left would lead to a very steep climb to Inspiration Point, closed to bikes since it is in the Carson-Iceberg Wilderness.)

This section is one of the nicest sections of trail on the ride. It rolls through the trees, offering views of the lake. Unfortunately it ends all too soon, about 2.9 miles, at the first of a series of rocky sections. Rocks of all sizes, from granite slabs to boulders to cobbles, conspire to make the next 0.4 mile a portage for most riders. At

Singletracking the Alpine Bypass Trail.

3.2 miles, curve left up the rocks—it's easy to miss the trail here.

At 3.3 miles you cross a creek—not an easy crossing by any means, even on foot. Climb out of the creek and, at 3.6 miles, reach a steep dirt road full of cobbles, signed Lakeshore Trail/Emigrant Trail. Head right and push/ride this first section. After that it's more up and down. At 3.7 miles pass through a gate (signed to Highway 4); be sure to close it behind you.

The 4WD road (7N17 on USFS maps) gets smoother as you pass the turnoffs to picnic areas and a campground. At 4.5 miles you reach Highway 4. Turn left for a 0.3-mile climb back to your parking spot.

Option: A new 3-mile trail now connects Bear Valley Village to Silvertip Campground. From the village turn left on Highway 4. Go 0.3 mile to the second paved driveway on the right. Turn in here and almost immediately go left onto the trail and into the woods. This trail crosses Emigrant Trail as it climbs up toward Lake Alpine. Eventually it deposits you at the back of Silvertip Campground. Make your way through the campground and out to Highway 4. Turn right and look for the Alpine Bypass trail on your left (see above). Although this option adds 3 miles of climbing, it adds 3 miles of fun descending on the return route.

86 Bear Trap Basin Loop

Distance: 10.3 miles; add 1.6 miles if riding from village
Difficulty: Moderately strenuous and technical with some very strenuous sections
Elevation: 7,200' to 8,400'
Ride Type: Loop on 4WD roads, motorcycle trails and singletrack
Season: Late spring to fall; check snow levels
Map: Tamarack
Comments: Emergency food and shelter available at the cabin in Bear Trap Basin. Don't let the low mileage fool you; this ride can take all day.

Highlights: Groves of quaking aspen and alpine meadows full of wildflowers reward cyclists on this scenic loop. Ridge riding provides views into Mokelumne Wilderness to the north. If that's not enough, throw in some challenging descents and fun singletrack.

Getting There: The ride starts at the junction of Highway 4 and Forest Service road 7N35 (also referred to as Corral Hollow 4WD Road), 0.8 mile west of Bear Valley Village. The road is marked by a small jeep sign. As soon as you turn off the highway, you can see a brown backcountry board. Park here. If you're staying in the village, ride from there—you'll need the warm-up.

Route: Begin by climbing Corral Hollow Road (7N35). This is a generally moderate climb through the trees on a relatively smooth(there are some big rocks) and shady jeep road. At 1.6 miles you enter a more open area. The road is more exposed here and thus hotter and drier. By August, OHV use has beat the soil to dust,

View of Mokelumne Wildernss from top of Corral Hollow Road.

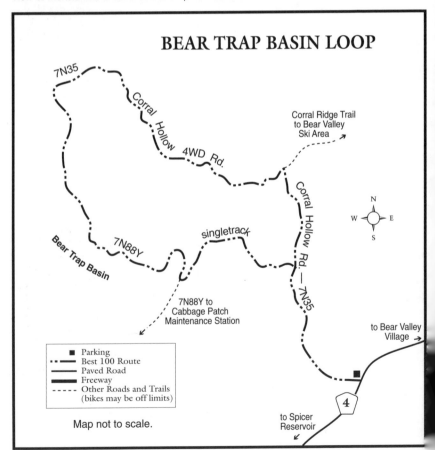

making traction difficult. Oh yeah, the grade gets steeper too.

At 1.9 miles the jeep road curves left and you can see The Wall. Mere mortals will have to hike-a-bike. Thank goodness it lasts less than 0.2 mile. After The Wall, the road continues to climb steeply, but it is rideable. At 2.3 miles you reach a junction with Corral Ridge Road (not to be confused with Corral Hollow Road, which is the jeep road you're on). Corral Ridge goes to the right toward Bear Valley ski resort. You continue around a 90-degree left on the Corral Hollow jeep road. Ignore the hiking trail which goes straight and enters Mokelumne Wilderness (closed to bikes).

Keep climbing until you summit at 2.9 miles. You have awesome views into the wilderness area from here. Definitely a photo op. When you're done gawking—and catching your breath—pass through the barbed wire gate and begin a fun, rolling section. Although there are some ups

Entering Bear Trap Basin.

and downs, the trend is downward. You may want to make use of the turnouts along this ridge since the great views continue on your right.

Cabin in Bear Trap Basin.

At 4.3 miles you really begin to lose elevation. The jeep road gets steep, loose and technical. Once again, motorcycles have churned up dirt and rock, making this descent a skidding, skating affair.

Things calm down as you enter a meadow, actually Bear Trap Basin, at 6.0 miles. Surrounded by aspens, the meadow shimmers in the summer sun. At 6.2 miles a little side trail off on the right leads 0.1 mile to a backcountry cabin in a large aspen grove. Fully stocked and furnished, it provides emergency shelter to cross-country skiers and other backcountry adventurers during the winter months. This makes a great rest or lunch stop. Look but don't disturb— unless of course you got a little carried away on that downhill and need some emergency help yourself.

Granite slab near ride's end—ride up and over it.

Returning from the cabin, you're back at the jeep road at 6.4 miles. Continue through the meadow on the jeep road. At 6.6 miles cross a stream and start to climb. You have a steep grunt of a climb out of the basin. Sections are very steep but rideable by the determined. At 7.5 miles, just before you summit a knoll, a doubletrack (more deteriorated than the jeep road) makes a sharp (almost 180 degree) turn on your left. Take this doubletrack and almost immediately pass through a barbed wire gate.

From here you have another 0.5 mile of climbing—a steep, granny gear push. At 8.1 miles, at the very lip of the ridge, is a singletrack to the right, marked by a vertical brown plastic post. The doubletrack continues to the left. Of course, you want the singletrack. Boy, do you want it. Ahead of you is nearly a mile of swoopy trail through the trees and down the other side of the ridge.

At 8.9 miles, the trail seems to run smack dab into a big slab of granite. Go up and over the slab. About 100 yards later the trail runs into the jeep road you began on. Turn right. The climb you started with is now a fast and fun descent. You are quickly back to Highway 4 at 10.3 miles.

Fragnoli

Elephant Rock Lake and meadow.

87 Elephant Rock Loop

Distance: 8.5 miles
Difficulty: Moderate with a few technical spots
Elevation: 6,800' to 7,100'
Ride Type: Loop on singletrack and dirt road
Season: Late spring to fall; check snow levels
Maps: Tamarack, Spicer Meadow Reservoir
Comments: No water or facilities. The trail skirts the Carson-Iceberg Wilderness; please stay on course and do not enter the wilderness (closed to bikes).

Highlights: Fun, rolling singletrack —there are a few technical sections— leads you past granite-dotted Union Reservoir, several meadows, tiny Elephant Rock Lake and pristine Summit Lake. The route concludes with a fast descent on a dirt road followed by a short, moderate climb and a final quick descent. Other than kayakers on Union Reservoir and a few backpackers heading to or from the wilderness area, you'll likely have the trail all

to yourself. Although the route is named for a rock formation, you never get a very good view of Elephant Rock from the trail.

Getting There: From Bear Valley Village, take Highway 4 west 3.6 miles to the signed Spicer Reservoir Road. Turn left on this paved road (7N01 on Forest Service maps). Continue on this road for 8 miles to the junction with dirt road 7N75, signed

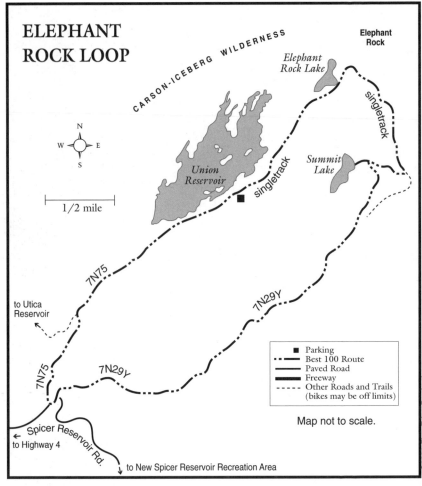

Utica Hydroelectric Project. Another sign indicates that Utica Reservoir and Union Reservoir are both 2 miles away. Go left up 7N75. At the fork in the road 0.7 mile later, go right on 7N75 toward Union Reservoir. This intersection is clearly signed. Follow 7N75 past a spur road to your left and to its end at a gravel parking area at Union Reservoir.

Route: The trail is on your right at road's end. It is signed Mountain Bicycle Trail—a designated bike trail.

Cool. Two brown wooden posts also mark the trail, which is more of a doubletrack here. Head up this trail, which almost immediately turns to singletrack.

At 0.3 mile you cross a creek. At 0.4 mile you hit a serious rock section. Most riders will portage most of the next 0.25 mile. Route finding can be tricky. LOOK FOR CAIRNS. There is one particularly tricky spot where the trail goes up a rock slab. I went straight here and ended up at a nice overlook of Union Reservoir. I

Summit Lake

you end up at the overlook you need
to backtrack, look for cairns, and go
up the rock. Don't let this section discourage you. It is the hardest section
of the whole ride. Your efforts will be
rewarded if you persevere.

Past the rocks is a sweet section of
trail, winding and packed down. At
1.4 miles you pass a trail sign on your
left, a gravel parking area on your
right, and two more trail signs, one
on the left and one on the right. Continue past the Elephant Rock trailhead sign on the right.

Soon you have views of a lake
(Elephant Rock Lake) and meadow to
your left. At the trail intersection at
1.7 miles you must turn right (signed
to Summit Lake). All other trails enter
the Carson-Iceberg Wilderness Area
and are closed to bikes. Immediately
after you make the right turn, you pass
the backside of a sign indicating that
mountain bikers should go in the
direction you just came from.

At 2.0 miles, you trace the edge of
a meadow to your left and begin

climbing. You may have to walk a
couple of short sections. At 2.9 miles
you reach a T-intersection. A trail sign
says Summit Lake is to your right and

Enjoying a view of Elephant Rock Lake.

Highland Lakes are to your left. *Note*: The Forest Service produces a route sheet which directs you to go left here. DO NOT. You will end up in a cow potty (an area that has been trampled and pooped to death by bovines), route finding becomes extremely difficult (I spent 45 minutes tromping around), and the only way out is via a VERY old, largely unrideable double-track. So, take my word for it and go right toward Summit Lake.

The trail rolls along to 3.2 miles where you pass a sign for Summit Lake trailhead. The trail enters a dirt parking area and crosses a dirt road (7N29Y). Cross the road and continue on the trail toward Summit Lake. Be polite—there may be hikers making the short trip from the parking area to the lake. You're at the lake at 3.3 miles. This small, very blue lake makes a great rest stop or lunch spot. Trees crowd right up to the shore, so you're sure to find some shade and a log to lean against.

Fragnoli

Singletrack on the way to Summit Lake.

Retrace your tracks to the dirt road, reached at 3.4 miles, and go right. It's flat at first, but then descends. Time to let off the brakes! Don't go totally nuts as the road can be washboarded and you do need to watch for vehicles.

After a quick couple of miles, the road crosses a creek and begins a moderate climb. Stay on the gravel road until it tops out at paved Spicer Reservoir Road. A sign on your left indicates that the paved road drops down to the New Spicer Reservoir Recreation Area. You continue straight and uphill for 0.1 mile.

At 6.5 miles, dirt road 7N75 intersects Spicer Reservoir Road. You should recognize this intersection from your drive in. Go right onto 7N75 and climb another 0.5 mile. At the intersection at 7.2 miles, go right toward Union Reservoir. Enjoy the downhill back to the parking area at road's end.

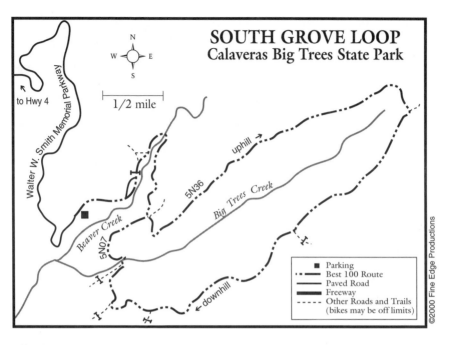

88 Calaveras Big Trees State Park/ South Grove Loop

Distance: 12.5 miles
Difficulty: Moderate, not technical
Elevation: 1,400' gain/loss
Ride Type: Loop on fire roads and pavement
Season: Spring through fall
Map: Dorrington. (Brochure and trail map available from the park office for $1.)
Comments: There is no water available at the south end of the park, so fill up at the more developed north end when you enter. There is a $5 park entry fee.

Highlights: Calaveras County seems to be famous for two things: as the setting for Mark Twain's short story "The Notorious Jumping Frog of Calaveras County" and as the home of two of the most impressive groves of giant sequoia trees in the state.

Commonly confused with redwoods, their coastal cousins, *Sequoiadendron giganteum* are stouter but shorter and thrive in a drier climate. Sacred to the local Indians, the Calaveras sequoias were brought to the

attention of whites in the 1850s when a lost hunter stumbled into the area by mistake. All hell broke loose after that, and several entrepreneurs cut down some of the most impressive specimens to cart around the country and exhibit for money.

Thankfully, two magnificent groves, the North Grove and the South Grove, have been preserved, largely through the work of the Save-the-Redwoods League and the Calaveras Grove Association. Today the

Rafters on the Stanislaus River.

park houses not only the two groves but also 6,000 acres of pine forest in the Stanislaus River and Beaver Creek watersheds.

Although all hiking trails are closed to bikes, you can enjoy the park on paved roads and dirt access roads. Most visitors are content to hike the trail through the North Grove and few make it to the South Grove; even fewer explore the fire roads. So relatively wild and remote is the South Grove that it has been given special status as a "natural preserve." Please behave accordingly when you visit.

Note: Please do not confuse the South Grove, which refers to a grove of trees, with the South Grove Trail, which is closed to bikes. Your route is on dirt roads which circle the South Grove.

Getting There: From Stockton, take Highway 99 to Highway 4 and head east. Follow Highway 4 past the junction with Highway 49 at Angels

Camp. The park is 4 miles past the town of Arnold. Take the park's main thoroughfare, the Walter Smith Memorial Parkway, for 8.3 miles to the parking area for the South Grove Trail. You can begin your ride here where there is plentiful parking, port-a-potties, picnic tables, and easy access to Beaver Creek for a post-ride dip. Or you can continue to Beaver Creek Picnic Area, which also has plentiful parking, port-a-potties and picnic tables. Or you can park in the small area at the end of the parkway—no facilities except one port-a-potty.

Route: Mileages are from the South Grove parking area. Leave the parking area and continue northeast on the park's main paved road. At 0.7 the pavement ends. Continue around a double gate (signed Beaver Creek, Gate 31) and onto a dirt road. Stay on the main smooth, graded road, veering right.

At 1.3 miles cross Beaver Creek on

a wooden bridge. This is a popular spot for fishing. Start a middle-chainring climb. The going isn't too tough on the smooth, lightly graveled road. The Bradley Grove Trail (closed to bikes) crosses the road at 1.8 miles. At 2.1 miles, road 5N07 comes in from the left and then, 100 feet later, veers off to the right. This road will be your return route. For now, you fork left to stay on 5N36 (signed).

Now comes the hard part. You have an exceptionally steep 0.1-mile climb, followed by another 0.4 mile of not-so-steep-but-still-plenty-steep climbing. At 2.6 you top out and have a nice easy roll to 3.2 miles. It gets steeper again from 3.2 to 3.4 miles, where you reach a clearing. From here the terrain is rolling with a few downhills, but with another steep pitch from 4.4 to 4.6 miles.

Fragnoli

Bridge over Beaver Creek.

From 4.6 to 4.9 miles you descend, then climb some more. You know the climb is about to top out when the road starts curving eastward and you can see a barbed wire fence marking the park boundary. From 5.2 to 6.9 miles you have rolling ridge riding. You pass some obviously unused spurs on your left. Stay on the main road.

At 7.7 miles, there is a big dirt road to the left. Stay straight and begin a steep descent. There's another dirt road on the left at 8.7 miles. Ignore it. At 9.1 miles, in a 90-degree right-hand corner, yet another dirt road comes in on the left. Ignore it as well. Again at 9.6 miles ignore the road to the left. You may not even notice some of these roads

as you head down, down, down.

At 9.7 miles cross Big Trees Creek. Watch your speed here since the South Grove Trail crosses the road immediately past the creek—you don't want to upset any unsuspecting hikers. At 10.4 miles the road you're on, 5N07, rejoins 5N36. This is the same intersection you hit at 2.1 miles on the way out. Go left on 5N36 to return the way you came: down to and over Beaver Creek and out to pavement. At 12.5 you're back at the South Grove parking area.

While you're here, why not go for a swim or take the time to hike the South Grove Trail? Be sure to take the spur out to the Agassiz Tree and the Palace Hotel Tree, the two largest trees in the park.

89 Merced River Trail

Distance: 14 miles one way, 28 miles out and back
Difficulty: Easy; areas where slides and washouts have occurred make the trail difficult in spots.
Elevation: 420' loss one-way
Ride Type: One-way with shuttle option or out-and-back
Season: Year-round; can get brutally hot in summer
Map: A trail guide (actually it's a boating trail guide) of the Merced River is available at the Briceburg Visitor Center.
Comments: You MUST call the Merced Irrigation District Parks Department at 209-378-2521 or 800-468-8889 to check water level at Bagby Recreation Area. Do NOT attempt this ride without calling. Water level MUST be under 820 feet. THIS IS NO JOKE. IF THE WATER LEVEL IS OVER 820 FEET, THE ENTIRE TRAIL IS COMPLETELY UNDER WATER.

Highlights: This route follows the old Yosemite railroad grade from the Briceburg Visitor Center to the Highway 49 bridge at Bagby Recreation Area. Briceburg is a popular put-in and take-out spot for boaters rafting the Merced River, and Bagby is the final take-out point. The trail parallels the river as it heads downstream to Lake McClure (Exchequer Reservoir). As is true of most railroad grades, this one is pretty level the whole way, never more than a 5 percent grade.

In addition to rafters, you may see modern-day prospectors working dredges. Miners first arrived here in the 1850s. The area is dotted with old mines, the most productive of which was Hite's Cove mine. It produced more than $3 million of gold before ceasing operations. Also keep your eyes peeled for lizards—the area is home to the rare limestone salamander.

The railroad was originally built to cart out timber cut by the Yosemite Lumber Company. The river's slopes used to be covered with sugar pine but, thanks to the logging, today's route is largely unshaded, which makes this an uncomfortably hot ride during the height of summer—

although opportunities to cool off in the river are plentiful. Besides timber, the railroad also carried tourists from Merced to El Portal. This was the most popular method for getting to Yosemite until the 1940s.

The river actually was named by a Mexican soldier. In 1806, Lieutenant Gabriel Moraga, exhausted after a 40-mile march, came upon the river. In his gratitude he called it *El Rio Nuestra Senora de la Merced* (The River of Our Lady of Mercy). It has since mercifully been shortened to Merced. Today much of the river belongs to the National Wild and Scenic River system.

The ride can be done as a one-way shuttle. Starting at Briceburg and ending at Bagby (the route described below), it yields an almost all-downhill ride. As an out-and-back of whatever length, the route is best done from Bagby. That way you go up on your way out and down on your way back. Try to at least make it to the waterfalls near the North Fork of the Merced.

No matter which way you ride the route, plan on making a day of it. A ranger I talked to recommended bringing a swimsuit, a snorkel and an

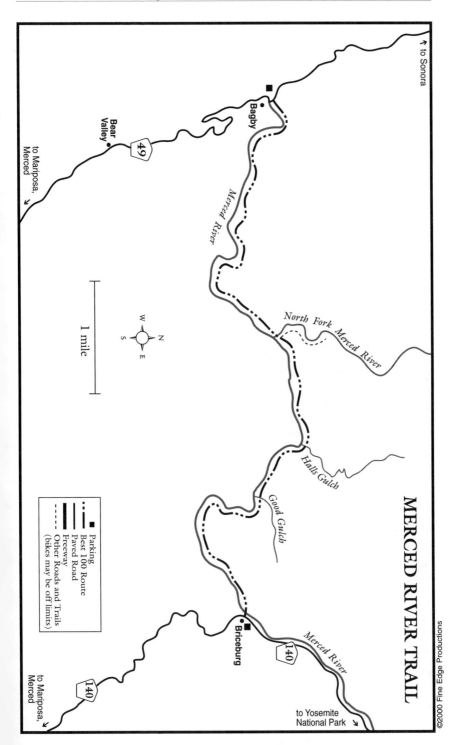

MERCED RIVER TRAIL

to Sonora

Bagby

Bear
Valley

49

to Mariposa,
Merced

Merced River

North Fork Merced River

1 mile

W
S
N
E

Halls Gulch

Good Gulch

Briceburg

140

Merced River

to Mariposa,
Merced

140

to Yosemite
National Park

Parking
Best 100 Route
Paved Road
Freeway
Other Roads and Trails
(bikes may be off limits)

sus

extra granola bar. Floating in the clear swimming holes you can watch enormous fish and look for elusive gold nuggets. Break off a bit of granola bar and watch the fish swarm.

Getting There: From Merced (on Highway 99), head east on Highway 140 to Highway 49 and go north. Past Bear Valley (not to be confused with the Bear Valley in Rides 85 - 87) you cross the Merced River at the Bagby bridge. If you choose the shuttle option, leave your shuttle vehicle in the vista point parking area on the north side of the bridge. Or you can pay the day-use fee ($5.50) and park at Bagby Recreation Area (water, toilets, campground) on the south side of the bridge.

To get to the ride's eastern end, backtrack to Highway 140 and go left (northeast). Follow Highway 140 through Midpines and down to Briceburg. Park at the Briceburg Visitor Center (open seasonally).

Route: The trail starts on the north side of the Merced River. Just over a mile later you pass Vanderkarr Crossing, a good swimming spot late in the summer. There are also toilets here should you need them.

At about 2.5 miles, you come to McCabe Flat Camp, an undeveloped campground. Here the river curves northward, a spot known to rafters as Corner Pocket. Just under 4 miles, you cross Good Gulch.

You pass Willow Placer and Railroad Flat, undeveloped campgrounds, at 5 miles. Both are popular with the boating crowd. Just past these you cross Halls Gulch. At about 5.5 miles you come to the remains of an old diversion dam.

In the next mile, the river really begins to churn as a major set of rapids serves warning of the upcoming North Fork Falls. Between 7 and 8 miles, the trail begins to degenerate. Here high water levels frequently wash out the trail.

At just under 8 miles, you come to where the

Miles of Smooth singletrack.

Fragnoli

North Fork runs into the main Merced River. In the spring, especially in heavy snow years, this may be impassable or may require a portage. Use your common sense. If it's too dangerous to cross, turn around and go back the way you came. It still makes for a nice ride. If you have to portage , you won't be alone—the main river is so rough at this point that rafters must make a mandatory portage.

If you can get past the North Fork you have 6 more undulating miles of river to follow. Miles 11 to 13 cross private land, so be sure to stay on the trail and behave yourself. Once you get to Bagby, you may want to hang out for a while. There is a campground as well as picnic facilities, and you can go swimming.

90 Yosemite National Park/ Valley Floor and Mirror Lake

Distance: Varies, depends on options taken; entire loop is about 17 miles
Difficulty: Easy, not technical
Elevation: Minimal elevation gain/loss
Ride Type: Loop on pavement and dirt
Season: Spring through fall
Maps: Wilderness Press produces a topo map of Yosemite Valley. Trails Illustrated makes one for Yosemite National Park.
Comments: All facilities are located in the valley.

Highlights: In *Desert Solitaire* (1968), Edward Abbey described Yosemite National Park as "a dusty milling confusion of motor vehicles and ponderous camping machinery" and went on to suggest that the park ". . . could be returned to relative beauty and order by the simple expedient of requiring all visitors, at the park entrance, to lock up their automobiles and continue their tour on the seats of good workable bicycles supplied free of charge by the United States Government. Let our people travel light and free on their bicycles . . . their backpacks, their tents, their food will be trucked in for them, free of charge, to the campground of their choice by the Park Service. Why not?"

Unfortunately, the Park Service has not heeded Abbey's advice and Yosemite Valley continues to be choked with motor traffic. Although shuttles have helped and plans are afoot to further minimize traffic, congestion can still be a problem. All the more reason then for you to take to two wheels. A bicycle is by far the easiest, most efficient, and healthiest way to tour Yosemite.

You are limited to paved roads and bike paths, with a section of dirt, so the riding is not hardcore mountain biking. Still, Yosemite houses some of the most incredible scenery in the world, and any kind of bike is a great way to visit the park's awesome sights.

Getting There: From the west, the most direct route is via Highway 140 from Merced. For those coming from the north, access is by Highway 120. Those coming from the east side of the Sierra have no choice but to take

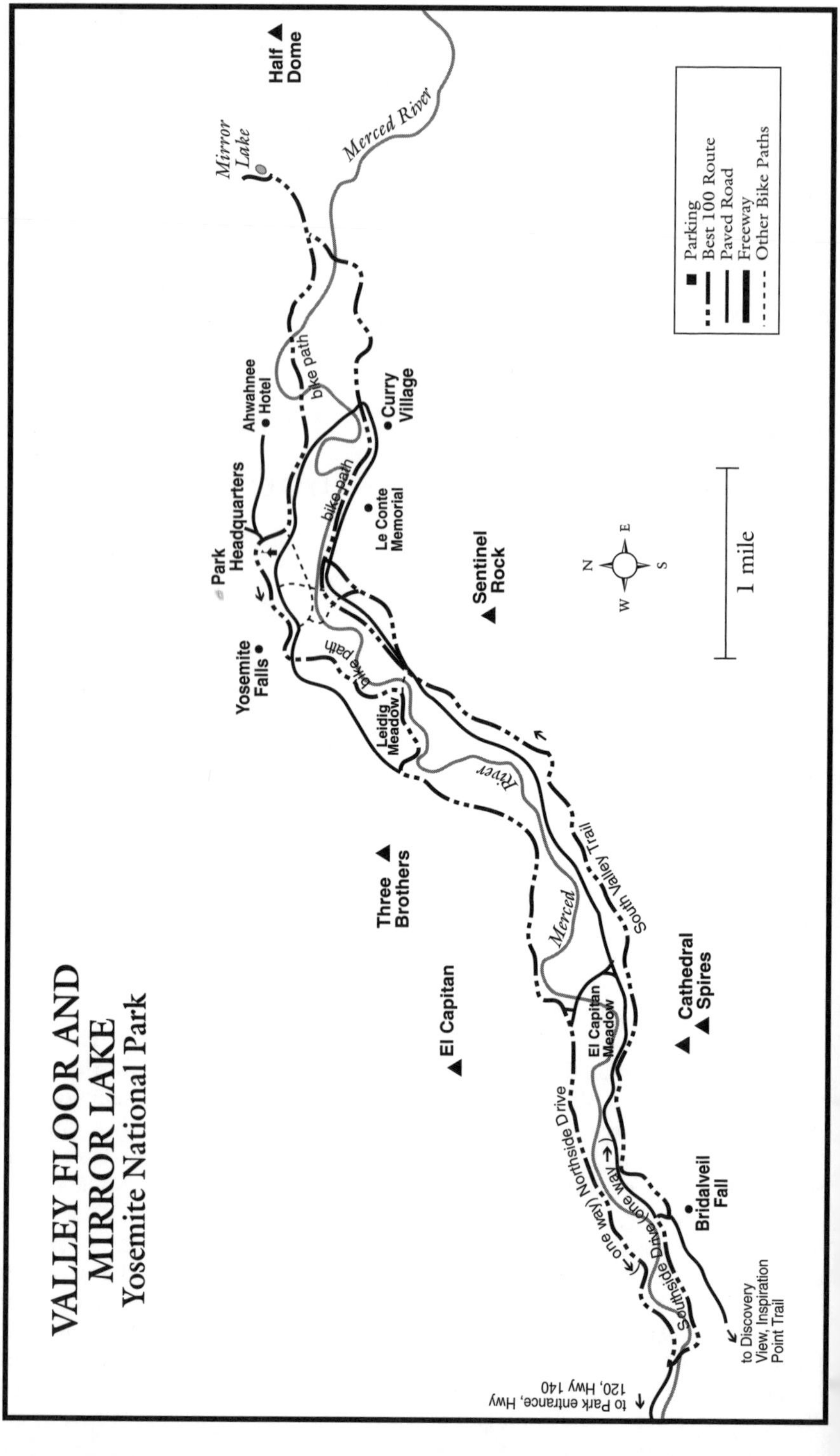

VALLEY FLOOR AND
MIRROR LAKE
Yosemite National Park

©2000 Fine Edge Productions

Half
Dome

Mirror
Lake

Merced River

Ahwahnee
Hotel

bike path

Curry
Village

Park
Headquarters

Le Conte
Memorial

Sentinel
Rock

Yosemite
Falls

bike path

Leidig
Meadow

River

Three
Brothers

Merced

South Valley Trail

El Capitan

El Capitan
Meadow

Cathedral
Spires

Bridalveil
Fall

one way) Northside Drive

Southside Drive (one way)

to Discovery
View, Inspiration
Point Trail

to Park entrance, Hwy
120, Hwy 140

Parking
Best 100 Route
Paved Road
Freeway
Other Bike Paths

N
W   E
S

1 mile

Interstate 395 to the junction with 120 near Lee Vining. From there, it's over Tioga Pass (check snow conditions as late as June or even July in a heavy snow year) and into the valley.

Route: You can start this ride virtually anywhere on the valley floor. Two one-way roads, Northside Drive and Southside Drive, basically circle the valley. A paved bike path parallels each road for much of the way, giving you freedom from vehicle traffic most of the time.

However, the bike path sees a lot of foot traffic and, increasingly, rollerbladers. Families with kids running every which way, joggers, tourists gaping at the scenery, parents pushing baby strollers—all combine to crowd the path. Be careful, watch for people stepping out in front of you suddenly, and keep your speed down. I've found that a bell helps immeasurably.

For lack of a better place, I'll start at the park headquarters in Yosemite Village. From here, the clearly-marked bike path heads west, paralleling Northside Drive. Your first scenic stop, Lower Yosemite Falls, comes up quickly, about 0.5 mile. Park your bike—there are bike racks—and walk up the asphalt to the base of the falls.

The bike path continues to head west, still paralleling Northside Drive. You cross the road and head south past Yosemite Lodge and down toward the Merced River. You contour along Leidig Meadow before circling back out to Northside Drive. You may want to stop at the meadow and look behind you for views of North Dome and Half Dome.

Past the meadow you have to get out on the road to continue your tour. (The North Valley Trail which leads from the meadow is closed to bikes.) There's no bike path for the next several miles, but there is a good shoulder.

If you're uncomfortable riding with vehicle traffic or have young children with you, I recommend that you do an out-and-back on the north or south side of the valley, or fashion a much shorter loop using the footbridge at Leidig Meadow or Sentinel Bridge.

As you merge onto the road, the towering rock formation above you is known as the Three Brothers because of its three distinctive ridgelines. You pass several picnic areas as you make your way around the Brothers and on to the base of world-famous El Capitan.

Just past the Devils Elbow Picnic Area, if you're tired already or want to do a short loop, take Northside over the El Capitan Bridge to Southside Drive and start heading back. For a longer loop, which takes you to Bridalveil Fall, continue west on Northside.

You pass the slight but graceful Ribbon Fall on your way to the intersection with Southside Drive. Be careful of traffic here as you cross over the Merced on Pohono Bridge and loop onto Southside Drive. All the traffic coming into the park has to take Southside Drive.

The terrain is a little hillier on the south side. So far your route has been gradually downhill and on the way back you have to gain back the elevation lost.

You will want to stop at Bridalveil Fall. Visiting Bridalveil is the primary reason for doing the longer loop in the first place. From the road which leads to Bridalveil you can pick up the South Valley Trail, a 6-mile dirt trail, sections of which are open to bikes (obey the signs). Cross a creek and head up an old road bed to the base of Cathedral Rocks.

The trail soon rejoins the road near a picnic area before continuing east. (This is a good spot to watch rock climbers on El Capitan across the valley—bring binoculars.) You cross Sentinel Creek and get a good look at Sentinel Fall, which runs in the spring. Just past here you can drop down to the pavement and pick up the paved bike path on the other side of the road.

Soon you pass Le Conte Memorial, a tribute to Berkeley's first geology professor, who was also a Sierra Club hero and supporter of Yosemite. Then you continue on to Curry Village.

Expect more traffic as you approach Curry Village. Near the village you can take the path left over Stoneman Bridge to see the architectural splendor of the Ahwahnee Hotel and complete your loop, or if you want to take a trip out to Mirror Lake, you can continue east past Stoneman Meadow.

Pass through Lower Pines and Upper Pines campgrounds and cross the Merced on Clark Bridge. Continue around the stables. At the fork go left and head northward toward Mirror Lake. At the next fork go right.

This is the only real hill in the whole loop as you head up to Mirror Lake. There is a horse path and a foot path, but you must stay on the pavement. (The pavement is closed to motor vehicles.) The climb doesn't last for long and soon deposits you at the lake. The lake may be a disappointment to you since it is quickly turning into a meadow and, thus, does not "mirror" much of anything anymore. Still, it's pretty, offers views of Half Dome looming above you, and makes a nice rest stop. Note that bikes are not allowed on the trail that loops around the meadow/lake.

Backtrack down the hill and watch your speed. At the fork go straight. Pass Indian Caves and circle around the group campground. Cross Sugarpine Bridge and head on to the Ahwahnee Hotel. Just past the hotel are the park headquarters. The entire loop is roughly 17 miles.

91 Goat Mountain Loop

Distance: 10 miles
Difficulty: Moderate, technical in spots
Elevation: 500' gain/loss; 4,000 high point
Ride Type: Loop on pavement, dirt road, singletrack
Season: Spring through fall
Map: Southern Yosemite Adventure Map
Comments: Facilities at Forks Campground

Highlights: A moderate climb leads to a lookout tower and a nothing-but-fun singletrack descent. The loop makes a great warm-up ride before you tackle the tougher routes in the area.

Getting There: The best place to start is at the dirt parking lot across the road from The Forks Resort at the junction of Road 222 (Bass Lake Road) and 426 (Crane Valley Road)

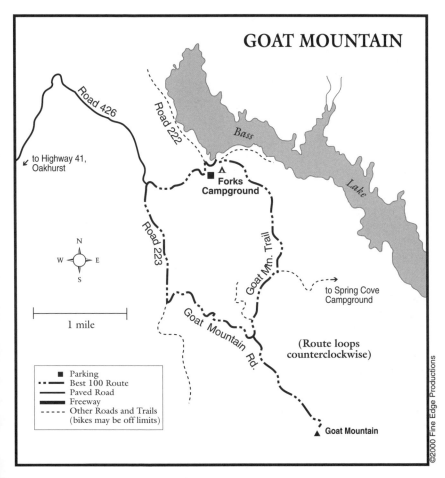

GOAT MOUNTAIN

to Highway 41, Oakhurst

Road 426

Road 222

Bass Lake

Forks Campground

Road 223

Goat Mtn. Trail

to Spring Cove Campground

Goat Mountain Rd.

(Route loops counterclockwise)

1 mile

Goat Mountain

■ Parking
∙∙∙ Best 100 Route
— Paved Road
▬ Freeway
--- Other Roads and Trails
    (bikes may be off limits)

©2000 Fine Edge Productions

on the southwest shore of Bass Lake. From Oakhurst, head east on Road 426. At the junction with Road 223 (Teaford Saddle Road) veer left to stay on 426 as it drops to the lake. Road 426 Ts into Road 222. The resort is on your left and the parking lot on your right. The cafe at the resort is a great greasy spoon for post-ride burgers, fries and shakes.

Route: Backtrack up Road 426 for 0.9 mile of fairly steep pavement, climbing to the T junction with Road 223. Go left. Roll along 223 until 2.3 miles. Look for dirt Goat Mountain

Road on your left and the sign: *Goat Mountain Trail, 1 mile; Goat Mountain Lookout, 3 miles*. A brown post designates this as Forest Service Road 7S23 and indicates no cars allowed. Head left up this road.

Soon a rougher dirt road goes down to the right—avoid it and keep climbing. Overall moderate, the ascent rises and abates in intermittently steeper and flatter sections . About 1.5 miles up the climb (3.8 miles total), you come to a Y-intersection at a saddle. A sign indicates the lookout is another 1.5 miles to the right. Continue toward the lookout.

Author at lookout tower atop Goat Mountain.

You soon begin a downhill. It seemed counterintuitive to me to be heading *down* to a lookout, but I need not have worried. The climbing begins again soon enough and grows steeper and rockier the closer you get to the lookout. Finally you reach a flattish spot but must go hard right up a final pitch to the tower. Here a picnic table invites you to rest and take in the surrounding mountains.

I have to confess that I found the view from the top a little disappointing. There is a brief view of the lake on the climb and you can barely make out the lake from one angle at the lookout.

Backtrack to the Y-intersection you passed on the way up. Keep your eyes peeled for a trail sign immediately before the Y. The sign indicates Goat Mountain Trail (22E04) to the right and says *Spring Cove Trail (22E18), 1.0 mile; Forks Camp-* *ground, 2.9 miles.* Take the trail through the manzanitas. It soon runs into a dirt road. Go right on the road for 0.2 mile to pick up the trail again off to the right. If you start climbing on the dirt road, you missed the trail turnoff. The trail is signed but it's easy to miss.

After a mile of bobbing and weaving over and around some rocky sections (watch for poison oak), you reach a junction with the Spring Cove Trail. Stay left on Goat Mountain Trail toward Forks Campground. From this point on, the trail is fast, swoopy, bermy fun. You won't want it to end.

After a couple of miles of whoop-and-holler fun, the trail deposits you in the campground. Go right, downhill. Stay on the main route through the campground to Road 222. Go left onto the pavement to the Forks to complete the loop.

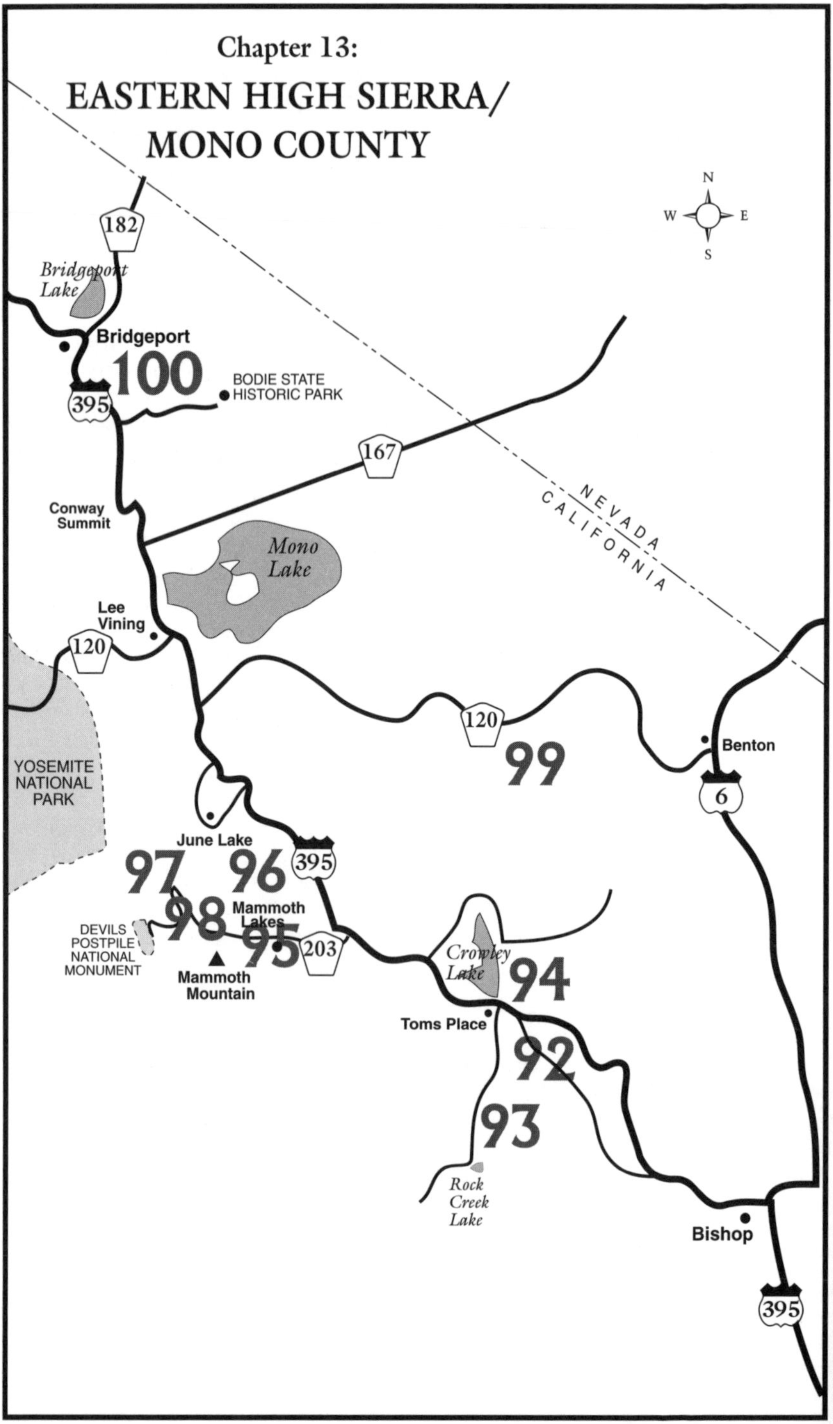

Chapter 13:

EASTERN HIGH SIERRA/ MONO COUNTY

182

Bridgeport Lake

Bridgeport

100

395

BODIE STATE
HISTORIC PARK

167

NEVADA
CALIFORNIA

Conway
Summit

*Mono
Lake*

Lee
Vining

120

120

99

Benton

6

YOSEMITE
NATIONAL
PARK

June Lake

97 **96** 395

98 Mammoth
Lakes

DEVILS
POSTPILE
NATIONAL
MONUMENT

95 203

▲
Mammoth
Mountain

*Crowley
Lake*

94

Toms Place

92

93

*Rock
Creek
Lake*

Bishop

395

Eastern High Sierra/ Mono County

by Réanne Hemingway-Douglass, Mark Davis, and Don Douglass

The Eastern High Sierra, home to some of the most scenic mountain and basin terrain in America, offers unlimited outdoor challenges in all seasons. Popular recreation includes camping, hiking, fishing, alpine and cross-country skiing, boating, hunting, horseback riding and packing. Mountain bike riding, four-wheel-driving, and snowmobiling are allowed in designated areas.

Approximately 98 percent of the land in Mono County is held in trust for the public. Among these lands are Inyo National Forest, Mono Basin National Scenic Area, Devils Postpile National Monument, Bureau of Land Management holdings, and the John Muir and Ansel Adams Wilderness areas.

The Inyo National Forest itself is one of the most highly visited areas of the country's national forest system. Its 1.9 million acres are managed primarily for recreation and wilderness preservation, with contracts held also for timber harvest, grazing, mining, and research. The Mono Basin National Scenic Area covers unique Mono Lake and its adjacent tufa-lined shores and pinyon forests—a total of 116,000 acres of Great Basin topography. Devils Postpile National Monument is administered by the National Park Service, while most of the large alluvial plains, valleys and meadows to the east of the Sierra Nevada are managed by the Bureau of Land Management.

92 Lower Rock Creek Trail

Distance: 3.3 miles or 8 miles (double the mileage if you ride it as a loop)
Difficulty: First half easy to moderate; second half moderate to advanced, with some technical sections
Elevation: 7,000' to 5,000' (500'-600' to 2,000' loss/gain)
Ride Type: One-way shuttle or loop on singletrack and pavement
Season: April to November; especially nice in early fall
Maps: USGS 7.5 min. series Toms Place, Casa Diablo Mountain, Rovana
Comments: Toilets, cafe and store at Tom's Place

Highlights: For a real mountain biking treat, the Lower Rock Creek Trail is hard to beat. This route follows an old fishermen's trail along the edge of Rock Creek as it flows south, creating its own gorge of natural scenic beauty. The upper section of the trail can be navigated with easy to moderate skill and simple care. Due to rocks and logs obstructing the lower section of the trail at certain points, the route becomes something of a trials competition requiring advanced skill. You can do part or all of the trail, depending upon your skill and love of adventure. Fortunately, a paved road crosses the trail at the appropriate bailout point. This trail is used by hikers and fishermen, so please yield to all others by stopping and dismounting if necessary. (It's a good idea to avoid the heaviest part of the fishing season to minimize traffic.)

Note: The BLM and USFS have been conducting a study regarding the designation of Rock Creek as a Wild and Scenic River. The agencies feel that current recreational use will be compatible with their findings, and they invite public input. Please contact the BLM in Bishop for information or to volunteer for trail work on the Rock Creek Trail. The Mammoth Area Mountain Bike Organiza-

tion (MAMBO) donates 150-200 hours of labor per year on this trail.

Getting There: From the junction of Highways 203 and 395, drive south 15.0 miles to a turnoff marked Swall Meadow, Lower Rock Creek. (When you pass the turnoff for Tom's Place, it's 0.85 mile to your turnoff.) About 75 yards south of Highway 395 on the west side of Lower Rock Creek Road, there is parking for four or five cars next to a sign marked: *Inyo National Forest Day Use Area, Lower Rock Creek.* Park here. To do the entire 8-mile downhill ride as a shuttle, drive a second car to Paradise Lodge, 8 miles down Lower Rock Creek Road, and park off the road beyond the lodge wherever you can find a place. Do not park behind the lodge or block their driveways.

Route: The trail takes off from the east side of the road between two small boulders. Head east down to Rock Creek, which flows in from a culvert under Highway 395. The trail narrows around the culvert, and it's best to walk your bike here. At 0.2 mile you pass a catch basin, then it's sandy for the next 100 yards until you come to the side of the creek. At 1.5 miles the trail narrows to handlebar-width among aspens.

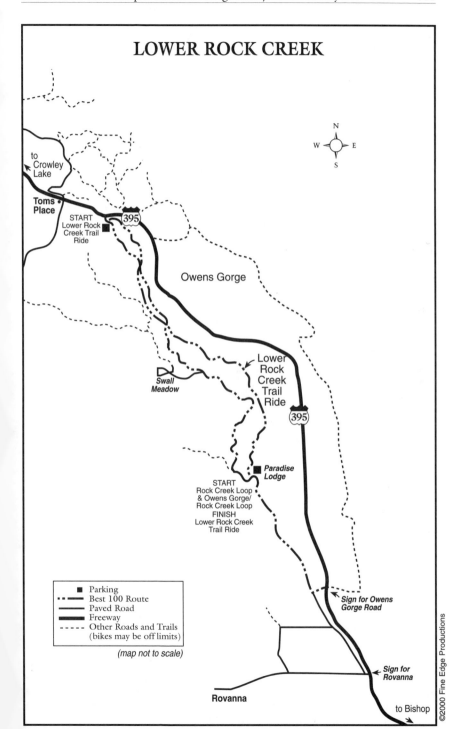

LOWER ROCK CREEK

N
W — E
S

to Crowley Lake

Toms Place

START Lower Rock Creek Trail Ride

395

Owens Gorge

Lower Rock Creek Trail Ride

395

Swall Meadow

Paradise Lodge

START Rock Creek Loop & Owens Gorge/ Rock Creek Loop
FINISH Lower Rock Creek Trail Ride

Sign for Owens Gorge Road

■ Parking
▪▪▪– Best 100 Route
—— Paved Road
—— Freeway
– – – Other Roads and Trails
(bikes may be off limits)

(map not to scale)

Sign for Rovanna

Rovanna

to Bishop

©2000 Fine Edge Productions

Courtesy BLM

Tight turns in Lower Rock Creek Canyon

The next section along the creek is frequently wet and muddy, and you may have to walk your bike. At 1.7 miles the trail is fast, but keep a lookout for rocks and logs. At 2.1 miles you cross a dry wash—carry your bike at this point. Make a hard right at 2.2 miles and drop down to the paved road. Then cross the bridge to the west side (uphill) of the creek and pick up the trail, continuing down the west side of the creek.

At 2.9 miles you ride across Witcher Creek Bridge. Within 75 yards there's another stream crossing without a bridge that you can usually cross without dismounting. At 3.2 miles, you're on a high-speed trail in the shade, but watch out for rocky outcroppings above the stream; it's very narrow at this point. At 3.3 miles you come back to the paved road at a parking area for about six cars.

The trail crosses the pavement at this point and continues down Rock Creek. You can bail out here and ride the 3.3 miles back up the pavement to your car. Or if you're an experienced, hearty cyclist and wish to continue down the trail, cross the road and pick up the trail down to the creek. (*Caution*: From here down, there are no bailout points, and only experienced cyclists should continue.) We don't recommend this lower section during times of earthquake swarms.

At 3.5 miles you pass an old rusty car, circa 1930. At about 3.8 miles the canyon starts to narrow, so watch out for brush. At the very bottom of Sherwin Hill, where you see several old rusted car bodies (4.0 miles), turn left and cross a log bridge. *Caution:* Watch the cracks between the logs! The canyon continues to narrow, and the trail becomes rocky for 100 yards. From here down, the canyon is deep with sheer cliffs.

At 4.2 miles a fallen tree, almost six feet in diameter, has been sawed through. For fun, count the rings of the tree to determine its age. At 4.4 miles the trail is blocked by a boulder half the size of a Volkswagen. During a 1985 earthquake, the pink rocks lying around this area split off from the east wall of the cliff above and

Davis

Rock Creek Lake

tumbled clear across the creek, taking numerous trees in their path. The large pink rock blocking the trail at 4.6 miles fell in a 1986 earthquake. If you look up the canyon wall to the east, you can see where the rock broke away. At 4.8 miles, ride the re-routed trail to the right of a 5-foot-wide boulder. Note that the original trail lies underneath that rock!

At 4.9 miles you pass a downed 6-foot-diameter "grandfather" tree. Look east up the canyon and notice the cabin-sized boulders that have tumbled down. There's a nice picnicking area along this particular stretch of the creek. You can also spot basaltic columns similar to those of Devils Postpile.

At 5.1 miles, where the stream flows more gently, there are several elbows where you can find primitive campsites. As you leave this area, the trail curves up a scree and talus slope. At 5.3 miles you return to the creek. At 5.8 miles heavy rocks cover much of the trail. The trail peters out on the east side and you have to cross to the west side of the creek.

Over the next nine-tenths of a mile, a series of bridges take you back and forth across the creek. (Crossing through the stream itself stirs up sediments which affect the ecology of the creek, so use the bridges.) You cross to the west side again at 7.0 miles on a wide bridge; continue on a high-speed trail, and within 0.2 mile, you pick up a jeep trail. At 7.5 miles, use the footbridge 30 feet downstream. There are 250 yards of singletrack to the right just after this last bridge.

At 8.0 miles, you reach Paradise Lodge and the paved road. The lodge is on private property, so please respect any signs posted. Pick up your shuttle vehicle here. If you're riding back to your starting point, instead turn right on Lower Rock Creek Road and return uphill on the pavement. Do not attempt to ride uphill on the trail.

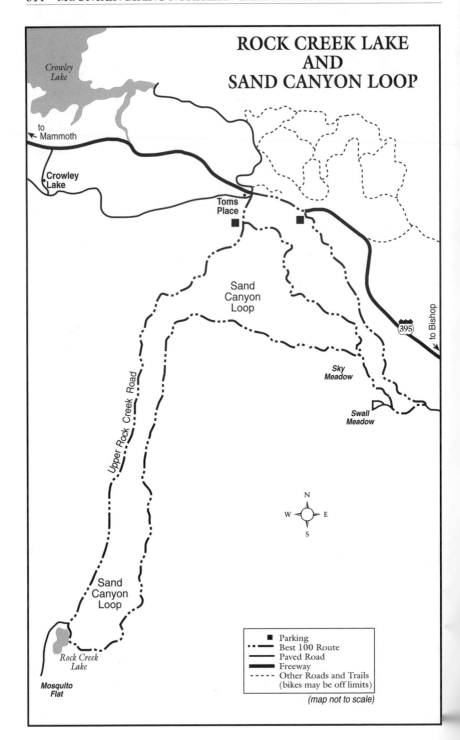

ROCK CREEK LAKE
AND
SAND CANYON LOOP

93 Rock Creek Lake/Sand Canyon

Distance: Approx. 22 miles (loop) or 14 miles as a shuttle
Difficulty: Strenuous due to the elevation and climb; technical
Elevation: 7,000' to 10,000'; 3,000' gain/loss
Ride Type: Loop on pavement, dirt roads and trail; or shuttle, leaving one car at Tom's Place and one at Rock Creek Lake Campground
Season: June through October
Maps: Fine Edge Eastern Sierra Recreation Topo Map; 7.5 min. series Mt. Morgan, Tom's Place
Comments: Toilets, café and store at Tom's Place; toilet, café and store at Rock Creek Lakes Resort

Highlights: This is a strenuous trip that covers a lot of ground over varied terrain with fantastic scenery. You can do this ride either as a loop or as a mostly downhill ride using a shuttle. If you're prepared for the brutal combination of elevation gain, "thin air," long distance, and some challenging bicycle handling, the entire loop trip may be for you. This route may get early snow, so carry extra clothing to be prepared for abrupt weather changes.

Be sure to carry adequate water. Springs that feed into Witcher Creek on the downhill run can be used, but all water must be treated. Note that since Rock Creek Canyon faces north-south, as you go up the canyon you are technically heading south. This route crosses the migration path for the Sherwin deer herd, and in both spring and fall, numerous deer

Views of Mount Tom/Owens Valley from Witcher Creek

Autumn cycling near Sand Canyon

travel along these slopes. Please be careful not to frighten them.

Getting There: From the junction of Highways 203 and 395 (near Mammoth Lakes), drive south 14.8 miles to Tom's Place. Turn west (right). If you plan to do the full pavement-dirt loop, park your car to the left on the pavement spur parallel to 395.

If you're planning to do the shuttle option, park one car on the pavement spur parallel to Highway 395 at Tom's Place and the second car in the day-use parking lot at Rock Creek Lake.

Route: For the full loop starting at Tom's Place, hop on your bike and head up the canyon on the paved road for 8 miles to Rock Creek Campground. Just after you pass Rock Creek Lakes Resort, turn left and head to the parking lot at the east end of the road at Rock Creek Lake. This

parking area is the starting point for the shuttle ride.

From here, pick up the dirt road that heads past the summer cabins on the slopes a little farther south.

Mt. Tom

Watch for and take the trail that leads sharply northeast (left), contouring across an open rock face. Across the face, the trail turns more easterly and climbs up a small, shallow canyon. As you reach the relatively flat Tamarack Bench at the 10,000-foot contour, you pick up a jeep road that starts a long 3,000-foot descent back out of the canyon. (There's a mile of single-track.) This beautiful, high area is seldom visited. (Do not be tempted to enter the John Muir Wilderness Area—bikes are prohibited.)

Six miles north of Rock Creek Lake, the road reaches the northern extreme of Wheeler Ridge, veers sharply east, and drops steeply down Sand Canyon. Walk your bike down the 1-mile stretch if necessary. The road can be badly rutted by runoff and 4WD vehicles, so use caution.

After climbing out of Sand Canyon, you pass through a stand of old-growth Jeffrey pine, and once again drop down a gnarly path that challenges the hardiest cyclists. At about the 6,700-foot elevation mark, you come out into the open along Witcher Creek. Just before the creek, take the power line road 4S54 left (north). This dirt road winds its way north for 5 miles, eventually rejoining Rock Creek Road just below Holiday Group Campground. A right turn take you back to Tom's Place.

94 The Great Wall of Owens Gorge Ride

Distance: 7.5 miles
Difficulty: Moderate
Elevation: 7,000' with about 300' loss/gain
Ride Type: Loop ride on pavement, singletrack, and dirt road
Season: Spring through fall
Maps: Fine Edge Eastern High Sierra Recreation Topo Map; USGS 7.5 min. series Tom's Place
Comments: Nearest facilities at Tom's Place; no water on this route

Highlights: This simple loop drops to the bottom of Owens River Gorge just below Long Valley Dam and circles back up the pavement. The trail section is an easygoing downhill ride except for occasional small pine trees and brush that obstruct the trail. The pavement section, just above the dam, is steep at first, but then rises fairly gently.

The stone walls seen in the early part of the ride were built by hand without mortar. The craftsmanship resembles that of the early Chinese laborers who worked on the Transcontinental Railroad, giving rise to its local name, "Great Wall of China." Who made the rock wall with such careful craftsmanship, what its purpose was, and when it was built no one knows for sure.

Getting There: Sixteen miles south of Mammoth Lakes Junction or 24 miles north of Bishop, turn east off Highway 395 at the Tom's Place/ Owens Gorge Road exit. Park by the mailboxes at the T-intersection.

Route: From the mailboxes, go left at the T-intersection on Owens Gorge Road (4S02), pass several cabins, loop

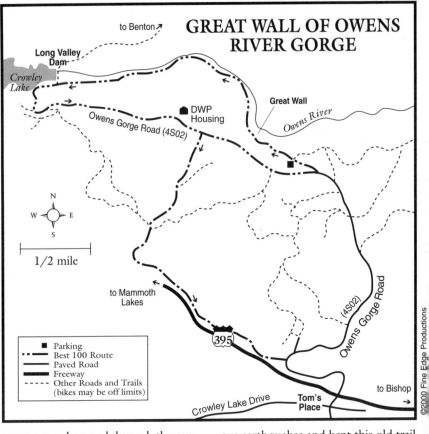

across a meadow, and through the center of the Sunny Slopes subdivision.

Follow 4S02 (about 1.8 miles) past a summit where it turns left (north) toward Crowley Lake. Turn right by two pine trees and take this sandy road across the flats toward the edge of Owens River Gorge. Cross the jeep road and take a faint singletrack that leads left and downhill into the gorge. Be cautious on your downhill—there may be hikers or other cyclists on the trail.

The singletrack follows the old road bed a little more than a mile to the bottom of the gorge. Toward the bottom of this trail, look below you to the right to see the "great wall." The fine rock work has withstood numer-

ous earthquakes and kept this old trail from washing out. Perhaps someday the story behind the wall will be uncovered. From a vantage point just above the wall, you can often see redtailed hawks, golden eagles, gulls and cranes, as well as deer, rabbits and coyotes. During the winter, you may spot a bald eagle or two.

When you reach the canyon floor, your loop route goes left on the graded dirt road, following the stream up-canyon to the top of Long Valley Dam (at the south end of Crowley). [Side trip: Turn right and head downstream to the end of the dirt road. The vegetation, birdlife and the view into Owens River Gorge are worth the extra time.]

Cycling in pure mountain air, solitude, and natural beauty

Resuming your loop route, curve left on 4S02 and climb steeply to the top of the rough pavement through a rock wonderland covered with juniper and Jeffrey pines, and passing the Los Angeles DWP housing. At the crest (5.3 miles), go right onto a closed road with broken pavement.

Cross the basin and go straight at the junction. Soon the road drops steeply to the base of the pink cliffs. Follow the fringe of wet meadow that parallels Highway 395. The dirt road ends in Sunny Slopes at Owens Gorge Road (4S02). Go right onto the pavement and follow this road back to your start.

95 Shady Rest Trail

Distance: 3 miles
Difficulty: Easy
Elevation: 200'
Ride Type: A loop on singletrack and paved bike trail
Season: May to October
Maps: Fine Edge Eastern High Sierra map; USFS handout
Comments: Toilets and water (seasonal) are available at the park.

Highlights: Shady Rest is a new trail built by the local bike club rehabilitating logging roads. It circles the town park, Shady Rest Park.

Getting There: This trailhead is off Forest Trail Road, just behind the Town of Mammoth Lakes Fire Station #1, on the right side. There is parking for 8-10 cars. Follow the brown signs with yellow bikes.

Route: The singletrack leads into the trees, then follows a fenceline of Old Shady Rest Campground. After the fence, the trail follows the base of a hill along the backside of the campground.

At about 0.5 mile, the trail makes a sharp left and parallels Shady Rest Road. This segment follows a water ditch which powered a sawmill on the site of Shady Rest Park circa 1915-1930. This segment passes the signed route on roads known as Knolls

Loop. Just past this is the wreck of a 1930s vintage truck. The trail winds through a forested flat.

When the trail ends at a road, go right, then pick up the trail again 20 yards farther on the left. This segment climbs to the crest of a small hill then descends the far side. At the bottom, the trail goes right, downhill, crosses a road, then in 100 yards, crosses the main dirt road, Sawmill Cutoff Road. After this, the trail heads south

Cyclists gather below Brass Mammoth, Mammoth Mountain Bike Park

150 yards then makes a sharp left, heading north to the base of a large hill, then bears right at a small meadow. The trail follows an old road along the base of the hill to a former mine site, now a small BMX track, then leads away from the base of the hill and downhill to the crossing of a powerline road.

The next section crosses a drainage and then another road, the Sawmill Road. Go right 10 yards and on the left side is the next section of trail which begins by ascending a short steep hill. The trail, now an overgrown logging road, follows the crest of a low rise between Shady Rest Park and Shady Rest Campground. This segment ends at the paved bike trail.

Take a left on the paved bike trail. In 30 yards, go right at three boulders and cross the paved Shady Rest Road. The loop closes here. Join the familiar trail along the base of the hill at the back of Old Shady Rest Campground. This follows a powerline, then bends left along the fence to the parking area on Forest Trail.

96 Inyo Craters Singletrack

Distance: 8 miles (up to 20 miles)
Difficulty: Moderate
Elevation: 8,000' to 8,600' to 8,000' and back
Ride Type: Out-and-back, mostly singletrack (possible loop once at Inyo Craters)
Season: June to October
Maps: Fine Edge Eastern Sierra Recreation Topo Map; USGS 7.5 min. series Old Mammoth, Mammoth Mountain
Comments: Pit toilets and interpretive kiosks at Inyo Craters

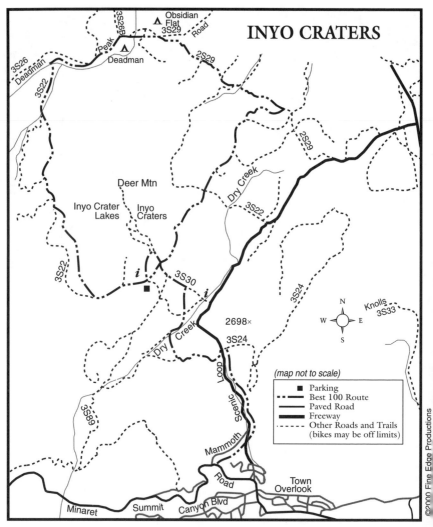

Highlights: Great singletrack, interesting geology of Inyo Craters, the most recent volcanic activity near Mammoth

Getting There: Start at the edge of Mammoth Lakes, North Village, where Highway 203 leaves town toward the ski area's Main Lodge and Devils Post Pile.

Route: Start up Highway 203 toward Main Lodge, or take Uptown singletrack to the left of the Highway. At the Scenic Loop (the first road on the right after Knolls Drive) about a mile, cross the Highway, ride 100 yards up Scenic Loop Road, and pick up a trail on the right side of the road by a road sign.

The Inyo Craters Trail climbs, paralleling the Scenic Loop Road. It crests the first climb then descends away from the road. At the bottom the trail turns left uphill, climbing through dense forest and approaching the road in several places. This section of trail ends at a dirt road, 3S24, at the top of the pass.

Cross the pavement and begin to follow the small brown and yellow bike signs at eye level. Follow the dirt road left and downhill 200 yards. The road turns sharply right and climbs two shelves. At the crest of this little climb you come to singletrack again. This section descends 600 feet with banked turns, rolls and dips. It is fast fun through old-growth red fir down to Dry Creek. A primitive bridge crosses the seasonal creek.

On the other side of the creek go right, downhill, on a jeep road. In 150 yards take a sharp left and cross the wide graded dirt road (3S30) to Inyo Craters. There is a small parking area and the start of the third section of singletrack. This trail rolls through alternating forest and meadow over a low hill, down to a second road crossing, and up a short steep hill to the parking lot for Inyo Craters.

Across the clearing a fourth trail leads a quarter-mile to the edge of Inyo Craters. These two large holes erupted 600 years ago, a violent gaseous explosion which buried the basin around it in 10-15 feet of pumice. There are excellent views of Mammoth Mountain and Joaquin Ridge from here. The Inyo Craters Loop, a popular 10.5-mile road loop, is signed from the Inyo Craters parking lot. Take the loop and ride the trail back to town for a 19-mile ride. For an 8-mile round trip, turn around and retrace your route. Follow the small brown signs with the yellow bikes.

97 Triple Trail Ride (Uptown, Mountain View and Hard Core trails)

Distance: 21.6 miles
Difficulty: Strenuous, but technically moderate
Elevation: 8,000' to 10,250', approximately 2,500' gain/loss
Ride Type: Out-and-back on singletrack mixed with jeep road
Season: June through October
Maps: Fine Edge Eastern Sierra Recreation Topo Map; USGS 7.5 min. series Old Mammoth, Mammoth Mountain
Comments: All facilities in the town of Mammoth Lakes

Highlights: This combination of Uptown, Mountain View and Hard Core trails is the longest collection of singletrack in the Mammoth Lakes area outside the Mammoth Mountain Bike Park. The ride accesses Minaret Vista and provides even better views along Joaquin Ridge. The ride features a progression of old growth red fir, Jeffrey pine, lodgepole pine, white fir, and at the highest elevations whitebark pine. The ride is infinitely variable. Turn around at any point and it is pretty much downhill back to town. This is a real mountain bike ride to the top of the mountains. Bring extra clothes as it can snow any day of the year. Don't forget your camera either.

Getting There: From Mammoth Lakes ride or drive to North Village where Highway 203 leaves town, heading toward the Main Lodge of Mammoth Mountain Ski Area. On the left side of the highway are two trails: Uptown to the right (closer to Highway 203) and Downtown to the left. These are one-way trails—Uptown is up and Downtown is down. Both are public access trails for 2.6 miles. Continued public access to these trails depends on mountain bikers leaving Mammoth Mountain Bike Park at the sign across Highway 203 from the Earthquake Fault. Otherwise you can purchase a Park trail pass to continue within the Mammoth Mountain Bike Park.

Route: Start at the bottom of Uptown on the edge of town. This one-way trail climbs through a mature old-growth forest of red fir. The openness between the trees, lack of other trees, and size of these giants are indicative of a mature forest. The trail winds, continuously climbing near Highway 203 past the Scenic Loop. At approximately 2.6 miles there is a sign for Mammoth Mountain Bike Park. This is the end of the public trail and a pass is required above this point.

Go right and follow the new brown and yellow bike signs across Highway 203. These metal signs are at eye level and Mountain View Trail is well marked. After 100 yards on the Earthquake Fault Road, the trail bears to the left, continuing through tall red fir. Mountain View climbs to a T-junction and bears right through a gap. Here the trail bears left and descends. The forest abruptly turns to a mix of lodgepole and Jeffrey pine. The trail traverses the hillside with good views of Crater Flat and Inyo Craters below. This first section of singletrack climbs to a road.

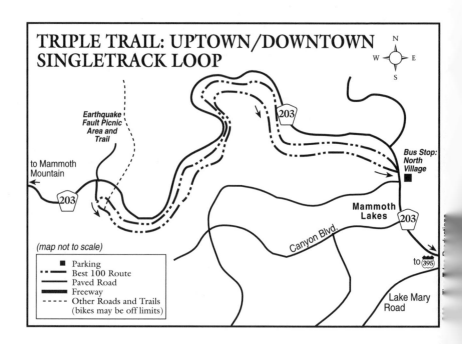

TRIPLE TRAIL: UPTOWN/DOWNTOWN SINGLETRACK LOOP

Earthquake Fault Picnic Area and Trail

to Mammoth Mountain

Bus Stop: North Village

Mammoth Lakes

Canyon Blvd.

203

to 395

Lake Mary Road

(map not to scale)

■ Parking
·—· Best 100 Route
—— Paved Road
▬▬ Freeway
---- Other Roads and Trails
        (bikes may be off limits)

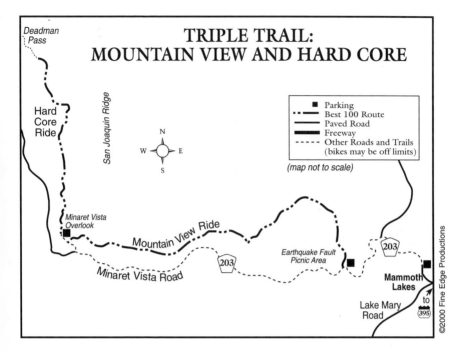

TRIPLE TRAIL:
MOUNTAIN VIEW AND HARD CORE

Deadman Pass

Hard Core Ride

San Joaquin Ridge

Parking
Best 100 Route
Paved Road
Freeway
Other Roads and Trails
(bikes may be off limits)

(map not to scale)

N
W—E
S

Minaret Vista Overlook

Mountain View Ride

Minaret Vista Road

203

Earthquake Fault Picnic Area

203

Mammoth Lakes

Lake Mary Road

to 395

©2000 Fine Edge Productions

Go right, downhill, on this road for 0.3 mile. The second singletrack section is on the left side just after a sharp turn. It immediately crosses twin bridges over Dry Creek (built in 1999 by the local bike club). Two miles of singletrack rolls through mixed Jeffrey pine and lodgepole forest, crosses two more bridges and ends at a T-junction at a road.

The second road section leads right, then quickly left at a slash pit. Follow the bike signs along a jeep road across sparse meadows in pumice bowls. The forest becomes entirely lodgepole pine. The first significant junction bears right. (The road left leads to Mammoth Mountain Inn.) The forest grows denser with elevation.

At 6.8 miles, the third section of singletrack begins. There is a transition to mixed old-growth lodgepole and silver fir. The trail climbs steeply with one last bridge. Then a pair of switchbacks leads through a grove of giant silver fir on a steep side slope. The grade eases into a low gap and you enter a stunted grove of whitebark pine. The trail ends at a jeep road by a kiosk.

This is the beginning of the San Joaquin Ridge OHV trail, called Hard Core; it is a signed bike route. Go right and continue uphill along the ridge. You pass through clustered groves of whitebark pine alternating with vast sparse alpine meadows. In early summer, the flowers are fantastic. The views are ever-expanding. At 2.5 miles from the top of Mountain View Trail, the jeep road ends at the site of a fire lookout. One full-circle look at the view explains why this is a classic ride. To the south is Mammoth Mountain. You look down from a perspective higher than the ski area's mid-chalet. East is the Long Valley Caldera, a basin left by the eruption of a massive volcano. You

Courtesy Mammoth Mountain Bike Park

Time for a rest before tackling Hard Core!

stand on one edge and on the other are the Glass Mountains, 15 miles away. To the north is Mono Lake and the Yosemite high country. And west is a sublime vista of Mount Ritter, Banner Peak, and the Minarets.

The return is a joy of a downhill. Retrace your route down San Joaquin OHV trail and Mountain View. After crossing Highway 203, take Downtown, the second trail, downhill to town.

98 Yost Lake Trail

Distance: 7 miles (loop option 15 miles)
Difficulty: Technically moderate, physically difficult
Elevation: 7,600' to 9,200'; loop is 7,000' to 9,700'
Ride Type: Out-and-back on singletrack; loop option is half singletrack with a return on dirt road and highway
Season: June to October
Maps: Fine Edge Eastern Sierra Recreation Topo Map; USGS 7.5 min. series Mammoth Mountain, June Lake
Comments: Stores, food, water, parking, restrooms, and lodging are available in June Lake at the start.

Highlights: The scenic highlights of this route include a high alpine meadow and mountain lake surrounded by dramatic peaks. The loop option is for skilled route finders as the middle section of singletrack is faint.

Getting There: The start is across

Highway 158 from the June Lake Fire Station on the east fringe of the town of June Lake, next to the giant balanced boulder.

Route: The trailhead is behind a couple of cabins across Highway 158 from the June Lake Fire Station. This faint old road switchbacks up to the crest of the canyon and enters a dense forest of lodgepole pine. It winds through forests to the June Mountain Ski Area and enters a wide clearing just above the main lodge of the ski area. A small wooden sign at the point of a triangle of trees guides you across the open area to the continuation of the trail into the forest west of the ski slope.

The trail continues climbing through forests and small meadows, crossing a creek. About 3 miles from the start, there is a junction of trails. The one to the right is closed to bikes. Take the left uphill to Yost Lake. This lake and meadow lie in the shadow of a dramatic cliff of the San Joaquin Ridge. The lake and meadow are your reward for the long climb. Most people turn around here.

Option: For adventurous mountain bikers with a good map and very good skills, there is a challenging route over a high pass to Glass Creek. The trail at this point becomes indistinct. It is actually several faint trails up the drainage, past the second Yost Meadow, and over the obvious gap. On the other side, take a drainage over a second gap to the left and into Glass Creek. Once down in Glass Creek Meadow, the trail becomes distinct. Follow the trail to the road,

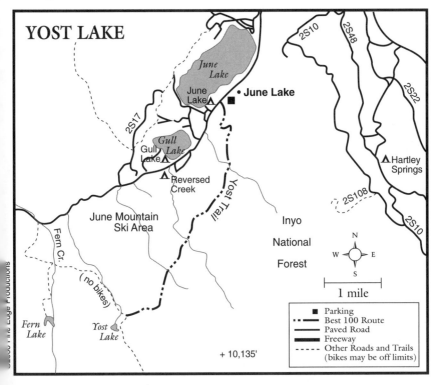

Eastern Sierra lakes

go left uphill, over a gap by Glass Flow Ridge, then downhill. Take the second road to the left, the one signed Hartley Springs Campground. Follow the road to and through the campground. On the far side, follow the small brown plastic signs downhill. From there, follow Highway 395 one mile north to June Lake Junction, a store at the junction of Highway 158. Take Highway 158 for 4 miles into the village of June Lake.

Caution: This is a difficult loop requiring a high level of navigational skill. It is easy to wind up in Upper Deadman's Creek instead of Glass Creek. Take a good map, compass, plenty of food and water, and a large measure of personal responsibility.

99 Sagehen Loop

Distance: 20 miles
Difficulty: Moderate, fairly strenuous
Elevation: Sagehen Summit 8,000'; highest point 9,000'
Ride Type: Loop ride on dirt road, jeep roads and pavement
Season: Late spring through fall. Fall colors are outstanding.
Maps: USGS 7.5 min. series Cowtrack Mtn., Dexter Canyon
Comments: This is a remote and scenic ride through Jeffrey pine forest and alpine meadows. Carry drinking water with you—a minimum of 2 quarts. Any spring water must be treated. Amenities are available in Lee Vining, Mammoth Lakes or June Lake Junction.

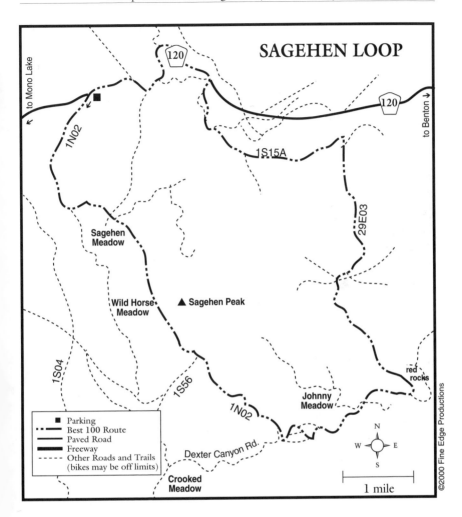

Highlights: Sagehen Loop is a classic ride through little-known country east of Mono Craters. This makes an excellent trip if you want to enjoy the fall colors. You need to be self-sufficient at all times.

Getting There: From Highway 395, turn east on Highway 120 (5 miles south of Lee Vining) and drive east to the signed Sagehen Meadow Summit. Park off the highway along Road 1N02.

Route: Head south on wide sandy road 1N02. The road winds around a big hill, gradually ascending through Jeffrey pine to Sagehen Meadow—a pumice flat covered by sparse grasses and alpine flowers. The road then veers toward Sagehen Peak, across a wide open ridge ascending to an aspen grove near the summit above Wild Horse Meadow (4.4 miles). There are marvelous views of Adobe Valley and the canyons on the east side of Glass Mountain Ridge.

Sagehen Peak

Descend through Wild Horse Meadow, a long alpine meadow lined with aspen. The road leads along a shelf before dropping toward Dexter Canyon. You join Dexter Canyon Road and turn left along the shelf, still on 1N02. The road then crosses the shelf and enters the trees.

At 8.6 miles there is an intersection with Johnny Meadows Road (signed). You continue straight toward a distinctive red rock outcropping. Turn left on a jeep road (29E03) by the outcropping (10.8 miles), into the trees, and over the ridge. Follow the road across a dry drainage, cross an intersection, and keep straight across a shelf to an old mine site where the road drops to North Canyon Creek.

Cross North Canyon Creek, turn west on 1S15A which leads out of the drainage and climbs an open ridge to a corral at Baxter Spring (about 16.3 miles) then bear north on 1S15 to Highway 120.

Go left at Highway 120 and follow it uphill around a curve and through a gap to Sagehen Summit. There is an animal watering trough on the left. From the gap, it is an easy downhill to your vehicle.

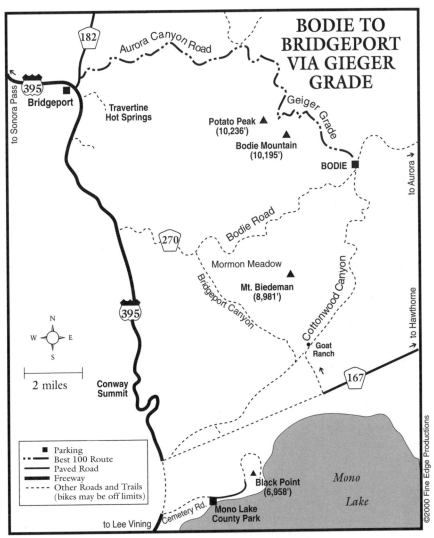

BODIE TO BRIDGEPORT VIA GIEGER GRADE

100 Bodie to Bridgeport via Geiger Grade/ Aurora Canyon

Distance: 16.7 miles
Difficulty: Strenuous, not technical
Elevation: 6,400' to 9,000'
Ride Type: Shuttle on dirt roads and pavement
Season: June through October
Maps: USGS 7.5 min. series Bodie, Dome Hill, Bridgeport
Comments: Toilet and water at Bodie State Park; all facilities in Bridgeport

Bodie Ghost Town in an "arrested state of decay."

Highlights: This ride gives you a chance to explore Bodie State Historic Park while you are fresh, and then take off into remote but easily accessible terrain. You will reach some lightly-forested areas and ride along open rolling hills. The discovery of gold in the Bodie Hills heralded the greatest gold bonanza in Mono County history. At its peak in the 1870s and mid-1880s, the mining camp held as many as 10,000 people before the mines closed in the late 1880s. Several hundred people remained until the last school finally closed its doors in 1940. The very Nevada-like terrain on this ride certainly allows your imagination to conjure up the lonely and rugged lifestyle of yesteryear's gold prospectors. In 1964 the site became a California State Historic Park and the town is now maintained in a state of "arrested decay;" its remaining buildings are furnished with authentic antiques.

Getting There: Leave a shuttle vehicle car in Bridgeport. Then from Bridgeport, drive south for 7 miles on Highway 395. Turn east on Highway 270 (Bodie Road) and drive 13 miles to the State Park (the last 3 miles are rough dirt road). Park in the parking lot (entrance fee for vehicles).

Route: After you've had a chance to explore Bodie, begin your ride on the north side of the parking lot. (The dirt road that heads east from the parking lot is signed: *Aurora 18 straight ahead; Hawthorne 41 straight ahead.* Do not confuse the historical site of Aurora ghost town with Aurora Canyon, which is in the opposite direction.)

Set your odometer to 0.0. Take

Davis

The view from Bodie Peak.

A rocky descent.

west leads to Bodie Mountain where there are outstanding views in all directions. Around 3.0 miles the road turns westerly toward Potato Peak (10,236'). Half a mile later the road gets rocky. If you're planning to camp, there's a primitive campsite to the right in a nice, quiet area. A road to the west climbs the saddle next to Potato Peak.

At 4.3 miles you reach the head of the canyon and contour to the north. You can find primitive campsites and short trails in this vicinity. By 6.0 miles you're on the ridge, and if you look left and down, you can see the pipeline grade for Old Bodie's water supply. Views of the Nevada peaks to the east and the Sweetwater Mountains to the north are outstanding.

Heading down, you come to a broad, shallow valley with an almost glaciated surface where you can see glacial erratic rocks lying about. There's a nice meadow here with a nearly year-round spring that once provided additional water for Bodie's development. (It's a good primitive campsite.)

At 6.7 miles, you come upon a weathered aspen grove and springs. Within less than a half-mile, you pass a well-graded road that heads east to the Paramount Mine. Continuing northwesterly you soon catch a view

the Geiger Grade Road (also known as the Old Pipeline Grade), which heads north, climbing toward Bodie Mountain (10,195'). (No sign identifies the Geiger Grade Road, which is perpendicular to the Aurora Road.) Immediately after you cross a cattleguard, you pass a sign: *Rough road. Travel at your own risk.* Bodie Mountain is to your left as you contour down through an open saddle. Watch your downhill speed—the road is rocky and grassy in some spots.

At 2.3 miles you pass the Sage Grouse and Antelope Habitat Improvement Project. The road to the

of Bridgeport Reservoir and the Sierra. Cross a cattleguard at 7.5 miles, and then at 8.7 miles you hit a saddle and the junction with Aurora Canyon Road. A sign painted on rock reads: *Masonic left 7 mi. Bridgeport left. Bodie back 7 mi.*

At the junction of Geiger Grade and Aurora Canyon roads, turn west and downhill toward Bridgeport. There's a cattle crossing at 9.1 miles. Then the road drops steeply downhill. Beware of rough and muddy conditions caused by runoff or small springs. At 9.7 miles a primitive campsite with a fire ring is located in the aspen grove to your left. Cross a stream at 11.1 miles. Sign: *Narrow cattleguard.*

Around the 14-mile mark the terraces you see to your left were caused by mining activity. Cross a cattleguard at 14.6 miles. A half-mile later (15.1 miles), the canyon opens out into a fan and Bridgeport is visible ahead.

At 15.3 miles the road to the left is signed: *D & B Enterprises. Private Mill Site. Mercury Health Hazard.* Stop for a moment to enjoy the view across the valley to the north—you can see the canyon through which the east fork of the Walker River flows, as well as the Sweetwater Mountains. At 15.8 miles you pass Bridgeport Ballpark and Sagebrush Road. Continuing downhill, guide to the left to intercept Highway 395 at 16.7 miles on the south side of Bridgeport. Head north (right) on Highway 395 to finish your ride and pick up your shuttle vehicle.

APPENDIX

About the Authors

 **Delaine Fragnoli,** former editor of *Mountain Biking* and *Southwest Cycling* magazines, is the co-editor of *Mountain Biking Southern California's Best 100 Trails* and the author of *Mountain Biking California's Central Coast* and *Mountain Biking North America's Best 100 Ski Resorts.* Her freelance work has appeared in *Bicycling, Women Outside, Women's Sports & Fitness, BIKE,* and *VeloNews.* She lives in the Sierra Nevada with her husband and baby girl.

Robin Stuart, co-author of *Mountain Biking For Women,* is a freelance writer whose work has appeared in numerous bicycling magazines. She lives and rides in the San Francisco area.

Carol Bonser co-author of *Mountain Biking North Lake Tahoe's Best Trails,* and *Mountain Biking South Lake Tahoe's Best Trails,* lives and rides in the central Sierra.

Mark Davis, a Mammoth Lakes resident, is active in the local Mammoth Area Mountain Bike Organization (MAMBO) and in local public land-access issues. He is an expert on Eastern Sierra bicycle trails. Mark has hiked the entire Pacific Crest Trail twice and has ridden his bike in all 48 contiguous states. He likes to say, "I live to ride my bike."

Don Douglass, one of the founders and the first president of the International Mountain Bicycling Association (IMBA), has written extensively on the need for environmentally-sound and responsible riding habits. He has been inducted into the Mountain Biking Hall of Fame.

Réanne Hemingway-Douglass, editor and freelance writer, published her first book, *Cape Horn: One Man's Dream, One Woman's Nightmare,* in 1994. She led the first women's cycling team to cross Tierra del Fuego. With her husband Don, she has pioneered many cycling routes in the Eastern Sierra.

R.W. Miskimins, owns and operates Great Basin Bicycles in Reno, Nevada, with his family. He is the author of *Mountain Biking Reno-Carson City's Best Trails* and the co-author of *Mountain Biking North Lake Tahoe's Best Trails* and *Mountain Biking South Lake Tahoe's Best Trails.*

Agencies, Visitor Centers & Mountain Bike Clubs

Andrew Molera State Park
c/o Pfeiffer Big Sur State Park
Big Sur, CA 93920
408-667-2315

Annadel State Park
6201 Channel Drive
Santa Rosa, CA 95409
707-539-3911

Auburn State Recreation Area
P.O. Box 3266
Auburn, CA 95604-3266
530-885-4527
http://auburn.parks.state.ca.us

**Bicycle Trails Council Marin
(BTCM)**
Box 494
Fairfax, CA 94978-0494
415-456-7512

**Bicyclists of Nevada County
(BONC)**
Box 444
Nevada City, CA 95959
530-274-DIRT

Big Sur Chamber of Commerce
P.O. Box 87
Big Sur, CA 93920
408-667-2100

Bodie State Park
P.O. Box 515
Bridgeport, CA 93517
760-647-6445

Bureau of Land Management
California State Office
2800 College Way
Sacramento, CA 95825
916-979-2805

Bureau of Land Management
Bishop Office
785 N. Main, Suite E
Bishop, CA 93514
760-872-4881

Bureau of Land Management
Clear Lake Resource Area
(for Cow Mountain Recreation
Area)
2550 N. State St.
Ukiah, Ca 95482
707-468-4071

Bureau of Land Management
Eagle Lake Resource Area
(for Bizz Johnson Trail)
2545 Riverside Dr.
Susanville, CA 96130
530-257-0456

Bureau of Land Management
Folsom Resource Area
63 Natoma Street
Folsom, CA 95630
530-958-4474

Bureau of Land Management
Redding Resource Area
(for Shasta area)
355 Hemsted Dr.
Redding, CA 96002
530-224-2100

Calaveras Big Trees State Park
P.O. Box 120
Arnold, CA 95223
209-795-2334

California Department of Forestry
(for Boggs Mountain Demonstration
State Forest)
P.O. Box 839
Cobb, CA 95426
707-928-4378

**California Department of Parks
and Recreation**
Attn: Public Affairs
P.O. Box 942896
Sacramento, CA 94296-0001
916-653-6995 Touch-Tone
Information

California State Parks
www.cal-parks.ca.gov

California State Parks
North Coast Redwoods District
(for Prairie Creek Redwoods State
Park and Jedediah Smith Redwoods
State Park)
707-445-6547

CalTrans
Road Conditions
800-427-7623

Campground Reservations
National Recreation Reservation
Service
1-877-444-6777
www.reserveusa.com

China Camp State Park
1455 East Francisco Blvd.
San Rafael, CA 94901
415-456-0766

DESTINET Camping Reservations
800-444-PARK

Donner Memorial State Park
530-582-7892

East Bay Regional Park District
11500 Skyline Blvd.
Oakland, CA 94619
510-562-PARK

**El Dorado National Forest
Headquarters**
100 Forni Road
Placerville, CA 95667
530-622-5061
www.r5.fs.fed.us/eldorado

El Dorado National Forest
Interpretive Association
3070 Camino Heights Drive
Camino, CA 95709
530-626-4833

Feather Falls Scenic Area
530-534-6500

**Folsom-Auburn Trail Riders
Action Coalition (FATRAC)**
Box 6356
Auburn, CA 95604
916-663-4626
www.jps.net/fatrac

Forest of Nisene Marks State Park
101 North Big Trees Park Road
Felton, CA 95018
831-335-4598

Henry W. Coe State Park
P.O. Box 846
Morgan Hill, CA 95038
408-779-2728

**Henry Cowell Redwoods State
Park**
101 North Big Trees Park Road
Felton, CA 95018
831-335-4598

Humboldt Redwoods State Park
P.O. Box 100
Weott, CA 95571
707-946-2409

International Mountain Bicycling
Association
P.O. Box 7578
Boulder, CO 80306-7578
303-545-9011
www.imba.com

Inyo National Forest
Headquarters
873 North Main
Bishop, CA 93514
760-873-2400
www.r5.fs.fed.us/inyo

Inyo National Forest
Lee Vining Ranger Station
P.O. Box 429
Highway 120
Lee Vining, CA 93541
760-647-3044

Inyo National Forest
Mammoth Ranger Station
P.O. Box 148
Highway 203
Mammoth Lakes, CA 93546
760-924-5500

J.D. Grant County Park
18455 Mt. Hamilton Road
San Jose, CA 95140
408-274-6121

Klamath National Forest
Headquarters
1312 Fairlane Rd.,
Yreka, CA 96097
530-842-6131
www.r5.fs.fed.us/klamath

Klamath National Forest
Goosenest Ranger District
37805 Highway 97
Macdoel, CA 96058
530-398-4391

Klamath National Forest
Oak Knoll Ranger District
22541 Highway 96
Klamath River, CA 96050
530-465-2241

Klamath National Forest
Salmon River Ranger District
P.O. Box 280
Etna, CA 96027
530-467-5757

Klamath National Forest
Scott River Ranger District
11263 South Highway 3
Fort Jones, CA 96032
530-468-5351

Lake Oroville State Recreation
Area
530-538-2200

Lake Tahoe Basin Management
Unit
P.O. Box 8465
South Lake Tahoe, CA 95731
530-544-6420
530-573-2600

Lassen National Forest
Headquarters
55 South Sacramento Street
Susanville, CA 96130
530-257-2151
www.r5.fs.fed.us/lassen

Lassen National Forest
Eagle Lake Ranger District
477-050 Eagle Lake Road
Susanville, CA 96130
530-257-4188

Mammoth Area Mountain Bike
Organization (MAMBO)
Box 2782
Mammoth Lakes, CA 93546
760-934-3708

Mammoth Lakes Visitors Center
2500 Main Street
P.O. Box 148
Mammoth Lakes, CA 93546
760-924-5500

Marin County Open Space District
415-499-6387

Marin Municipal Utility District
220 Nellen Ave.
Corte Madera, CA 94925
415-459-5267

Mendocino National Forest Headquarters
825 N. Humboldt
Willows, CA 95988
530-934-3316
www.r5.fs.fed.us/mendocino

Mendocino National Forest
Corning Ranger District
2000 Corning Road
P.O. Box 1019
Corning, CA 96021
530-824-5196

Mendocino National Forest
Covelo Ranger District
78150 Covelo Road
Covelo, CA 95428
707-983-6118

Mendocino National Forest
Stonyford Ranger District
P.O. Box 160
5080 Lodoga-Stonyford Road
Stonyford, CA 95979
530-963-3128

Mendocino National Forest
Upper Lake Ranger District
P.O. Box 96
10025 Upper Middle Creek Road
Upper Lake, CA 95485
707-275-2361

Merced Irrigation District Parks Department
(for Merced River Trail)
209-378-2521
800-468-8889

Mid-Peninsula Regional Open Space District
330 Distel Circle
Los Altos, CA 94022
650-691-1200

Mono Basin Scenic Area Visitors Center
P.O. Box 429
Highway 395
Lee Vining, CA 93541
760-647-3044

Mono Lake Committee
Visitors Center
P.O. Box 29
Highway 395
Lee Vining, CA 93541
760-647-6595

Mt. Diablo State Park
Box 250
Diablo, CA 94528
510-837-2525

Mt. Tamalpais State Park
801 Panoramic Highway
Mill Valley, CA 94901
415-388-2070

Outside Inn
575 East Broad Street
Nevada City, CA 95959
530-265-2233
outsideinn@gv.net

Plumas County Visitors Bureau
P.O. Box 4120
Quincy, CA 95971
800-326-2247

Plumas National Forest
Headquarters
159 Lawrence St.
P.O. Box 11500
Quincy, CA 95971-6025
530-283-2050
www.r5.fs.fed.us/plumas

Plumas National Forest
Beckwourth Ranger District
Mohawk Ranger Station
Mohawk Road, P.O. Box 7
Blairsden, CA 96103
530-836-2575

Plumas National Forest
Oroville Ranger District
875 Mitchell Avenue
Oroville, CA 95965-4699
530-534-6500

Plumas National Forest
Quincy Ranger District
39696 State Highway 70
Quincy, CA 95971
530-283-0555

Redwood National Park
1111 Second Street
Crescent City, CA 95531
707-464-6101

**Redwood Natural History
Association**
707-464-9150

**Responsible Organized Mountain
Pedalers (ROMP)**
Box 1723
Campbell, CA 95009-1723
408-982-0660

**Robert Louis Stevenson Memorial
State Park**
3801 St. Helena Highway 29
Calistoga, CA 94515
707-942-5370

Samuel P. Taylor State Park
Box 251
Lagunitas, CA 94938
415-488-9897

Shasta-Trinity National Forest
Headquarters
2400 Washington Ave.
Redding, CA 96001
530-246-5222
www.r5.fs.fed.us/shastatrinity

Shasta-Trinity National Forest
Mount Shasta Ranger District
204 W. Alma
Mt. Shasta, CA 96067
530-926-4511

Shasta-Trinity National Forest
Shasta Lake Ranger District
6543 Holiday Dr,
Redding, CA 96003
530-275-1587

Sierra National Forest
Headquarters
1600 Tollhouse Road
Clovis, CA 93612
209-487-5155
www.r5.fs.fed.us/sierra

Sierra National Forest
Interagency Visitor Center
Highway 140 at 49 North
P.O. Box 747
Mariposa, CA 95328
209-966-3638

Sierra National Forest
Mariposa Ranger District
41969 Highway 41
Oakhurst, CA 93644
559-683-4665

Southern Yosemite Mountain Guides
Box 301
Bass Lake, CA 93604
800-231-4575
www.symg.com

Stanislaus National Forest Headquarters
18777 Greenley Road
Sonora, CA 95370
209-532-3671
www.r5.fs.fed.us/stanislaus

Stanislaus National Forest
Calaveras Ranger District
P.O. Box 500
Hathaway Pines, CA 95233
209-795-1381

Sugarloaf Ridge State Park
2605 Adobe Canyon Road
Kenwood, CA 95452
707-833-5712

Tahoe Area Mountain Bike Organization (TAMBO)
3430 Highway 50
South Lake, CA 96150
530-541-7505

Tahoe National Forest Headquarters
Nevada City Ranger District
631 Coyote Street
Nevada City, CA 95959-2250
530-265-4531
www.r5.fs.fed.us/tahoe

Tahoe National Forest
Downieville Ranger District
North Yuba Ranger District
15924 Highway 49
Camptonville, CA 95922-9707
530-288-3231

Tahoe National Forest
Foresthill Ranger District
22830 Foresthill Road
Foresthill, CA 95631
530-367-2224

Tahoe National Forest
Truckee Ranger Station
10342 Highway 89 North
Truckee, CA 96161
530-587-3558

Toiyabe National Forest
Bridgeport Ranger Station
P.O. Box 595
Bridgeport, CA 93517
760-932-7070

Whiskeytown-Shasta-Trinity
National Recreation Area
Whiskeytown Unit
P.O. Box 188
Whiskeytown, CA 96095
530-241-6584

Yosemite Association
P.O. Box 230
El Portal, CA 95318

Yosemite National Park
Public Information Office
P.O. Box 577
Yosemite National Park, CA 95389
559-372-0200

Yosemite Sierra Fat Tire Association
P.O. Box 669
Oakhurst, CA 93644
559-683-3379
www.sierranet.net/fat-tire

Northern California Ski Resorts with Mountain Biking Programs

**Bear Valley Cross-Country Ski
and Adventure Company**
P.O. Box 5120
Bear Valley, CA 95223
209-753-2834
www.bearvalleyxc.com

This rustic resort in the Stanislaus National Forest, three hours east of San Francisco on Highway 4, boasts 150 miles of trails (no trail fee; open May to November, daily 9-5), mostly singletrack and rugged jeep trails. The terrain tends to be steep and rocky. Some routes are designated for mountain biking only. The resort has a good working relationship with the surrounding national forest and new trails are always being added. Lifts open only for races and special events. Trail maps, mountain biking tours, rentals and a bike shop are all available on site. The Lodge at Bear Valley (209-753-2327) offers mountain biking/lodging packages.

Donner Ski Ranch
P.O. Box 66
Norden, CA 95724
530- 426-3635

Located less than 90 miles east of Sacramento off I-80, Donner offers lift-served mountain biking with access to 50 miles of trails for a day-use fee, open daily 9-4, late June through early September. Rentals are available through the Sport Shop. Donner also hosts the Rage'n At The Ranch mountain bike race series.

Eagle Mountain
P.O. Box 1566
Nevada City, CA 95959
800-391-2254
www.eaglemtnresort.com

An hour's drive east from Sacramento at the Yuba Gap exit, Eagle Mountain opens its cross-country ski trails (you must buy a park pass) to cyclists in the summer (late May to mid-October) on weekends and holidays, 9-6. (Call about weekday availability.) The resort claims over 400 miles of mountain bike trails and specializes in organizing a variety of camps, races and events, including the very popular RocktoberFest Enduro. There's a lodge with food service on site. The resort offers lessons, packages, rentals, hot showers and tent cabin camping (includes park pass).

Mammoth Mountain Bike Park
Mammoth Adventure Connection
P.O. Box 24
Mammoth Lakes, CA 93546
800-228-4947
760-934-0606

As soon as the snow melts, Mammoth Mountain Ski Area (MMSA) turns into one of the best mountain biking parks in the West. The first ski area in the U.S. to lift bicyclists and their bikes to the peak by gondola, Mammoth Mountain burst upon the mountain biking scene in 1985 with its famous Kamikaze Downhill. That year, approximately 150 entrants rode up the gondola and screamed four miles down the side of 11,053-foot Mammoth Mountain. Nowadays, that number has increased more than fivefold, and the full-fledged park offers trails for cyclists of all abilities. You can cruise the flats, challenge your uphill muscles, or try your skills on an obstacle course. New trails are being added yearly, and in addition, the Park offers clinics, guided tours and mountain bike vacation packages. Weather permitting, the Park opens July 1 and operates daily through late September, then weekends through early October. Hours are 9-6. Maps of the Park trails are available at Mammoth Mountain Bike Center.

Mt. Shasta Ski Park
104 Siskiyou Avenue
Mt. Shasta, CA 96067
530-926-8610
530-926-8686
(Summer Information Line, 24-hour recorded message)

You can find bike tours, rentals, chairlift access (for a fee), organized events, and lots of other services all in the shadow of spectacular 14,162' Mt. Shasta at the Ski Park, located off Highway 89 just east of I-5, 65 miles north of Redding. Trails range from wide, semi-improved gravel and dirt roads, such as the thrilling 1,100' Coyote Road downhill trail, to 6 miles of singletrack. The resort is open to cycling from mid-June to Labor Day, and offers tours, bike rentals, accessory retail and special events. There's dining on-site as well as lodging and dining in nearby Mt. Shasta City, McCloud and Dunsmuir.

Northstar-At-Tahoe
P.O. Box 129
Truckee, CA 96160
530-562-1010
800-GO-NORTH

The backroads and forested trails on Northstar's Mount Pluto and Lookout Mountain offer some of the best riding in the area, with spectacular views of Lake Tahoe, the Martis Valley, meadows, pine forests and aspen groves. Three chairlifts (fee, but trail map is free) provide access to over 100 miles of backroads and trails. There's even a slalom course and an obstacle course. The terrain varies from smooth, beginner-friendly cross-country ski trails to rocky, technical singletrack. A full-service resort, Northstar offers everything from guided tours to classes to child care to bike rentals to lodging packages to complimentary on-site transportation. The resort is open from late May to mid-September, daily from 9:30-4:00.

Squaw Valley, USA
1960 Squaw Valley Road
Olympic Village, CA 96146
800-545-4350
530-583-5585
530-583-6955

Located off Highway 89 between Truckee and Tahoe City, Squaw has 10 miles of lift-served (fee) mountain-bike-only singletrack and more than 30 miles of multi-use trails. Seventeen dirt trails and 7 miles of paved trail provide scenic excursions for cyclists. Terrain includes singletrack, long straight-aways and technical steeps. The resort offers rentals, special events, a free map detailing four area rides, and lodging and dining on site. The cycling season usually runs from Memorial Day to mid-October.

Recommended Reading

General Cycling

Friel, Joe, *The Cyclist's Training Bible*. Velo Press, 1996.

Nealy, William, *Mountain Bike! A Manual of Beginning to Advanced Technique*. Birmingham: Menasha Ridge Press, 1992.

———, *The Mountain Bike Way of Knowledge*. Birmingham: Menasha Ridge Press, 1989.

Skillbeck, Paul, *Singletrack Mind*. Velo Press, 1996.

Smith, Jill, *The Mountain Bikers' Cookbook*. Velo Press, 1997.

Stuart, Robin and Cathy Jensen, *Mountain Biking for Women*. Waverly, New York: Acorn Publishing, 1994.

Zinn, Leonard, *Zinn and the Art of Mountain Bike Maintenance*. Velo Press, 1996.

Backcountry Travel and First Aid

Graydon, Don, ed., *Mountaineering, The Freedom of the Hills*, 5th edition. Seattle: The Mountaineers, 1992.

Lentz, M.S. Macdonald, and J. Carline, *Mountaineering First Aid*. Seattle: The Mountaineers, 1990.

Meyer, Kathleen, *How to Shit in the Woods*. Berkeley: Ten Speed Press, 1989.

Literary

Gilbar, Steven, ed., *Natural State: A Literary Anthology of California Nature Writing*. Berkeley: University of California Press, 1998.

McPhee, John, *Assembling California*. New York: Farrar, Straus and Giroux, 1993.

Yogi, Stan, ed., *Highway 99: A Literary Journey Through California's Great Central Valley*. Berkeley: Heyday Books in conjunction with the California Council For The Humanities, 1996.

References

Alt, David and Donald Hyndman, *Roadside Geology of Northern California*. Mountain Press.

Dodd, K., *Guide to Obtaining USGS Information*. U.S. Geological Survey Circular 900, 1986.

Gudde, Erwin G., *California Place Names*, 4th edition. Berkeley: University of California Press, 1998.

Little, Elbert L., *National Audubon Society Field Guide of North American Trees*. New York: Alfred A. Knopf, 1980.

Stellenberg, Richard, *National Audubon Society Field Guide of American Wildflowers—Western*. New York: Alfred A. Knopf, 1979.

Stratton, George, *The Recreation Guide to California National Forests.* Helena, Montana: Falcon Press, 1991.

Udvardy, Miklos, *National Audubon Society Field Guide to North American Birds—Western Region.* New York: Alfred A. Knopf, 1998.

Regional Guides

Elliot, Chuck, *Cycling the California Outback with Bodfish: Northern California National Forests.* Bodfish Books, 1993. (The trail information in this book is dated.)

Lyon, James, et. al., *California and Nevada Travel Survival Kit.* Hawthorn, Australia: Lonely Planet Publications, 1996.

Rice, Andrew, *Adventure Guide to Northern California.* New York: Macmillan, 1996.

Shuman, John, *Mountain Biking Whiskeytown.* Self-published, 1995. (For all intents and purposes this book is out of print, although several bike shops in Redding still have copies. It's worth searching for if you ride a lot in the area.)

Route Index

Outdoor Publications from MountainBikingPress.com

RECREATION TOPO MAPS

(with Mountain Biking, Hiking and Ski Touring Trails,
6-color, double-sided, includes trail profiles & route descriptions)

Eastern High Sierra-Mammoth, June, Mono, 2nd Ed., ISBN 0-938665-77-4	$9.95
Santa Monica Mountains, ISBN 0-938665-69-3	$8.95
San Bernardino Mountains, ISBN 0-938665-32-4	$9.95
San Gabriel Mountains—West, ISBN 0-938665-13-8	$8.95
North Lake Tahoe Basin, 2nd Ed., ISBN 0-938665-34-0	$8.95
South Lake Tahoe Basin, 3rd Ed., ISBN 0-938665-68-5	$8.95
The Great Flume Ride, ISBN 0-938665-75-8	$3.95

MOUNTAIN BIKING GUIDEBOOKS

Mountain Biking California's Central Coast Best 100 Trails,
by Fragnoli ISBN 0-938665-59-6
(classic routes, 90 detailed maps, 272 pages) $18.95

*Mountain Biking Southern California's
Best 100 Trails,*
2nd Ed., Fragnoli & Douglass, Eds.,
ISBN 0-938665-53-7
(classic routes, 80 detailed maps, 352 pages) $16.95

*Mountain Biking Northern California's Best 100
Trails* by Fragnoli & Stuart,
ISBN 0-938665-73-1
(classic routes, 90 detailed maps, 360 pages) $18.95

Mountain Biking the Eastern Sierra's Best 100 Trails,
by Hemingway-Douglass, Davis,
and Douglass, ISBN 0-938665-42-1 $18.95

*Mountain Biking Santa Monica Mountains'
Best Trails,* by Hasenauer & Langton,
ISBN 0-938665-55-3 $14.95

Mountain Biking North America's Best 100 Ski Resorts
by Fragnoli, ISBN 0-938665-46-4 $16.95

Mountain Biking the San Gabriel Mountains' Best Trails
with Angeles National Forest and Mt. Pinos
by Troy & Woten, ISBN 0-938665-43-X $14.95

Mountain Biking South Lake Tahoe's Best Trails
by Bonser & Miskimins, ISBN 0-938665-52-9 $14.95

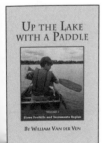

Mountain Biking North Lake Tahoe's Best Trails
by Bonser & Miskimins, ISBN 0-938665-40-5 $14.95

Lake Tahoe's Top 20 Bike Rides on Pavement & Dirt
by Miskimins, ISBN 0-938665-36-7 $5.95

Guide 10, San Bernardino Mountains
by Shipley, ISBN 0-938665-16-2 $10.95

Guide 11, Orange County and Cleveland N.F.,
2nd Ed. by Rasmussen, ISBN 0-938665-37-5 $11.95

Mountain Biking Reno/Carson City's Best Trails
by Miskimins, ISBN 0-938665-66-9 $10.95

OTHER GUIDEBOOKS

Up the Lake with a Paddle, Canoe & Kayak Guide, Vol. I,
Sierra Foothills, Sacramento Region,
by Van der Ven, ISBN 0-938665-54-5 $18.95

Up the Lake with a Paddle, Vol. II
by Van der Ven, ISBN 0-938665-70-7 $18.95

Favorite Pedal Tours of Northern California,
by Bloom, ISBN 0-938665-12-X $12.95

To order any of these
items, see your local dealer
or order direct from
FineEdge.com

MountainBikingPress.com

13589 Clayton Lane
Anacortes, WA 98221
Phone: 360-299-8500
Fax: 360-299-0535

Prices are subject to change.

AN IMPRINT OF
FINE EDGE PRODUCTIONS

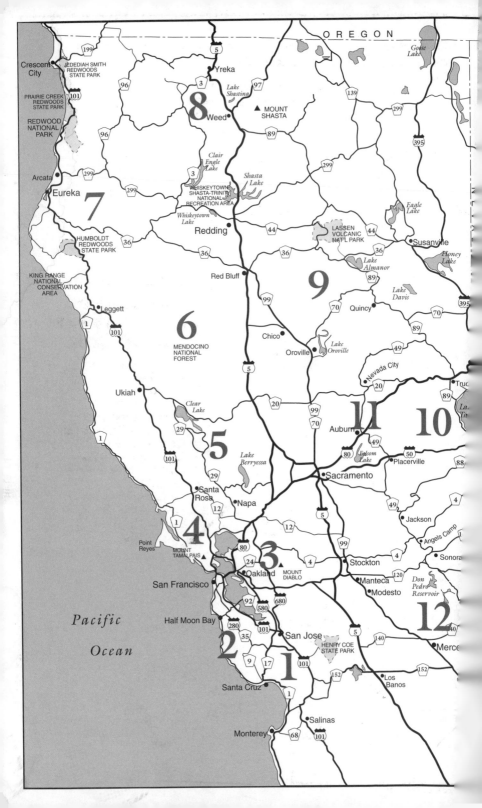